FROM SCHOOLHOUSE TO COURTHOUSE

FROM SCHOOLHOUSE TO COURTHOUSE

The Judiciary's Role in American Education

JOSHUA M. DUNN AND MARTIN R. WEST

editors

THOMAS B. FORDHAM INSTITUTE
Washington, D.C.

BROOKINGS INSTITUTION PRESS
Washington, D.C.

Copyright © 2009
THE BROOKINGS INSTITUTION
1775 Massachusetts Avenue, N.W., Washington, D.C. 20036
www.brookings.edu

Library of Congress Cataloging-in-Publication data

From schoolhouse to courthouse : the judiciary's role in American education / Joshua M. Dunn and Martin R. West, editors.
    p.   cm.
Includes bibliographical references and index.
    Summary: "Law, political science, and education policy experts test supporters' and critics' claims about education litigation concerning judicial efforts promoting school desegregation and civil rights; high-stakes testing and school finance in NCLB era; school discipline, special education, and district management; and the relationship between religious freedom, student speech, and school choice"—Provided by publisher.
    ISBN 978-0-8157-0307-5 (pbk. : alk. paper)
    1. Educational law and legislation—United States. 2. Political questions and judicial power—United States. I. Dunn, Joshua M. II. West, Martin R. III. Title.
    KF4119F76 2009
    344.73'071—dc22   2009023370

9 8 7 6 5 4 3 2 1

Printed on acid-free paper

Typeset in Adobe Garamond

Composition by Cynthia Stock
Silver Spring, Maryland

Printed by R. R. Donnelley
Harrisonburg, Virginia

Contents

Foreword

Primary-secondary education is scarcely the exclusive realm of increased litigation and court involvement in social policy, much less the only field in which the fruits of such litigation have sometimes turned out to be rotten. It is most assuredly not the only sphere where policy disputes and reform initiatives—and resistance to these—have been fought out in courtrooms as well as legislative corridors and voting booths. In the three decades since Donald Horowitz penned *The Courts and Social Policy* (Brookings, 1977), many forests have been cut down to produce the paper on which were inscribed hundreds of thousands of court decisions in countless areas of domestic affairs. (Consider, just as a beginning, disability law, family law, welfare, health, immigration, housing and, of course, law enforcement.)

Our principal concern at the Thomas B. Fordham Institute, however, is primary-secondary education and its improvement, above all the strengthening of academic performance by students and the expansion of quality schooling options for needy families and children. Fordham is an education-policy think tank focused on what it takes to revitalize American schools and reduce obstacles to the reform enterprise.

These obstacles take myriad forms, many but not all of them governmental. We've examined, for instance, the extent to which teacher union contracts constrain the capacity of principals to make crucial personnel decisions for their schools, the malign effect of statewide "caps" on the power of charter schools to afford decent educational alternatives to youngsters who need them, and the way that some of the compromises built into the federal No Child Left Behind act (NCLB) have attenuated standards-based reform at the state level.

Although we have ample company in studying the executive and legislative branches of government, both state and federal, in relation to K–12 education, we—and most other analysts—have sorely neglected the judicial branch. We simply did not know enough about it—and neither, so far as we could tell, did anybody else.

To what extent, we wondered, is court involvement an obstacle to desired reforms in primary-secondary education in twenty-first century America? To what extent is it a distraction? Might it possibly turn out to be an asset?

We could easily recount several famous decisions, particularly by the U.S. Supreme Court, that seemed to advance important education reforms (such as *Brown* and *Zelman*) and could point to others (especially state court rulings on school finance) that tended to push in the opposite direction, particularly by emphasizing resources over results and uniformity over diversity and choice. A 2003 book by Richard Arum had highlighted the courts' tendency to exacerbate the challenges of school discipline and a 1997 book by Mark Kelman introduced us to the gnarly complexities of special education law.

But all of this was piecemeal, addressing specific facets of K–12 schooling and their interaction with the judiciary rather than mapping this entire rocky landscape. To find a reasonably comprehensive treatment of the whole topic, one had to look back to 1978, long before many key developments in education policy. Over the past thirty years, as best we could tell, nobody had surveyed these questions from 30,000 feet. Yet there was so much that seemed important to find out. Is education litigation still on the rise? In which policy spheres? Federal or state courts? Constitutional, statutory, or regulatory? In what domains might judicial activity be fostering needed reforms and in which is it retarding them—or consuming so much attention and resources as indirectly to have that effect? What about the hot-button issues of segregation, special education, school discipline, and No Child Left Behind?

This was important territory for Fordham to explore, but we needed our own Lewis and Clark to lead the expedition. So we turned to two of the ablest young education-policy scholars and political scientists in the land, Harvard University's Martin West and Joshua Dunn of the University of Colorado at Colorado Springs.

They set out to recruit a stellar cast of chapter authors for this volume, while we at Fordham set out to determine which outside funders might help smooth the way for its creation. To our delight and lasting gratitude, the Searle Freedom Trust and the Achelis Foundation came through with most of the financial assistance needed for this ambitious project.

In the end, besides the eleven terrific chapters that readers will find in these pages (including a perceptive overview and introduction by the coeditors), the project incorporated a stimulating, packed-house conference at the American Enterprise Institute, where drafts were discussed by a well-chosen cadre of astute and constructive critics, then prepared for review and publication by the Brookings Institution Press. Accustomed as we are to organizing our own Fordham events and publishing our own studies, we are honored to have brought this project across the finish line with Washington's two most highly regarded think tanks as teammates.

What, exactly, have we learned from this undertaking? Four points strike me as particularly noteworthy.

First, some areas where we expected to find enormous amounts of litigation (notably special education and NCLB) reveal far less than anticipated, even as others (such as school choice and free speech) display more than we imagined—and as a few domains that once dominated the field (desegregation, school finance) appear to be approaching something like a steady state if not dormancy.

Second, several realms where it briefly seemed that a climactic Supreme Court decision might clear the air and settle the matter (for example, the *Zelman* holding that properly structured voucher programs do not violate the establishment clause) have instead remained fraught with lawsuits, showing how a controversial resolution under the federal Constitution does not quash the ability of agitated interest groups to continue litigating in state courts.

Third, as Mr. Dooley noted of the Supreme Court in Finley Peter Dunne's classic fin de siècle works, judges do follow the election returns—and they also possess policy minds of their own, including ideological predilections and sometimes a sense of superior wisdom. Litigation in education, as in other domains, is not something that arises in outside-the-courtroom disputes between rival interests and views, then enters the courtroom for objective resolution by disinterested and Olympian jurists. Too often, alas, it is the work of judges seeking particular policy (or political) outcomes and finding (or crafting) legal pathways to their desired destinations.

Fourth and finally, while judges are surely adept at finding and pursuing such pathways, the consequences for education are frequently mischievous if not downright damaging. The multiple roles assumed, and decisions issued, by state and federal courts in this domain in recent years add up to a large, mixed bag of influences, many of them malign, on the K–12 education enterprise and earnest efforts to reform and renew it. Most jurists know plenty about the law, but few know much about schools and the conditions in which those responsible for teaching in and leading them are most apt to succeed. As a result, the outcome of education litigation often works better in the courtroom than in the classroom or principal's office.

A few judges seem to have figured this out and to be stepping back from efforts to micromanage schools and state or local education systems from the bench. But they are still outnumbered by jurists willing to conspire with litigants and their attorneys—there is no dearth of either—to enact (or block) policies and programs via the courtroom when they cannot prevail in the legislative or executive branches of government. We ought not to be so dazzled by some of the great, transformative court rulings of yesteryear—*Brown* above all—as to suppose that any large fraction of the 7,000 or so education-related decisions now being rendered annually by federal and state judges are having a salutary effect on American schools or children's learning.

If this volume serves only to illuminate and document that vexing conclusion, it will more than match our high hopes for it.

CHESTER E. FINN JR., President
Thomas B. Fordham Institute

Acknowledgments

A ll books are collective efforts, especially edited volumes—and this one more than most. We are particularly grateful to Chester Finn and Michael Petrilli at the Thomas B. Fordham Institute for encouraging us to tackle this project and for providing support and counsel throughout. We also appreciate the financial support they helped us to recruit from the Searle Freedom Trust and the Achelis Foundation.

Drafts of each chapter were first presented at a conference at the American Enterprise Institute (AEI), which generously allowed us to use its space. We would like to thank the following scholars and experts who served as discussants at that event: Alan Bersin, Clint Bolick, Robert Gordon, Paul Hill, Peter Schuck, Ross Weiner, and Jonathan Zimmerman. Their insightful criticisms of the drafts helped make this a stronger work. Christina Hentges of Fordham and Rosemary Kendrick of AEI provided outstanding logistical support before, during, and after the event.

Publishing the final product with Brookings Institution Press has been a true pleasure. Acquisitions editors Chris Kelaher and Mary Kwak shepherded the manuscript through the review process with unusual speed. Fastidious editing by Vicky Macintyre improved each chapter enormously, while Susan Woollen handled the cover design with her usual creativity, thoughtfulness, and care. Janet Walker, Larry Converse, and Anthony Nathe provided valuable expertise in overseeing the editorial and production aspects of the book. We remain grateful to Robert Faherty, director of the press, for his sustained commitment to producing timely and readable scholarly books on American education.

Finally, we must acknowledge the sacrifice made by Richard Arum and Doreet Preiss, whose initial title for their conference paper was so apt that we decided (with their permission) to use it for the book.

PART I

Context

1

The Supreme Court as School Board Revisited

MARTIN R. WEST AND JOSHUA M. DUNN

In 1948 Justice Robert H. Jackson warned his colleagues on the U.S. Supreme Court against establishing themselves as a "super board of education for every school district in the nation."[1] Clearly troubled by the Court's invalidation of a Champaign, Illinois, program allowing students to attend religious classes in public school buildings, he worried that the decision lacked constitutional grounding and would spawn a steady stream of complaints challenging established practices nationwide. Oddly, however, Jackson could not bring himself to follow his own advice: he concurred with the Court's judgment in the case. His evident ambivalence in doing so foreshadowed, in microcosm, debates about the propriety of judicial involvement in American education that persist to this day.

That involvement has, by any measure, grown exponentially over the past sixty years. Seemingly no aspect of education policy has been too insignificant to escape judicial oversight. Schools and districts now regularly face lawsuits over discipline policies, personnel decisions, holiday celebrations, and more. Even in areas where formal complaints are rare, the threat lingers. And a single decision, by establishing new legal principles, can have far-reaching ramifications. It comes as no surprise, then, that a national survey conducted in 2004 by Public Agenda found that 82 percent of public school teachers and 77 percent of principals practiced "defensive teaching" in order "to avoid legal challenges."[2]

Both conservatives and liberals on the current Supreme Court have voiced concern over the extent of judicial involvement in education. In the 2006 case *Morse* v. *Frederick,* Justice Clarence Thomas bemoaned the passing of *in loco parentis,* the doctrine that assigned to school officials the authority of parents and made courts "reluctant to interfere in the routine business of school administration." While hardly arguing for a return to *in loco parentis,* Justice Stephen G. Breyer nonetheless worried that "the more detailed the Court's supervision becomes, the more likely its law will engender further disputes among teachers and students. Consequently, larger numbers of those disputes will likely make their way from the schoolhouse to the courthouse. Yet no one wishes to substitute courts for school boards, or to turn the judge's chambers into the principal's office."[3]

The path from schoolhouse to courthouse is already well traveled. This volume considers the implications of this development through fresh analyses of the areas of education policy in which the judiciary has been and remains most active. In this introduction, we review the causes of increased education litigation, the forms it now takes, and the scholarly debates it has provoked. While dogmatism would be unjustified, we conclude that the courtroom is rarely the optimal venue for education policymaking. The problematic incentives of adversarial litigation and the judiciary's own institutional limitations are aggravated in the context of K–12 schooling by the difficulty of monitoring educators' behavior and their tendency to tread cautiously so as to avoid legal challenges. In short, Justices Thomas and Breyer have good reason to worry about the judicialization of American education.

The Causes of Education Litigation

Widespread education litigation is, for all intents and purposes, a phenomenon of the second half of the twentieth century. After trending slowly upward through the Depression era, the average number of education cases decided each year in state and federal courts swelled from 1,552 in the 1940s to 6,788 in the 1970s and has fluctuated about that new level since.[4] As the pace of decisions accelerated, their content also changed. The bulk of pre-1950 cases involved narrow disputes over tax policies, bond offerings, and the alteration of school district boundaries—important matters, to be sure, but ones far removed from the core educational tasks of teaching and learning. Post-1950 litigation, in contrast, encompassed not only the high-profile issues of segregation and the separation of church and state, but also such aspects of day-to-day school management as discipline policies and the due process rights of teachers facing dismissal.[5]

Of course, education was not alone in this regard. The judiciary's role in social policymaking expanded broadly in the course of the rights revolution of the 1960s, as the public's thirst for "total justice" combined with novel legal doctrines, increasingly long and complicated federal statutes, and the emergence of well-funded advocacy organizations to generate a surge of litigation across policy domains.[6] Federal courts came to supervise nearly all of the core functions of state and local government: police, prisons and mental hospitals, for example, in addition to schools.[7] With education, the increase in judicial involvement and changes in litigation practices coincided with a growing ferment over the performance of the nation's schools and an urgent—at times seemingly frenetic—search for solutions. Competing reform movements with bases of support in universities, foundations, and civil rights organizations advanced proposals for more spending, greater accountability, and expanded parental choice, to mention only the most prominent. These efforts invariably provided occasion for litigation and, as in the case of school finance reform, sometimes worked primarily through it.

The starting point for any systematic explanation of this change in the governance of public education would have to be the announcement by courts of novel doctrines that effectively invited new types of litigation.[8] For instance, when the Supreme Court in 1947 interpreted the First Amendment's establishment clause as requiring a "wall of separation" between church and state, it created unending opportunities for claims that this barrier had been breached.[9] Likewise, when a trio of state courts in 1989 found in their states' constitutions a right to an "adequate" education and ordered that state spending on education increase, copycat lawsuits proliferated nationwide.[10] By 2008 courts in seventeen other states had ruled their school finance systems unconstitutional on similar grounds.[11]

The steady expansion of federal involvement in education after the passage of the Elementary and Secondary Education Act in 1965 also generated its share of legal disputes. As Congress took on greater statutory obligations and imposed still more on states and school districts, conflict inevitably arose over the government's performance of those new duties. Congress often invited litigation by creating "private rights of action" that empower individuals to file suit if they dislike how a statute is being enforced. Private rights of action in turn facilitated the adoption of new regulations by outsourcing their enforcement to the courts. Title IX of the 1972 Education Amendments, for example, prohibited federal aid for entities engaging in gender-based discrimination but failed to define that crucial term. Though the statute did not explicitly grant a private right of action, the Supreme Court inferred that one was implied. Naturally, as disagreements developed over the scope and meaning of discrimination, federal courts were enlisted to fill in the details.

In areas in which the federal government lacked the license or capacity to shape education policy directly, officials used government-sponsored litigation to advance reform. The 1967 creation of the Legal Services Program within the

Office of Economic Opportunity marked a shift in federal policy away from subsidizing legal advice for the poor and toward filing test cases intended to alter policy nationwide. Education cases supported by Legal Services included *Serrano* v. *Priest,* the landmark school finance equity claim decided by the California Supreme Court in 1971, and *Goss* v. *Lopez,* in which the U.S. Supreme Court in 1975 extended "rudimentary" due process rights to students facing short-term suspensions.[12]

While private rights of action opened up the courts to new types of statutory claims, the rise of modern class-action litigation in the late 1960s allowed for an even wider range of disputes.[13] Class actions allow all "similarly situated" individuals to pursue a claim in a single lawsuit, dramatically lowering the cost of litigation and thereby increasing the consumption of it. Particularly in education, a class action often begins with an attorney seeking out plaintiffs rather than plaintiffs seeking an attorney. A striking example is *Missouri* v. *Jenkins,* a long-running Kansas City desegregation case initially filed in 1977.[14] This case, which culminated in the Supreme Court's approval of judicially imposed tax increases to support over $2 billion in school improvements, was instigated not by local parents or traditional civil rights organizations. Instead, a local attorney found a handful of parents willing to let their children serve as plaintiffs and went on to be recognized by the court as the representative for every student in the district.[15]

Finally, the rewards for going to court increased. Modern education litigation pays—sometimes literally. The Civil Rights Attorney's Fees Award Act of 1976 empowered judges to award fees to lawyers prevailing in civil rights cases. Thus attorneys working in such areas as religion, free speech, desegregation, and school discipline, who previously donated their services or relied on charitable contributions, could reasonably expect an independent source of funding in successful cases. In other contexts, the payoff from litigation comes in the form of changed policy. A legal victory may be part of a larger political effort, with the courts serving to accentuate pressure for statutory changes. A series of appellate-level decisions in federal court, for example, provided the impetus for the landmark 1975 Education for All Handicapped Children Act (EAHCA), as advocates for the disabled pressed Congress to codify the judicially announced right to a "free appropriate public education" in the "least restrictive environment" into law. But often the payoff is immediate and direct—as when a judge requires a school to provide a religious student group with access to its facilities.

The Categories of Education Litigation

These developments spawned a vast array of education cases argued on widely varying grounds and at all levels of the American judicial system. Whether a claim is constitutional or statutory and whether it is filed in federal or state court matter greatly for the character of the judicial involvement that results. But the fact that specific cases can be placed into distinct boxes does not mean that advocates for a particular cause must choose only one. Just as America's famously fragmented political institutions provide multiple points of access for citizens and interest groups, so does its legal system. If a constitutional claim fails, a variety of statutory claims may yet be available. Likewise, if the Supreme Court forecloses federal litigation on an issue, state courts are often willing to entertain a similar complaint on the basis of their own constitutions. As a result, education litigation is often hydra-headed: when one legal avenue closes, others remain open.

Constitutional versus Statutory Litigation

Because Supreme Court rulings are binding across all fifty states and offer the last word on constitutional questions, winning a federal constitutional claim is the most definitive kind of legal victory. In fact, modern education litigation arose largely out of constitutional disputes over religion and segregation. It was an establishment clause decision that caused Justice Jackson's consternation in 1948. And the battle to desegregate America's schools, based on the Fourteenth Amendment's equal protection clause, became the Court's signature venture into education oversight.

Yet both areas of litigation illustrate the difficulty with staking education reform on constitutional guarantees. The Court's invocation of the principle of strict separation on religious matters sounded straightforward but proved devilishly complex to apply in a consistent and coherent manner. The end result, as Justice Jackson feared, was a "legal 'wall of separation between church and state' as winding as the famous serpentine wall designed by Mr. Jefferson for the University he founded."[16] Likewise, desegregation cases began with a claim for simple justice but over time drew courts into profoundly complicated remedial plans governing the minutest details of school district operations. It is also noteworthy that the Court's interventions in these areas were met with significant resistance. Its 1963 proscription of school prayer was for years routinely ignored throughout much of the country—and undoubtedly is still ignored in some places.[17] And massive resistance to *Brown* v. *Board of Education* prevented virtually any progress toward the end of de jure segregation in the South until the passage of the Civil Rights Act of 1964.[18]

A different dynamic is evident when courts engage in statutory interpretation. If a clear majority in Congress disagrees with the judiciary's reading of a law, that majority can amend it. When the Supreme Court in 1984 ruled that plaintiffs in successful special education cases could not collect attorneys' fees, for example, Congress effectively overturned the Court's decision within two years.[19] Of course, revising a law in response to a judicial decision is not always as simple as it sounds. By endorsing a particular reading of a law, courts alter the status quo and create new beneficiaries who can be expected to oppose subsequent changes. But it is ultimately the legislature that has the last word.

Legislatures can, if they so choose, limit the pace of statutory litigation on even controversial measures—and therefore the extent of judicial involvement in their implementation. For example, although the courts articulated the principles underlying EAHCA and its successor, the Individuals with Disabilities Education Act, the total volume of litigation generated by these laws is much lower than one might expect (see chapter 6). The No Child Left Behind Act, too, has led to surprisingly little litigation given its vast scope and complexity (see chapter 10). With both, one reason for the relatively low levels of litigation was the creation of quasi-judicial administrative procedures to channel disputes. No Child Left Behind also does not include a private right of action, and over the past decade the courts have grown reluctant to infer that such rights are implied.

Federal versus State Courts

Despite growing federal regulation, primary responsibility for public education continues to rest with state and local governments. When federal courts order changes in education policy, they therefore speak as a superior to an inferior and are more likely to see their orders put into action. In *Missouri* v. *Jenkins,* for example, a federal judge successfully ordered tax increases to support an ambitious plan of facilities improvement with little backing in the local community required to foot the bill. In contrast, state courts hearing education cases are asked to command a coequal branch of government, better positioning the legislature or governor to offer effective resistance. Moreover, most state judges are either initially elected to their positions or subject to retention elections and can therefore be expected to assess the political winds carefully before issuing new mandates. The federal judiciary therefore is ordinarily the more attractive route for those trying to engage the courts in education reform.

Nonetheless, state courts often provide an alternative when federal litigation is not viable. In 1977 Justice William Brennan of the Supreme Court famously advised civil rights attorneys to pursue litigation in the states should the federal courts become inhospitable to their goals. State constitutions, he said, offered independent grounds for judicial action and could serve as "fonts of individual liberties, their protection often extending beyond those required by the Supreme Court's interpretation of federal law."[20] In the case of school finance litigation, the process Brennan described was already under way. When the

Supreme Court's 1973 decision in *San Antonio* v. *Rodriguez* effectively ended federal litigation over school finance, plaintiffs simply shifted their focus to the states, waging a state-by-state campaign that continues today.

State-level litigation also offers plaintiffs the advantage of a wider variety of constitutional clauses from which to choose. Teachers unions and other opponents of private school choice had to rely on the establishment clause when challenging school voucher programs in federal courts, a strategy that proved unsuccessful when the Supreme Court in 2002 issued its *Zelman* v. *Simmons-Harris* decision upholding a Cleveland program.[21] Even before that decision was issued, however, the general counsel of the National Education Association said that his organization would use whatever "Mickey Mouse" provisions it could find in state constitutions to fight private school choice programs in the states.[22] In the years since *Zelman,* opponents have challenged voucher programs on the basis of state constitutional language prohibiting the use of public funds to support religious schools (commonly known as Blaine amendments), mandating "uniformity" within the state school system, and guaranteeing local control over public schools. The smorgasbord of arguments advanced in a typical complaint allows judges to pick and choose which clauses to use when striking down a program. The Florida Supreme Court, for example, relied on its state's uniformity mandate rather than its Blaine amendment to strike down that state's Opportunity Scholarship Program in 2006.[23] Doing so foreclosed an appeal of its decision to the U.S. Supreme Court testing whether Blaine amendments, if interpreted as prohibiting neutral school choice programs, violate the federal Constitution's guarantee of the free exercise of religion (see chapter 8).

The Debate over Education Litigation

As in other areas of American public policy, the advent of "adversarial legalism" in education has occasioned fierce scholarly debate.[24] Critics of judicial policymaking contend that courts are ill-equipped to resolve the sorts of "polycentric" problems in which education reformers have sought to involve them. Judges are generalists by training, and many lack the skills and institutional knowledge needed to process specialized information central to policy debates. Instead they must rely on partisan expert witnesses who may be inclined to simplify and mislead in order to persuade. Moreover, the legal process tends to force complex issues onto a procrustean bed of rights, making compromise or consideration of opportunity costs all but impossible. Because courts can properly address only the legal question before them, they cannot consider related issues that may nonetheless be essential in order to craft an effective remedy.[25]

In contrast, defenders of judicial capacity, who gained prominence in the 1970s, emphasize the courts' advantages over other institutions. At the heart of their case is the courts' relative insulation from electoral pressures, which they suggest allows judges to pursue what is best rather than what is politically convenient. Moreover, they contend that the adversarial nature of the legal process produces powerful incentives for the parties to produce sufficient information for judges to make informed decisions.[26]

It is now hard to find scholars so sanguine about judicial capacity. Most contemporary proponents of judicial policymaking do not defend the courts at all. They instead accept the criticisms leveled at the judiciary but go on to question the capacity of other institutions. All forms of social regulation are problematic: markets have transaction costs, legislatures and executives can be swayed by an uninformed public or captured by special interests, and litigation is costly and time-consuming. As a result, the courts in some instances might represent the "least-imperfect" alternative. Evaluating judicial policymaking therefore requires an issue-specific consideration of which venue offers the best prospects for desirable reform.[27]

America's experience with education litigation, however, offers ample reason to doubt the judiciary's claim on the title of the least-imperfect branch. Courts often explicitly announce their goals and, in many areas, it is obvious that they have fallen well short of reaching them. Indeed, the judiciary's attempt to desegregate the public schools has become the leading example for scholars bemoaning the limits of court-led reform.[28] While the broader effects of *Brown* and its progeny on American race relations are debated, it is clear that few de jure segregated school systems were eliminated before 1964. With new backing from Congress and the executive branch, the Supreme Court in 1968 required previously segregated school districts to adopt a remedial plan that "promises realistically to work now" to produce racially balanced schools.[29] This renewed effort yielded considerable progress, particularly in the South, but soon provoked hostility not only from white parents but also from blacks, many of whom lost faith in the potential of busing programs to enhance their children's educational opportunities. In the pivotal 1974 case, *Milliken* v. *Bradley,* the Court limited the scope of desegregation remedies to districts found to have engaged in de jure segregation. It proceeded to muddle through until the 1990s, when, despite continued racial imbalance, it directed lower courts to begin withdrawing from the supervision of school districts.[30]

Similarly, there is scant evidence that the numerous school finance judgments issued by state courts since the 1970s have measurably improved student outcomes, and recent decisions indicate that state courts are increasingly doubtful that judicially manageable standards exist that would ensure better results.[31] Both equity- and adequacy-based claims effectively reduce education policy choices to the deceptively simple metric of money, which years of experience and voluminous research suggest is unlikely on its own to improve the quality of education. Yet when courts have delved into the details of reform, the results have not been encouraging. Peter Schrag, a longtime proponent of school finance litigation, regretfully concludes "that the courts are rarely great places to make educational policy. . . . Where they try to detail specific remedies . . . the courts may soon find themselves deeper in the business of imposing across-the-board educational programs . . . than they are equipped to manage."[32]

Why have judicial interventions in education policy so often yielded disappointing results? Perhaps the most important reason is that schools, as Shep Melnick explains in chapter 2, are a quintessential example of what political scientist James Q. Wilson termed "coping organizations." This simply means that it is difficult both to monitor what the organization does and to measure how well it has done it. Students' academic outcomes reflect not only the quality of their schools, but also a host of factors outside of those schools' control. Those directly responsible for managing public education, such as principals, school board members, and superintendents, struggle to know how well teachers are doing their job. The courts, which only engage educational institutions intermittently, have even more difficulty in determining whether their reforms have been successful—or even if they have been implemented at all.

The informational problems confronting courts are also exacerbated in education cases. The legal process, Nathan Glazer has pointed out, tends to "exaggerate theoretical considerations and reduce practical considerations." For example, he notes, "in a school desegregation case, it is not a teacher or principal who will testify, but experts and administrators from distant universities on both sides of the argument."[33] Education research is notoriously inconsistent in quality and often so narrowly focused as to provide only limited guidance for policy, yet it is precisely this research that courts must use to order reforms. The strongest evidence for the benefits of early childhood education, for instance, comes from small-scale, intensive interventions for highly disadvantaged students and may not apply to other types of programs and populations. In a similar way, experimental evidence suggests that smaller class sizes in the early grades can raise student achievement, but it is not at all clear that broad class-size reductions represent the most effective use of funds. Nonetheless, these two reforms have proven popular with judges responding to school finance adequacy claims.[34]

Furthermore, the absence of strong performance incentives in public education increases the likelihood that court decisions will produce unintended consequences. Under *Wood* v. *Strickland,* all public school employees are personally liable for disciplinary actions that violate student rights.[35] In a condition of legal uncertainty, teachers and school administrators can therefore be expected to behave defensively even when doing so conflicts with educational goals. Such goal displacement seems to occur even when the legal position of schools is strong: since the 1970s courts have increasingly adopted a "pro-school" position in school discipline cases, yet conflict-averse school officials go out of their way to accommodate exceptionally disruptive behavior (see chapter 11). Leaving aside the time and disruption of a lawsuit, the personal costs to officials of defending themselves can be significant if they are unable to obtain free legal counsel, insurance, or indemnification. And access to free counsel raises its own set of concerns as officials can be understandably anxious about the quality of representation provided by government attorneys of uncertain skill and motivation.[36]

Each of these judicial imperfections is most apparent when courts are asked to play the leading role in ambitious reform efforts. In such circumstances, courts must create an ongoing enforcement regime despite unstable doctrine and a lack of judicially manageable standards. They seem to founder or succumb to exhaustion as a result.

In contrast, courts asked to command elected officials to stop a program or action face a far simpler task. Recent decisions striking down school voucher programs in Arizona, Colorado, and Florida eliminated those programs. And when a school denies access to a gay/straight alliance in violation of free speech doctrine and the Federal Equal Access Act, it is easy for courts to craft an effective remedy and see that it is enforced. When courts create durable change, it therefore tends to be on issues requiring comparatively simple proscriptions, like lifting restrictions on student speech, or when legal mobilization is combined with political action, as was the case with the exclusion of students in need of special education. It is for this reason that the volume of litigation in a particular area can be a misleading indicator of the extent of judicial influence. Where the courts establish clear and enforceable standards, the number of cases filed will fall as compliance increases. Moreover, if legislatures or agencies incorporate judicial standards, the role of the courts will be camouflaged.

Durable change, though, does not necessarily mean successful reform. As the following chapters illustrate, there is often disagreement about the merits of judicial policymaking in education precisely because court decisions have been effectual. That *Goss* v. *Lopez* had an effect on school discipline policies is obvious.[37] It is whether the effects were positive or negative that is in dispute. Likewise, when courts strike down school choice programs, the question of whether those programs would have expanded educational opportunities remains. Considering the policymaking limitations of courts, deferring to representative branches would seem to be the more prudent course of action—particularly, as with school choice, when the constitutional texts in question are at best unclear.

The Organization of the Volume

In surveying the areas of education policy in which courts have been most active, it seems clear that the most intensive period of judicial policymaking has passed. Recent decisions make it difficult to envision dramatic new developments involving desegregation, school finance, and special education. Tinkering at the doctrinal edges seems more likely in these areas.

This does not ensure that judicial influence will fade, however, nor even that the total volume of education litigation will decline. In areas such as school choice, religion, free speech, and school discipline, courts are being called upon to resolve controversies at an increasing rate. These areas are distinguished by the combination of ambiguous legal doctrine and constituencies eager to exploit that ambiguity to pursue their objectives. The Supreme Court's notoriously indeterminate reading of the establishment clause, for example, entices both the American Civil Liberties Union and its religious counterparts to litigate perceived violations. In much the same way, the legal standards for school discipline are sufficiently vague to generate an increasing number of cases challenging the decisions of school officials, despite the fact that judges have grown more reluctant to second-guess those decisions. In 1988 the Supreme Court said that "the education of the Nation's youth is primarily the responsibility of parents, teachers, and state and local school officials, and not of federal judges."[38] And in a recent case challenging the use of timeouts to control an emotionally disturbed and violent student, the Tenth Circuit said that federal courts should not "displace educational authorities regarding the formulation and enforcement of pedagogical norms."[39] Even so, it is more likely now than ever that a school official will face a lawsuit.

This admittedly imprecise division—between areas where judicial activity has tapered off and those where it appears to be holding steady or increasing—guides the organization of the essays that follow. The remainder of part 1 examines the judicialization of American education broadly from the perspective of courts and school district officials. In chapter 2, Shep Melnick analyzes the remedial strategies courts have developed in recent decades to help manage public agencies, arguing that each of them suffers from infirmities that are particularly acute when applied to schools. In chapter 3, Frederick Hess and Lance Fusarelli explore how (often exaggerated) legal concerns affect the behavior of district superintendents. They suggest that by training and socialization most superintendents seek to avoid conflict and that they have few professional incentives to defend school districts vigorously in court even when they are likely to succeed. Superintendents from nontraditional backgrounds with strong political backing, however, appear more inclined to push legal boundaries to advance an agenda of reform.

The second part of the volume considers four areas in which courts have played a pivotal role in the past but now seem to be more marginal actors. Surveying the history of school desegregation litigation through the Supreme Court's 2006 invalidation of voluntary integration plans, James Ryan argues in chapter 4 that these cases tell more about the courts' willingness to engage in broad social reform than about their capacity to do so effectively. School finance is among the education issues on which courts have most often sided with plain-tiffs. As John Dinan explains in chapter 5, however, recent rulings from numer-ous states suggest that school finance litigation has lost momentum, with judges increasingly disinclined to undertake ongoing supervision of school finance sys-tems. Another area in which active judicial involvement has waned is special education, which Samuel Bagenstos discusses in chapter 6. The judiciary, he explains, helped shape federal laws concerning special education but now plays a surprisingly limited role in their implementation. A similar trajectory is evident in the development of test-based accountability policies. In chapter 7, Michael Heise examines how early litigation worked to soften high-stakes testing regimes and why any additional challenges are unlikely to be consequential.

The final part of the volume covers areas where litigation retains the poten-tial to shape education policy significantly in the near future. For advocates of private school choice, *Zelman* v. *Simmons-Harris* appeared to draw their long struggle to establish the constitutionality of voucher programs to a triumphant conclusion. As Martin West shows in chapter 8, however, ongoing litigation under state constitutions now threatens not only programs involving religious private schools but also measures to provide new schooling options within the public sector. The nexus of religion and education has always presented vexing legal issues. Indeed, a majority of the Supreme Court's decisions demarcating the lines between church and state have involved K–12 schooling. In chapter 9, Joshua Dunn explains how the strategy of religious litigants to bring claims on the grounds of free speech has clarified matters but argues that significant ques-tions about the boundaries on religious speech in schools remain unresolved. One would expect legislation as broad and controversial as the No Child Left Behind Act to trigger an avalanche of litigation. Martha Derthick shows in chapter 10 that that has not happened—yet. This could easily change, however, if Congress yields to the demands of advocates urging that it be modified to include a private right of action. School discipline has followed a strange path since the Supreme Court's landmark decision in *Tinker* v. *Des Moines,* with the number of cases declining in the 1980s before commencing a steady increase over the past twenty years.[40] In chapter 11, Richard Arum and Doreet Preiss document the recent run-up in cases and misperceptions of the current legal environment on the part of students and school officials.

The collective import of these studies, in our view, is to urge courts to be cautious before wading into educational disputes. This is not a quixotic call for an end to litigation. There will always be, we believe, lawsuits and rumors of lawsuits. Nor is it a call for courts to ignore clear rights violations, which are as inevitable as they are unfortunate. But courts should consider whether implementable and effective remedies exist for the alleged violations before launching into far-reaching reforms. And when courts do engage in education policymaking, they should strive to contain the pernicious effects of litigation by offering clear standards that minimize legal uncertainty.

Notes

1. *McCollum v. Board of Education,* 333 U.S. 203 (1948).

2. See commongood.org/schools-reading-cgpubs-polls-10.html (August 5, 2008).

3. 127 S. Ct. 2618 (2007).

4. Perry Zirkel, "The 'Explosion' in Educational Litigation: An Update," *Education Law Reporter* 114 (January 1997): 341–51.

5. David Tyack, Tom James, and Aaron Benavot, *Law and the Shaping of Public Education, 1785–1954* (University of Wisconsin Press, 1987).

6. Lawrence M. Friedman, *Total Justice* (New York: Russell Sage Foundation, 1985).

7. Phillip Cooper, *Hard Judicial Choices: Federal District Court Judges and State and Local Officials* (Oxford University Press, 1988).

8. For a thorough analysis of the causes of American litigiousness, see Thomas F. Burke, *Lawyers, Lawsuits, and Legal Rights: The Battle over Litigation in American Society* (University of California Press, 2002).

9. *Everson v. Board of Education,* 330 U.S. 1 (1947).

10. Martin R. West and Paul E. Peterson, eds., *School Money Trials: The Legal Pursuit of Educational Adequacy* (Brookings, 2006).

11. See www.schoolfunding.info/litigation/AdequacyDecisions08.pdf (December 8, 2008).

12. *Serrano* v. *Priest,* 5 Cal. 3d 584, 487 P2d 1241 (1971); *Goss* v. *Lopez,* 419 U.S. 565 (1975).

13. While representative actions involving numerous plaintiffs have always existed in American law, modern class actions date back only to the 1966 revisions to the Federal Rules of Civil Procedure.

14. *Missouri* v. *Jenkins,* 515 U.S. 70 (1995).

15. Joshua M. Dunn, *Complex Justice: The Case of Missouri v. Jenkins* (University of North Carolina Press, 2008).

16. *McCollum v. Board of Education,* 333 U.S. 203 (1948).

17. *Abington Township School District* v. *Schempp,* 374 U.S. 203 (1963). For evidence of sustained resistance, see Joseph Viteritti, *The Last Freedom: Religion from the Public School to the Public Square* (Princeton University Press, 2007) p. 107.

18. Gerald N. Rosenberg, *The Hollow Hope: Can Courts Bring About Social Change?* 2nd ed. (University of Chicago Press, 2008).

19. *Smith* v. *Robinson,* 468 U.S. 992 (1984).

20. William J. Brennan, "State Constitutions and the Protection of Individual Rights," *Harvard Law Review* 90 (1977): 489.

21. 536 U.S. 639 (2002).

22. See Clint Bolick, *Voucher Wars: Waging the Legal Battle over School Choice* (Washington: Cato Institute Press, 2003), p. 156.

23. *Bush* v. *Holmes,* 919 So. 2d 392 (Fla. 2006).

24. Robert Kagan, *Adversarial Legalism: The American Way of Law* (Harvard University Press, 2001).

25. The starting point for this debate is Lon Fuller, "The Forms and Limits of Adjudication," *Harvard Law Review* 92 (1978): 354–409. While not published until 1978, this essay was written in the 1950s and was distributed in manuscript form among "legal process" scholars who were skeptical of judicial policymaking. The most comprehensive treatment remains Donald L. Horowitz, *The Courts and Social Policy* (Brookings, 1977).

26. See Abram Chayes, "The Role of the Judge in Public Law Litigation," *Harvard Law Review* 89 (1976): 1281–1316; and Owen M. Fiss, "Foreword: The Forms of Justice," *Harvard Law Review* 91 (1979): 1–58.

27. This movement has been called the "new legal process" school. For a thorough analysis, see Edward L. Rubin and Malcolm M. Feeley, "Velazquez and Beyond: Judicial Policymaking and Litigation against the Government," *University of Pennsylvania Journal of Constitutional Law* 5 (2003): 617–64.

28. Rosenberg, *Hollow Hope.*

29. *Green* v. *New Kent County School Board,* 391 U.S. 430 (1968).

30. 418 U.S. 717 (1974).

31. For the most recent analysis, see Eric A. Hanushek and Alfred A Lindseth, *Schoolhouses, Courthouses, and Statehouses: Solving the Funding-Achievement Puzzle in America's Public Schools* (Princeton University Press, 2009).

32. Peter Schrag, *Final Test* (New York: New Press, 2003), p. 233.

33. Nathan Glazer, "Should Judges Administer Social Services?" *Public Interest* 50 (1978): 78.

34. Joshua M. Dunn and Martin R. West, "Calculated Justice: Education Research and the Courts," in *When Research Matters: How Scholarship Influences Education Policy,* edited by Frederick M. Hess (Harvard Education Press, 2008), pp. 155–76.

35. 420 U.S. 308 (1975).

36. For an analysis of the effect of personal liability on the behavior of government officials, see Peter Schuck, *Suing Government: Citizen Remedies for Official Wrongs* (Yale University Press, 1983).

37. 419 U.S. 565 (1975).

38. *Hazelwood School District* v. *Kuhlmeier,* 484 U.S. 260 (1988).

39. *Couture* v. *Board of Education,* No. 07-2133 (10th Cir. 2008).

40. 393 U.S. 503 (1969).

2

Taking Remedies Seriously:
Can Courts Control Public Schools?

R. SHEP MELNICK

Midway through the twentieth century, federal court rulings on elementary and secondary education were rare events. Today they are commonplace. A 2004 survey of public school law devotes over 500 pages to such diverse topics as "church-state relations," "school attendance and instruction issues," "student classifications," "rights of students with disabilities," "student discipline," "teachers' substantive constitutional rights," "discrimination in employment," and "tort liability." Of the 300 U.S. Supreme Court cases listed in its index, only a handful were issued before 1954.[1] Since the Supreme Court reviews only a tiny percentage of the state and federal court decisions handed down each year, it is clear that dealing with courts has become a regular part of running public schools.

To anyone who studies educational policy or the courts, this shift is old news. There are a number of convincing explanations for the new judicial role: *Brown* v. *Board of Education* and the decades-long effort to desegregate public schools, the incorporation of the Bill of Rights into the due process clause of the Fourteenth Amendment, the enactment of landmark civil rights legislation in the 1960s and 1970s, the steady expansion of the federal role in education policy after 1965, and the creation of an extensive litigational infrastructure that provides a constant stream of litigants, intellectual support, and political encouragement for "adversarial legalism."[2]

One might ask why it took so long. After all, the new role of the courts reflects very old elements of American political culture. Virtually all studies of American exceptionalism emphasize that Americans understand equality to mean equality of *opportunity,* not equality of economic condition. What can the government do to ensure that everyone has an equal start in life? The most obvious answer is education. While the United States was late in developing a welfare state, it led the way in developing the common school. The more important that education became for economic success, the more ominous loomed the barriers to equal educational opportunity. As Chief Justice Earl Warren wrote in *Brown,* "In these days it is doubtful that any child may reasonably be expected to succeed in life if he is denied the opportunity of an education."[3] It is thus not surprising that once the Supreme Court began to treat the equal protection clause as more than an unavailing "usual last resort of constitutional argument," it would take a hard look at educational practices that reinforce rather than ameliorate existing inequalities.[4]

If schools play a central role in promoting equality of opportunity, they also constitute a potentially dangerous form of government authority. Since individualism and distrust of government authority are also key elements of American political culture, courts have sought to impose limits on the power of an institution that is compulsory for millions of ordinary citizens. Early in the twentieth century, the Supreme Court restricted the authority of the state to "interfere with the liberty of parents and guardians to direct the upbringing and education of the children under their control."[5] This meant, among other things, that parents have the option of exit, so long as they provide their children with adequate private schooling. This was one strand of the old constitutional law that survived the constitutional "revolution" of 1937. Because schools inevitably engage in the sensitive task of shaping students' character and opinions, they became a breeding ground for First Amendment cases once the Court had incorporated the Bill of Rights into the Fourteenth Amendment and applied it to the states.

The most important barrier to federal court involvement in educational matters, of course, was federalism. From the nation's founding through the 1950s, education was nearly universally viewed as the preserve of states and localities, not the federal government. Unlike state constitutions, the federal Constitution is silent on education. Until the 1960s Congress imposed few restrictions on state and local school systems. As a result, there was little federal law for federal courts to apply.

It is tempting to say that the courts' role in education grew as judges' understanding of federalism changed. But it is probably more accurate to say that federal judges' understanding of federalism underwent a sea change as they battled racial inequality in education. The struggle that began with judicial efforts to desegregate southern schools—and eventually became a much broader campaign to destroy Jim Crow "root and branch"—led to a fundamental shift in judges' evaluation of state and local governments. As Martha Derthick has put it, "With a view invariably to southern racism, which tainted states and localities as a class, Supreme Court majorities repeatedly rendered decisions that were more than indifferent to federalism; they were inimical."[6]

Since the Court's federalism doctrines were largely self-created, they were relatively easy to revise. At the very time that courts were imposing more constitutional demands on state and local school systems, Congress was funneling many forms of school litigation into federal chambers. Federalism's concerns with protecting the autonomy, sovereignty, and "dignity" of the states made Congress more likely to rely on judges than on administrators to set and enforce national guidelines on education. Everyone seemed to agree that "federal bureaucrats"—especially those in the much-maligned Department of Education—should not order state and local school officials around. But federal judges have a constitutional responsibility to enforce the "supreme law of the land," which includes federal statutes as well as the Constitution. As a result, judges are more central to the regulation of state and local agencies than they are to the regulation of organizations in the private sector.

As judges handled more and more school issues ranging from desegregation to special education, due process, and the use of standardized tests, it soon became evident that they faced a more pervasive, more practical, and more daunting obstacle: school officials, especially those "street-level bureaucrats" called teachers, wield substantial discretionary authority over which courts have limited leverage. How can judges hope to change the behavior of teachers in their classrooms or principals in their offices? Over the preceding century and a half, judges had accumulated little experience with the difficult job of changing the behavior of large public bureaucracies. Most of the bureaucracies federal judges had confronted in the past—primarily regulatory commissions such as the Interstate Commerce Commission and Federal Communications Commission—were relatively small and rule-bound. Once judges started to oversee schools (and police departments), they faced a humbling task: supervising far more bureaucracies with many more employees who exercised much more discretion and directly affected the daily lives of millions of Americans.

Some scholars argue that fundamental "attributes of adjudication" make it nearly impossible for courts to handle polycentric issues effectively.[7] Defenders of judicial activism such as Abram Chayes and Owen Fiss reply that courts have the ability to reshape their doctrines, procedures, and instruments to deal effectively with the new set of issues before them—or at least to do so more effectively than the administrators and legislators who previously dominated policymaking.[8] For them, new forms of judicial remedies provide convincing evidence of the adaptability of judicial institutions.

These new remedies have allowed plaintiffs to take the offensive. In the traditional judicial challenge to action by a government official, the plaintiff claims that the statute or regulation upon which the official has relied is invalid and thus not enforceable in a court of law. A court decision invalidating a law or regulation becomes a shield against further enforcement action. When government officials must routinely go to court to impose penalties on those who violate their rules, judges retain significant leverage over administrative discretion as well as agency rulemaking. The classic example is the courts' use of the exclusionary rule in criminal proceedings: judges can bar from trials evidence obtained in ways they consider unacceptable. This gives them the opportunity to review discretionary judgments by police and prosecutors on such matters as searches, interrogations, and arrests. But what about institutions—like schools—that do not rely on courts for accomplishing their daily tasks? Here judges must do more than offer plaintiffs a defensive shield; they must find a way to reach inside these organizations to change their policies, structures, and incentives. Courts basically wield two forms of offensive weapons: the injunction, a court order backed by the threat of contempt of court proceedings; and monetary damage awards.

Two factors complicated federal courts' efforts to deploy these offensive weapons in suits against government agencies. First, before the 1960s the injunction had "been deemed an 'extraordinary' remedy, to be used only when all else fails."[9] Second, requiring government officials to pay monetary damages ran headlong into judicial doctrines on sovereign immunity. In suits against private parties, monetary damages are favored over injunctions. But in suits against public entities, sovereign immunity had the odd effect of pushing judges to rely more heavily on "extraordinary" injunctive relief.

During the 1960s and 1970s, both inhibitions faded away. The federal courts gradually developed three sets of tools for supervising public institutions. This chapter traces the evolution of these remedial tools and examines their strengths and weaknesses for supervising public schools.

The best-known remedial instrument to emerge during this period is the structural injunction. Structural injunctions are detailed, frequently revised court orders that seek to restructure large government organizations. They tend to remain in place for years, even decades, and usually involve the appointment of special masters, monitors, or receivers by the judge. Initially developed in desegregation cases, the structural injunction was soon used to reform prisons, welfare agencies, state hospitals, and police departments.

Just as important—and far more pervasive—is the Section 1983 suit. First enacted as part of the Ku Klux Klan Act of 1871, the key provision of Section 1983 reads as follows:

Every person who, under color of any statute, ordinance, regulation, custom, or usage, of any state . . . subjects, or causes to be subjected, any citizen of the United States or other person within the jurisdiction thereof to the deprivation of any rights, privileges, or immunities secured by the Constitution and laws, shall be liable to the party injured in an action at law, suit in equity, or other proper proceeding for redress.

The most important feature of Section 1983 is that it allows those alleging a "deprivation of rights" to file suit in federal district court, which in turn is authorized to award monetary damages as well as to issue injunctions. In other words, under Section 1983 constitutional violations are converted into "constitutional torts," with federal courts defining both the nature of the violation and the extent of compensation. The Supreme Court's 1961 decision in *Monroe* v. *Pape* was the first of a long series of Court rulings that expanded the opportunity for students, parents, and teachers to seek monetary damages in suits against schools, school boards, and school administrators.[10] In 1976 Congress encouraged such litigation by allowing federal judges to award attorneys' fees to successful plaintiffs.[11] The total number of Section 1983 suits filed annually in federal court rose from about 200 before *Monroe* v. *Pape* to more than 20,000 in the mid-1970s, over 35,000 in the mid-1980s, and almost 58,000 by 1995.[12]

Starting in the 1970s, the federal courts developed a third remedial tool by recognizing "private rights of action" to enforce federal mandates such as the nondiscrimination provisions of Title VI of the Civil Rights Act and Title IX of the 1972 Education Amendments. When a court recognizes a private right of action under a statute, it authorizes private citizens to file suit to enforce its provisions. In the 1970s and 1980s, federal courts went even further, entertaining private suits to enforce administrative regulations promulgated under these federal statutes. By the early 1990s, the Supreme Court had also authorized lower courts to award monetary damages to victorious plaintiffs in these cases. The result was a potent court-agency alliance recently lauded by Justice John Paul Stevens as an "inspired model" for "attacking the often-intractable problem of racial and ethnic discrimination."[13]

Schools as Coping Organizations

Since each of these judicially created remedies was a response to the difficulties judges faced in reforming public schools, it is important to understand the nature of those challenges. A useful place to start is James Q. Wilson's discussion of the compliance problem in various types of public agencies. "From a managerial point of view," says Wilson, "agencies differ in two main respects": the first is the extent to which managers can observe the *activities* of the organization's "operators," that is, the people (such as teachers) who do the most important work of the organization; the second is the extent to which managers can observe and measure the *results* of these activities. Wilson calls bureaucracies in which it is difficult either to observe operators' activities or to measure outcomes "coping organizations," the leading examples being police and schools. "A school administrator," Wilson notes, "cannot watch teachers teach (except through classroom visits that momentarily may change the teacher's behavior) and cannot tell how much students have learned (except by standardized tests that do not clearly differentiate between what the teacher has imparted and what the student has acquired otherwise)."[14]

Given these limitations, managing coping organizations is a particularly difficult job. What operators do on the job is likely to be affected more by their personal beliefs, training, and incentives than by directives issued from above. "Situational imperatives"—above all, the need to maintain order and to protect operators' personal safety—tend to be especially powerful in coping organizations. Operators expect managers to "back them up" when conflict arises, but otherwise to stay out of their way. Managers may be able to improve the performance of their organization by motivating their workforce or by choosing good workers (an inherently difficult task made all the harder by union rules), but they tend to spend much more time dealing with complaints (especially from politically influential constituencies) and constraints than trying to shape the behavior of operators: "Complaints can be rejected when the manager can show that the complained of behavior did not occur or they can be partially deflected when the manager can argue that the outcomes achieved justified the action in question. But coping agencies are precisely those that do not know with confidence what behavior occurred and cannot show with persuasiveness what outcomes resulted."[15] As a result, effective management "is almost impossible" in coping organizations.[16] If managers have a hard time controlling what goes on at the bottom of their organizations, what hope do more distant judges have of revising bureaucratic practices?

Wilson notes that ambitious managers and persistent critics of coping organizations dream of turning them into "production agencies" in which it is possible to observe the most important behavior of operators and to measure the most important accomplishments of the organization. This may not be impossible, but such efforts are rarely successful. Observing teachers in the American classroom, notes Rick Hess, is particularly difficult because of its current design:

The "egg crate" construction of classrooms gives teachers little sustained contact with one another, making it difficult to force reforms into classroom practice. Isolated in this way, teachers cannot be easily supervised and are able to buffer themselves from the school around them by simply closing the classroom door. In this context, lasting change in teaching and learning practices requires that reforms be delivered into each classroom separately and then infused into the school culture by sustained administrative effort.[17]

Perhaps the United States can move teachers out of their "egg crates," offer them substantially more supervision, establish rigid standard operating procedures, and insist that teachers throughout the country teach each subject in the same way. This, of course, would require extraordinary changes in the way education is organized. It would also conflict with the ethos, powerful both within the teaching profession and in the courts, that expects teachers to take into consideration the *individualized* needs of students. Suffice it to say that judges have shown little interest in standardizing curricula or establishing a rigid regimen for teaching.

It might also be possible to devise better measures of the effectiveness of schools and teachers, turning schools into what Wilson calls "craft" organizations—those in which one can accurately measure outcomes but not directly observe the activities of operators. Efforts to develop better outcome measures and to use them to spur competition and school improvement have been at the heart of education politics since the 1990s. Some people have derided these measures as worse than useless, saying they lead schools to substitute "teaching to the test" for "real" education. Others view them as useful but highly imperfect aggregate indicators of how various schools are doing. No one believes, however, that all or even most of the important things that schools should be doing can yet be accurately measured.

To those who study education policy, the basic features of school life no doubt seem too obvious to deserve much attention. Yet the voluminous legal literature on judicial supervision of schools seldom considers the enormous challenge they pose for judges, who are far removed from the activities of operators, only sporadically involved in education issues, and accustomed to governing by issuing general rules. This does not mean that the dilemmas of dealing with coping organizations have not left their mark on judicial practices. Few aphorisms are more overused than Oliver Wendell Holmes's remark that "the life of the law has not been logic; it has been experience." But here it does apply: since the early 1960s experience has produced three new judicial remedies, each of which has sought to address the inadequacies of previous approaches to educational reform.

Structural Injunctions

When the Supreme Court decided *Brown* v. *Board of Education* in 1954, its remedial arsenal was severely limited. Never before had the federal judiciary engaged in institutional reform on this scale. It took more than a decade after *Brown II* for the lower courts to develop—and the Supreme Court to approve— the first major tool of institutional reform, the structural injunction.

The structural injunction is used in virtually all school desegregation cases, as well as in most school finance litigation. Its development has been celebrated by legal scholars such as Fiss and Chayes, who consider it a prime example of the flexibility and inventiveness of the judicial branch. Critics argue that it poses a threat to democratic institutions and stretches judicial capacity to the breaking point.[18] No form of judicial remedy has been the focus of so many detailed case studies.[19] And none has been subjected to *less* review by the Supreme Court.

In retrospect, it is remarkable how quickly federal judges jumped to the con- clusion that school desegregation should be achieved through liberal use of the previously disfavored injunction. *Brown II* announced that "in fashioning and effectuating the decrees," lower courts would be "guided by equitable princi- ples." According to the Supreme Court's short and cryptic explanation, "Tradi- tionally, equity has been characterized by a practical flexibility in shaping its remedies and by facility for adjusting and reconciling public and private needs."[20] Ironically, the Court initially relied upon this extraordinary, weakly defined power in order to ease southern school systems into compliance with- out inciting an immediate confrontation with southern officials and parents. A remedy that looked only to future action rather than past mistakes fit well with the Court's strategy of avoiding recriminations and encouraging voluntary compliance. The fact that *Brown* was a class action suit made it particularly unlikely that the Court would focus on damages (which would have been nearly impossible to calculate for such a large and amorphous class) rather than injunctive relief.[21]

In 1955 the justices assumed that the decrees developed by district court judges with the help of school officials would remain fairly simple, confined to the basic elements of school attendance rules. In oral argument, Thurgood Marshall of the National Association for the Advancement of Colored People (NAACP) assured the Court that "the only thing that we are asking for is that the state-imposed racial segregation be taken off, and to leave the county school board, the county people, the district people, to work out their solu- tions of the problem to assign children on any reasonable basis they want to assign them on." Drawing new district lines on a nonracial basis would be so simple that it "might take six months to do it one place and two months to do it another place."[22]

Obviously, things did not turn out that way. After more than a decade of delay, the Fifth Circuit and the Supreme Court finally got serious about deseg- regation, and the "flexibility" of "equitable principles" was employed in ways that no one could have imagined a decade earlier. As Paul Gewirtz has noted, it was the massive southern resistance to desegregation "that required the courts to intrude with such coercion, with such detail, with such stubborn patience and courage, and with strategic and managerial preoccupations that strained the boundaries of the traditional judicial function."[23] As tricks and evasions multiplied, so, too, did the length and intrusiveness of judicial orders. The Supreme Court was reluctant to impose limits on the use of equitable remedies, lest it appear to undercut the often-heroic efforts of lower-court judges.

Southern resistance was not the only reason for expanding judicial supervision of school practices. Common sense dictated that judges pay attention to the many factors other than school assignment rules that could affect the long-term success of desegregation. Desegregating schools meant reassigning teachers as well as students. School siting decisions obviously have a big impact on the future composition of individual schools. It made little sense to integrate school buildings but then allow administrators to resegregate classrooms through their decisions on tracking. Were too many minority students being assigned to special education classes? Were they receiving harsher punishments and more frequent suspensions? Were they being excluded from extracurricular activities? Were minority students who spoke languages other than English being left behind? Given the track record of southern schools and the growing evidence that school officials in the north, too, had engaged in systematic racial discrimination, there seemed little reason for judges to rely on the good faith of school officials.

To complicate matters further, lower courts increasingly understood their task as eliminating all the "vestiges" of segregation. Since de jure segregation in the South and more subtle forms of discrimination elsewhere in the country had denied African American students equal educational opportunity for generations, this seemed to suggest that schools had an obligation to provide them with compensatory programs that would bring them up to the educational level they would have attained in the absence of such unconstitutional state action.[24] How else could they "be made whole"? The longer federal courts struggled with desegregation suits, the murkier the meaning of "desegregation" became.

The most prominent feature of the structural injunction is that the district court judge has very broad power to issue orders, to revise them as he or she sees fit, and to enforce them by threatening to hold violators in contempt of court. This includes decrees requiring state and local governments to raise revenues sufficient to pay for services mandated by the court. Public officials who fail to comply with these court orders can be fined or even imprisoned. Of course, this rarely happens. But as the well-publicized Yonkers, New York, housing desegregation case shows, such threats tend to focus the mind.[25] When Alexander Hamilton wrote that the judiciary "has no influence over either the sword or the purse," he demonstrated that he had never encountered a structural injunction.

Given the potential sweep and coerciveness of structural injunctions, Supreme Court guidance on the use of injunctions has remained remarkably vague.[26] The Court regularly repeats that "the scope of the remedy is determined by the nature and extent of the constitutional violation" but seldom explains how one gets from the latter to the former. "Generally uninterested in procedural and tactical details in school cases," it has failed to "set out principles to govern the use of experts, masters, or supervisory committees" or to clarify the crucial issues of "intervention and participation, or of permissible strategies of inducing settlement."[27] Although the Rehnquist court made it somewhat easier for district courts to terminate desegregation orders, it offered only the vaguest guidance on when they must do so.[28]

The Court's most extended discussion of the use of equitable remedies in desegregation cases came in Chief Justice Warren Burger's 1971 *Swann* opinion. Unfortunately, that text reads more like a speech by Polonius than a careful legal exegesis. Most apparent was the extensive delegation of authority to district court judges familiar with facts on the ground:

> The scope of a district court's equitable powers to remedy past wrongs is broad, for breadth and flexibility are inherent in equitable remedies. The essence of equity jurisdiction has been the power of the Chancellor to do equity and to mould each decree to the necessities of the particular case. . . . In this area, we must of necessity rely to a large extent, as this Court has for more than 16 years, on the informed judgment of the district court in the first instance and on courts of appeals.

The chief justice insisted that there were limits on the district court's authority to bus young children and to require numerically balanced schools, yet he seemed incapable of enunciating them. Indeed, Burger announced that "in seeking to define the scope of remedial power or limits on remedial power of courts in an area as sensitive as we deal with here, words are poor instruments to convey the sense of basic fairness inherent in equity."[29] But the words contained in judicial opinions are virtually the only mechanism the Supreme Court has for directing lower courts. Certainly the words of Chief Justice Burger were poor instruments for imposing any limits on them.[30]

The most prominent feature of the structural injunction is that it concentrates authority in the hands of the district court judge and those he anoints as his principal lieutenants. In this sense, as Owen Fiss has put it, the structural injunction "represents the antithesis of separation of powers."[31] It also represents a striking departure from widely accepted norms of impartial adjudication. "Once we enter the enforcement phase," Fiss notes, "it is likely that the triadic structure will collapse, or at lease get blurred, and realignment will occur, with the judge and plaintiff now aligned against the defendant."[32] As a result, the injunction "becomes an expression of a person, as much as an expression of an office, and represents a striking instance of the personification of the law." Thus "when we speak of the decisional authority in the injunctive process we often talk not of *the law* or even of *the court,* but of Judge Johnson or Judge Garrity."[33]

The extensive powers wielded by district court judges armed with structural injunctions contrasts starkly with the decidedly modest accomplishments of desegregation litigation outside the South. Since the mid-1970s, desegregation litigation has generated enormous controversy but produced little racial integration or improvement in the education of minority children. Those on the left blame these shortcomings on the Supreme Court's decision in *Milliken* v. *Bradley,* which prevented the lower courts from mandating busing between central cities and the surrounding suburbs. But it is quite likely that if the four dissenters in *Milliken* had managed to pick up an additional vote, "white flight" would simply have taken the form of moving to more distant suburbs or an even larger exodus from public to private schools. One of the few things judges armed with structural injunctions cannot control is student enrollment. The exit option, the Court had announced decades before, is a constitutional right.

Clearly, courts have been less successful in reforming schools than in improving conditions in state mental hospitals, schools for the developmentally disabled, or even prisons.[34] It is worth asking why. The answer, I suggest, lies in the two defining features of coping organizations: (1) their lack of measurable outcomes and (2) the difficulty of observing and controlling the activities of street-level bureaucrats. Consider, first, how judges have defined the goals of desegregation, and then how they have tried to monitor the behavior of schools' "operators."

Running through almost all court opinions on desegregation—from the Supreme Court to the circuit courts to the district courts—is a stunning lack of clarity and candor on the meaning of desegregation. From 1954 through 1968, the Supreme Court made no effort to define this key term. Then, with the help of the Fifth Circuit, the Court started to explain what it means to dismantle a "dual" school system "root and branch" and replace it with a "unitary" system. According to the case law developed between 1968 and 1974 in *Green, Swann, Keyes,* and *Milliken,* "desegregation" meant that each school within a school district found guilty of intentional discrimination (which by now meant almost all school systems with a significant minority population) had to achieve a racial balance roughly the same as the proportion of minority students in the school system as a whole.[35] That is, if a system was 70 percent white and 30 percent black, then each school should be roughly 70 percent white and 30 percent black. And if the system was 80 percent minority and 20 percent white, those remaining white students should be distributed evenly among the schools in the system—even if that was almost certain to produce further white flight.

This definition of desegregation was the product not of systematic analysis, but of piecemeal decisionmaking by an increasingly divided Court. *Green* and *Swann* mandated racial balance in schools previously segregated by law. *Keyes* extended this requirement to northern school systems that had engaged in more subtle forms of discrimination. *Milliken* ensured that in most large cities almost all of these "racially balanced" schools would remain primarily black and Hispanic. During the 1980s the Court did not issue a single decision modifying or clarifying this exceedingly odd position. In the early 1990s the Court made it somewhat easier for lower courts to terminate decades-old desegregation cases but did little to change their underlying legal rationale.

It is a testament to the good sense of federal district court judges that few considered this understanding of desegregation—desegregation by the numbers in school systems with fewer and fewer whites—an adequate guide for action. For them, the "promise of *Brown*" went well beyond such counterproductive measures. Desegregation was not an end in itself, but a means for improving the education provided to minority students, for ensuring that educational opportunity is, in Chief Justice Warren's words, "made available to all on equal terms."[36] The broader purposes of desegregation were summarized by Judge Richard Matsch, who oversaw the desegregation of Denver schools:

> A unitary school system is one in which all of the students have equal access to the opportunities for education, with the publicly provided educational resources distributed equitably, and with the expectation that all students can acquire a community defined level of knowledge and skills consistent with her individual efforts and abilities. It provides a chance to develop fully each individual's potential, without being restricted by an identification with any racial or ethnic group.[37]

As urban schools became majority black and Hispanic, improving educational opportunities for minority students became more important than keeping a few white kids in each class. Perhaps improving schools would increase the "desegregative attractiveness" of these schools, that is, draw in white students from the suburbs. At any rate, it would improve the education and the life chances of the minority students remaining in failing urban schools.

The Supreme Court seemed to endorse this understanding of "effective" desegregation when it approved the compensatory programs mandated by the district court judge in the second round of the Detroit litigation. A unanimous Court ruled that the district court could require Detroit to establish (and the State of Michigan to help pay for) new magnet and vocational schools as well as "in-service training for teachers and administrators, guidance and counseling programs, and revised testing procedures." The Court deferred to the lower court's judgment that such educational matters were "needed to remedy effects of past segregation, to assure a successful desegregative effort, and to minimize the possibility of resegregation." Taken as a whole, the mandated educational programs would "restore the victims of discriminatory conduct to the position they would have enjoyed" had public officials not acted unconstitutionally. In *Milliken II* the Court concluded that federal courts cannot "close their eyes to inequalities . . . which flow from a longstanding segregated system."[38]

Who could possibly disagree with this? The problem was that judges had *replaced a clear but unreasonably narrow goal with a commendable but amorphous one*: improving education in urban schools. Consequently, they faced the same problem confronting school reformers past and present: how to improve a sprawling school system without clear performance measures, without proven techniques or technologies, with little short-run control over personnel, and with no control over the lives of children outside the classroom.

Compared with school superintendents, judges have two glaring deficiencies: they have no previous experience running schools or special training in educational policy, and they can devote only a fraction of their time to school matters. But they also possess one great advantage: they can force state governments and local school districts to spend more money on education.

Case studies on the development of structural injunctions repeatedly show judges to be negotiators rather than dictators.[39] Initially they almost always rely on school leaders—usually superintendents—to propose desegregation plans. School officials can offer judges detailed plans and crucial assistance in carrying them out. Judges, in turn, can help school officials garner the money and other resources they need to do so. They can also insulate them from political pressures. Frequently these suits (and similar suits involving prisons and state facilities for the mentally ill and developmentally disabled) are close to collusive. In fact, in Kansas City it was the school board itself that filed the initial desegregation case. The judge then realigned the school district as a defendant and searched for lawyers to represent the "plaintiffs," who were quickly recruited to create the appearance of a live "case or controversy."[40] In the Detroit suit, the school district switched sides immediately after the completion of the liability phase of the litigation.[41]

It seldom takes long for this cozy alliance to fall on troubled times. Plaintiffs' attorneys become impatient with the schools' lack of progress. Their experts offer more aggressive and innovative reform ideas. Expected to produce a plan that "promises realistically to work *now*," as the Supreme Court mandated in *Green,* judges are sorely tempted to delegate power to academic experts who promise to overhaul the entire educational system on the basis of the most up-to-date academic findings. The superintendent of the Denver schools conceded that "some of us find it so comfortable working for judges rather than our normal bosses that we may not actually want to be out from court orders." But the constant revisions and additions suggested by plaintiffs' experts and lawyers create "moving goalposts" that produce seemingly endless conflict between school administrators and litigants.[42]

Structural injunctions, case studies show, invariably centralize control over school policymaking not in the hands of a heroic or dictatorial judge but in a new set of repeat players that Ross Sandler and David Schoenbrod aptly call the "controlling group."[43] This includes lawyers for the plaintiffs, school superintendents and their lawyers, and the special master or compliance officers appointed by the court. This centralized body does some things relatively well. It can supervise the construction of new facilities, hire personnel with specialized training, and establish new protocols for assessing students and meting out punishments. All these tasks are susceptible to centralized monitoring and control. Even in the dysfunctional Kansas City school system, the capital improvement phase of the court-mandated program proceeded relatively smoothly.[44]

What the centralized "controlling group" has not proved capable of doing is changing the behavior of teachers in the classroom. The Kansas City desegregation case provides a particularly graphic (and tragic) example of this. The magnet school plan ordered by Judge Russell G. Clark required the school system to spend hundreds of millions of dollars on new facilities. The goal was to produce "theme" schools that would energize both teachers and students. But, as Josh Dunn has explained, neither teachers nor students actually chose their schools on the basis of special academic interests. Teachers almost always decided to stay at their current school, and to teach in the same manner they had taught before. Students predictably chose their school on the basis of where their friends were going. Physically, the classrooms changed, but what happened inside them did not.[45]

Another example comes from the long-running New York City special education litigation. Lawyers for the plaintiffs had considerable success in hiring specialized personnel and changing evaluation procedures, but much less in achieving mainstreaming within regular classrooms. As their lead counsel, Michael Rebell, explained: "Substantial improvements in mainstreaming practices undoubtedly would require a sustained commitment . . . by the entire school system. Extensive institutional impediments posed by the union contract, teacher apathy, administrators' resistance, and space limitations had to be overcome. Meaningful mainstreaming would also require sensitive preparation of children in the regular classes and of the handicapped students and their parents."[46] Ever the judicial optimist, Rebell expressed confidence that these issues could be successfully resolved by 1989—ten years after the parents and their lawyers had signed the initial consent decree in the case. His co-counsel, John Gray, was not so sure: "Courts are effective in getting enough money into the system, and getting planning, staff, and data. But courts are not so good on quality of the program like achieving the least restrictive environment."[47]

Much of the literature on judicial supervision of schools focuses on the special institutional capabilities and limitations of the judiciary. I am more struck by the *similarities* between reforms pursued through structural injunctions and the superintendent-led reform efforts described by Rick Hess. In both superintendent- and court-led efforts, reformers relish the task of announcing bold new plans "but pay insufficient attention to making them work."[48] They concentrate on what can be controlled from the center—the expenditure of new funds, the creation of specialized programs, the hiring of new personnel, the announcement of new procedures—and put on the back burner the arduous task of changing the incentives, the routines, the training, and the motivating of classroom teachers. The churning of personnel and reform proposals and the growth of central office staff that Hess considers fatal to significant educational change are particularly apparent in school systems subject to judicial supervision.

School systems under court order do differ in one key respect from those described by Hess: they are more insulated from political pressure and from parents' complaints. In theory, these cases are brought on behalf of students and their parents. In practice, "this is lawyer-initiated and lawyer-controlled litigation."[49] Given the many ways in which short-term political demands and constraints can inhibit significant change in educational policy, political insulation might be considered a major advantage of judicial supervision. But it also means that judges and the "controlling groups" they empower are never held accountable for the results (or non-results) of their efforts. In Kansas City, the court's failure to listen to complaints of black parents—who repeatedly argued that the exotic themes of the judicially created magnet schools ignored the needs of minority students who were failing basic math and English—eventually led to a political revolt against the entire plan.[50]

Charles Sabel and William Simon have recently shown that judges are shifting "away from command-and-control, injunctive regulation" toward "experimentalist intervention."[51] Judges appear to have become disillusioned with the "top-down, fixed-rule regimes" because they end up focusing too much attention on inputs rather than outputs and because they discourage rather than stimulate public participation. Too often "the operations of the agencies depended on the street-level conduct of myriad subordinates far below the court's view." While it is not clear what Sabel and Simon mean by "experimentalist intervention," at the very least it includes developing new ways to measure the consequences of educational reforms. Their main example of a successful shift in the focus of litigation is the Baltimore school desegregation case. Here a detailed and unsuccessful twenty-year-old injunction was replaced with a "Consent Order

Approving Ultimate Measurable Outcomes," a six-page document that "speci-
fies sixteen outcomes and procedures for measuring progress toward attaining
them." This new approach, Sabel and Simon note, has "been influenced by the
'new accountability' movement in educational reform."[52]

If courts and litigants could come up with reliable methods for measuring
important educational outcomes, then they surely would improve the quality of
judicial supervision of schools. This, of course, is what all educational alchemists
seek: a method for turning "coping" organizations into more tractable "craft" or
"production" agencies. And if pigs could fly. . . . This is not to suggest that
improving methods for measuring outcomes is not valuable. But it is hard to see
how courts will improve upon the efforts spurred by No Child Left Behind and
similar state legislation. Court-led efforts to establish objective quantitative
measures of the essential elements of an "adequate" education do not inspire
confidence.[53] It is also unclear what incentives courts can employ in these sys-
tem-wide cases to improve the performance of schools and teachers. In short,
the deficiencies of "command-and-control" regulation by injunction are more
apparent than the success of the "experimental" alternative.[54]

Section 1983 and Constitutional Torts

Injunctions are rare—and becoming rarer all the time in education. Most court
cases against school districts and officials are now brought under Section1983
by teachers, students, and parents seeking money damages and relatively specific
changes in school policy. Indeed, over the past four decades Section1983 has
become "the centerpiece of federal court relief against local governments and
state and local officers."[55]

In many ways Section1983 suits for monetary damages are the mirror image
of cases culminating in structural injunctions. They are usually brought by ordinary citizens dissatisfied with or angered by particular school actions, not by
interest groups seeking systemic reform. They focus on past misconduct rather
than a prospective policy change. As a form of tort litigation, Section 1983 suits
are specifically designed to shift the incentives structure of street-level bureaucrats and their managers—a consideration strangely absent from structural
injunctions litigation, as already mentioned. Appellate rulings on liability,
immunity, and damages under Section 1983 are as numerous and convoluted as
Supreme Court guidance on structural injunctions is sparse and ambiguous. In
fact, court precedents on Section1983 are so complicated and shifting that
entire casebooks and law school courses are devoted to them—which makes it
all too easy to lose sight of the central issue, which is how these suits are likely to
change the behavior of government officials.

The 1961 Supreme Court decision that triggered the growth of Section 1983 litigation provides some insight into why members of the Supreme Court as well as most lower court judges and commentators have found it so important to offer this judicial sword to those alleging a violation of legal rights. *Monroe* v. *Pape* was a Section 1983 suit filed by a black Chicagoan and his family against police officers who, without a search warrant, "broke into petitioners' home in the early morning, routed them from bed, made them stand naked in the living room, and ransacked every room."[56] The police took Mr. Monroe to the police station, where they detained him for ten hours, interrogating him about a recent murder without providing him with a lawyer. Since Monroe was eventually released without being charged with a crime, the abusive constables could not be punished through the exclusion of evidence at his trial: no trial, no application of the exclusionary rule. Monroe's only available remedy was either a tort sued in Illinois court or a Section 1983 action in federal court. Justice Felix Frankfurter argued that he should be required to proceed first to state court, invoking Section 1983 only if state redress proved unavailing. But Justice William O. Douglas, who wrote for the majority, had less faith in state judges. He read Section 1983 to allow plaintiffs to proceed directly to federal court without first exhausting their state remedies.

Justice Douglas's opinion did not interpret Section 1983 to authorize suits against the city of Chicago, but only against the rogue officers who had apparently acted contrary to official city policy. Permitting suits against individual officials rather than directly against state and local governments allowed the Court to sidestep the difficult issue of sovereign immunity. This had the unintended effect of focusing courts' attention on the behavior of particular street-level bureaucrats rather than on the training and supervision provided by public agencies. It also made it difficult for victorious plaintiffs to collect the damages awarded by the court. After all, street-level bureaucrats seldom have deep pockets. Most states and localities, though, now provide defendants in Section 1983 suits with legal counsel and pay damage awards from public funds—which forces them to pay attention to the costs of losing such suits.[57]

Monroe v. *Pape* illustrates several of the most important characteristics of the Warren court: determination to take aggressive action to protect civil rights, commitment to increasing judicial supervision of police and prosecutors, distrust of states' capacity to correct civil rights violations, and willingness to develop novel readings of constitutional provisions and statutes to achieve these goals. More surprising is the Burger court's expansion of government liability under Section 1983. The allegedly conservative Burger court was almost as activist as the Warren court, albeit in a less ostentatious and overtly constitutional manner. Not only did the Burger court introduce *Bivens* actions in 1971, but from 1977 to 1980 it announced a series of decisions that expanded the reach of Section 1983 and narrowed the defenses available to government officials.[58] Most important, the Court reversed its position in *Monroe* v. *Pape* that municipalities could not be sued under Section 1983, concluding that not only can municipalities be required to pay money damages, but unlike individual officials, they are not entitled to "good faith" immunity.[59] Furthermore, a local school district "is more like a county or city than it is an arm of the State" and thus is "not entitled to assert any Eleventh Amendment immunity from suit in federal court."[60] The Court subsequently developed an elaborate set of rules on liability, immunity, and damages to apply to school districts and school board members as well as teachers, principals, and superintendents.

Why did the Burger court, which in many other respects was more reluctant to impose judicially imposed standards on state and local governments, spearhead this expansion of Section 1983? Perhaps as judges and commentators became more aware of the difficulties courts face in imposing systemic change in large government institutions, they felt Section 1983 suits could help curb the worst abuses within these institutions without exceeding the institutional capacity of the judicial branch. In the Court's 1982 opinion in *Youngberg* v. *Romeo,* for example, Justice Lewis F. Powell's majority opinion paints Section 1983 litigation as a way to "minimize" the "interference by the federal judiciary with the internal operations of these institutions" without completely abandoning the field.[61] Structural injunctions epitomize the free-wheeling judicial policymaking that critics claim is more appropriate for legislators and administrators than for judges. Constitutional tort law seemed to fit more easily into the traditional role of judges working within the adjudicatory process.

Unlike cases culminating in structural injunctions, Section 1983 litigation is designed to create powerful disincentives for the abuse of discretionary authority by street-level bureaucrats and strong incentives for managers to provide their agents with the training, standard operating procedures, and supervision needed to minimize misuse of authority. Court opinions on Section 1983 are filled with discussions of the deterrence provided by such litigation. By requiring agencies to compensate those harmed by official misconduct, this form of tort law could (in theory at least) force agencies to internalize the social costs of the actions of their employees and thus impel them to establish mechanisms for effective internal control.

Despite the voluminous literature on Section 1983 and the central role of incentives and deterrence in the debate over constitutional torts, there are few empirical studies of the effects of these liability rules on street-level bureaucrats in organizations such as schools, prisons, and police departments. The only sustained effort to think about how Section 1983 actions are likely to affect the use of discretion in such organizations was published by Peter Schuck more than twenty-five years ago.[62] No one has yet provided a convincing critique of his analysis of the perverse incentives created by federal court doctrines.[63]

While I cannot hope to do justice to Schuck's sophisticated argument here, its outlines are worth repeating. Many government officials, he points out, exercise significant discretions in conditions of great uncertainty and, sometimes, personal danger. They routinely exercise coercion over identifiable—and often angry, resentful, and indignant—members of the public. Unlike those working in the private sector, public officials cannot profit from aggressive pursuit of their organization's goals. Liability under Section 1983 significantly increases the costs to individual officials and to the organization as a whole of making a mistake—for example, being overly aggressive in arresting, searching, or pursuing a suspect or being too harsh in punishing a student.

Taking action in situations when the risks and the legal rules are uncertain exposes the official to legal liability. But *failure* to take action does not: "When a school official disciplines a student, he may do so unjustly; when he fails to impose discipline, he may impair the learning opportunities of many others. . . . The risks of being sued for choosing one course of action rather than the other are not equal. Remedies are strongly biased in favor of the highly visible victim."[64] "As a result," Schuck argues, "the official's caution is likely to assume proportions that can reduce his willingness to pursue the objectives that his agency is required to advance."[65] The "asymmetric pressures on officials confronted with the risk of personal liability" produce the "tactics of inaction, delayed action, formalism, and selection of the least risky decision alternative." Those "who ultimately bear the costs of such behavior tend to be 'silent victims,' probably either unaware that they are being injured or ignorant that their victimization is the consequence of another's personal risk-minimizing behavior." They tend to be people "who must rely heavily upon street-level public services to assure their safety and well-being; they are almost certainly disproportionately poor and dependent."[66] In other words, litigation tends to recognize the concentrated costs imposed on those who are the visible victims of official misconduct, but not the widely dispersed costs that stem from officials' risk-adverse behavior.

One way to compensate for this asymmetry would be to allow these "silent victims" to sue for the government's failure to provide adequate services or protections. The Supreme Court inched in that direction in the early 1980s, when it invoked something akin to a medical malpractice negligence standard to decide whether a patient in a state institution had been provided constitutionally adequate care and habilitation.[67] But in noncustodial situations the federal judiciary has been understandably reluctant to establish constitutional standards for the provision of government services and protections. The Supreme Court has explicitly refused to recognize Section 1983 claims against child services agencies and police departments that fail to protect vulnerable people from violent behavior by other private citizens. In a recent case, the Court announced that Section1983 simply does not "create a system by which police departments are generally held financially accountable for crimes that better policing might have prevented."[68]

These government protection cases present in graphic form the problem that haunts all Section 1983 cases: the difficulty in developing "judicially manageable standards" for defining either official misconduct or government effectiveness. The truth is that federal courts have had a difficult time doing this even in misconduct cases, which would seem to be simpler than effectiveness cases. Time and again, they have fallen back on the highly subjective and frequently criticized "shocks-the-conscience" test."[69] The Supreme Court has been understandably reluctant to impose stiff penalties on officials who could not have known whether the action they took would "shock the conscience" of the judges who happen to hear the case.[70] Section 1983 litigation may be an effective mechanism for punishing particularly egregious conduct, but, so far at least, it has been significantly less successful in establishing clear codes of conduct for public officials or improving the quality of the services provided by them.

Private Rights of Action and Federal Mandates

What if the courts could address these challenges by discovering a way to increase the specificity of their rules, to offer advanced warning to administrators, and to provide democratic legitimacy to the entire endeavor? In effect, this is what federal courts have tried to do in "private right of action" cases enforcing conditions on federal grants, particularly nondiscrimination mandates such as Title VI and Title IX. According to this model of judicial supervision—developed in a halting way with little explicit explanation by any of its architects—Congress establishes the basic structure of federal regulation, thus supplying democratic legitimacy. Federal agencies provide the expertise and rulemaking capacity necessary to turn vague constitutional and statutory commands into clear, enforceable standards. And the federal courts offer access and remedies to those injured by state and local officials' failure to comply with federal guidelines.

When Congress imposes mandates on state and local governments, it sometimes explicitly authorizes court suits to enforce these requirements.[71] Usually, though, Congress neither authorizes nor forbids such suits, leaving it to federal judges to decide whether such a remedy is "implied" by the statute's structure, language, or legislative history. When it enacted the most sweeping and controversial federal mandates—Title VI of the Civil Rights Act of 1964, which bans discrimination on the basis of race and national origin in federally funded programs; Title IX of the Education Amendments of 1972, which prohibits discrimination on the basis of gender in all education programs funded by the federal government; and Section 504 of the 1974 Rehabilitation Act, which prohibits those receiving federal funding from discriminating on the basis of disability—Congress was completely silent on the issue of private enforcement. Neither the language of these statutes nor their pre-passage legislative histories devoted any attention to this important matter. Nonetheless, the Supreme Court has consistently (but hardly unanimously) ruled that these statutory mandates incorporate "implied" private rights of action.

Title VI of the Civil Rights Act set the pattern for the enforcement process that grew up around these mandates. Title VI was originally viewed as a mechanism for replacing costly, time-consuming constitutional litigation with decisive administrative action. As President John F. Kennedy explained, "Indirect discrimination, through the use of Federal funds, is just as invidious" as direct discrimination, "and it should not be necessary to resort to the court to prevent each individual violation."[72] There was little dispute about this during the long debate over the act, with "almost no attention . . . to Title VI, the sleeper that would become by far the most powerful weapon of them all."[73]

Title VI contains two key provisions. The first proclaims: "No person in the United States shall, on the ground of race, color, or national origin, be excluded from participation in, be denied the benefits of, or be subjected to discrimination under any program or activity receiving Federal financial assistance." The second requires federal agencies to promulgate rules to achieve this goal and authorizes them to enforce their rules through termination of federal funds or "any other method authorized by law." The House and the Senate imposed several constraints on the use of this administrative power: the rules must be approved by the president himself, state and local governments are entitled to a public hearing prior to termination of funds and judicial review after the fact, federal agencies must give Congress thirty days' advance warning of terminations, and terminations apply only to the particular program found guilty of discrimination, not the entire institution receiving funds. In marked contrast to Title VII of the act, which prohibited racial and gender discrimination by private employers and originally authorized *only* private enforcement suits, there was no discussion of private enforcement of Title VI. This is not surprising given the purpose of this section of the act, namely, to empower federal agencies to pursue an administrative *alternative* to litigation. Since it was already unconstitutional either for state and local governments to discriminate on the basis of race or for the federal government to support such activity, suits by aggrieved private individuals were already available under Section 1983—which was just too cumbersome to be effective. This explains why the private right of action issue received no mention from a Congress that was so attentive to the role of the courts in other sections of the Civil Rights Act.

From detailed accounts of southern school desegregation and the development of affirmative action programs in the construction industry, it is clear that
administrative action under Title VI initially proved a potent weapon for
change.[74] But it did not take long for most federal agencies to discover that termination of funding is too blunt and extreme a sanction to be politically palat-
able or administratively attractive in ordinary times. In a report highly critical of
federal agencies' enforcement of Title VI, the Commission on Civil Rights identified a central dilemma facing funding agencies: "Although funding termination may serve as an effective deterrent to recipients, it may leave the victim of
discrimination without a remedy. Funding termination may eliminate the benefits sought by the victim."[75] Just as important, funding cut-offs threaten to damage relations between the federal agency and state and local officials with whom
it worked on a regular basis—not to mention antagonize members of Congress
upon whom administrators rely for appropriations.

In the early 1970s, civil rights advocates blamed the shortcomings of Title VI
enforcement on the Nixon administration and launched the Dickensian case of
Adams v. *Richardson* (1973) to force the Department of Health, Education, and
Welfare (HEW) to be more aggressive.[76] After years of unproductive litigation,
it became evident that the central problem lay not in the political motives of
Republican administrations so much as in the administrative mechanisms created by Title VI. Meanwhile civil rights groups were slowly and haphazardly
developing an alternative for putting teeth in Title VI: private suits to enforce
the rules promulgated by federal agencies but not aggressively enforced by them.
If these agency rules had merely tracked court rulings defining racial discrimination under the Fourteenth Amendment, such litigation would have been of little
significance. But agency rules under Title VI usually went far beyond what the
courts had deemed constitutionally required. In order to provide specific guidance to recipients of federal funding, agency rules created a strong presumption
in favor of racial proportionality. They took a hard line against practices that
have a "disproportionate impact" on racial minorities without being intentionally discriminatory.

Bilingual education provides a good example of the division of labor that
developed between courts and agencies under Title VI. In 1970 HEW's Office
of Civil Rights (OCR) announced that a school's failure to provide bilingual
education to students not speaking English as their first language constituted
discrimination on the basis of national origin. Idealistic young lawyers in OCR
(encouraged by White House officials eager to court Hispanic voters) wrote
guidelines explaining the new federal bilingual education mandate. But they did
virtually nothing to force schools to comply, or even to figure out how many
school districts had instituted acceptable practices. In its 1974 decision in *Lau* v.
Nichols, the Supreme Court both approved HEW's rules and suggested that

they could be enforced in federal court. HEW subsequently issued more specific bilingual education rules—known appropriately as the "*Lau* remedies"—and federal district courts in New York and New Mexico ordered school districts with large numbers of Hispanic students to comply with them.[77]

These developments transformed a mechanism initially designed to create an administrative alternative to litigation into one that combined broad rulemaking authority for federal agencies with judicial enforcement through private suits. Title VI was clearly designed to give agencies authority to issue "prophylactic" regulations that extend beyond the basic requirements of the Constitution. At the same time, significant restrictions were placed on the agency's power to promulgate and enforce these rules. Everyone knew that termination of funding would be a highly visible action that most agencies would take only in unusual circumstances. Termination requires the expenditure of a considerable amount of political capital.

Judicial enforcement changed this political equation significantly. Now agencies could write broad Title VI regulations and allow others to take the political heat for enforcing them, something civil rights organizations and federal judges were happy to do. Even more important, federal judges could enforce these rules not by ordering the termination of funding—by far the most obvious remedy for the violation of Title VI—but by issuing injunctions requiring recipients to alter their practices in specific ways to comply with agency rules. After all, private parties did not go to court to end the funding of programs in which they participated; they wanted state and local officials to use federal money in different ways. Remarkably, the Supreme Court heard many cases under Title VI and its various "clones" for years without directly addressing the underlying questions of who could file suit and what kind of relief could be ordered at the courts. The lower courts understandably took the Supreme Court's silence as a green light to entertain private rights of action and to issue injunctions requiring compliance with agency rules.[78] Not until 1979 did the Court squarely address the former issue, cryptically declaring that the administrative funding cut-off should be supplemented by the injunctive power of the courts because the process explicitly created by Congress was insufficient to protect the rights established in agency rules.[79]

In the 1970s private rights of action under Titles VI and IX were usually brought by civil rights organizations. Not only were these cases too expensive for most private individuals to pursue, but prospective injunctive relief promised few benefits for those initially aggrieved. The 1976 Civil Rights Attorneys Fees Awards Act made suits under Titles VI and IX more attractive to these groups by allowing judges to award fees and costs to the "prevailing parties." Oddly, Congress included both titles in this legislation without explicitly authorized private suits under them. Congress was clearly more favorably disposed to aggressive enforcement of these rules in the mid-1970s than it had been a decade before, yet it remained curiously silent on key issues.

An even more important spur to litigation came from the Supreme Court: it authorized federal judges to award *monetary damages* to plaintiffs in Title VI and Title IX cases. The court first permitted the award of back pay in a splintered, garbled decision on racial discrimination in the employment practices of the New York City Police Department.[80] A decade later the Court announced that federal courts could require public schools to pay damages to students who have been subjected to sexual harassment by teachers.[81] Soon thereafter it ruled that a student could sue a school district for monetary damages when it fails to take adequate steps to prevent sexual harassment by a fellow student.[82] In each case the Court placed substantial weight on sexual harassment guidelines issued by the Department of Education, which, it argued, had afforded schools clear notice of what was expected of recipients of federal funding. In authorizing monetary damages, the Court argued that the "general rule" is that "absent clear direction to the contrary by Congress, the federal courts have the power to award *any* appropriate relief in a cognizable cause of action brought pursuant to a federal statute."[83] Since the causes of action under Titles VI and IX are "implied" not explicit, they establish no limitations on awards. As Justice Antonin Scalia pointed out, this creates the odd rule "that the most question-able of private rights will also be the most expansively remediable."[84]

The combination of attorneys' fees and monetary damages significantly increased incentives for private parties to file suits under Titles VI and IX. Eventually a private bar developed to litigate these cases. This had the effect not just of increasing the number of cases filed but also of augmenting the political support for this enforcement mechanism.[85]

In 2001, Justice Stevens argued that the "integrated remedial scheme" developed by the courts, Congress, and agencies under Title VI "reflects a reasonable—indeed inspired—model for attacking the often-intractable problem of racial and ethnic discrimination." The letter of the law prohibits overt discrimination. "With regard to more subtle forms of discrimination (such as schemes that limit benefits or services on ostensibly race-neutral grounds but have the predictable and perhaps intended consequence of materially benefiting some races at the expense of others)," Stevens claimed, "the statute does not establish a static approach but instead empowers the relevant agencies to evaluate social circumstances to determine whether there is a need for stronger measures." This division of labor "builds into the law flexibility, an ability to make nuanced assessments of complex social realities, and an admirable willingness to credit the possibility of progress."[86]

Since the issue in this case was virtually identical to the one decided by the Court a quarter-century earlier in *Lau* v. *Nichols,* Stevens considered it particularly easy to resolve.[87] Surprisingly, though, he lost. In a decision that Stevens bitterly and accurately described as "unfounded in our precedent and hostile to decades of settled expectations," the Court held that while private parties could sue to enforce the explicit statutory mandate contained in the first section of Title VI, they could not sue to enforce agency *regulations* issued under the second section of that provision.

Alexander v. *Sandoval* was in large part a reflection of the Rehnquist court's hostility to affirmative action and to "effects" tests in discrimination cases. The Court's five-member majority in essence said, "Since we interpret Title VI to outlaw only *intentional* discrimination, we will not allow agencies to impose a broader definition through the rulemaking process." But *Sandoval* also indicated that some members of the Court—perhaps a majority, but a fleeting one at best—entertained serious doubts about the entire set of institutional arrangements that have grown up around Titles VI and IX. Under the new regime created by *Sandoval,* it would seem, when agencies seek to go beyond the Court's interpretation of Title VI, they are on their own in the enforcement process. They must invoke the awkward funding termination process rather than rely on court-based enforcement by private parties.

It is too early to write the obituary for Stevens's "inspired model" for attacking discrimination. In a 2005 "retaliation" case brought under Title IX, a closely divided Court seemed to retreat from *Sandoval's* narrow interpretation of the judicially enforceable rights contained in broad federal mandates.[88] The direction the Court will now take depends largely on the number of judicial appointments made by President Barack Obama. It is also quite possible that a Democratic Congress could amend the relevant statutes to explicitly authorize private damage suits enforcing agency rules. When Democrats controlled Congress in the 1980s and 1990s, they repeatedly reversed Supreme Court decisions restricting civil rights litigants' access to the federal courts.[89] One of the very first bills President Obama signed into law in 2009 overturned a Supreme Court decision that had imposed a very short statute of limitations on Title VII discrimination suits.[90]

It is more useful to examine the reasons for the growth of this enforcement regime than to speculate about the likelihood of its demise. The institutional arrangements that evolved under Titles VI and IX were the product of two convictions. The first is that for every federal right there should be an effective federal remedy, created, if necessary, by the courts. As the Supreme Court stated in *J. I. Case* v. *Borak* (1964), "It is the duty of the courts to be alert to provide such remedies as are necessary to make effective the congressional purpose."[91] The second is that neither the tools wielded by civil rights agencies under these statutes nor those previously employed by the courts—most notably structural injunctions and Section 1983 suits—were adequate for uprooting subtle yet invidious forms of discrimination. Implicit in the Court's marrying of private damage suits with administrative regulation under these statutory provisions is a recognition that the federal judiciary cannot go it alone in creating a federal common law on sexual harassment, bilingual education, special education, and so many other education issues.

How well has this "inspired model" worked in practice? The truth is that no one knows. No sooner had the Court put the finishing touches on this new form of remedy by adding monetary damages, than it placed the future of the entire venture in doubt. Legal scholars have been slow to recognize the nature of this new set of arrangements, and more empirically oriented scholars have generally ignored it—with one important exception.

The most fully developed example of this form of privately enforceable federal mandate is special education. Nowhere else has Congress been so explicit in authorizing private suit and establishing specific procedural and substantive guidelines for school systems. It is fair to say that the federal mandates developed under the Individuals with Disabilities Education Act have substantially improved the quality of education for children with disabilities. Furthermore, since 1975 improvements in special education have not come from large-scale class-action litigation such as the *Jose P.* case in New York City, but from the pressure exerted by innumerable parents and special education professionals in individualized education plan conferences, administrative hearings, and court suits on the placement of individual students.[92] The empowerment of parents, students, and special education experts through private suits is far more potent than centralizing structural injunctions.

Special education is unusual in important respects. For one thing, it was not hard to improve upon the abysmal education many schools provided to disabled children before the 1970s. More important, special education reforms are usually educational "add-ons." As James Q. Wilson notes, bureaucratic change is easiest when "a new program is added on to existing tasks without changing the core task or altering the organizational culture."[93] Special education has been most successful when it has rested on the recruitment of new employees with strong professional norms rather than required changes in the training and routines of existing staff. Nor can one overlook the costs imposed by these gains. The adversarial nature of proceedings under federal law produces substantial transaction costs, psychological as well as monetary. The ever-growing special education budget of most school systems has drained funds from other programs, raising significant questions about the relative cost-effectiveness of these expenditures. At the very least, one can conclude that the combination of federal mandates and private enforcement can be a potent method for changing school policy. Whether this is a change for the better is, as usual, a much more difficult question to answer.

Conclusion

This chapter has two themes. The first is that judicial remedies are not set in institutional or constitutional stone but are constantly evolving as courts try to respond to new challenges and to learn from their previous mistakes. All the remedial tools examined here were the product of the post-1960 civil rights era. Judges resorted to "equitable remedies" to escape from ordinary legal constraints on their authority. The Supreme Court's guidance to lower courts amounted to little more than "do whatever it takes." Court decisions on Section 1983 and private rights of action under federal mandates regularly departed from ordinary norms of statutory construction. Judges played fast and loose with statutory interpretation in order to create remedial instruments they believed would protect constitutional and statutory rights that courts had previously announced but failed to vindicate. Disputes over remedies may seem technical but frequently spark ideological divisions in the courts. The remedies examined here were generally created by the activist Warren court, expanded by an ideologically divided Burger court, and then pruned by a more conservative Rehnquist court. In cases shaping these remedies, judges not only revealed their assumptions about the proper functions of the institutions created by the U.S. Constitution but were forced to make practical judgments about how well various remedial arrangements are likely to work once placed in motion.

Second, in order for these remedies to work well, they must be adapted to the peculiar features of the target organization. Coping organizations such as schools are particularly hard nuts for courts to crack. The lower courts developed structural injunctions in order to take a comprehensive look at school practices and to bring wholesale change to previously segregated school systems. Over the years, the considerable shortcomings of this centralized, command-and-control regulation became apparent. Section 1983 litigation is more attuned to the complaints of individual parents and teachers, and more attentive to the incentives facing street-level bureaucrats. But it reinforces the tendency of coping organizations to be complaint- and constraint-driven. Private rights of action under federal statutes seem to combine the advantages of Section 1983 suits with the rulemaking authority of expert agencies. How well this combination works in practice is something not yet fully understood. Since judges must frequently make (at best) educated judgments about the way these remedial schemes will affect the behavior of government officials, it is unfortunate that empirically minded law-and-courts scholars have paid so little attention to this topic.

Sweeping claims about the inability of courts to achieve "social change" or their lack of control over either "the sword or the purse" ignore the many ways in which federal courts have augmented their enforcement power since the

1960s, often with assistance from Congress and the executive. At the same time, examination of why courts felt compelled to expand their remedial powers reminds us of the inherent difficulty of the many tasks they have undertaken and the concomitant danger of producing serious unintended consequences. Only studies that pay attention to the routines and incentives of street-level bureaucrats can determine whether the courts' new tools have proved adequate for achieving their ambitious new tasks.

Notes

1. Nelda H. Cambron-McCabe, Martha M. McCarthy, and Stephen B. Thomas, *Public School Law: Teachers' and Students' Rights*, 5th ed. (Boston: Allyn & Bacon, 2004).

2. Steven M. Teles, *The Rise of the Conservative Legal Rights Movement: The Battle for Control of the Law* (Princeton University Press, 2008); Thomas Burke, *Lawyers, Lawsuits, and Legal Rights: The Battle over Litigation in American Society* (University of California Press, 2002); Charles R. Epps, *The Rights Revolution: Lawyers, Activists and Supreme Courts in Comparative Perspective* (University of Chicago Press, 1999); Robert Kagan, *Adversarial Legalism: The American Way of Law* (Harvard University Press, 2001).

3. *Brown* v. *Board of Education*, 347 U.S. 483, 493 (1954).

4. Justice Holmes's famous and dismissive characterization of the equal protection clause came in his infamous opinion in *Buck* v. *Bell*, 274 U.S. 200 (1927).

5. *Pierce* v. *Society of Sisters*, 268 U.S. 510 (1925); *Meyer* v. *Nebraska*, 262 U.S. 390 (1923).

6. Martha Derthick, *Keeping the Compound Republic: Essays on American Federalism* (Brookings, 2001), p. 152.

7. Donald L. Horowitz, *The Courts and Social Policy* (Brookings, 1977).

8. Abram Chayes, "The Role of the Judge in Public Law Litigation," 89 *Harvard Law Review* 1281 (1976); Owen Fiss, "The Forms of Justice" 93 *Harvard Law Review* 1(1979).

9. Owen Fiss, *The Civil Rights Injunction* (Indiana University Press, 1978), p. 1.

10. *Monroe* v. *Pape*, 365 U.S. 167 (1961). For detailed discussion of the extensive case law on Section 1983, see Erwin Chemerinsky, *Federal Jurisdiction*, 3rd ed. (New York: Aspen, 1999), chaps. 8 and 9; Michael G. Collins, *Section 1983 Litigation*, 3rd ed. (St. Paul, Minn.: West Group, 2006); and Richard S. Vacca and H. C. Hudgins Jr., *Liability of School Officials and Administrators for Civil Rights Torts* (Charlottesville, Va.: Michie, 1982).

11. Civil Rights Attorneys' Fees Award Act of 1976.

12. Chemerinsky, *Federal Jurisdiction*, pp. 450, 455–56.

13. *Alexander* v. *Sandoval*, 532 U.S. 275 (2001). See the more extensive discussion of this case later in the chapter.

14. James Q. Wilson, *Bureaucracy: What Government Agencies Do and Why They Do It* (New York: Basic Books, 1989), p. 168.

15. Ibid., pp. 169–70.

16. Ibid., p. 175.

17. Frederick M. Hess, *Spinning Wheels: The Politics of Urban School Reform* (Brookings, 1999), p. 38.

18. Donald L. Horowitz, "Decreeing Organizational Change: Judicial Supervision of Judicial Institutions," 1983 *Duke Law Journal* 1265 (1983); Peter Schuck, *Suing Government:*

Citizen Remedies for Official Wrongs (Yale University Press, 1983), pp. 150–81; Paul Mishkin, "Federal Courts as State Reformers," 35 *Washington and Lee Law Review* 949 (1978); and Gary McDowell, *Equity and the Constitution: The Supreme Court, Equitable Relief, and Public Policy* (University of Chicago Press, 1982).

19. Among the most important are the following: Joshua Dunn, *Complex Justice: The Case of Missouri v. Jenkins* (University of North Carolina Press, 2008); Malcolm Feeley and Edward Rubin, *Judicial Policy Making and the Modern State: How the Courts Reformed America's Prisons* (Cambridge University Press, 1998); John J. DiIulio Jr., *Governing Prisons: A Comparative Study of Correctional Management* (New York: Free Press, 1987); DiIulio, ed., *Courts, Corrections, and the Constitution: The Impact of Judicial Intervention on Prisons and Jails* (Oxford University Press, 1990); Phillip J. Cooper, *Hard Judicial Choices: Federal District Court Judges and State and Local Officials* (Oxford University Press, 1988); Barbara Flicker, ed., *Justice and School Systems: The Role of the Courts in Education Litigation* (Temple University Press, 1990); James Fishman and Howard Kalodner, eds., *Limits of Justice: The Courts' Role in School Desegregation* (Temple University Press, 1978); Eleanor Wolf, *Trial and Error: The Detroit School Desegregation Case* (Wayne State University Press, 1981); Ross Sandler and David Schoenbrod, *Democracy by Decree: What Happens When Courts Run Government* (Yale University Press, 2003); Michael Rebell and Arthur Block, *Educational Policymaking and the Courts* (University of Chicago Press, 1982).

20. *Brown v. Board of Education* II, 349 U.S. 295, 300 (1955).

21. In addition, relying on equitable remedies meant that desegregation cases would be heard by federal judges unencumbered by local juries: the Seventh Amendment only guarantees the right to a jury trial in civil suits "at common law."

22. Quoted in Richard Kluger, *Simple Justice: The History of Brown v. Board of Education and Black America's Struggle for Equality* (New York: Vintage Books, 1975), pp. 571–72.

23. Paul Gewirtz, "Remedies and Resistance," 92 *Yale Law Journal* 588 (1983).

24. This understanding is presented in Justice Marshall's dissent in *Board of Education of Oklahoma City v. Dowell,* 498 U.S. 237 (1991). Marshall suggested that "the poor quality of a system's schools may be so severe that nothing short of a radical transformation of the schools within the system will suffice to achieve desegregation and eliminate all of its vestiges."

25. Peter Schuck provides a description of this dramatic litigation in *Diversity in America: Keeping Government at a Safe Distance* (Harvard University Press, 2003), pp. 234–57.

26. This is one of the features of structural injunctions on which scholars on the left and the right can agree. See, for example, William Fletcher, "The Discretionary Constitution: Institutional Remedies and Judicial Legitimacy," 91 *Yale Law Journal* 635 (1982); and John Yoo, "Who Measures the Chancellor's Foot? The Inherent Remedial Authority of the Federal Courts," 84 *California Law Review* 1121 (1996).

27. Fletcher, "The Discretionary Constitution," p. 682.

28. *Board of Education v. Dowell,* 498 U.S. 237 (1991); and *Freeman v. Pitts,* 503 U.S. 467 (1992).

29. *Swann v. Charlotte-Mecklenburg Board of Education,* 402 U.S. 1, 15, 31 (1971).

30. David Zaring points out that practical difficulties also place sharp limitations on *circuit court* review of district court judges' use of injunctions. "National Rulemaking through Trial Courts: The Big Case and Institutional Reform," 51 *UCLA Law Review* 1045 (2004).

31. Fiss, *The Civil Rights Injunction,* p. 27.

32. Ibid., p. 30.

33. Ibid., p. 28.

34. See, for example, Malcolm M. Feeley and Edward Rubin, *Judicial Policymaking and the Modern State: How the Courts Reformed America's Prisons* (Cambridge University Press, 1998); and Cooper, *Hard Judicial Choices.*

35. *Green* v. *New Kent County School Board,* 391 U.S. 430 (1968); *Swann* v. *Charlotte-Mecklenburg Board of Education,* 402 U.S. 1 (1971); *Keyes* v. *Denver School District #1,* 413 U.S.189 (1973); and *Milliken* v. *Bradley,* 418 U.S. 717 (1974).

36. David Armor lays out the commonly accepted judicial understanding of the link between desegregation and educational opportunity in *Forced Justice: School Desegregation and the Law* (Oxford University Press, 1995), chap. 2.

37. Cited in James Fishman and Lawrence Strauss, "Endless Journey: Integration and the Provision of Equal Educational Opportunity in Denver's Public Schools," in Flicker, *Justice and School Systems,* p. 201.

38. *Milliken* v. *Bradley II,* 433 U.S. 267, 282–83 (1977).

39. The best explanation of this role remains Colin Diver, "The Judge as Political Power-broker: Superintending Structural Change in Public Institutions," 65 *Virginia Law Review* 43 (1979).

40. Dunn, *Complex Justice,* pp. 47–55.

41. Cooper, *Hard Judicial Choices*; and Eleanor P. Wolfe, *Trial and Error: The Detroit Desegregation Case.*

42. Quoted in Robert Wood, ed., *Remedial Law: When Courts Become Administrators* (University of Massachusetts Press, 1990), pp. 38–39. This book provides a good portrait of the love-hate relationship between administrators and litigants.

43. Sandler and Schoenbrod, *Democracy by Decree.*

44. Dunn, *Complex Justice,* p. 113.

45. Ibid., pp. 128–31.

46. Michael Rebell, "*Jose P.* v. *Ambach*: Special Education Reform in New York City," in Flicker, *Justice and School Systems,* p. 50.

47. Quoted in Sandler and Schoenbrod, *Democracy by Decree,* p. 91.

48. Hess, *Spinning Wheels,* p. 89.

49. Horowitz, "Decreeing Organizational Change," p. 1279.

50. Dunn, *Complex Justice,* chaps. 6–7.

51. Charles Sabel and William Simon, "Destabilization Rights: How Public Law Litigation Succeeds," 117 *Harvard Law Review* 1019 (2007), p. 1019, emphasis deleted.

52. Ibid., pp. 1028, 1026.

53. See Mathew Springer and James Guthrie, "The Politicization of the School Finance Legal Process," and Eric Hanushek, "The Alchemy of 'Costing Out' an Adequate Education," in *School Money Trials: The Legal Pursuit of Educational Adequacy,* edited by Martin West and Paul Peterson (Brookings, 2007).

54. The most troubling aspect of the Sabel and Simon article is their romantic assumption that "destabilizing" an institution will somehow lead to its improvement. Common sense argues that destabilizing institutions usually makes them worse. For evidence that poorly performing institutions can always become even more dysfunctional, see Josh Dunn's description of the evolution of schools in Kansas City in *Complex Justice.*

55. Chemerinsky, *Federal Jurisdiction,* pp. 457, 451.

56. 369 U.S. 167, 169 (1961).

57. John C. Jeffries Jr., "In Praise of the Eleventh Amendment and Section 1983," 84 *Virginia Law Review* 47 (1998). Peter Schuck did not find this to be the case when he wrote *Suing Government.* This is one of those many issues on which there is little empirical evidence.

The emotional costs of being named a defendant in a Section 1983 suit are no doubt significant even if the public agency covers all the monetary costs.

58. Schuck provides a detailed examination of these cases in "Suing Our Servants: The Court, Congress, and the Liability of Public Officials for Damages," *Supreme Court Review* (1980), p. 281.

59. *Monnell* v. *New York City Department of Social Services,* 436 U.S. 658 (1978); and *Owen* v. *City of Independence,* 445 U.S 622 (1980).

60. *Mt. Healthy City School District Board of Education* v. *Doyle,* 429 U.S. 274 (1977).

61. *Youngberg* v. *Romeo,* 457 U.S. 307 (1982).

62. Schuck, *Suing Government,* and "Suing Our Servants."

63. Two excellent law review articles that survey the recent literature on this topic find no convincing rebuttal to Schuck's argument about the incentives created by Section 1983 suits: Jeffries, "In Praise of the Eleventh Amendment and Section 1983"; and John C. Jeffries Jr. and George A. Rutherglen, "Structural Reform Revisited," 95 *California Law Review* 1387 (2007).

64. Schuck, "Suing Our Servants," p. 302.

65. Ibid., p. 286.

66. Ibid., pp. 313, 314.

67. *Youngberg* v. *Romeo,* 321–24.

68. *Castle Rock* v. *Gonzales,* 545 U.S. 748, 758 (2005). The other important case is *DeShaney* v. *Winnebago County Department of Social Services,* 489 U.S. 189 (1989).

69. See, for example, *City of Sacramento* v. *Lewis,* 523 U.S. 833 (1998).

70. See, for example, *Wilson* v. *Layne,* 526 U.S. 603 (1999). The justices seem to have a particularly hard time defining what constitutes negligent police pursuit of fleeing suspects. Apparently, though, they "know it when they see it." Just as this amorphous standard required the Court to watch a number of pornographic movies in the 1960s, the justices now seem to be watching frequent outtakes from the television show *COPS*. See the video provided by the Court in *Scott* v. *Harris* 550 U.S.372 (2007).

71. A leading example is the 1975 Education for All Handicapped Children Act, revised and renamed the Individuals with Disabilities Education Act in 1990, discussed later in the chapter.

72. Quoted in U.S. Commission on Civil Rights, *Federal Title VI Enforcement to Ensure Nondiscrimination in Federally Assisted Programs* (June 1996), p. 27.

73. Hugh Davis Graham, *The Civil Rights Era: Origins and Development of National Policy* (Oxford University Press, 1990), p. 83.

74. Stephen Halpern, *On the Limits of the Law: The Ironic Legacy of Title VI of the Civil Rights Act* (Johns Hopkins University Press, 1995); Gary Orfield, *The Reconstruction of Southern Education: The Schools and the 1964 Civil Rights Act* (New York: John Wiley and Sons, 1969); Hugh Davis Graham, "Since 1964: The Paradox of American Civil Right Regulation," in *Taking Stock: American Government in the Twentieth Century,* edited by Morton Keller and R. Shep Melnick (Washington: Woodrow Wilson Center Press, 1999); John Skrentny, *The Ironies of Affirmative Action* (University of Chicago Press, 1996).

75. U.S. Commission on Civil Rights, *Federal Title VI Enforcement,* p. 40.

76. For extended accounts of this case, see Jeremy Rabkin, *Judicial Compulsions: How Public Law Distorts Public Policy* (New York: Basic Books, 1989); Rosemary Salomone, "Judicial Oversight of Agency Enforcement: The *Adams* and *WEAL* Litigation," in Flicker, *Justice and School Systems*; and Halpern, *On the Limits of the Law.*

77. *Lau* v. *Nichols,* 414 U.S. 563 (1974). This discussion of bilingual education relies on Gareth Davies, *See Government Grow: Education Politics from Johnson to Reagan* (University

Press of Kansas, 2007), chap. 6; and John Skrentny, *The Minority Rights Revolution* (Harvard University Press, 2004), chap. 7.

78. See R. Shep Melnick, *Between the Lines: Interpreting Welfare Rights* (Brookings, 1994), pp. 48–51.

79. *Cannon* v. *University of Chicago*, 441 U.S. 677 (1979). This case involved Title IX, not Title VI. Since Title IX was explicitly modeled on Title VI, it seemed obvious to the justices that a similar private right of action existed under Title IX. Indeed, recognizing a private right of action to enforce Title IX was an even bigger reach than recognizing a private right of action to enforce Title VI. One could argue that Title VI was passed to protect *constitutional* rights, and thus that both Congress and the courts have broad power to remedy violations by state and local governments. But the courts had never held that gender is a "suspect classification" under the Fourteenth Amendment. Many forms of gender discrimination—such as providing more funding to male sports than to female sports—would never be considered unconstitutional. Title IX was enacted under the spending clause, not Section 5 of the Fourteenth Amendment. Congress simply determined that it would not spend federal money on programs that failed to provide equal benefits to women. Termination of funding is a particularly appropriate remedy for violation of a law enacted under the spending clause.

80. *Guardians Association of NYC Police Dept.* v. *Civil Service Commission*, 463 U.S. 582 (1983).

81. *Franklin* v. *Gwinnett County Public Schools*, 503 U.S. 60 (1992); and *Gebser* v. *Lago Vista Independent School District*, 524 U.S. 274 (1998).

82. *Davis* v. *Monroe County Board of Education*, 526 U.S. 629 (1999).

83. *Franklin* v. *Gwinnett County Public Schools*, 71.

84. Ibid., 77–78.

85. For an excellent examination of this dynamic under Title VII, see Sean Farhang, "The Political Development of Job Discrimination Litigation 1963–1976," Working Paper 59 (University of California at Berkeley Center for the Study of Law, 2008).

86. *Alexander* v. *Sandoval*, 532 U.S. 275 (2001), 306–07.

87. The state of Alabama had refused to comply with Department of Justice rules requiring drivers' tests to be conducted in Spanish as well as English. The department claimed that Alabama's English-only rule would have a disproportionate impact on those born outside the United States and therefore violated Title VI.

88. *Jackson* v. *Birmingham Board of Education*, 544 U.S.167 (2005).

89. Two notable examples are the 1988 Civil Rights Restoration Act (commonly known as the Grove City Act after the court decision it overturned) and the Civil Rights Act of 1991, which reversed multiple court rulings.

90. Sheryl Gay Stolberg, "Obama Signs Equal-Pay Legislation," *New York Times*, January 30, 2009, p. A1.

91. 377 U.S. 426, 432–33 (1964).

92. I provide an extended analysis of these court decisions in *Between the Lines*, chaps. 7–8.

93. Wilson, *Bureaucracy*, p. 225.

3

School Superintendents and the Law: Cages of Their Own Design?

FREDERICK M. HESS AND LANCE D. FUSARELLI

While the formal impact of the law on school funding, equity, and discipline is widely recognized, far less consideration has been paid to the significant impact of law on the culture and nature of district leadership.[1] In a 2003 *Newsweek* article, Alan Bersin, then superintendent of San Diego City Schools, termed the threat of a lawsuit "'the anaconda in the chandelier'—It hangs constantly overhead, threatening to strike at any time."[2] In a 2003 Public Agenda survey, 47 percent of superintendents said they would operate differently if "free from the constant threat of litigation."[3] A Public Agenda study from the same year concludes, "For many principals and superintendents, avoiding lawsuits and fulfilling regulatory and due process requirements is a time-consuming and often frustrating part of the job."[4] According to the nonprofit coalition Common Good, 88 percent of superintendents complain that special education parents, for example, are "too quick to threaten legal action to get their way."[5] Seventy-seven percent of superintendents think that making it easier "to remove bad teachers" would be desirable.[6]

Although legal and contractual constraints can arguably have socially desirable effects, research suggests that they also hinder efforts to pursue systemic improvement. Because of the provisions in collective bargaining agreements (CBAs), district and school leaders have "virtually lost the ability to choose

We thank Thomas Gift and Juliet Squire for their research and editorial contributions.

teachers, make work assignments, fire ineffective teachers, and manage budgets," says the University of Washington's Paul Hill.[7] If not found in contracts, notes the National Council on Teacher Quality, those agreements may be "embedded elsewhere, such as local school board policies . . . or, critically, in state laws and regulations."[8] A 2004 Common Good study cataloguing the statutes and regulations governing a typical public high school in New York City identified more than sixty separate sources of rules and thousands of distinct obligations, among them "The New York State Education Law, which is 846 pages long; 720 pages of regulations issued by the New York State Commissioner of Education; 15,062 decisions—contained in 43 volumes—made by the New York State Commissioner of Education . . . ; the [204-page] New York City teachers' contract."[9] The report also lists required procedures for administrators, such as the eighty-three steps and legal considerations to fire an inept teacher or the thirty-two steps and considerations to enter a negative evaluation into a teacher's file.

How Constrained Are Superintendents?

In view of these mounting obligations, it is essential to know how tightly these bonds confine administrators in practice or how fully district leaders employ their existing authority. Education law scholar Perry Zirkel, for one, believes administrators are less hamstrung by statute than is often supposed: their complaints reflect a "distorted assessment of education and the law," he says, and "knowledge deficits" have led them to "overestimat[e] legal requirements."[10] In an analysis of work rules, teacher compensation, and personnel policies in collective bargaining agreements in the nation's fifty largest school districts, Frederick Hess and Coby Loup found "considerable ambiguity" in the labor agreements, which "may represent a less substantial barrier to school improvement than critics have suggested, making it essential for school leaders to take advantage of their autonomy."[11] Vanderbilt University professor Dale Ballou similarly finds that in Massachusetts "on virtually every issue of personnel policy there are contracts that grant administrators the managerial prerogatives they are commonly thought to lack. . . . When more flexible language is negotiated, administrators do not take advantage of it . . . [but] blame the contract for their own inaction."[12]

Some superintendents wield the law as a tool of reform, acting in ways that had been deemed off-limits before. In 2008 Washington, D.C., schools chancellor Michelle Rhee moved to restrict seniority rights by dusting off a decade-old statute permitting principals to weigh other factors alongside seniority in staffing. The law had remained unused even as district officials complained that they could do nothing when senior teachers displaced younger peers. "Bumping rights had been viewed as a problem for those of us trying to get quality teachers in the classroom," says Kevin Chavous, a D.C. Council member when the law passed; but "even after the law was passed, superintendents operated under the assumption that bumping rights were still there."[13]

In a similar example, John Deasy, outgoing superintendent of Prince George's County Public Schools in Maryland, who has attracted national attention for introducing merit pay and for substantial gains in his district's worst-performing schools, says superintendents are free to do more than they think they can do and the extensive tools that are at their disposal are generally unused by colleagues.[14] During his three-year tenure, Deasy has taken unprecedented steps, including transferring hundreds of the district's 10,800 teachers to new schools and initiating a voluntary pay-for-performance system for teachers. He has done this in a district with a CBA judged to be among the nation's most restrictive.[15] "Nothing prohibited any of this," Deasy argues. "Why does it not happen? . . . Most people see the contract as a steel box. It's not. It's a steel floor with no boundaries around it. You've just got to push and push and push."

Joel Klein, chancellor of the New York City Public Schools, created the Teacher Performance Unit (TPU), a cadre of experienced attorneys who advise principals and litigate cases against ineffective, tenured teachers. New York City Department of Education's chief executive for labor policy and implementation, attorney Dan Weisberg, explained in a November 2007 memo to the district's principals: "The creation of TPU represents a significant infusion of resources that will ensure we have the capacity to seek the removal of all ineffective tenured teachers who, in spite of receiving the time and support sufficient to allow them to substantially improve, won't or can't do so."[16] This approach, says Klein, has encouraged principals to act because "when action must be taken, the disciplinary system for tenured teachers is so time-consuming and burdensome that . . . relatively few principals are willing to tackle it."[17] Klein reports that deploying attorneys specifically to help principals remove ineffective teachers has altered behavior even in the absence of contractual changes. Although "there are some places where you can't bend," adds Weisberg, "there's typically a gray area."[18]

Presuming a Defensive Posture

Such examples of aggressive legal maneuvering are few and far between, however. A greater concern is how districts and district leaders can stay out of court. As Paul Houston, former executive director of the American Association of School Administrators (AASA), points out, the fear of getting sued is at times more limiting than the law itself.[19] In October 2007 AASA's magazine, *School Administrator,* dealt exclusively with subjects relating to schools and the law:

new technologies (such as disciplining students for online activity), the recent U.S. Supreme Court ruling on racial integration, avoiding lawsuits by speaking carefully to parents, the accountability movement's role in paving the way for litigation based on a student's right to competent instruction, and a superintendent's efforts to stem litigation through "prudence and diligent follow-up."[20] Every article focused on how superintendents might comply with requirements and avoid litigation; not one mentioned that superintendents might use the law as a tool of reform or suggested how they might do so. This is not so surprising, given that the legal training most school leaders receive (whether in their administrator preparation programs or through state professional development seminars) focuses on avoiding lawsuits and staying out of the newspapers.

Issues of the similarly influential *American School Board Journal,* which publishes a monthly column on school law by an attorney and education professional, tell the same tale. Twenty of the twenty-four columns written between August 2006 and August 2008 seek to help school leaders comply with statutory changes and navigate legal pitfalls on questions such as religious freedom, personnel issues, and free speech. The other four discuss diversity, equitable financing, parental involvement, and collective bargaining with an eye to keeping district officials out of trouble. Not one column suggests how district officials might use the law to push improvement.

In the view of Maree Sneed, an education lawyer and partner at the national law firm Hogan & Hartson, "the law isn't pure—it's political," and superintendents should understand that legal questions often do not have yes or no answers: "Lawyers shouldn't decide what is done—their job is to say 'here are the parameters. Here is a way to do it—but there is some risk.'"[21] Francisco Negron, associate executive director and general counsel for the National School Boards Association, puts it more baldly: "A good general counsel . . . will tell you how to achieve what you want and how to do it within the law."[22] For that reason, he notes, "forward thinking leaders would be wise to include legal counsel on their [reform] teams" because legal advice can often determine what reforms superintendents pursue.

What Superintendents Do versus What They Can Do

The relationship between superintendents and the law can be analyzed in two dimensions: the legal and contractual context in which superintendents operate, and the way they choose to operate in that environment. Legal and contractual environments can in turn be divided into two extreme types: "inhibited" and "autonomous." Inhibited environments are those in which collective bargaining agreements and statutes tightly restrict superintendents. Autonomous environments are those in which formal constraints are relatively lax. As already

Figure 3-1. *Four District Environments*

	Assertive	*Passive*
Autonomous		
Inhibited		

mentioned, contextual constraints have been widely studied in various locales so we focus here on how superintendents operate in a given legal context.

Superintendents exhibit two behavioral extremes in their responses to legal and contractual requirements: "assertive" and "passive." Assertive superintendents use organizational resources to challenge constraints and do not shy away from conflict. Passive superintendents favor a collaborative approach, emphasize consensus, and work within existing legal and contractual arrangements to ensure the support of all major stakeholders. Experts disagree on the relative merits of these two general approaches. To better understand them, it is helpful to divide superintendencies into four broad categories according to their context and response: assertive-autonomous, passive-autonomous, assertive-inhibited, and passive-inhibited (see figure 3-1).

Assertive-autonomous districts are those in which substantial change is most likely because superintendents act aggressively to challenge the status quo in a relatively permissive environment. Their polar opposite is the passive-inhibited district, in which leaders seek to avoid conflict in the face of restrictive CBAs, statutes, and other legal considerations. An assertive-inhibited district is one in which superintendents moving aggressively routinely clash with relatively binding constraints. Passive-autonomous districts present few formal constraints, but superintendents here move only as quickly as collaboration and consensus permit.

How Superintendents Approach Constraints

How superintendents respond to the law—whether proactively (assertively) or reactively (passively)—appears to be influenced by three major factors: their mindset (socialization and legal preparation), their resources and arrangements, and their political environment.

Superintendents' Mindset

A leader's mindset is a product of socialization, experience, and familiarity and comfort with the law, all of which affect one's approach to legal issues. The majority of superintendents are acculturated to regard conflict as an unproductive response and to favor a more collegial approach. Fully 80 percent of superintendents follow a career path that leads from teacher, to principal, to the superintendency (with two-thirds serving in the district central office en route).[23] Given the dispositions of most entrants into teaching, the predominant values in schooling, and the nature of K–12 professional development, it is not surprising that most superintendents accept existing practices and interpretations without question. In the course of their professional experiences inside districts and schools of education, few superintendents have been exposed to assertive models of leadership. Prince George's County superintendent John Deasy, an unconventional leader who has followed a conventional career ladder, says that when it comes to pushing the boundaries of what is permissible, his most formative experiences "developed almost entirely in relationships and mentorships with noneducators."

Even the training of educational leaders seems to discourage conflict in favor of consensus. For instance, in his widely read volume *What's Worth Fighting for in the Principalship?* Michael Fullan believes that "the starting point for what's worth fighting for is not system change, not change in others around us, but change in ourselves."[24] Furthermore, note Frederick Hess and Andrew Kelly, the most widely assigned texts in school leadership "shy away from blunt discussion of why, when, or how principals might use evaluation to light a fire under teachers."[25]

As for familiarity with the law, superintendent preparation and professional development emphasize legal nuts and bolts and collaboration rather than "envelope-stretching." As AASA's Paul Houston points out, the vast majority of education school classes focus on tort avoidance and legal history instead of helping superintendents understand the elasticity of the law, its ambiguities, or how it can be interpreted advantageously.

District Legal Resources and Arrangements

Exploiting legal opportunities requires not only the inclination but also the means and the wherewithal to do so. In other words, districts must have sufficient expertise, dollars, and staff to address legal concerns. A district's financial resources can have a significant effect on whether superintendents approach the law with a defensive or an offensive mindset. The National School Board Association's Francisco Negron, for example, says that superintendents often decide whether to settle or fight a legal case simply by estimating its cost. Similarly, Houston notes that settling is often less expensive than going to court—even when a district is likely to prevail—and this creates a strong incentive to adopt a defensive or passive posture.

As for their expertise in legal matters, districts vary in how they organize the make-up of their legal teams. While some rely on in-house counsel or retain counsel on a fee basis, most appear to employ some combination of the two approaches. Systematic data on the recruitment or retention of school lawyers are in short supply, but figures available for 2006 show attorneys entering the public sector with a median starting salary of just $36,000, compared with a median of $95,000 for a first-year associate at a private law firm.[26] This clearly puts districts at a disadvantage when it comes to pursuing legal talent. It is unclear whether such counsel are likely to be savvier or bolder than outside counsel, or how varied arrangements may affect the quality of legal advice. These would seem to be pressing questions, which have received surprisingly little or no consideration to date.

Political Support

Whatever a superintendent's inclination and resources, improvement efforts ultimately depend on political support. The willingness of the school board (or mayor) to tolerate conflict and the relationship with the superintendent influences a superintendent's decision to proceed on legal issues. As the University of Memphis's Thomas Glass observes: "In districts where superintendents and principals know their boards are going to support them, they are more likely to take risks aimed at bringing about reform. But superintendents unsure of what their board members want or insecure about how they will respond to controversy are reluctant to stick their necks out in an effort to bring about change."[27]

The state of superintendent–board relations, particularly in large and contentious districts, is at the center of much discussion. Although only one of twenty superintendents surveyed by Public Agenda in 2001 termed their relationship with the board "mostly contentious," just 52 percent said they could "virtually always" count on board support when a crisis or controversy hits the district.[28] This is one reason that advocates of mayoral control, including New York's Joel Klein and Washington's Michelle Rhee, deem mayoral involvement crucial. Although school boards "keep power in check" and "provide a link to the democratic process," Deasy finds that political considerations "absolutely" limit the pace of his improvement agenda. Yet superintendents may be hesitant to speak openly about the relationships with their boards and mayors, even though such discussion can affect the pursuit of their reform agendas.

Five Cases of District Leadership

To explore how superintendents interact with the law, we offer brief profiles of five current or former superintendents. Our cases include two of the nation's most notable "nontraditional" superintendents (both former attorneys) and three respected career superintendents with a more conventional set of formative experiences. These individuals operated districts large and small, across different states, and faced different challenges. We selected them merely to illustrate the variation in educational leaders' approaches to legal issues, not to suggest the ones most likely to be effective.

Alan Bersin: "If the law says that, the law is an ass."

Alan Bersin, formerly an influential attorney in private practice and then U.S. attorney for the Southern District of California and the attorney general's southwest border representative, served as superintendent of the San Diego Unified School District (SDUSD) from 1998 to 2005.[29] SDUSD is one of the nation's largest school systems, with 134,000 students enrolled in 202 schools.[30] The district employs 13,442 staff, including 7,199 full-time teachers, and has an annual budget of $2.1 billion.[31]

After a tumultuous tenure marked by a divided school board and much national attention, Bersin was tapped by Governor Arnold Schwarzenegger to serve as California's secretary of education and a member of its board of education.[32] Bersin, famous for introducing the mantra "Do it fast and do it deep" to characterize his reform effort, made it clear from the outset that his goal was to overhaul the district's culture and practices to improve student achievement.

MINDSET. Bersin concedes that he often found SDUSD's approach to the law to be excessively compliance-driven:

> What struck me right away was how virtually every issue seemed to be reduced by educators in schools and the central office alike to a rule-based response believed by them to be legally required. Much of both district and school management as a result was super-formalistic and hyper-procedural. I became aware early on that district lawyers were playing policy roles in ways that were foreign to my experience in the corporate world— framing questions in "is this permissible" terms, followed by yes or no answers purporting to be dispositive.

This simple approach, he explains, is never used in the private sector, which observes the necessary interaction of facts and law through significant analysis about how to frame and resolve a problem. If a question can be answered yes or no, he thinks it does not constitute an issue. But this was how genuinely difficult legal matters were being dealt with in the district: "I remember in the first year getting one-page memos where lawyers would cite a case or two with no real discussion of how they supported the particular conclusion reached. That's a prime indication of third-rate lawyering." Bersin's time in private law practice showed him that both business and nongovernment sectors were growing more sophisticated about the uses of law and lawyers in accomplishing organizational objectives, while education remained far behind.

Bersin believes that it is essential for reform-minded superintendents to understand how law shapes policy: "District leaders don't need law school, but they do need to get smarter about the law and legal process. The law is not a black box and shouldn't be treated as such. It's a matter of judgment. Lawyers must be asked for risk assessments, not for decisions masked in the form of advice. If we keep asking 'Can I do this?' we shouldn't be surprised if we keep getting yes or no answers." Attorneys who sense a desire to minimize conflict are far more likely to say no than yes. If a lawyer told Bersin that he could not do something, for instance, he would always ask, "Why, and what are the circumstances or changes that could permit us to do it?" because in his view that is the attorney-client dialogue that ought to occur: "A good lawyer would never just say that you can't do something (except in the most extreme cases), and a competent CEO would never take just that as a final answer."

DISTRICT LEGAL RESOURCES AND ARRANGEMENTS. SDUSD's legal department houses one general counsel, two assistant general counsel, and four support staff. The annual budget for the Office of the General Counsel in 2008 was about $1.1 million. When Bersin became superintendent, the district had a law office of five attorneys and staff with a budget for outside counsel that was limited "only by the number of cases filed against us." There was also a separate unit of three attorneys for labor issues. He moved quickly to hire an administrative law judge and former legal aid lawyer from outside education to join the district as his general counsel and supported her reorganization of the legal office. Although the district continued to use outside counsel on a broad range of issues, from personal injury to desegregation, "the business given to these law firms was more tightly managed and the legal advice given by them more carefully scrutinized."

From day one, Bersin sought to dramatically restructure the district's legal approach: "We brought in lawyers from outside of education who were inclined to view, and capable of analyzing, legal problems in ways more consistent with my experience before coming to the school district. They were prepared to make arguments that pushed and probed in search of novel conclusions. They took nothing for granted." One major change was to give lawyers a more central role in shaping reform strategies. A reform team needs a lawyer who understands the legal process as a problem-solving one, he emphasizes. Otherwise, the attorneys themselves and the advice they give become significant obstacles: "They become the shields on which interests which resist change depend. School leaders who lean back from reforms frequently take cover behind lawyers."

POLITICAL SUPPORT. During Bersin's tenure, the board split 3 to 2 in support of his efforts on the legal front. Although dissenting members, in cahoots with recalcitrant union leaders, never accepted the legitimacy of the majority's actions, the board conferred complete authority—and power—to proceed in new directions on legal decisions. These included, among others, the dismissal of administrators and teachers on instructional incompetence grounds and a dramatic reallocation of Title I funding. Both "legal innovations" ultimately were upheld by the courts. As it turned out, even a supportive school board was not always enough to eliminate political impediments:

> This was a system in which procedural rules, custom, and practice could routinely overwhelm the substance of the work. People would tell me we had to do something because it's the law. My favorite response was to quote Mr. Bumble in *Oliver Twist,* saying, 'If the law says that, then the law is an ass.' And I'd ask our lawyers, who were not then behind the status quo, to go see what we could do instead within the rule of law.

William Harrison: "My lawyer is bigger than your lawyer."

William Harrison has been a superintendent for seventeen years and served as superintendent of North Carolina's Cumberland County Public Schools (CCPS) from 1996 to 2008.[33] CCPS, located in Fayetteville, is the fourth largest school district in the state, with approximately 53,000 students enrolled in eighty-seven schools. The superintendent oversees an annual budget of $420 million. Harrison was a homegrown superintendent, having taught and served as principal in CCPS. Nearly half the district's students are African American, and slightly more than one-third Caucasian. Under Harrison's leadership, this "majority-minority" district made significant strides in narrowing the achievement gap.

MINDSET. Some superintendents are afraid of the law, says Harrison, and "are constantly looking over their shoulders and don't do anything," while others, either in disregard or ignorance, "behave recklessly." Harrison himself is a balanced leader who is willing to move toward taking a risk. It has never been his nature to fear lawsuits, even as a rookie superintendent and even as superintendent in Hoke County, North Carolina, when the famous *Leandro* school finance lawsuit was initiated. Experience has taught him that he will likely prevail, especially if "my lawyer is bigger than your lawyer."

Harrison generally does not find legal constraints, regulations, or contracts to be an obstacle. Nor has he had to challenge statutes or contract language, or maneuver in murky terrain to move his improvement efforts forward. He cannot recall any occasion when his attorneys have found ways to take steps thought to be prohibited.

Harrison's legal background includes two law classes taken in his master's program and two more in the course of his doctoral preparation. In addition, Harrison has taught school law to aspiring school leaders. "My disclaimer," he notes, "is always that I'm not an attorney. I don't pretend to be an attorney. I know enough about the law that I have an attorney sit right next to me. We spend a lot of time together." When Harrison served as superintendent of CCPS, he interacted with his attorneys at least twice a week and was especially grateful for the time they helped save on contracts, which were reviewed before they got to his desk.

From his experience teaching education law, Harrison thinks most superintendents fail to push aggressively enough for improvement. He found that having his attorney in the office next door provided a "convenient sounding board" and enabled him to take risks that he might not otherwise have taken. The attorney helped him talk through policies, procedures, and due process, and without this resource, "I don't think I would risk doing [some things] on my own."

DISTRICT LEGAL RESOURCES AND ARRANGEMENTS. CCPS budgets $332,000 annually for legal expenses, which breaks down into $232,000 for the in-house legal staff and $100,000 for outside counsel. From 2007 to 2008, the district spent only $3,700 for outside counsel.

When he served as superintendent, Harrison's in-house attorney took part in district strategy, was a member of the superintendent's cabinet, and attended weekly meetings, which may be "atypical": "I know other superintendents do not talk with or include attorneys in their cabinet because, technically, [the attorney] works for the board, rather than me." But Harrison thinks the attorney really needs to understand a district's education mission and what it is doing to this end. The attorney advised Harrison not only on policy issues and changes in state regulations but also on teacher removal and disciplinary issues, especially with regard to due process. When Harrison was superintendent in Hoke County, the annual budget was much smaller, which made a difference in the types of action he could take. For example, an investigation in Cumberland into employee misconduct could cost as much as $65,000 and was doable there, whereas the "economy of scale in these things" would have made the same expense prohibitive in Hoke County.

Joel Klein: "If we're winning every case we bring, we're not bringing enough cases."

Joel Klein has served as chancellor of the New York City school system since 2002.[34] He was appointed by Mayor Michael Bloomberg, who rapidly moved to eliminate the city's traditional school board in favor of a mayorally appointed body. During his tenure, Klein has pushed a number of aggressive changes, including a reshaping of the collective bargaining agreement with the United Federation of Teachers. In recognition of its achievement gains, the district was awarded the 2007 Broad Prize for Urban Education.

New York City is the nation's largest school system, with 1.1 million students and 95,000 teachers.[35] The district spends more than $20 billion a year, which would rank it among the nation's 125 largest corporations if it were a private firm.[36] Before becoming chancellor, Klein served two years as chairman and chief executive officer of Bertelsmann, Inc., a media firm with annual revenues in excess of $20 billion and more than 76,000 employees in fifty-four countries.[37]

MINDSET. A heralded litigator who clerked for Supreme Court Justice Lewis Powell and headed the U.S. Department of Justice's antitrust division under President Bill Clinton, Klein came to the chancellorship with substantial legal experience.[38] This legal background has helped make him more comfortable charging into gray areas and telling his legal team to push the envelope, whereas the normal instinct of a lawyer in the public sector is "first do no harm," which "may not improve the outcomes for kids."

Klein explains that he is playing a "long game" in New York City, much as he did during his time in the federal government:

> When I was at the Justice Department, I used to say, "If we're winning every case we bring, we're not bringing enough cases." And that's a guiding principle for me in the way I approach these challenges. If somebody says, "Well, there's a 60 percent chance we'll lose this arbitration," I'd say the value of winning is worth enough that if I have a 40 percent chance of winning, I'll do it.

Klein also finds it imperative for reform-minded superintendents to view their legal team as problem-solvers rather than as safeguards: "My lawyer's job is not simply to protect me but to figure out how I can get done the things I need done. I didn't come here to keep out of controversy. If I wanted a lawyer like that, I would've hired somebody different."

Weisberg, Klein's chief attorney for labor affairs agrees: "My task is counseling the client, finding ways to help them reach the goal, and giving assessments of risk—they'll make the final call. . . . Joel has taught us to push the envelope. In the past, what they'd get from central or legal is, 'You can't do it.' Now, it's, 'How can we achieve the goal, even if there's risk involved.'" Tactically, he says, attorneys want to push people into the field as much as possible in order to orient themselves more toward the goals of principals than those of people in central offices, and to enable principals to be the key decisionmakers. When attorneys go too far and do not enforce central mandates, they may have to be reined in, of course, but "you want them pushing for the interests of the people closest to the schools and the kids."

POLITICAL SUPPORT. It is impossible to push reforms in a contentious environment without political support, says Klein: "A lot of it is the politics. While I'm a big believer in mayoral control, I think it's necessary though not sufficient. I mean, if you don't have the right mayor, or the mayor is easily rolled politically, you can't get things done." Even with a supportive mayor, he sees school board politics as the politics of paralysis, which makes it very difficult for a bold leader to do much. Although many superintendents think that seeking partnership with the union is the strategy that will work best, Klein believes "it's more complicated than that," because the ecosystem in which reforms take place is often more significant than the black-and-white constraints in contracts. In fact, he sees probably more flexibility inside some contracts than gets exercised partly because of a simple lack of knowledge: "When I got there, I was astonished at how few principals knew they had authority to do things." The culture of the system is another major factor, which together with informal norms can minimize problems posed by restrictive contract language: "In schools which are well led and where teachers and administrators are on one page . . . the regulatory significance of the contract is much diminished."

While degrees of freedom are important as a legal matter, Klein's larger concern is that "power matters much more," as illustrated in an incident when he began as chancellor. The union did not like two principals and things got negotiated out: "There's a tremendous amount of, if you will, bartering in the system. . . . The union would say, 'Well look, we could go to the newspaper and make a big deal out of [something problematic about one principal], and you'll have to get rid of him anyhow. But if you want to get rid of the other one, too, we can keep this all in the family.'"

Robert Holster: "We are challenged more by everyone today. . . . Everyone has a lawyer."

Robert Holster, superintendent of the Passaic, New Jersey, school system for sixteen years, is the longest-serving superintendent in the state. [39] The Passaic City School District is the ninth largest district in the state, with more than 13,000 students, and is one of the largest of the school districts (named *Abbott* districts) covered by a 1990 decision of the New Jersey Supreme Court ordering remedies to funding inadequacies in urban schools. Passaic has an operating budget of $232 million and spends more than $14,000 per pupil. Approximately 84 percent of Passaic students are Hispanic.

Owing to two decades of *Abbott* equity finance litigation, says Holster, the law is never too far from discussions of school improvement. Holster spends 10 to 15 percent of his time daily on legal questions—mainly on accountability regulations or legal issues that come up in connection with the operation of the district. The district's special education budget amounts to $55 million and is growing, thanks to today's parents, who are very informed, and a lot of advocacy for special education children, "rightfully so." As a result, they are always going to court on issues where parents of children eligible for special education services feel their children are entitled to greater amounts of funding: "Sometimes we disagree with [parents] and the next thing we know we are in some hearing over the entitlements they feel they should get."

MINDSET. Over the years, Holster has become inured to the threat of lawsuits. At first, he was "a little concerned" whenever he got lawyers' letters, but now he laughs them off: "Anyone can sue, but not many people win their suits. So, if it's in the best interests of kids and the district, we accept the challenge." That said, he tries not to let legal considerations drive his decisions: "I don't look at the legal outcome, but I try to look at the ethical one—am I doing the right thing? You can't have in your mind, 'Does this put me in the corner legally?'"

At the same time, Holster has challenged some statutes or contract language, particularly when the district has been in court seeking more funding from the state because "you have to prove that you have extraordinary needs" under existing regulations. Working in an *Abbott* district, Holster views the legal process as a key means of procuring more dollars for his district: "If we feel the state is not providing enough, that's where we've gone before the Supreme Court, in administrative hearings. We have [a suit] pending right now, a big one; we feel we are entitled to more money for safety and health issues under the *Abbott* decision and the state is dragging its feet and we are taking the state to court to provide the necessary funding to repair roofs, to remove oil tanks." Holster has been in court regarding *Abbott,* particularly administrative court, twenty to twenty-five times and is proud of a plaque from the state recognizing him as the rogue superintendent in New Jersey for the number of suits he has brought against the state. He considers that "a badge of honor."

Holster thinks most superintendents fail because they are not aggressive enough, and so shy away from conflict. The objective in public education today, he feels, is to survive at all levels: "You might get some that are aggressive up to a point, but I think they get easily intimidated." As a result, much professional development is focused on staying abreast of changing rules to keep up to date on regulations and laws, particularly in special education. By contrast, much of his legal training has focused on due process.

DISTRICT LEGAL RESOURCES AND ARRANGEMENTS. On average, Holster's district spends about $3 million to $5 million a year on legal fees (out of a total district budget of $232 million). The district employs three outside attorneys, with four additional attorneys for every collective bargaining cycle. Holster interacts with his outside counsel almost daily. The board attorney is not a full-time staffer, and there is no full-time in-house attorney. The board attorney makes $90,000 per year, plus $150 an hour for services above a set number of hours. There is also a special counsel for litigation pursuing additional state funds. Holster has been in court quite a bit about that, "winning 100 percent each time—which brings millions in additional funding into the district."

Holster involves his attorneys in planning because regulations require strategic plans to be submitted when seeking new funds and money must be spent for permissible purposes. The attorney advises whether it falls within the realm of the regulations: "Regulations are driven by law and [that] is the template for decisions superintendents have to make when it comes to the operation and administration of a district." Holster's attorneys sometimes prevent him from taking steps he deems appropriate if they borderline on legally improper or inappropriate decisions. Since a superintendent's best interest is in children and the operation of schools, at times one could overlook things that might be legally inappropriate. Therefore he runs a lot of decisions by legal counsel, getting input as to their legality: "It seems like we are challenged more by everyone today—from students to parents to staff. Everyone has a lawyer," he explains. "Quite often, I'm on the phone almost daily with one of the three attorneys. It's really a safeguard."

POLITICAL SUPPORT. Running schools is a very complex culture, Holster emphasizes. The political component is a board of education. The legal part is the administration of schools through laws and regulations. And the ethical and the character part is what is best for children: "So you try to balance the three and it's extremely difficult. You have to be aggressive and alert and do what is best for your students."

The politics of schooling, he observes, is much more legalistic than it was fifteen years ago: "Today, everything is driven by some regulation or state law or governed by the courts or legal decisions" rather than "leadership and management of schools." Hence the largest source of legal concerns is new regulations issued by the state department of education, which puts greater stress on superintendents, who are the real focus when it comes to efficiency and accountability for schools. "Those regulations really impact me on a daily basis," he says, because as one of the *Abbott* districts, Passaic is particularly heavily regulated.

Ronald Valenti: *"The dirty little secret is that many people don't want real change."*

A former priest, and a superintendent for twenty-eight years, Ronald Valenti recently served as superintendent of Blind Brook School District in Rye Brook, New York, for five years.[40] Valenti also served as the superintendent of Blind

Brook from 1980 to 1988 before leading three larger school districts in Westchester and on Long Island. Blind Brook is a suburban district in Westchester County, serving approximately 1,500 students in three schools with a budget of approximately $38 million. Recognized since the 1980s by the U.S. Department of Education as a "blue ribbon" district, Blind Brook also boasts Blind Brook High School, which has consistently ranked among the top 100 public high schools in the country, according to *U.S. News and World Report.*

MINDSET. Valenti took one class on education law in his master's program and another in his doctoral work. Yet it is his legal training in the priesthood that has had a lasting impact: "I studied Canon Law for four years. You develop a legal mind whether the law is ecclesiastical or educational, and learn to problem-solve legally." Although Valenti does not feel administrators need to be trained school attorneys, they do need help in becoming "more knowledgeable and more conversant about the law and its capacity for school reform."

Superintendents should be cautious in legal and financial matters, Valenti warns, "because mistakes can come back to bite you. I don't know of any superintendent terminated because he or she introduced the wrong reading curriculum. I know of several superintendents who have lost their job because of financial mismanagement or legal misjudgments." The legalization of education has become more pervasive, Valenti says, with the superintendent or principal no longer "captain of the ship," but a much more constrained leader. Back in 1980, when Valenti first became a superintendent, it was considered sufficient for a textbook on school law to contain one chapter on the students. "Today, there's not only a chapter for regular education, there's another for special education, a third treating student safety issues, and additional chapters on student discipline, technology, journalistic freedoms, and so on. There has been exponential growth in laws regarding schooling."

"In this business," Valenti states, "superintendents should all be more conservative than not" and follow the example of attorneys, who tend to be a conservative lot, often cautioning, like the fiddler on the roof, "On the one hand, but on the other. . . ." He recalls moving carefully when he sought to shift several full-time aides to part-time status. After extensive consultation with his attorneys and the unions, he saw that that he could be hauled into federal court. As a result, "something fiscally and educationally prudent was held up for legal reasons." Valenti sees a contradiction between rhetorical demands for school reform and public resistance to the substance of reform:

> Superintendents are running into more and more problems because they are recruited as change agents, but the dirty little secret is that many people don't want real change. They say, "Yes, we want a new direction, new energy, and reform," but school communities, trustees, and employee

unions, by nature, can at best only tolerate evolutionary and incremental change. Any superintendent intent on achieving revolutionary and systemic changes is going to be severely impeded by entrenched interests and often sorely disappointed.

As to the other roles of lawyers in education, Valenti does not rely on attorneys much in strategic planning but is more likely to involve them in staff development: "I have brought them into workshops with my administrators and sometimes involve key union people so that we are all getting the same message—[on] suspension of students, dealing with sexual harassment issues, teacher evaluation." With all the changes in the law, at times he brings attorneys in to update his administrators and school board.

Some attorneys are more helpful and a little more "creative" than others when it comes to dealing with legal challenges, Valenti comments: "Some experienced attorneys will say, 'Look, here is a way to do it; here's a way to go about that,' particularly in collective bargaining. I had a negotiation a couple years ago [and was seeking] to save some money. This attorney had ideas in terms of lengthening the salary schedule so that we'd pick up some money over a period of years by hiring people at a certain lower rate."

DISTRICT LEGAL RESOURCES AND ARRANGEMENTS. When he served as superintendent, Valenti spent 20 percent of his time dealing with legal matters. In the absence of in-house counsel, he spoke with outside counsel several times each week, sometimes calling on them "just to check out the obvious." The district's legal expenses, approximately $200,000 a year—which Valenti worked hard to keep as low as possible—amount to about one-half of 1 percent of the total district budget. "We're all very conscious of how we're going to use our resources, and so we've got to prioritize," notes Valenti. "We try to avoid grievances or settle them so it doesn't go to arbitration, which can become another expensive process."

Valenti handled collective bargaining without the benefit of an attorney at the table and worked to negotiate a good deal for teachers and students:

> I've worked closely with the union and was able to save $35,000 to $45,000 negotiating directly with the union, absent an attorney. Afterwards, I forwarded the Memorandum of Agreement (MOA) to our attorney for tweaking. In New York State, the superintendent enjoys considerable latitude as the chief negotiator for the school district. I've taken full advantage of this legal authority and recently, with the full involvement of the school board, and sans legal counsel, negotiated a "merit only salary agreement" with the administrators' association, again saving considerable resources better used for student learning.

POLITICAL SUPPORT. Of the constraints on superintendents, collective bargaining, which can be "extremely burdensome," ranks very high on Valenti's list. With experience, however, he thinks superintendents become more creative and develop negotiation strategies to venture where others fear to tread—for example, increased instructional time or performance-based pay. At the same time, he finds that being a superintendent in a strong union state such as New York and confronting the New York State United Teachers with its political muscle in Albany imposes an automatic constraint: "In fact, the whole purpose of unions is to constrain management."

Valenti also sees constraints in a variety of state regulations, contracts, district policies, established routines, and statutes. "Commissioners' regulations and commissioners' decisions in New York State have the force of law," he explains. "Beyond these are collective bargaining agreements and school board policies that restrict as well as inform managerial flexibility. Finally, there is what we call 'past practice,' which can have the force of law." He cites the example of a newly appointed superintendent who learns the district's secretaries have traditionally worked shorter hours during the summer months, even though the written contract is silent on this point. If shorter workdays during the summer have become a consistent practice over several years and have been tacitly accepted by both management and the union, past practice may have the same force as the written contract: "You can't wave your magic wand to abolish a past practice. Overlay these legal constraints with competing interests of stakeholders and you are attempting to create change within very close quarters."

The political environment in which superintendents operate today, says Valenti, is packed with regulatory constraints and legislative mandates "on every corner." Seeking constructive change is "not a Sunday drive through the countryside": "Rather, you're navigating some very congested city streets during rush hour. The essential question remains: 'How do I make this a better school system despite the legal obstacles and other regulatory roadblocks that do exist?' I think that's the twenty-first century challenge for the new superintendency."

Conclusion

Whatever the degree of legal constraint they face, superintendents vary in how aggressively they exploit the leeway that does exist. Which approaches are successful in this regard is not at issue here. Rather, the point is that the mindset, resources, district context, and political environment of school superintendents shape their responses. These differences raise important questions about how to tackle school improvement. Five kinds of differences emerged in our interviews.

First, almost all of the interviewees count themselves as being unusually savvy about taking full advantage of the law and regard their own legal efforts as examples of purposive leadership. Even superintendents who appear less willing to wield the law as a tool of reform believe they are doing so already, and successfully. At the same time, superintendents seem to vary in the assertiveness with which they approach legal questions and in their willingness to countenance risks. The careerist superintendents appeared more passive, more likely to avoid legal conflict, less likely to push the boundaries of permissible practice, and inclined to think their lawyers were there to keep them out of trouble.

Second, while many superintendents regard lawyers as their defense against litigation, others view them as partners in reform. Alan Bersin and Joel Klein, whose formative experiences took place outside education and who possess legal backgrounds, both emphasize the role of lawyers as agents of change. As Bersin notes, some look at a reform proposal and say, "Yes, you can do this" or, "No, you can't." Other attorneys provide the parameters for action and frame the law as an instrument of change, urging instead, "How can we achieve the goal?" Embracing an approach that Klein deems largely alien to K–12 schooling, both he and Bersin focus more than the careerist superintendents on altering rules governing the hiring, assignment, and removal of personnel—and believe that changing the makeup of their legal teams is key to this effort.

Third, the careerists, with uneven staff support and whose professional training encourages consensus-building, seem to lack an aggressive legal strategy. While all three are accomplished district leaders, they appear sympathetic to Valenti's view that it is better to be too cautious than too aggressive. On occasion, the careerist superintendents used their legal teams as agents of reform but for the most part considered attorneys a means of staying out of trouble. Holster tends to ask his attorneys, "Is this the legal decision to make?" However, Valenti usually dispenses with their assistance in collective bargaining to save money. The interviewees make it clear that superintendents are acting quite rationally when they assume a defensive posture. Superintendents hope to satisfy stakeholders (especially their school boards), bolster their professional standing, and receive laurels when steering clear of legal clashes. Lawsuits and litigation can drain resources almost dry and distract superintendents from instructional efforts, especially if they have little incentive to resist familiar legal or contractual constraints.

Superintendents varied in the resources at their disposal, the caliber of their district's attorneys, and the ease of recruiting and retaining talented practitioners. It may be that large districts with high-profile reform agendas are able to attract lawyers from the more lucrative private sector, although this is merely speculation. While some districts have in-house, salaried attorneys, others work with outside counsel. Little information has been compiled on the nature of various arrangements, much less on their ability to support systemic improvements. This is a substantial omission that provides a fruitful avenue for research and reflection.

Fourth, context matters. The extent to which superintendents engage the law to pursue reform reflects, to some degree, the environments in which they operate. Klein and Bersin lead or have led large urban school districts suffering from dismal school performance, expansive collective bargaining agreements, restrictive work rules and regulations, large bureaucracies, and they both enjoy strong mayoral support. The imperative for change was overwhelming and decisive leadership essential. Harrison, on the other hand, led a much smaller, higher-performing district in a right-to-work state free of unions and collective bargaining. Although both Holster and Valenti operate in heavily regulated, unionized states, their districts are small—one-tenth and one-hundredth the size of Los Angeles, respectively. Furthermore, Valenti's was generally a high-performing district, which made it less necessary to "shake things up."

Fifth, the inclination and ability of superintendents to push existing boundaries are partly a product of the political support they receive. Even if that support is tenuous, superintendents can accomplish reforms, as demonstrated by Bersin's aggressive action despite the 3-2 vote of his board. In Klein's experience, mayoral support was the catalyst for enacting change in an otherwise restrictive environment. All five district leaders alluded to political support as an important consideration but seemed reticent to speak too explicitly about the dynamics of these relationships. Clearly, researchers need to examine the impact of politics on the ability of superintendents to deal with contractual or regulatory impediments, ideally through systematic and anonymous surveys. At present, it is reasonable to suppose that attitudes toward constraints are a function of how leaders maximize political support and minimize political barriers—which means systemic change is a dynamic, all-encompassing endeavor rather than a simple knocking down of obstacles. As Barry Bull and Martha McCarthy noted more than a decade ago, "School administrators do not just follow the law; they also make and interpret it."[41]

Contrary to the defensive view that characterizes most discussions of district leadership and the law, superintendents are not merely bound by statute, code, and contract—they are agents in crafting the environments they face. Superintendents who seek to reshape system routines and culture, challenge existing constraints, and have the legal resources and political support to do so may well find the impediments more manageable than is often imagined. How, when, and why a new generation of leaders might accomplish this reshaping are questions of pressing importance for America's schools.

Notes

1. A related, notable exception is Gerald Grant's insightful book, *The World We Created at Hamilton High* (Harvard University Press, 1988), which explores the impact of court rulings on the culture and behavior of school-level personnel over the course of several decades.

2. Steward Taylor Jr. and Evan Thomas, "Lawsuit Hell: How Fear of Litigation is Paralyzing Our Professions," *Newsweek*, December 15, 2003.

3. Steve Farkas, Jean Johnson, and Ann Duffett, "Rolling Up their Sleeves: Superintendents and Principals Talk about What's Needed to Fix Public Schools," Public Agenda, 2003 (www.wallacefoundation.org/NR/rdonlyres/B51FB0B9-D280-4ED8-B276-8BB2ED4872 E9/0/rolling_up_their_sleeves.pdf [July 31, 2008]), p. 18.

4. Jean Johnson and Ann Duffet, "I'm Calling My Lawyer: How Litigation, Due Process and Other Regulatory Requirements Are Affecting Public Education," Public Agenda and Common Good, 2003 (www.publicagenda.org/files/pdf/im_calling_my_lawyer.pdf [July 31, 2008]), p. 8.

5. Ibid., p. 9.

6. Jean Johnson, Ana Maria Arumi, and Amber Ott, "The Insiders: How Principals and Superintendents See Public Education Today," Public Agenda, Reality Check 2006, Issue 4 (www.publicagenda.org/files/pdf/rc0604.pdf [July 31, 2008]), p. 4.

7. Paul T. Hill, "The Costs of Collective Bargaining," in *Collective Bargaining in Education: Negotiating Change in Today's Schools*, edited by Andrew J. Rotherham and Jane Hannaway (Harvard Education Press, 2006), p. 89.

8. Emily Cohen, Kate Walsh, and RiShawn Biddle, "Invisible Ink in Collective Bargaining: Why Key Issues Are Not Addressed," National Council on Teacher Quality (July 2008) (www. nctq.org/p/publications/docs/nctq_invisible_ink_20080801115950.pdf [August 14, 2008]).

9. Common Good, "Overruled: The Burden of Law on America's Public Schools," 2004 (http://commongood.org/burden-of-law.html [July 31, 2008]).

10. Perry A. Zirkel, "Paralyzing Fear? Avoiding Distorted Assessments of the Effect of Law on Education," *Journal of Law and Education* 35, no. 4 (2006): 461–96.

11. Frederick M. Hess and Coby Loup, "The Leadership Limbo: Teacher Labor Agreements in America's Fifty Largest Districts" (Washington: Thomas B. Fordham Institute, 2008) (http://commongood.org/assets/attachments/22.pdf [July 31, 2008]), p. 9.

12. Dale Ballou, "Teacher Contracts in Massachusetts," White Paper (Pioneer Institute for Public Policy Research, 2000) (http://eric.ed.gov/ERICDocs/data/ericdocs2sql/content_ storage_01/0000019b/80/19/8a/76.pdf [July 31, 2008]), pp. viii–ix.

13. V. Dion Hayes, "Rhee Seeks Tenure-Pay Swap for Teachers," *Washington Post*, July 3, 2008, p. B1.

14. Unless otherwise attributed, all quotations in this section are drawn from John Deasy, interview with authors, August 14, 2008.

15. Hess and Loup, "The Leadership Limbo," p. 124.

16. Daniel Weisberg, "Memorandum Re: Labor Support Unit/Peer Intervention-Plus Program/Teacher Performance Unit," November 14, 2007 (http://schools.nyc.gov/Offices/ GeneralCounsel/Disciplinary/TPU/default.htm [September 16, 2008]).

17. Elissa Gootman, "A New Effort to Remove Bad Teachers," *New York Times*, November 15, 2007, p. B1.

18. Unless otherwise attributed, all quotations in this section are drawn from Daniel Weisberg, interview with authors, June 27, 2008.

19. Unless otherwise attributed, all quotations in this section are drawn from Paul Houston, interview with authors, April 3, 2008.

20. American Association of School Administrators (AASA), *Legal Fallout,* special issue of *School Administrator,* October 2007.

21. Unless otherwise attributed, all quotations in this section are drawn from Maree Sneed, interview with authors, April 21, 2008.

22. Unless otherwise attributed, all quotations in this section are drawn from Francisco Negron, interview with authors, April 23, 2008.

23. Thomas Glass, Lars Bjork, and Cryss C. Brunner, "The 2000 Study of the American School Superintendency: A Look at the Superintendent of Education in the New Millennium" (Arlington, Va.: AASA, 2000), cited in Margaret Terry Orr, "Learning the Superintendency: Socialization, Negotiation, Determination" (Columbia University Teachers College, 2002), p. 5 (www.superintendentresource.org/CMT/Resources/orr.pdf [August 1, 2008]).

24. Michael Fullan, *What's Worth Fighting For in the Principalship?* (New York: Teachers College Press, 2008), p. 24.

25. Frederick M. Hess and Andrew P. Kelly, "Textbook Leadership: An Analysis of Leading Books Used in Principal Preparation," Program on Education Policy and Governance at Harvard University, 2005 (www.hks.harvard.edu/pepg/PDF/Papers/Hess_Kelly_Textbook_Leadership_PEPG05.03.pdf [July 31, 2008]), p. 26.

26. National Association for Law Placement (NALP), "NALP Publishes New Report on Salaries for Public Sector and Public Interest Attorneys," press release, September, 1, 2006 (www.nalp.org/2006nalpnewreportonsalaries [February 12, 2009]); NALP, "What Do New Lawyers Earn?" *NALP Bulletin,* September 2007 (www.nalp.org/2007septnewlawyers [February 12, 2009]).

27. Education Writers Association, "Effective Superintendents, Effective Boards: Finding the Right Fit," Special Report, 2004 (www.ewa.org/library/2004/leadership.pdf [August 1, 2008]), p. 6.

28. Ibid., pp. 43, 9.

29. Alan Bersin, interview with authors, June 20, 2008.

30. Anthony Garofano and Jennifer Sable, "Characteristics of the 100 Largest Public Elementary and Secondary School Districts in the United States: 2004–5," U.S. Department of Education, Common Core of Data, table A-1 (http://nces.ed.gov/pubs2008/2008335.pdf [August 1, 2008]).

31. San Diego Unified School District, "2008-09 Budget Book and District Profile," June 2008, p. 43 (www.sandi.net/depts/budget/pdf/0809budgetbook.pdf [August 1, 2008]).

32. For a comprehensive review of Bersin's tenure, see Frederick M. Hess, ed., *Urban School Reform: Lessons from San Diego* (Harvard Education Press, 2005).

33. William Harrison, interview with authors, July 21, 2008.

34. Joel Klein, interview with authors, July 16, 2008.

35. New York City Department of Education, "About Us," 2007 (http://schools.nyc.gov/AboutUs/default.htm [August 1, 2008]), and "Statistical Summaries," 2007 (http://schools.nyc.gov/AboutUs/DOEData/Stats/default.htm [August 1, 2008]).

36. "Fortune 500: Our Annual Ranking of America's Largest Corporations," *Fortune Magazine* (http://money.cnn.com/magazines/fortune/fortune500/2008/full_list/101_200.html [August 1, 2008]).

37. New York City Department of Education "Chancellor's Biography: Joel I. Klein," 2006 (http://schools.nyc.gov/Offices/mediarelations/ChancellorsBiography/Chancellors+Bio.htm [August 1, 2008]).

38. U.S. Department of Justice, "Joel Klein Named Antitrust Division Deputy for Regulatory Affairs," press release, February 23, 2007 (www.usdoj.gov/atr/public/press_releases/1995/0121.htm [August 1, 2008]).

39. Robert H. Holster, interview with authors, July 16, 2008.

40. Ronald Valenti, interview with authors, July 31, 2008.

41. Barry L. Bull and Martha M. McCarthy, "Reflections on the Knowledge Base in Law and Ethics for Educational Leaders," *Educational Administration Quarterly* 31, no. 4 (1995): 613–31.

PART II

Settled Issues

4

The Real Lessons of School Desegregation

JAMES E. RYAN

I n their sharp dispute over the efficacy and propriety of court involvement in
education reform, courts, commentators, and politicians inevitably cite the
half-century experience with school desegregation to prove their point. Some
use the experience to argue that courts cannot produce lasting change in the face
of public opposition, at least in the context of public education.[1] The underlying assumption is that courts, especially the U.S. Supreme Court, acted aggressively to integrate schools but largely failed in that effort.

That assumption is at least half right: the Court failed to integrate public
schools. To be sure, the Court succeeded in dismantling laws that intentionally
and explicitly segregated students by race, and this was, and remains, a major
accomplishment. But the Court did not produce stably integrated schools in
either the short or long term. Very little integration occurred during the first
decade after *Brown* v. *Board of Education*.[2] Although integration increased with
the advent of busing, those gains have since disappeared. Schools today are as
segregated as they were in the late 1960s before busing began. Currently, more
than 70 percent of black and Hispanic students attend predominantly minority
schools; more than 30 percent attend schools that are greater than 90 percent
minority. The average white student attends a school in which more than 80
percent of the students are white.[3]

Some take these disappointing results as proof that the Court lacked the
capacity to produce social change. Others suggest that it lacked the *will* and thus

73

did not do enough to ensure integrated schools. The underlying assumption, sometimes made explicit, is that greater effort would have produced stably integrated schools across the country. Noted constitutional law scholar Erwin Chemerinsky, for example, has suggested that if key desegregation cases had been decided differently, "the nature of public education today would be very different."[4]

The school desegregation experience also features in the related debate about the propriety of court involvement in education reform. Although the decision to intervene in *Brown* is no longer controversial, there is lingering disagreement about the Court's subsequent decisions to require integration and to authorize busing for that purpose. Some suggest that the Court went too far in those decisions, while others argue that the Court was justified in authorizing aggressive remedial efforts.[5] The debates about efficacy and propriety tend to intertwine as views about the propriety of court intervention are influenced by views about its efficacy. One might still question the propriety of effective court interventions, for example, but few would argue in favor of futile interventions.

I believe the Court's experience with school desegregation reveals something less and something different than many suppose. It is not the case, as some contend, that school integration failed despite strong efforts by the Court to achieve that goal. The Court did act aggressively, at least eventually, in ordering integration and requiring busing.[6] On the whole, however, the Court was quite restrained.[7] At several important forks in the road, the Court either stayed its hand or intentionally limited the reach of school desegregation. School desegregation cases thus reveal not a liberal, activist Court committed to integrating schools regardless of political or practical obstacles. Instead, they reveal a fairly conservative Court that did as much, if not more, to limit integration as to promote it, as explained later in the chapter.

It does not follow, of course, that a stronger effort by the Supreme Court or lower federal courts would have produced substantially different results. Just as important, it does not follow that the results would have been exactly the same. The truth is that one can never know what would have happened had the Court acted differently. Whether districts and parents would have complied with or resisted firmer and broader desegregation remedies is a matter of speculation. Some evidence, from school districts like Charlotte-Mecklenburg in North Carolina, suggests that broader remedies may have indeed been successful. But such evidence is too sparse to do anything more than rebut the facile assertion that stronger efforts necessarily would have been futile. In short, school desegregation offers surprisingly little insight into the ability of the Supreme Court, or any other court, to produce successful education reforms.

The desegregation cases do shed some light on the unending debate over court involvement in education reform. This debate tends to break down along partisan lines. In general, politically conservative commentators, politicians, and judges are more likely to question the propriety of court involvement, whereas liberals are more likely to embrace it.[8] The Court's desegregation decisions, from the very first to the most recent, do not show that one side or the other is right; that debate will never be resolved. Instead, they tend to show that neither side holds fast to its views on this issue.

Many at the time criticized the Court for overreaching in *Brown*. Today, the decision is accepted as legitimate by liberals and conservatives alike, which suggests that views about the propriety of court interventions can change over time. The Court's most recent decision, in *Parents Involved in Community Schools* v. *Seattle School District No. 1,* in turn suggests that views about the legitimacy of court involvement may depend on the nature of the reform. In *Parents Involved,* the Court placed significant restrictions on even voluntary efforts to integrate schools, regardless of local political will.[9] The decision is decidedly conservative, but it is hardly an example of judicial restraint. To those who champion judicial restraint, the obvious question is whether *Parents Involved* constituted illegitimate activism. Precisely the same question can be posed to those who embrace aggressive court involvement in education. To the extent that the outcome in *Parents Involved* is supported by those who normally applaud judicial restraint and is opposed by those who welcome court activism, it suggests that views about the legitimacy of court-ordered reform are unstable and depend, ultimately, on what the court is trying to achieve.

Forks in the Road

The Court undoubtedly acted boldly in declaring intentional school segregation unconstitutional in *Brown* v. *Board of Education*. The decision overturned settled practices throughout the South and was wildly unpopular in that region. Even this courageous decision, however, should be considered in context. *Brown* came more than half a century after *Plessy* v. *Ferguson,* the infamous 1896 decision in which the Court gave its blessing to segregation. By the time the Court decided *Brown,* in 1954, the country had become much more tolerant of school desegregation. Indeed, national polls revealed a slight majority in favor of the *Brown* decision. The Court acted against the wishes of the South, but from a national perspective, *Brown* was not strongly countermajoritarian.[10]

All Deliberate Speed

The Court also failed to specify a remedy in *Brown II,* which was devoted entirely to this issue. The decision is famous for its oxymoronic phrase, "all deliberate speed," which the Court used to describe the pace at which states needed to desegregate their schools.[11] Less appreciated is the fact that the Court did not clarify what, exactly, school districts needed to do. On the one hand, the Court suggested that students should be admitted to schools on a nondiscriminatory basis, which might require little more than repealing laws mandating segregation. This might not result in much integration, but presumably it also would not take much time. Yet the Court seemed to envision something more, as evidenced by its discussion of the need to remove "a variety of obstacles," by which the Court must have meant obstacles to integration. But even if the Court imagined that some integration was required to remedy the constitutional violation, it remained silent about the degree of integration necessary to cure the harm. In other words, the Court offered no benchmarks that lower courts could use to determine if states and school districts had satisfied their remedial obligations.

For more than a decade, the Court left this remedial question unanswered. Scholars at the time and ever since have debated whether the Court was right to allow the South some time to get used to *Brown* and transition away from segregated schools. Had the Court been more forceful and required swift action, some argue, the South would have put up some resistance but then would have buckled and become used to integrated schools. Quite the contrary, others say: pushing the issue would have led to greater and fiercer resistance. Better to go slowly than to incite violence.[12]

That debate is beyond resolution but also beside the point in some respects, as Judge J. Harvie Wilkinson III has explained cogently. One could defend the Court's decision to move somewhat slowly in *Brown II*, but it is hard to defend the Court's virtual absence from the field of desegregation until the late 1960s. After *Brown II* in 1955, the Court issued a few decisions making clear that outright defiance of *Brown* was not allowed. So Little Rock, Arkansas, was not exempt from *Brown* simply because people there did not like the decision. And schools in Prince Edward County, Virginia, could not remain closed while schools were open in other parts of the state. But these decisions simply marked what was clearly outside the boundaries of constitutional responses to *Brown*; they did not provide any more guidance about what *Brown* actually required.[13]

This left lower-court judges with all the discretion in the world. Some opposed desegregation and therefore were inclined to do little. Others faced intense community pressure to move slowly. Federal judges are appointed for life and therefore immune from political pressure, at least in theory. But judges live in the same communities affected by their rulings, and life tenure on the bench does not guarantee a life without pressure or criticism. Because the Supreme Court left the issue so open-ended, even judges who wanted to order more integration knew they would be blamed for the result. They could not point to a ruling from the Supreme Court and claim that their hands were tied.[14]

The South took full advantage of this unhelpful dynamic by enacting all sorts of schemes that seemed on the surface to comply with *Brown* but in reality led to little change. Most judges went along with this wink-and-nod approach to compliance, which is why, a decade after *Brown,* no more than 2 percent of black children in the South attended schools with whites. As historian James Patterson points out: "Virtually all Southern black children who had entered first grade in 1954 and who remained in Southern schools graduated from all-black schools twelve years later."[15]

The Bus Comes Late

After thirteen years of silence, the Supreme Court announced in its 1968 decision in *Green* v. *New Kent County* that formerly segregated school districts must actually integrate their schools. In an opinion written by Justice William J. Brennan Jr., the Court declared the end of "all deliberate speed" and spoke as if the duty of school districts had been clear all along. *Brown II* charged school boards "with the affirmative duty to take whatever steps might be necessary to convert to a unitary system in which racial discrimination would be eliminated root and branch." The school board had to come forward with a plan that promised "realistically to work, and . . . realistically to work *now.*" What the Court meant by a plan that had to "work" was clear: the plan had to result in integration and convert the district "promptly to a system without a 'white' school and a 'Negro' school, but just schools."[16]

Three years later, in *Swann* v. *Charlotte-Mecklenburg,* the Court unanimously approved the use of busing as one tool in a desegregation remedy. In districts where neighborhood schools would be segregated because of residential segregation, courts could thus order officials to transport students out of their neighborhoods. The decision in *Swann,* like that in *Green,* applied only to states and school districts that had previously intentionally segregated students. The Court did not create an affirmative obligation to integrate all schools across the country.

Green and *Swann* represented the high-water mark of the Court's efforts to integrate schools.[17] *Green* transformed *Brown II*'s vague language about desegregation into a clear mandate to integrate, and *Swann* endorsed the controversial use of busing to accomplish the goal. The Court without doubt acted aggressively in these two decisions; according to some contemporary justices, it also acted improperly in converting *Brown* from a prohibition against intentional segregation into a mandate requiring integration.[18]

The implicit accusation of illegitimate activism fails to recognize, however, that the South in some ways invited a strong response from the Court. For more than a decade, southern officials either completely resisted school desegregation or engaged in tokenism, using a variety of race-neutral student assignment criteria that technically complied with *Brown* but also maintained segregated schools. Southern judges acquiesced for the most part. Even when they required the admission of a black student to a formerly all-white school, these judges often limited relief to a single plaintiff or small group of plaintiffs, indicating that integration might have to occur one or two students at a time.[19] Had the South been less determined to resist all but token levels of integration, or had judges been a bit less tolerant of such obvious ruses, perhaps the Court would have allowed the South to go its own way.[20] Both *Green* and *Swann* arguably exceeded the scope of *Brown II,* if only because the scope of that decision was so vague. But they may well have been necessary to put an end to the South's shenanigans. From this perspective, the decisions look more like attempts to enforce the law than attempts to create from whole cloth a new integration mandate.

The Court in *Swann,* moreover, made clear that desegregation remedies would be temporary. Courts could order busing for a while, but "at some point," the Court emphasized, these school authorities and others like them would "have achieved full compliance with the Court's decisions in *Brown I.*"[21] Once that point was reached—once school systems achieved "unitary" status— courts would lose their authority to require busing in the absence of new intentional attempts to segregate schools. Thus in the same decision that endorsed the expansive scope of a district judge's remedial power, the Court indicated that this power would not last forever. Exactly how long desegregation decrees could or should remain in place was left unanswered. But at the very least the Court's emphasis on the temporary nature of busing cast a cloud over its use and helped preclude long-term commitments to using whatever means available to maintain integrated schools. School desegregation could thus be seen, even in the early 1970s, as an aberration and temporary deviation from neighborhood schools, and thus as a burden to endure temporarily or to avoid while it ran its course.

Many chose the latter option. Indeed, by the time the Court ordered integration and the use of busing, it was too late in many districts for meaningful integration to occur. The demographics of many urban districts changed fairly dramatically during the period between *Brown I* in 1954 and *Swann* in 1971. Middle-class whites decamped for the suburbs in significant numbers. Some, though hardly all, were driven by a desire to avoid school desegregation.

Richmond, Virginia, is as good an example as any. In 1954 the school population was 57 percent white and 43 percent African American. By 1970 more than 70 percent of the students were African American.[22] White Richmonders, it seems, used the period of defiance and delay following *Brown* to move out of the school system altogether. Even with busing, a predominately black school district might be difficult to integrate—and efforts to do so might be self-defeating by spurring even more white flight. Indeed, a study of the Richmond school attendance patterns released in 1971 concluded that the only realistic way to integrate the district's schools would be to merge Richmond with surrounding Henrico and Chesterfield counties, which were overwhelmingly white.[23]

Congress and the president, meanwhile, were late to become involved in school desegregation, and they did not remain active supporters for very long. Before 1964 the executive and legislative branches of the federal government offered little assistance to school desegregation. The 1964 Civil Rights Act authorized the Department of Justice to intervene in desegregation cases and also allowed the Department of Health, Education, and Welfare (HEW) to withhold funding from school districts that did not desegregate. HEW eventually issued guidelines requiring districts to achieve some level of integration.[24] In 1968, in *Green,* the Court made clear that it, too, would require integration. Less than one year later, however, Richard Nixon occupied the White House, and he kept his campaign promise to slow down school desegregation. He instructed the Justice Department and HEW officials to ease their efforts and to oppose the National Association for the Advancement of Colored People (NAACP) in some desegregation cases.[25]

Thus just as the Court was getting serious about desegregation, the executive branch was putting on the brakes. For a mere seven months after *Green* and before Nixon's inauguration, one could fairly say that all three branches of government were committed not just to desegregation but to integration. At every other point, from the time *Brown* was decided until today, at least one branch of the federal government has either acted to limit the reach of *Brown* or done little to enhance the likelihood that black and white students would actually attend school together.[26] To say that desegregation failed even though all three branches of the federal government supported it is no more accurate than to suggest that it failed despite strong efforts by courts alone.

Holding Fast to the De Jure–De Facto Distinction

The next fork in the road arose when desegregation headed north. In the aftermath of *Green* and *Swann,* southerners complained that the Court was treating the South unfairly and applying a double standard. Southern schools, they argued, were segregated in 1970 not because of the lingering effect of old laws requiring segregation, but because of residential segregation. If the South had to overcome residential segregation through busing, why not the North as well?

Justice Lewis F. Powell Jr., the only white southerner on the Court, took up this charge in a concurring opinion in *Keyes* v. *School District No. 1,* decided in 1973. The Court in that case ruled that northern districts would have the same obligation to desegregate if, but only if, it were shown that officials had acted intentionally to segregate schools.[27] Put differently, the Court concluded that informal policies, just like statutes or constitutional provisions, could constitute de jure segregation, or segregation by law. The Court also made clear that only de jure segregation, as opposed to de facto segregation, violated the U.S. Constitution.[28] Segregation that occurred because of individual choices about where to live, for example, was beyond the reach of courts because the equal protection clause of the Fourteenth Amendment, which provided the legal basis for challenges to segregation, applied only to state action, not to private discrimination.

Justice Powell argued for the abandonment of the de jure–de facto distinction. He did not claim that the Fourteenth Amendment should apply to private actions. Instead, he contended that school segregation could always be traced to public action or inaction. He did not believe, in other words, that de facto school segregation really existed. State and local officials, for example, had the responsibility to draw attendance zones and choose sites for new buildings. If they acted with the knowledge that some choices would maintain or increase school segregation, then they should be held responsible for those choices. Similarly, if they failed to do anything to combat segregation, despite having options available, they should also be held responsible, argued Powell.[29] In advocating this approach, Powell sought to place northern and southern school districts on the same footing.

Four other justices appear to have agreed that the de jure–de facto distinction should be abandoned.[30] But this majority of justices failed to join a single opinion in *Keyes* because of a disagreement about busing. Powell disliked busing and opposed its use as a remedial tool. The four others endorsed busing. Instead of joining Powell's opinion only insofar as it called for jettisoning the de jure–de facto distinction, the other four remained silent, and the issue was dropped. After *Keyes,* Powell relied on the de jure–de facto distinction, and it has remained a part of the Court's desegregation jurisprudence ever since.

The decision to maintain the distinction, though somewhat accidental in *Keyes,* was nonetheless significant. If the Court had abandoned it, school officials would have had an ongoing responsibility to tackle segregated schools. Although the extent of their remedial obligations might remain a subject of contention, school officials would have been indefinitely liable for any and all segregation over which they could exercise some control. This liability necessarily would have extended to state officials. Because of their own constitutions, states are ultimately responsible for education and, in particular, for drawing school district boundaries. And because a great deal of segregation occurs between rather than within districts, state officials would presumably have had some obligation to redraw district boundaries or otherwise allow students to cross those boundaries in order to ameliorate segregated conditions among schools in a particular region.

By maintaining the de jure–de facto distinction, the Court required states and districts to remedy only intentional acts of segregation. It thereby limited both the temporal and geographical scope of desegregation. The resulting efforts to integrate schools would presumably take a period of time, but at some point the violation would be cured and the remedial obligation lifted from school districts.

Moreover, the obligation to integrate would arise in the first place only where there was proof of intentional acts of school segregation. Such proof was not always easy to amass in the North, for it meant demonstrating that officials made decisions with the *purpose* of segregating students rather than simply with an *awareness* that segregation would be a byproduct of their actions.[31] Many northern districts, especially metropolitan regions, had single-race schools owing to a combination of residential segregation, neighborhood schools, and school district boundaries. Unless plaintiffs could show that officials assigned students with the specific intent of segregating them, districts would not be found liable. Similarly, once districts fulfilled their remedial obligations, they would only be liable for school segregation again if it was fairly plain that one assignment plan or another was designed with the hope that it would produce segregation. Whether most school districts have changed their ways or simply learned not to flaunt their old ways, such proof of intentional segregation has been hard to find.

Sealing Off the Suburbs

The next restriction, and perhaps the most important of all, came in the year following the *Keyes* decision. In *Milliken* v. *Bradley*, decided in 1974, the Court essentially placed the suburbs beyond the reach of court-ordered desegregation.[32] The case arose out of Detroit, where state and local officials were found guilty of intentionally segregating the schools. The question in the case had to do with the scope of the remedy. The district court judge, Stephen Roth, concluded that busing limited to Detroit would be futile or self-defeating because Detroit was already majority-minority. More busing, he believed, would simply lead to more white flight to the suburbs. In order to have an effective remedy, Roth reasoned, the suburbs needed to be included. And that is exactly what he ordered. To be precise, the judge approved a busing plan that would have included fifty-three suburban districts surrounding Detroit.[33]

The Supreme Court, by a vote of 5-4, reversed the decision. Four of the justices in the majority were relatively new to the Court, having been appointed by President Nixon. The Court started from the proposition that the scope of the remedy could not exceed the scope of the violation. This sounds reasonable enough, but the principle played little role in earlier cases like *Swann* and *Keyes*, where the desegregation remedies clearly exceeded the scope of the initial constitutional violation. In *Milliken,* however, the Court sought to protect local control over schools and thus demanded stringent symmetry between violation and cure: an interdistrict remedy could only be used for an interdistrict violation. Absent proof that school district lines had been intentionally gerrymandered to promote segregation, for example, school buses would not be allowed to cross into the suburbs for the purpose of desegregating city schools.[34]

Such proof was necessary, it bears mentioning, in part because of the de jure–de facto distinction and the lingering effect of *Keyes.* Had the distinction been abandoned, *Milliken*'s rationale for limiting desegregation would have made no sense. With that distinction in tact, plaintiffs had to show that local or state officials took actions or devised policies with the intent of segregating not just schools but districts. Such proof was hard to find, in part because housing discrimination kept most African Americans out of the suburbs.[35] There was thus no need to play around with school district boundaries in order to keep suburban schools mostly white.

It is difficult to discount the importance of *Milliken.* Because interdistrict violations were hard to find or prove, most school desegregation plans were limited to urban districts. Trying to integrate urban schools, however, was a losing proposition by the early 1970s because of the demographics of urban districts. Thus just three years after the Court approved busing in *Swann,* it effectively halted the progress of school desegregation. Indeed, *Swann* and *Milliken* were a fairly deadly combination. The former required all-out busing in urban districts, which gave middle-class whites a reason to depart, while the latter ensured that those who made it to the suburbs would be spared from busing.[36]

In order to reach the result in *Milliken,* the Court had to duck the issue of residential segregation. Judge Roth had rested his decision in part on the ground that state and local officials bore some responsibility for residential segregation within the Detroit metropolitan area. The court of appeals did not rely on this evidence, reasoning that Roth's decision could be upheld even absent proof of housing discrimination. The Supreme Court used this as an excuse not to deal with the issue of residential segregation, despite the fact that unlike the court of appeals, it *reversed* Judge Roth's decision. It is one thing to ignore one of two possible bases for a decision if one alone is sufficient to uphold it; it is quite another to ignore one of two independent rationales if the decision is being reversed.[37]

If state or local officials discriminated with regard to housing and therefore helped cause residential segregation between urban and suburban districts, these acts might well justify cross-district busing. Whether school officials should be held responsible for the actions of housing officials might pose tricky legal questions, for sure, but one could reasonably conclude that a state or local government could not avoid responsibility for race discrimination by dividing up authority among different agencies.

Ironically, this is how Justice Potter Stewart saw the issue in *Milliken.* He supplied the fifth vote and wrote separately to make clear that if state officials had caused segregation among school districts "by purposeful racially discriminatory use of state housing or zoning laws, then a decree calling for transfer of pupils across district lines or for restructuring of district lines might well be appropriate."[38] Yet having made this concession, Justice Stewart did not so much ignore as refuse to take seriously the evidence regarding state responsibility for residential segregation.

What was true in *Milliken* was true of other school desegregation cases. The gaping hole in the Court's school desegregation jurisprudence is the absence of any real attention to government responsibility for housing discrimination. For at least the past forty years, the primary cause of school segregation has been the combination of neighborhood school assignments and residential segregation. The causes of residential segregation are numerous and intertwined and include such factors as economics, preferences, and private discrimination. But every level of government, as the district judge found in *Milliken,* has played an integral and underappreciated role in fostering residential segregation by race.[39]

In school desegregation cases, however, the Court elided the issue of housing discrimination, and most lower courts followed suit. The Court dodged the issue in *Swann* by relying on the aphorism that one school case, like a vehicle, "can carry only a limited amount of baggage."[40] The Court, in particular Justice Stewart, ignored the evidence of housing discrimination again in *Milliken.*[41] By the 1990s, when the Court began to encourage lower courts to dissolve desegregation decrees, it essentially explained housing choices as purely private decisions and thus beyond the power of courts to address in desegregation cases.[42]

There is no doubt that a different outcome in *Milliken* would have generated intense opposition. Cross-district busing had relatively few ardent supporters and many passionate opponents. Whether the decision would have been resisted, ignored, or evaded is impossible to know, however, as is usually the case with counterfactual hypotheticals. That said, it is simply wrong to assume that requiring cross-district busing would have been futile and thus that the decision in *Milliken* was in some sense irrelevant.

Indeed, the experience in Charlotte-Mecklenburg suggests that urban-suburban desegregation plans might well have worked. Charlotte-Mecklenburg was a single school district that encompassed both the city of Charlotte and its surrounding suburbs in Mecklenburg County. District lines did not need to be crossed, but suburban parents, at least initially, strongly opposed busing. Over time, however, urban-suburban desegregation gained the support of voters in Charlotte-Mecklenburg, who defeated school board candidates pledging to end busing, and it became a source of pride for the region. Experience with integrated schools changed opinions in Charlotte-Mecklenburg, and the schools remained stably integrated there for over twenty years.[43]

This is not to say that what happened in Charlotte-Mecklenburg would have been repeated in metropolitan regions across the country if *Milliken* had come out the other way. But the experience in Charlotte-Mecklenberg does give lie to the claim that any effort by the Court to integrate suburban and urban schools would have been futile.

Shutting Down

For a little more the fifteen years after the *Milliken* decision, school desegregation proceeded along the path marked by *Swann,* on the one hand, and by *Milliken,* on the other. The only significant addition to the Court's desegregation jurisprudence was a subsequent opinion in the *Milliken* case, in which the Court approved the inclusion of compensatory funding as one part of a desegregation remedy. Students in formerly segregated schools often performed below par, and the Court in *Milliken II* concluded that they were entitled to financial assistance to fund additional counseling and academic services.[44] Gone was the strong concern, in *Milliken I,* about maintaining a close connection between the scope of the violation and the scope of the remedy, as it would have been quite difficult to establish any but the loosest connection between segregation that occurred years or decades earlier and the academic performance of current students.

The most important aspect of *Milliken II* remedies involved state contributions. The Court required the state to share the burden of these financial remedies, which had the effect of transforming a number of school desegregation cases. Lawyers for plaintiffs in urban districts recognized the futility of busing within a predominantly minority district and began to focus on *Milliken II* funding. School districts themselves, once the defendants in school desegregation cases and opponents of court involvement, saw *Milliken II* relief as an opportunity to obtain more funding from the state. As a result, they either joined forces with plaintiffs or became very friendly defendants, and desegregation cases became as much about money as about moving students around.[45]

In the early 1990s, the Court returned to the field and signaled that it was time to dismantle desegregation decrees. In a trio of decisions between 1991 and 1995, the Court established criteria for lower courts to use when deciding whether to end court supervision of formerly segregated school districts. If school districts had complied in good faith with desegregation decrees and eliminated "the vestiges of past discrimination . . . to the extent practicable," they should be declared unitary and the decree dissolved either in part or in whole.[46]

Similarly, the Court instructed, *Milliken II* relief should not be considered endless and tied to overly ambitious achievement goals.[47]

More important than the criteria or doctrinal niceties of the opinions was their overall message: court-ordered school desegregation has gone on long enough and should be dismantled soon. As Justice Antonin Scalia said in a concurring opinion, in characteristically blunt fashion, "We must acknowledge that it has become absurd to assume, without any further proof, that violations of the Constitution dating from the days when Lyndon B. Johnson was president, or earlier, continue to have an appreciable effect upon current operation of schools. We are close to that time."[48] No other justice joined that opinion. But notice that the test for unitary status relies strongly, if implicitly, on the passage of time. Whether "good faith" compliance is shown must turn, in part, on the length of time the decree was in place, and the same is true with the determination of whether vestiges have been eliminated "to the extent practicable." The longer the decree is in place, the more likely a court can conclude, regardless of what the district looks like, that things are not likely to get much better.

In these three decisions, the Court essentially kept its promise to make desegregation a temporary aberration from neighborhood school assignments. In doing so, it again stressed the importance of returning schools to state and local control as opposed to maintaining courts as their overseers. The Court also took these steps fully aware that dismantling desegregation decrees and returning to neighborhood schools would increase school segregation in a number of districts. Oklahoma, involved in one of the cases, is a good example. The record indicated that ending the desegregation decree there would result in a fairly significant increase in racial isolation among district schools. For this reason, the lower court refused to lift the decree.[49] To the Court, however, the resegregation of schools upon a release from a desegregation decree was and remains an irrelevant factor.

Lower federal courts have heeded the Supreme Court's message and have been dissolving desegregation decrees for more than a decade. The pace of dissolution has been slower than some have imagined, and perhaps slower than the Court would have liked. Part of the reason has to do with *Milliken II* relief, which takes away the incentives of school districts to seek relief from court orders. Indeed, a number of desegregation cases have ended as a result of consent decrees that endorse an agreement by states to pay a lump sum to school districts. States, in essence, have bought out these districts. In addition, a surprisingly large number of decrees remain in place out of sheer inertia. They do not require much on the part of school officials, or they are simply ignored; either way, they are not imposing much cost on anyone and therefore do not attract much attention.[50]

All of that said, there is no doubt that court-ordered desegregation is in its twilight phase. It may be dying a slow death, but it is clearly dying and unlikely to be resurrected. Although commentators sometimes lament the departure of federal courts from the desegregation scene and express some hope they will become involved again, the odds of federal or state courts jumping back on the desegregation bandwagon seem vanishingly slim.[51]

Conservative Activism and "Voluntary" Integration

The Supreme Court's most recent desegregation decision, *Parents Involved in Community Schools* v. *Seattle School District No. 1,* limits the extent to which school districts can use racial classifications in order to create or maintain racially integrated schools.[52] A small percentage of school districts across the country have created so-called voluntary integration plans. They are deemed voluntary not because parents or students have a choice as to whether race is considered, but to distinguish plans adopted by elected officials from those that are mandated by courts. In *Parents Involved,* a fractured court struck down two voluntary integration plans, one from Seattle and the other from Jefferson County, Kentucky. Both districts allowed for some choice among schools, but the choices were constrained by the goal of maintaining racially integrated schools. Whether a student ultimately would be assigned to a particular school turned, in some instances, on the race of the student.

The Court applied strict scrutiny to the plans, which is now the test used to assess all laws that explicitly make racial classifications, regardless of whether those laws are designed to disadvantage or benefit racial minorities. Under this test, the law or policy must be deemed necessary to achieve a compelling interest and be narrowly tailored to accomplish its goals. Few laws or policies survive this intensive review, although the Court fairly recently upheld an affirmative action admissions policy at the University of Michigan Law School.[53] In *Parents Involved,* the Court struck down the voluntary integration plans at issue because the districts failed to show that the use of racial classifications was necessary to produce racially integrated schools; neither district, for example, had demonstrated that race-neutral methods of achieving racially integrated schools would have been futile.[54]

The ruling for the Court was fairly narrow, as was the five-justice majority that endorsed it. Five of the justices wrote additional, separate opinions, either concurring in the judgment or dissenting from it, to express their own views. Chief Justice John Roberts, who was joined by three other justices, suggested that voluntary integration does not advance a compelling interest, which would completely preclude the use of race in student assignments.[55] Clarence Thomas made a similar point in a separate concurrence.[56] Four justices dissented. They argued that strict scrutiny should not be applied to these plans and, even if it were, the plans should be upheld.[57]

Anthony M. Kennedy split the difference between Roberts and the dissenting justices. He wrote separately to make clear that he would approve the consideration of race in student assignments in certain ways and under limited circumstances. In Kennedy's view, racial classifications should be avoided unless absolutely necessary. Instead, school districts should use race-neutral but race-conscious measures to integrate their schools, such as siting new schools or drawing attendance zones with an eye toward integration. They might also use proxies for race, such as place of residence or socioeconomic status. Only if these methods fail should school districts consider the race of an individual pupil when assigning or admitting students, and even then, race should not be dispositive but one of several factors guiding assignment or admission.[58]

Justice Kennedy's opinion, though joined by no other justice, is effectively controlling for the Court on the issue of when and how school districts can take race into account when assigning students. The four dissenting justices would allow school officials more latitude to consider race than would Justice Kennedy. It follows as a matter of logic that they would tolerate the more limited consideration of race endorsed by Kennedy.

Parents Involved is at once both unimportant and momentous. On a practical level, the decision will have little immediate impact, for two reasons. First, the decision affects very few of the roughly 16,000 school districts in the United States. Although precise figures are hard to come by, only a few hundred and at most 1,000 take race into account when assigning students to schools. Even these figures exaggerate the use of race insofar as they count districts in which only a few schools take race into consideration, while most others rely on neighborhood school assignments. But even if the highest estimate is accepted, that still leaves 15,000 districts that do not rely on race in assigning students. For the vast majority of districts, therefore, this decision is simply irrelevant because they did not consider race in student assignments before *Parents Involved*.[59]

The relatively low number of districts that do take race into account certainly signals some lack of interest in racially integrated schools. That said, it is important to recognize that most districts could not create integrated schools even if they were interested in doing so. The plain, somewhat shocking truth is that the majority of school *districts*—not schools, but districts—are either *at least* 90 percent white or 90 percent minority. In these districts, demographics make the question of integrated schools moot.[60]

Even those districts that currently consider race may be able to continue to do so, given Justice Kennedy's concurring opinion. It all depends on how race is used, and this varies from district to district. In the few districts where race is used as the sole factor to determine whether a student can attend a particular school, assignment policies will have to be changed. On the other hand, in districts where schools require an application for admission and some consideration is given to race but race is not dispositive, it may be that nothing needs to be changed. Even in districts where current policies need to be altered to satisfy Justice Kennedy's criteria, officials are not without recourse. Those who remain interested in racial integration can turn to proxies like socioeconomic status or place of residence, both of which are perfectly constitutional bases for school assignments. The use of such proxies may not achieve precisely the same level of racial integration as would the explicit consideration of race, but they will surely achieve more integration than simple neighborhood assignments.

In short, the decision affects few districts directly, and those it does affect still have some room to maneuver. It is for this reason that some states and school districts that considered race before *Parents Involved* have announced that they will leave their programs unchanged, or that they will alter them slightly in order to comply with Justice Kennedy's somewhat vague restrictions.[61] This does not mean that *Parents Involved* will be completely irrelevant. The Seattle district, for example, has abandoned efforts to integrate its schools, and the Court's decision in *Parents Involved* certainly helps explain why.[62] The point is simply that the impact of the decision will necessarily be slight given the paucity of districts that consider—or are even in a position to consider—race in student assignments.

Despite its limited practical importance, the decision nonetheless represents a significant addition to the Court's desegregation jurisprudence. In some ways, the decision is a fairly radical departure from prior cases. At the most basic level, the Court prohibited some school districts—those previously under desegregation decrees—from doing what courts had been ordering them to do for decades. Before districts under desegregation decrees achieve unitary status, they *must* take race into account in an effort to achieve some level of integration. The most straightforward way to do that, and the way endorsed by countless desegregation decrees, is to classify students on the basis of race and assign them accordingly. It now appears that after districts receive unitary status, they *must not* take race into account, at least insofar as that consideration involves individual racial classifications. What was required one day becomes prohibited the next.

In addition, the Court in the past had explicitly endorsed voluntary integration. In the *Swann* opinion, the Court made clear that school officials could of their own volition assign students so that each school featured "a prescribed ratio of Negro to white students reflecting the proportion for the district as a whole."[63] The only way to achieve such a precise ratio would be to classify individual students by race. Chief Justice Roberts, in his plurality opinion, tried to dismiss this language from *Swann* as dicta and therefore not binding.[64] This was correct as a technical matter but ignored the more fundamental point. The

Court that decided *Swann* would surely have upheld the plans at issue in *Parents Involved*, as well as other assignment plans that used racial classifications to achieve integrated schools.[65] To suggest that *Parents Involved* did not involve a change in doctrine, as Roberts argued, is thus both technically correct and profoundly misleading.

The decision also reflects a degree of activism missing from earlier decisions that limited the scope of school desegregation remedies. When the Court limited the reach of desegregation decrees in *Milliken*, and when it called for their dissolution in the 1990s, one could fairly call the decisions conservative. They limited the power of courts to achieve integration, a result championed by President Nixon and other conservatives. The decisions themselves were written or joined by the more conservative justices on the Court. At the same time, these earlier decisions represented exercises in judicial restraint. In each case, the Court deferred to local control of public education and used this principle to justify limiting both the scope and the duration of court-ordered desegregation.

In *Parents Involved*, by contrast, none of the justices who joined the majority or wrote opinions supporting the result, including Justice Kennedy, offered much deference to local control. The notion that local and state officials should be in charge of school assignments, so prominent in earlier decisions curtailing desegregation, is nowhere to be found in these various opinions. Instead, four of the justices strongly embraced the notion of a colorblind constitution, which is a cause célèbre for political and judicial conservatives.[66] Kennedy distanced himself from the plurality's stance by admitting that the consideration of race is still necessary in some instances. But he did not trust local officials to use their discretion and instead placed significant restrictions on their ability to take race into account when trying to create or maintain integrated schools.[67]

The charge of judicial activism is made loosely and often. It is a mostly meaningless criticism because there is not much agreement on what activism comprises. There is nonetheless a common implication that activist courts improperly interfere with democratic decisionmaking; that is, they overturn legislative or executive decisions without having a strong basis in constitutional law for doing so. Activism thus connotes illegitimacy. One cannot know for sure, of course, but the charge (still) seems to come more often from those on the right, who continue to criticize courts for being too liberal and activist despite the fact that Republicans dominate the federal judiciary.[68] In any event, busing for desegregation would, in some eyes, constitute a perfect example of liberal activism.

Parents Involved challenges the surprisingly enduring assumption that liberalism and activism go hand in hand. To the extent that activism constitutes unjustified interference with democratic decisionmaking, *Parents Involved* can fairly be called activist. The rules created by the Court in that case lack a strong foundation in either the text or history of the Constitution, as does the color-blind principle more generally.[69] Precedent, in turn, points in different directions, depending on whether one looks to *Swann* or to the more recent affirmative action cases.[70] This is not to say that the decision is completely indefensible on policy or moral grounds, but rather to argue that the result is hardly *commanded* by the plain text of the Constitution, the historical understanding of that text, or precedent.

Parents Involved thus offers an interesting challenge to conservatives and liberals alike. For conservatives who champion judicial restraint and deference to democratic decisionmaking, at least in the context of public education, the question is whether the Court's activism and intervention in *Parents Involved* was nonetheless justified. If so, the obvious follow-up question is whether intervention would also be justified to right other wrongs. If it is proper for courts to curtail voluntary efforts to integrate schools, regardless of local political sentiment, is it also proper to equalize school funding? If not, why not?

For liberals who are comfortable with court intervention, even without a completely solid basis in constitutional text or precedent, *Parents Involved* is something of a cautionary tale. Once intervention is endorsed, the obvious risk is that the outcome will have a great deal to do with the inclinations of the particular justices who are intervening. One would be hard pressed to defend, as principled, the notion that courts should intervene only if they will reach a politically liberal result. Thus the case raises similar questions for liberals, just in reverse. If it is proper for courts to intervene in school funding decisions, why is it improper for them to interfere with voluntary integration policies?

Conclusion

It is always tempting, and sometimes useful, to generalize from a particular experience. There are risks, however, that the wrong lesson will be learned. The Supreme Court's experience with school desegregation does not demonstrate, as some believe, that the Court is unable to produce lasting social change. The most that can be said is that, for whatever reason, the Court was unwilling to press hard to achieve lasting school integration. Whether greater effort would have produced different results remains in the realm of speculation. At the very least, the experience in Charlotte-Mecklenburg cautions against the conclusion that any further effort by the Court would have been futile.

None of this suggests, of course, that the Supreme Court—or any court, for that matter—might be a reliable partner in efforts to reform education. Whether a court refuses to press for reform or is unable to achieve it, the result will be the same: preservation of the status quo. A court convinced of its powerlessness, moreover, may be more inclined to stay its hand, so willingness and ability are undoubtedly linked at some level. But they are not the same thing.[71] And to the extent that successful reform is more a matter of will rather than capacity, it does suggest some hope for court-ordered reform. Rather than giving up on the idea altogether, reformers might instead focus on whether and how courts can be persuaded to act more forcefully. And here the importance of judicial appointments cannot be overstated. *Milliken* and *Parents Involved,* for example, were both 5-4 decisions. In the former, four of the five justices were relatively new Nixon appointees; in the latter, all five were appointed by Presidents Ronald Reagan, George H. W. Bush, and George W. Bush. It may be true, as a general matter, that the Court is unlikely to stray too far from dominant public opinion. But it is also undoubtedly true that the outcomes in some cases depend on the political inclinations of particular judges.

Even if courts can be persuaded to act, and can act successfully to reform public education, it does not follow that they should. Some contend, with justification, that courts should leave education issues to legislative and executive branch control, at least in the absence of clear constitutional violations. Others believe that the political process cannot be trusted to reform public education given that reforms will often involve the redistribution of resources or other unpopular measures. To both sides in this debate, *Parents Involved* offers a serious challenge, and it provides some insight into the nature of the debate about court involvement in education reform. If, as I suspect, most who normally champion judicial restraint supported the outcome in *Parents Involved,* while those who generally favor court involvement opposed it, arguments about the legitimacy of court involvement should be seen for what they are: cover for underlying disagreements about the end results.

Notes

1. See, for example, Gerald N. Rosenberg, *The Hollow Hope: Can Courts Bring About Social Change?* (University of Chicago, 1991) (arguing that courts have limited ability to produce lasting change on their own, and using desegregation as key example); Wendy Parker, "The Future of School Desegregation," *Northwestern Law Review* 94 (Summer 2000): 1185 (noting that "critics have long questioned whether litigation produces integrated school systems" and that "increasing segregation starting in the 1980s has further called into question the ability of court orders to produce integration"); Raymond Wolters, "From *Brown* to *Green* and Back: The Changing Meaning of Desegregation," *Journal of Southern History* 70 (May 2004): 323 (arguing that the trend toward resegregation "suggests that the Supreme Court can achieve social change only when its orders are consistent with the larger tendencies of the times"). For a nuanced, careful, and balanced discussion of this issue, which nonetheless suggests that court efforts to integrate failed because of factors beyond the control of courts, see Michael Heise, "Litigated Learning and the Limits of Law," *Vanderbilt Law Review* 57 (November 2004): 2417–61.

2. 347 U.S. 483 (1954).

3. The figures come from Erica Frankenberg, Chungmei Lee, and Gary Orfield, "A Multiracial Society with Segregated Schools: Are We Losing the Dream?" Harvard Civil Rights Project, 2003 (ww.civilrightsproject.ucla.edu/research/reseg03/resegregation03.php).

4. Erwin Chemerinsky, "The Segregation and Resegregation of American Public Education: The Court's Role," *North Carolina Law Review* 81 (May 2003): 1601. Chemerinsky qualifies his claim later in the piece, writing that "desegregation *likely* would have been more successful, and resegregation less *likely* to occur, if the Supreme Court had made different choices" (p. 1620).

5. See Wolters, "From *Brown* to *Green* and Back," pp. 317–26.

6. It required integration, as opposed to desegregation, in *Green* v. *New Kent County School Board*, 391 U.S. 430 (1968), and it approved the use of busing in *Swann* v. *Charlotte-Mecklenburg Board of Education*, 402 U.S. 1, 29–31 (1971).

7. To avoid confusion, it should be emphasized that desegregation and integration are related but not identical concepts. Desegregation refers, essentially, to the prohibition against intentional segregation. At a basic level, school desegregation cases simply established a right to be free from intentionally segregated schools; whether schools that were once intentionally segregated would necessarily become or have to become integrated remained unclear until well after the *Brown* decision, as explained later in the chapter. Actual integration, eventually ordered by the Supreme Court in 1968, was a remedy for schools that were once intentionally segregated—that is, the Court eventually required schools formerly segregated by law to be integrated. Thus looking to whether schools were integrated became a measure of the success of school desegregation cases. But neither the Supreme Court nor lower courts ever endorsed a freestanding right to integrated schools.

8. See, for example, Michael Kinsley, "Who Are the Activists Now? Judges That Rule for Bush Escape That Nasty Label," *Los Angeles Times*, November 14, 2004, p. M5.

9. 127 S. Ct. 2738 (2007).

10. Michael J. Klarman, *From Jim Crow to Civil Rights: The Supreme Court and the Struggle for Racial Equality* (Oxford University Press, 2004), pp. 308–10.

11. *Brown* v. *Board of Education*, 349 U.S. 294 (1955).

12. James T. Patterson, Brown *v.* Board of Education: *A Civil Rights Milestone and Its Troubled Legacy* (Oxford University Press, 2001), pp. 113–17.

13. J. Harvie Wilkinson III, *From* Brown *to* Bakke: *The Supreme Court and School Integration: 1954–1978* (Oxford University Press, 1979), pp. 86, 101–02.

14. Ibid., pp. 80–82.

15. Patterson, Brown *v.* Board of Education, p. 113.

16. All quotations in this paragraph are from *Green* v. *New Kent County*, 430–45.

17. They were also quite effective, as even Gerald Rosenberg, who is skeptical of the capacity of courts to produce social change, concedes. The proportion of black students in the South attending schools with white students nearly tripled from 32 percent in the 1968–69 school year to 91 percent in the 1972–73 school year. As Rosenberg acknowledges, this was "a period of court efficacy in civil rights." Rosenberg, *Hollow Hope*, p. 54. He suggests that courts were more successful during this period than before because they had the backing of the other branches of the federal government, but that explanation ignores the fact that the Court left the remedies for school desegregation unspecified before *Green*. After *Green*, it was clear that school districts needed to integrate to remedy past segregation, and they did. At the very least, this dramatic change in results is as supportive of the argument that judicial will, not capacity, explains the pattern of school integration as it is of the idea that courts needed the backing of other branches to succeed.

18. See, for example, Justice Scalia's concurring opinion in *Freeman* v. *Pitts,* 503 U.S. 467, 503–05 (1992).

19. See, for example, *Bradley* v. *Richmond School Board,* 317 F.2d 429 (1963) (affirming a district court decision to limit admission of black students to formerly all-white schools to the few black plaintiffs who brought suit).

20. Wilkinson, *From* Brown *to* Bakke, pp. 100–01 (suggesting that "when confronted with case after case of obvious obstruction, [the Court] had no choice but to broaden federal judicial oversight over local schools, and finally to order student busing").

21. 401 U.S. 31.

22. James E. Ryan, *Five Miles Away, A World Apart: Two Schools, One City, and the Story of Educational Opportunity in Modern America* (Oxford University Press, forthcoming 2009), pp. 36, 44.

23. Ibid., p. 44.

24. Wilkinson, *From* Brown *to* Bakke, pp. 102–08.

25. See, for example, "David S. Tatel, Judicial Methodology, Southern School Desegregation, and the Rule of Law," *New York University Law Review* 79 (October 2004): 1089–97.

26. One historian credits the Nixon administration with helping to ensure southern compliance with *Green* and the subsequent case of *Alexander* v. *Holmes,* 396 U.S. 19 (1969), in which the Court strongly rejected the Nixon administration's request to delay school desegregation. Gareth Davies, "Richard Nixon and the Desegregation of Southern Schools," *Journal of Policy History* 19, no. 4 (2007): 367–89. But counseling against massive resistance to court orders and encouraging compliance with them is not the same thing as leading the way, and no one claims, for good reason, that the Nixon administration had any interest in pushing for more integration than was required by the Court. See Davies, pp. 388–89 (emphasizing that Nixon had no interest in pushing for integration but merely in complying with court orders). Indeed, after easing compliance with *Green* and *Holmes,* the Nixon administration opposed the use of busing for desegregation, ordered in *Swann* in 1971, and Nixon appointed four justices (out of the five) who voted to limit the reach of desegregation in *Milliken.* See, for example, Wilkinson, *From* Brown *to* Bakke, p. 217 (noting that because of the Nixon administration's opposition to busing, "the job of urban school desegregation thus fell almost entirely on private organizations").

27. 413 U.S. 189 (1973).

28. Ibid.

29. Ibid., pp. 217–54 (Justice Powell concurring).

30. John C. Jeffries Jr., *Justice Lewis F. Powell, Jr.* (New York: Scribner, 1994), pp. 302–06.

31. See *Personnel Administrator of Massachusetts* v. *Feeney,* 442 U.S. 256 (1977) (defining purposeful discrimination as an action taken "at least in part 'because of,' not merely 'in spite of' its adverse effects upon an identifiable group").

32. 418 U.S. 717 (1974).

33. *Bradley* v. *Milliken,* 338 F. Supp. 582, 585–87 (E.D. Mich. 1971).

34. 418 U.S. 745.

35. See James E. Ryan "The Supreme Court and Voluntary Integration," *Harvard Law Review* 121 (November 2007): 140.

36. James E. Ryan, "Schools, Race, and Money," *Yale Law Journal* 109 (November 1999): 275–84; Jeffries, *Justice Powell,* p. 318.

37. 418 U.S. 728, n. 7.

38. Ibid., p. 755 (Justice Stewart concurring).

39. Ryan, "Supreme Court and Voluntary Integration," pp. 140–41.

40. 402 U.S. 22.

41. 418 U.S. 724, 728, n. 7.

42. See, for example, *Freeman* v. *Pitts,* 467, 495–97.

43. For an excellent history of the desegregation experience in Charlotte-Mecklenburg, see Matthew D. Lassiter, *The Silent Majority: Suburban Politics in the Sunbelt South* (Princeton University Press, 2006).

44. 433 U.S. 267 (1977).

45. See Ryan, "Schools, Race, and Money," pp. 261–66.

46. *Board of Education* v. *Dowell,* 498 U.S. 237, 248–51 (1991); *Freeman* v. *Pitts,* 485–500.

47. *Missouri* v. *Jenkins,* 515 U.S. 70, 98–103 (1995).

48. *Freeman* v. *Pitts,* 506 (Justice Scalia concurring).

49. *Board of Education* v. *Dowell,* 244, 255–56.

50. Ryan, "Supreme Court and Voluntary Integration," pp. 141, 147.

51. See, for example, Chemerinsky, "Segregation and Resegregation of American Public Education," p. 1622, n. 190.

52. 127 S. Ct. 2738 (2007).

53. *Grutter* v. *Bollinger,* 539 U.S. 306 (2003).

54. 127 S. Ct. 2759–60.

55. Ibid., pp. 2755–59, 2767–68 (opinion of Chief Justice Roberts).

56. Ibid., p. 2787 (Justice Thomas concurring).

57. Ibid., pp. 2797–800 (Justice Stevens dissenting), pp. 2800–37 (Justice Breyer dissenting). Justices Stevens, Souter, and Ginsburg joined Justice Breyer's dissent.

58. Ibid., pp. 2791–93.

59. See Ryan, "Supreme Court and Voluntary Integration," pp. 144–45.

60. Ibid., p. 145, n. 91.

61. See, for example, Editorial, "Metco, Now More than Ever," *Boston Globe,* September 24, 2007, p. A12. See generally Craig Heeren, "'Together at the Table of Brotherhood': Voluntary Student Assignment Plans and the Supreme Court," *Harvard BlackLetter Law Journal* 24 (Spring 2008): 133–89.

62. Linda Shaw, "Integration No Longer a Top Priority for District," *Seattle Times,* June 3, 2008, p. A1. See also Joseph Pereira, "Rollback: School Integration Efforts Face Renewed Opposition," *Wall Street Journal,* October 11, 2007, p. A1.

63. 402 U.S.16.

64. 127 S. Ct. 2752, n. 10.

65. See, for example, ibid., pp. 2797–2800 (Justice Stevens dissenting).

66. Ibid., pp. 2767–68 (opinion of Chief Justice Roberts).

67. Ibid., pp. 2791–97.

68. See, for example, Kinsley, "Who Are the Activists Now?" p. M5.

69. See Ryan, "Supreme Court and Voluntary Integration," pp. 150–51.

70. Ibid., pp. 151–54.

71. Gerald Rosenberg, in his well-known book on courts and social change, often conflates the two, suggesting that courts have inherent limits in their capacity to produce social change. One of the inherent limits he identifies is the unwillingness of courts to push too hard for social change, which arises from the fact that judges are not sufficiently independent from the other political branches. See Rosenberg, *Hollow Hope,* pp. 13–15. This, however, is

not an inherent limit of courts, akin to their inability to superintend, say, the details of teachers in a classroom. It is partly a function of the judges on the courts. It may well be true, as history suggests, that courts will not often rule in a strongly countermajoritarian way, but it is also true that some courts are more conservative or liberal, activist or restrained, than others, depending in part on the individual justices serving at any particular time. The *Green* Court that ordered integration in 1968, for example, was more activist than the *Brown II* Court in 1954 that required desegregation at all deliberate speed. The ongoing controversy over judicial appointments illustrates the same point.

5

School Finance Litigation: The Third Wave Recedes

John Dinan

The legal challenges brought against school finance systems in forty-six states since the 1960s have by several measures been quite successful.[1] State courts have frequently sided with plaintiffs, both the initial challengers of interdistrict spending disparities and the more recent litigants contending that overall spending levels are inadequate. Moreover, the legislative reforms passed in response to these court rulings have generally reduced spending disparities and boosted the state share of school spending.

Numerous state court rulings of the past several years indicate, however, that the school finance litigation movement may have peaked, in that many judges are now disinclined to undertake continuing supervision of school finance policies. It is true that several state courts have yet to terminate jurisdiction over long-standing cases. Also, litigants continue to file state suits, and an increasing number are mounting federal challenges to school finance mechanisms. Even so, separation-of-powers concerns about the propriety, effectiveness, and wisdom of judicial intervention have persuaded a number of state judges to terminate long-standing jurisdiction or to decline invitations to embark on another round of intervention.

The History of School Finance Litigation

Scholars have identified three waves of school finance litigation. Although a number of cases do not fit neatly into this scheme, litigants initially brought equity suits grounded in federal equal protection claims, then generally concentrated on equity suits based on state equal protection clauses, and then turned to adequacy challenges grounded in state education clauses.[2] The federal challenges stalled in 1973 with the Supreme Court's rejection of a federal equal protection suit. The state equity suits from 1973 to 1988 had only mixed success, while the post-1989 state adequacy challenges have been more successful.

The initial round of federal equal protection suits originated in and drew support from Arthur Wise's "one dollar, one scholar" model, as well as a quite different proposal for "fiscal neutrality" in district taxing power by John Coons, William Clune, and Stephen Sugarman.[3] The earliest challenges, in federal courts in the Northern District of Illinois in 1968 and Western District of Virginia in 1969, were rejected on the ground that courts were ill suited to identify judicially manageable standards for determining school finance policy.[4] As the three-judge federal panel in Illinois explained, "There are no 'discoverable and manageable standards' by which a court can determine when the Constitution is satisfied and when it is violated."[5] Plaintiffs had more success in pressing the federal equal protection clause argument in the California Supreme Court, which in *Serrano* v. *Priest* (1971) invalidated the state school finance system and directed the trial court to fashion a remedy.[6] In *San Antonio* v. *Rodriguez* (1973), however, the U.S. Supreme Court overturned a three-judge federal district court panel that had ruled in favor of plaintiffs challenging the Texas school finance system, thereby bringing to a halt any further federal constitutional challenges.[7] Writing for the Court, Justice Lewis Powell noted that because wealth was not a suspect classification and education not a fundamental right, Texas need only show a rational basis for its system. And the five-justice majority found reasonable the state's contention that its system furthered local control over and participation in education policy and therefore should be sustained, especially in light of federalism and separation of powers concerns.[8]

Within two weeks of the *Rodriguez* ruling, in *Robinson* v. *Cahill* the New Jersey Supreme Court issued what would be the first of seven state supreme court decisions around the country between 1973 and 1988 relying on state constitutional provisions to invalidate school finance systems.[9] For the most part, courts issuing this second wave of rulings sought to achieve interdistrict spending equity through interpretation of state constitutional equal protection clauses—hence their categorization as equity decisions. But New Jersey and Washington courts rested their rulings on their state education clauses. And in West Virginia, the ruling was as much an adequacy as an equity decision in that it called for the state to meet across-the-board educational achievement standards rather than reduce spending disparities.[10] Despite the success in securing these seven favorable rulings, plaintiffs did not post any victories after 1983 and lost more cases than they won during the entire 1973–88 period in that fifteen other state supreme courts sustained school finance systems against constitutional challenges.[11]

A 1989 Kentucky Supreme Court ruling in *Rose* v. *Council for Better Education,* along with rulings in Montana and Texas that same year, started the third wave of litigation, challenging the adequacy of school financing on the basis of state education clauses.[12] Some courts during this period still grounded decisions in state equal protection clauses, as in Tennessee.[13] And many rulings ostensibly concerned with adequacy actually targeted inequality of funding and achievement.[14] But on balance, post-1989 rulings have centered on the adequacy of school funding and anchored their arguments in education clauses. Plaintiffs have enjoyed their greatest success during this period: twenty-one state courts have invalidated school finance systems in whole or in part;[15] only eleven have rejected challenges.[16]

These third-wave rulings are notable both on account of their nonoriginalist approach to constitutional interpretation and their sweeping and detailed remedial orders. Although it is not uncommon for today's judges to depart from the original understanding of constitutional provisions, the recent reliance on education clauses to overturn school finance systems presents a particularly striking example of nonoriginalist interpretation. To be sure, nonoriginalism has its share of academic and judicial defenders.[17] However, in the context of school finance rulings, the distance between the original intent of state education clauses and the uses to which they are now being put is so vast that it is exceedingly difficult to derive from their general language any judicially manageable standards for distinguishing in meaningful fashion between adequate and inadequate funding levels.[18]

Education clauses were adopted from the late eighteenth century through the late twentieth century for various reasons.[19] Some draw from language in the Massachusetts Constitution of 1780 or Northwest Ordinance of 1787 and are intended to serve a hortatory purpose, whether to introduce substantive provisions in a constitution's education article or to announce aspirational goals that legislators are encouraged to attain.[20] Others are obligatory in the sense that they commit legislators to fulfill certain discrete tasks. The concern in some of these states was to ensure the establishment of a state school system rather than to maintain an existing patchwork of local systems.[21] Other states specified the level of schooling that the legislature was obliged to provide, which in some cases was an "efficient system" of common schools providing a basic education and in other cases required that schools "promote intellectual, scientific, moral, and agricultural improvement."[22] Several state constitutions mandated that schools be "free" of charge for students.[23] And several provided for a "uniform" system, ensuring that all localities would operate schools for a minimum number of months each year.[24]

However, except for a few post-1960 amendments, historical records offer scant evidence that education clauses were intended to enable judicial superintendence of legislative judgments regarding school financing.[25] Judges who have put these clauses to use in service of such an outcome have therefore been led to engage in various forms of nonoriginalist interpretation, as in a 1995 Wyoming Supreme Court decision invalidating the state's school finance system:

> Although the text of the constitutional provision in question must be given the common and ordinary meaning understood by the majority of voters which ratified it, we must be mindful our state constitution is, in a sense, a living thing, designed to meet the needs of progressive society, amid all the detail changes to which society is subject. Recognizing educational philosophy and needs change constantly, we believe the language of those education article provisions requiring "a complete and uniform system of public instruction" and "a thorough and efficient system of public schools, adequate to the proper instruction of all youth of the state" must not be narrowly construed.[26]

To the extent that courts have consulted the relevant constitutional records en route to invalidating school finance systems, they have generally discerned a general and undeniable commitment to education but offered no specific support therein for an expectation of judicial superintendence of legislative decisionmaking regarding funding levels. A 1989 ruling in Kentucky, for instance, drew on comments of a key delegate to the Kentucky Convention of 1890–91 that reflected "the framers' cognizance of the importance of education and, emphasized that the educational system in Kentucky must be improved." In part on the strength of these comments the court imputed a substantive component to the education clause and invalidated the entire school system.[27] Similarly, the Massachusetts Supreme Court determined that the state's "framers created a Constitution which by its words and its structure states plainly that providing for the education of the people is both duty and prerequisite for a republican government," a conclusion that is as unobjectionable as it is unhelpful in determining what funding levels are necessary to sustain republicanism and whether this is a matter of legislative or judicial provenance.[28] And the Ohio Supreme Court in 1997 discerned in the Ohio Convention of 1850–51 debates a recognition that:

> It was the state's duty to both present and future generations of Ohioans to establish a framework for a "full, complete and efficient system of public education." Thus, throughout their discussions, the delegates stressed the importance of education and reaffirmed the policy that education shall be afforded to every child in the state regardless of race or economic

standing. Furthermore, the delegates were concerned that the education
to be provided to our youth not be mediocre but be as perfect as could
humanly be devised. These debates reveal the delegates' strong belief that
it is the state's obligation, through the General Assembly, to provide for
the full education of all children, within the state.[29]

On the basis of this passage, which represents the entirety of their examination
of the constitutional debates, the judges concluded that the school finance system violated the "thorough and efficient" clause.

Equally notable, these post-1989 rulings have gone beyond merely invalidating school finance mechanisms to the point of issuing sweeping remedial orders.
Before the late 1980s, courts were generally content to declare a school finance
system unconstitutional and defer the fashioning of a remedy to the legislature.[30] But the Kentucky Supreme Court in its 1989 *Rose* decision went further
than any prior—or later—court in declaring "Kentucky's *entire system* of common schools," "all its parts and parcels," unconstitutional. "This decision," the
court ruled, "applies to the statutes creating, implementing and financing the
system and to all regulations, etc., pertaining thereto. This decision covers the
creation of local school districts, school boards, and the Kentucky Department
of Education to the Minimum Foundation Program and Power Equalization
Program. It covers school construction and maintenance, teacher certification—
the whole gamut of the common school system in Kentucky."[31]

The New Jersey Supreme Court's *Abbott* v. *Burke* rulings from 1990 onward
highlight a related trend: a focus on detailed prescriptive remedies rather than
general proscriptive pronouncements. In prior school finance rulings in other
states, the court noted, "almost invariably the remedy extended no farther than
the observation that the Legislature will presumably revise the system to conform with the Court's decision, the Court frequently reserving jurisdiction in
order to impose a judicial remedy if the Legislature failed to act."[32] This court
was prepared to go further: it identified twenty-eight "poorer urban school districts" and required that they "have a budget per pupil that is approximately
equal to the average of the richer suburban districts," which in the previous year
would have amounted to an additional cost of "approximately $440 million."[33]
The Kansas Supreme Court was just as specific in one of a series of rulings during a protracted battle with the legislature: "No later than July 1, 2005, for the
2005–06 school year, the legislature shall implement a minimum increase of
$285 million above the funding level for the 2004–05 school year."[34]

Furthermore, post-1989 courts have not confined their remedial orders to
school operating expenses.[35] Courts in Alaska, Arizona, New Mexico, and Idaho
have ordered changes in methods of financing school construction and other
capital expenses. Some courts have also directed legislatures to institute new

programs such as prekindergarten classes. In fact, more and more school finance litigants are seeking to include prekindergarten requirements in judicial remedial orders.[36] The New Jersey Supreme Court in 1998 directed the commissioner of the Department of Education to "implement whole-school reform; implement full-day kindergarten and a half-day pre-school program for three- and four-year-olds as expeditiously as possible; implement the technology, alternative school, accountability, and school-to-work and college-transition programs" in the (now thirty-one) poorer urban districts.[37] The court went even further in a 2000 ruling, calling on the state to adhere to specific teacher-student ratios: it rejected a policy of "one teacher and two aides for every twenty students as permitted by the Department's new regulation" and "reaffirmed the requirement of one teacher for every fifteen preschool children."[38]

Still other courts have ordered changes in school governance, such as the centralization of authority and additional state oversight of local districts. Most notably, the New Hampshire Supreme Court held in 2002 that the current system of accountability did not comply with the state education clause, which stipulates in part: "It shall be the duty of the legislators and magistrates, in all future periods of this government, to cherish the interests of literature and the sciences." Currently, noted the court, "even if the assessment results show that all the students in a school are at novice level, neither the school district nor the department of education is required to do anything." The district is "merely encouraged to develop a local educational improvement plan, and if it opts to do so, the department of education is available to assist. Nothing more is required." In directing the legislature to construct a new system, the court wrote: "An output-based accountability system that merely encourages local school districts to meet educational standards does not fulfill the State's constitutional duty."[39]

Legislative Reactions to School Finance Rulings

Although public law scholars such as Gerald Rosenberg have highlighted difficulties that courts encounter in producing social reform, especially in the absence of political support, state courts have in a number of instances been effective in compelling legislative reform of school finance systems.[40] It is true that in some states school finance rulings have enjoyed substantial political support, which has helped speed and ease the passage of legislative reform. State defendants, too, have occasionally supported the plaintiffs' goals and gained cover and political support from the resulting school finance judgments. But court rulings in a number of other states have generated strong opposition and at times spurred proposals for court-constraining constitutional amendments. Even in these instances, courts have often succeeded, albeit after protracted and bitter struggles, in compelling enactment of legislative reforms that increased school spending, reduced spending disparities, and centralized school governance at the state level.

In several states, legislatures supported reform even before courts invalidated school finance systems. The Washington legislature enacted a reform law during the course of the litigation process, in anticipation of the court's 1978 decision.[41] In Kentucky, reform legislation was already under consideration and was given a boost (and supportive politicians given political cover) by the court's decision in 1989.[42] In Vermont, legislation had already passed one house and enjoyed strong support in the other house in advance of the court's 1997 ruling.[43] And in Massachusetts, legislation had passed both houses before the court issued its 1993 ruling and was signed into law by the governor shortly afterward.[44] As Peter Enrich has written, these school finance judgments were "part of a broader political effort pointing in the same general direction," and their principal contribution was to "serve as a goad or as a backstop to the legislature's accomplishment" of school finance reform.[45]

In the vast majority of states, school finance judgments have met with political opposition, albeit in varying degrees and from various quarters, depending on the nature of the ruling. As expected, equity rulings have generated more opposition than adequacy rulings, because reforms designed to narrow spending disparities tend to reduce state contributions to wealthier districts, whereas adequacy rulings usually elicit general spending increases. As one would also expect, prescriptive and detailed remedial orders have tended to generate more opposition than rulings that defer the fashioning of a remedy to the legislature. But even the more deferential adequacy rulings have met with some political resistance. At times, opposition has stemmed from political interest. Wealthier districts usually lose out in some fashion or are not treated as well as property-poor districts, even when general spending is increased to respond to adequacy rulings, given that many adequacy judgments are grounded to some degree in a concern with spending inequity. Moreover, taxpayers often balk at the tax hikes proposed to pay for increased state spending. At other times, political opposition is rooted in principle: politicians and the public may question whether judges are better positioned than legislators to give priority to spending for schools rather than for roads and prisons or to require greater centralization of spending and decisionmaking.

Political resistance to school finance rulings has taken several forms, ranging from no action to delayed response or action that falls short of what the judges wanted. Admittedly, it can be difficult sometimes to determine whether reform statutes on the short side of judicial requirements were actually an expression of resistance or simply uncertainty about what levels of increased spending would be necessary to pass judicial muster, especially when the initial ruling purported to defer to the legislature the fashioning of a remedy. In fact, some legislators adopted reforms that they believed would meet with judicial approval on the basis of an earlier court opinion, only to find the reforms unacceptable, as occurred in Texas in the early 1990s.[46] Despite uncertainty about what counts as legislative nonacquiescence, there is no denying that legislators in a number of states actively resisted school finance rulings, whether by initially declining to respond, as in Arizona in the mid-1990s;[47] failing to increase spending by the full amount directed by the court, as in New York in the 2000s;[48] or neglecting to meet court-imposed deadlines, as in Arkansas in the 2000s.[49]

The flexibility of state amendment processes and prevalence of state judicial elections offer additional avenues for resistance to state court rulings.[50] Several states considered constitutional amendments to limit judicial intervention in school finance policy or to alter the education clause to legitimate the current policy. Such proposals arose in Texas in 1992–93, in New Jersey in 1992 and 1994, in New Hampshire from 1997 to 2008, and in Kansas in 2005.[51] On a few occasions, opponents have made school finance rulings an issue in judicial elections, as in Texas in 1996. In Ohio in 2002, opponents even went so far as to actively campaign against judges who voted with the majority in these cases.[52]

In the end, political resistance to school finance rulings has in nearly all instances been overcome by state courts that eventually compelled enactment of reform legislation. None of the proposed court-constraining amendments was approved by a legislature, let alone submitted to voters. And only in Ohio, the one clear case in which political resistance was responsible for ending judicial intervention, did the prominence of the school finance issue lead to a reconstituted supreme court that halted judicial intervention.[53]

It is true that it took some courts a long time to pressure recalcitrant legislatures into enacting desired reforms, as demonstrated by the string of roman numerals affixed to some leading cases. Topping the list is the New Jersey Supreme Court's long-running *Abbott* v. *Burke* litigation. The first ruling was issued in 1985. The most recent decision, in 2009, is labeled *Abbott* v. *Burke XXI*.[54] This followed an earlier series of *Robinson* v. *Cahill* rulings in New Jersey that began in 1973 and concluded in 1976. In Texas, a string of Supreme Court rulings that began in 1989 concluded in 1995 with *Edgewood Independent School District* v. *Kirby IV*. Although the New Hampshire Supreme Court dispensed with roman numerals in its *Claremont School District* rulings, it remarked in a 2002 decision: "In the nearly nine years since this court issued the decision in *Claremont I,* we have rendered eight subsequent opinions directly related to that initial decision."[55]

At times, courts prevailed only after heated interbranch conflicts that were finally resolved only when judges threatened to close the schools unless legislators acquiesced to their demands.[56] The Arizona Supreme Court issued such threats on two occasions during its string of *Roosevelt Elementary* decisions from

1994 to 1998. First, it approved a November 1996 superior court judge's ruling ordering schools to be closed unless the legislature equalized school construction costs in an acceptable fashion by the end of June 1998. Then, after the Arizona legislature enacted what the court deemed an unacceptable response, the state supreme court issued a June 1998 ruling giving the legislature sixty days to comply before the shutdown would take effect.[57] The legislature in July 1998 approved a plan that the court finally deemed acceptable.[58] The Kansas Supreme Court also threatened in June 2005 to close the schools in the midst of a series of *Montoy* rulings that year. The legislature capitulated within a month and increased school spending by the amount ordered by the court.[59]

Notwithstanding the protracted and bitter judicial-legislative confrontations over school finance policy, overall, courts have been successful in compelling enactment of reform legislation even in the face of significant political opposition. As Matthew Bosworth remarked in a conclusion to a Texas study that is equally applicable to other states, "The judicial system convinced policymakers to pass laws that they would not have otherwise by a mixture of persuasion and threat."[60] Courts have generally prevailed in these interbranch battles in part by issuing threats and imposing costs on legislators for noncompliance and in part because they have benefited from public ambivalence toward school finance reform. As Bosworth notes, public opinion "is typically quite general and diffuse" and "uninformed concerning specific state school funding mechanisms," thereby leaving "quite a bit of policy leeway for legislatures and courts to operate within."[61] One might add that media reporting and editorializing thus become all the more influential, and that the media have often sided with courts in these battles.[62]

Legislative reforms enacted in response to school finance judgments have taken several forms, the most common being increased state spending on schools, at least initially. In Kentucky, for example, overall revenue per pupil "dramatically increased 42 percent in real terms between the 1986–87 and 1991–92 school years," as a result of the state's 1990 reform legislation.[63] In Kansas, "as a result of adequacy litigations, state funding for public schools . . . will increase by $755.6 million, or 26 percent, from 2004–05 to 2008–09. In New York City, funding is slated to rise by $5.2 billion, or about 30 percent, from 2006–07 to 2010–11."[64]

A number of legislatures have responded to court rulings by boosting state spending in property-poor districts in particular. Some states, most notably California, altered funding formulas so as to achieve near equity in per pupil spending among local districts. Other states, such as New Jersey, have targeted spending increases to property-poor high-needs districts.

Some legislatures have also limited the funds that property-rich districts can raise and spend on their own behalf, and in some cases have adopted "Robin

Hood" plans requiring these districts to contribute funds, either directly or indirectly, to poorer districts. The Washington legislature limited the amount of excess property taxes that local districts could levy in support of schools.[65] The Kentucky legislative reform limited to 49.5 percent the amount by which local districts can exceed a specified minimum funding level.[66] The Texas, Vermont, and New Hampshire legislatures have gone even further: each has ordered the "recapture" of local tax revenues, whereby wealthy districts must send revenues to poor districts, whether by direct payment or by transfer to the state for redistribution to these districts.[67]

Some legislatures have also increased state taxes or created new taxes, both to pay for the spending hikes and to increase the state share of school spending and reduce reliance on local taxes. For instance, New Jersey opted to increase income and sales taxes following a 1990 ruling, Tennessee raised its sales tax after a 1993 decision, and Vermont and New Hampshire introduced statewide property taxes in response to 1997 rulings.[68]

Results are more mixed, however, on the crucial question of whether states subject to school finance judgments have increased their share of spending and reduced spending inequities to a greater degree than other states.[69] A comprehensive study in 2007 by Christopher Berry found "substantively small and statistically insignificant effects of school finance judgments. The exceptions are an increase in the state's share of education funding and a modest (perhaps 16 percent) decline in spending inequality related to school finance judgments."[70] The effect on the centralization of school funding to the state level, which is the most notable consequence of court-induced reform, has, moreover, been relatively modest and occasionally fleeting. States such as New Hampshire, Vermont, and Massachusetts have substantially increased the state share of school spending. But other states subject to school finance judgments—including New Jersey, Kentucky, Texas, and Tennessee—have seen little change and even an occasional reduction over time in the state share of school spending.[71] "The typical legislative response," concludes Bosworth, "has been moderate, including a funding increase, but not fundamental change."[72]

As for the question of whether court-induced legislative reforms have produced gains in student performance, scholars have not reported strong evidence in support of such a connection. In introducing a 2004 volume that looked at "whether state aid reform leads to an increase in student performance, particularly for districts in which performance is relatively low," John Yinger noted that the question has been "difficult to study" and "no consensus on the answer has yet emerged." He concluded that "although some of the evidence indicates that state aid reform can boost student performance, none of the findings are definitive, and some of them are quite ambiguous."[73]

Recent and Future Trends in School Finance Cases

Despite plaintiffs' post-1989 courtroom victories and state courts' success in compelling legislative reforms even in the face of substantial political opposition, judges appear to be growing concerned about the legitimacy, capacity, and wisdom of judicial intervention in school finance policy.[74] Some state courts have concluded long-standing judicial interventions. Some that were once engaged in the supervision of school finance systems have declined to embark on another round of intervention. And some have rejected lawsuits inviting an initial round of intervention. To be sure, several state courts have yet to end long-standing interventions, and plaintiffs continue to file state suits and are contemplating more challenges in federal courts. Hence the school finance litigation movement has not yet run its course. But if recent state court rulings are an indication, it appears that judicial intervention is unlikely to displace the political process as the main forum for school-finance policymaking, despite the hopes of some movement leaders.[75]

Some of the strongest evidence of a trend toward judicial pullback comes from the many state courts that have terminated jurisdiction over long-standing school finance litigation in recent years: Alabama (2002), Ohio (2002), West Virginia (2003), Massachusetts (2005), New York (2006), Kansas (2006), Tennessee (2006), Arkansas (2007), Wyoming (2008), New Hampshire (2008), and New Jersey (2009). In 2002 the Alabama and Ohio Supreme Courts ended jurisdiction over school finance suits that originated in state supreme court rulings dating from 1997.[76] In 2003 a West Virginia circuit judge declared his intention "to address, with a degree of finality, all of the remaining issues" in a class action filed in the Circuit Court of Kanawha County in 1975: "From this day forward, unless this matter is properly returned to this Court, decisions regarding the classroom are out of the courtroom and into the halls and offices of the legislative and executive branches of government."[77]

Several of the 2005–08 rulings proved particularly disappointing to plaintiffs, including a 2005 Massachusetts Supreme Judicial Court decision that "lifted its 1993 finding of constitutional violation and decisively terminated twenty-seven years of litigation."[78] This was followed in 2006 by rulings of the New York Court of Appeals and Kansas Supreme Court ending judicial interventions that began with high court rulings in 1995 and 2003, respectively.[79] The New York high court ruling was especially notable as it modified a lower court ruling that had ordered at least $4.7 billion in extra spending; the 2006 decision scaled this back to $1.93 billion, which was the lowest figure put forth by a gubernatorial commission established to study school funding needs. Moreover, in ending this long-standing intervention, the court emphasized: "Devising a state budget is a prerogative of the Legislature and Executive; the

Judiciary should not usurp this power. The legislative and executive branches of government are in a far better position than the Judiciary to determine funding needs throughout the state and priorities for the allocation of the State's resources."[80] Also in 2006, a Tennessee trial court terminated jurisdiction over a suit that dated back to a 1993 state supreme court ruling.[81] Then in 2007 the Arkansas Supreme Court ended jurisdiction of a lawsuit that had its origin in a 2002 state supreme court ruling.[82] In 2008 the Wyoming Supreme Court ended jurisdiction over school finance litigation that originated in a 1995 state supreme court ruling and followed an earlier round of litigation stemming from a 1980 ruling.[83] Also in 2008, the New Hampshire Supreme Court declined to retain jurisdiction over a suit dating back to a 1993 state supreme court ruling.[84]

None of these recent rulings was more significant than a unanimous May 2009 New Jersey Supreme Court decision upholding a 2008 School Funding Reform Act and terminating longstanding remedial orders regarding spending on the special-needs *Abbott* districts. Noting that the resolution of conflicting predictions about the effect of the new funding formula "is, in the first instance, a judgment for the Executive and Legislature to make," and cautioning, "We do not sit to second guess those nuanced and complex education funding decisions," the court concluded that the "political branches of government . . . are entitled to take reasoned steps, even if the outcome cannot be assured, to address the pressing social, economic, and education challenges confronting our state. They should not be locked in a constitutional straitjacket."[85]

These post-2000 rulings have been handed down for various reasons. Several can be attributed to substantial reforms that courts—though not necessarily plaintiffs—deemed to be in compliance with prior rulings, as in Massachusetts, Kansas, Tennessee, Arkansas, and Wyoming. In West Virginia and New Hampshire, some reforms had been enacted, and courts sought to permit them to be assessed in the absence of judicial supervision. In several other cases, however, legislatures had done little to comply with prior court orders, or at least had done less than what was ordered, but courts agreed to permit future school funding levels to be determined by the legislature, as in Alabama, Ohio, and New York.

Additional evidence of a trend away from judicial intervention comes from state courts that had already completed at least one round of intervention but recently declined to embark on another round, as in Texas (2005), Kentucky (2007), and Arizona (2007). From 1989 to 1995, the Texas Supreme Court overturned various school finance mechanisms before finally approving a legislative reform package. When the court again ruled on multiple challenges to the school finance system in 2005, however, a majority of judges declined to find a violation of the state education clause.[86] The Kentucky Supreme Court had also issued a 1989 decision, and that ruling led to a speedy and wholesale legislative reform of the school finance system. But when plaintiffs returned to the Kentucky courts seeking another round of judicial intervention in 2007, a Franklin County circuit judge rejected their challenge and they opted not to appeal.[87] And in 2007 the Arizona Supreme Court declined to embark on a second round of judicial intervention when it rejected a challenge to the adequacy of funding for at-risk students. This followed a string of decisions from 1994 to 1998 that forced the legislature to bring about more equalization of school construction spending.[88]

Judicial pullback is also evident in recent rulings rejecting challenges that would have led courts to embark on an initial round of judicial intervention. Both the Nebraska and Oklahoma Supreme Courts rejected adequacy challenges to school finance systems in 2007 on the ground that plaintiffs' claims were nonjusticiable.

At the same time, the school finance movement is still filing new lawsuits in an aggressive fashion—most recently in Illinois in August 2008.[89] Furthermore, it continues to benefit from the financial support of leading foundations and the political support of teachers' unions and sympathetic public officials. Campaign for Fiscal Equity (CFE), co-founded in 1995 by Michael Rebell, filed the recently settled New York case and has a national presence, raising over $7.4 million in a five-year period from contributors that included the Ford Foundation, Bill and Melinda Gates Foundation, Robin Hood Foundation, and Rockefeller Foundation.[90] And the National Access Network, an outgrowth of the Campaign for Educational Equity (CEE) at Teachers College, Columbia University, and also headed by Rebell, provides extensive updates on the progress of school finance suits and holds an annual conference that brings together litigators and activists for strategy sessions.[91] At the network's June 2008 conference, Massachusetts Supreme Court justice John M. Greaney, who voted with the winning side in a 1993 plaintiffs' victory and the losing side in a 2005 plaintiffs' defeat, spoke about how to prevail in school finance suits. Plaintiffs' advocates, he advised, should examine the history of a particular state court "getting into arguably purely legislative issues, like prison management," and "address remedy issues head-on," by showing "that court involvement can be had without encroaching on separation of powers and that involvement will not consume so much of the court's time that [it] will not want to step in." He also urged advocates to secure amicus briefs from "professors and teachers at colleges and community colleges who can speak to the vast number of students they have to deal with who are unprepared for higher education and need remedial work" and, among other sources, "high school dropouts who can speak to the disadvantages they incur because they did not receive an adequate education."[92]

In addition, despite the general trend toward terminating or declining jurisdiction in school finance cases, plaintiffs have persuaded some state courts to maintain jurisdiction over long-running suits. In particular, courts in North

Carolina, South Carolina, and Idaho retain jurisdiction over suits that have been in progress for more than a decade in most instances.

In a sign that school finance litigators are adjusting to the recent judicial pullback at the state level but remain intent on pursuing judicial relief, more plaintiffs are considering and occasionally prevailing in federal litigation, even though the Supreme Court's *Rodriguez* decision seemingly foreclosed federal equal protection challenges to interdistrict spending disparities. In some states, plaintiffs are alleging that school finance systems are in violation of the Civil Rights Act of 1964 and the federal equal protection clause because state statutes or constitutional provisions have a disparate racial impact or were adopted out of racial animus. Such is the argument in a 2008 federal suit claiming that long-standing property tax limitations in the Alabama Constitution were adopted for racially discriminatory purposes and should therefore be invalidated, thereby generating more education revenue.[93]

Plaintiffs in Arizona, meanwhile, have relied on the Equal Educational Opportunities Act of 1974 in contending the state is providing inadequate funding for English Language Learner (ELL) programs. The U.S. District Court of Arizona has generally been receptive to these claims, issuing a series of *Flores* v. *Arizona* decisions from 2000 to 2007 ordering the state to increase funding for the programs and at one point fining the legislature for noncompliance; it also stipulated that until the state came into compliance, ELL students would be exempt from taking the required high school exit exam.[94] In 2007 U.S. district judge Raner Collins invalidated the legislature's latest effort to comply with these orders, and a Ninth Circuit Court panel in 2008 sustained his ruling and denied a request by state legislators and the state superintendent for public instruction to bring an end to the district court's jurisdiction.[95] In June 2009, however, in *Horne* v. *Flores,* the U.S. Supreme Court reversed the lower courts. Arguing that "the Court of Appeals improperly substituted its own educational and budgetary policy judgments for those of the state and local officials to whom such decisions are properly entrusted," the Court remanded the case for reexamination of whether changed circumstances "warrant the granting of relief" from the original injunction.[96]

Academic supporters of school finance litigation are also researching creative new federal constitutional challenges. Arguing that "even if we were to eliminate disparities between school districts within each state, large disparities across states would remain," Goodwin Liu, a Berkeley law professor and National Access Network advisory board member, is urging "a national approach to the distribution of educational opportunity." In his view, the citizenship clause of the Fourteenth Amendment, together with its enforcement clause, "entails substantive rights that Congress is both authorized and duty-bound to enforce."[97] At present, Liu's argument is directed at Congress. Many state courts, Liu points out, have "faulted state legislatures for fashioning educational policy based on political or budgetary compromises rather than educationally relevant factors" and have "held that state legislatures are constitutionally obligated to develop policy based on rational, empirically supported judgments of what constitutes an adequate education." "The Fourteenth Amendment," he concludes, "demands no less of Congress,"[98] whose "annual appropriations for elementary and secondary education are not based on any rational determination of what resources are necessary to meet children's educational needs."[99] It would be surprising if law professors and litigators did not follow up on ways that these arguments could be pressed into service by federal courts.[100]

Despite these signs of resilience and ingenuity in the school finance litigation movement, state courts are continuing to move away from judicial intervention, especially long-term supervision, in school finance cases. Their reluctance to embark on new rounds of intervention or to continue supervising long-standing cases is attributable in part to a renewed judicial respect for what Rebell has referred to (disparagingly) as "anachronistic concepts of separation of powers."[101] In recent years, many judges have come to view separation-of-powers principles not as an anachronism but as cause to reconsider the legitimacy of judicial intervention in an area that meets the classic criteria of a "political question."[102] This concern about legitimacy clearly influenced the majority in a New York Court of Appeals ruling in 2006 that ended a long-standing lawsuit. "Deference to the Legislature's education financing plans is justified," said the court, "not only by prudent and practical hesitation in light of the limited access of the judiciary 'to the controlling economic and social facts,' but also by our abiding 'respect for the separation of powers upon which our system of government is based.' We cannot 'intrude upon the policymaking and discretionary decisions that are reserved to the legislative and executive branches.'"[103]

Separation-of-powers principles also influenced a 2007 Oklahoma Supreme Court ruling that deemed the plaintiffs' challenge nonjusticiable: "The plaintiffs are attempting to circumvent the legislative process by having this Court interfere with and control the Legislature's domain of making fiscal-policy decisions and of setting educational policy by imposing mandates on the Legislature and by continuing to monitor and oversee the Legislature. To do as the plaintiffs ask would require this Court to invade the Legislature's power to determine policy."[104] Similarly, a 2007 circuit court judge's decision to reject a suit by Kentucky plaintiffs seeking a second round of judicial intervention rested on the belief that "ultimately, increases in education funding must be the product of political will, not judicial decree."[105]

The judicial pullback is also being spurred by a renewed concern among judges about their capacity to make effective decisions on questions of school funding. Public law scholars such as Donald Horowitz have long argued that the judicial process is ill suited for making complex policy judgments. On this view, courts are an improper forum for policymaking not so much because they remove issues from democratic control, but rather because judges are rendered incapable of making effective policy by the very nature of adjudication, which "inhibits the presentation of an array of alternatives and the explicit matching of benefits to costs."[106] Judges have recently demonstrated a keen awareness of the limits of judicial capacity in this sense, as seen in Massachusetts chief justice Margaret Marshall's majority opinion in a 5-2 ruling in 2005 terminating jurisdiction over a long-standing lawsuit. In rejecting a lower-court judge's determination that jurisdiction should be continued and a cost study ordered, Marshall argued that the "study the dissenting Justices would order is rife with policy choices." Noting that the study assumed preschool programs would be required to address the needs of at-risk children, Marshall responded that "other options might be equally effective," "such as remedial programs (policy choices that in the judge's view should not be a mandatory component of public education); nutrition and drug counseling programs or programs to involve parents more directly in school affairs. Each choice embodies a value judgment; each carries a cost in real, immediate tax dollars; and each choice is fundamentally political. Courts are not well positioned to make such decisions."[107]

Yet another factor behind the state judicial pullback is judges' increasing awareness of the difficulties that courts in previous decades have encountered in promulgating judicially manageable standards for school spending. State courts follow closely the school finance rulings handed down in other courts, as seen in their extensive citations to both the earlier wave of equity decisions and later wave of adequacy decisions.[108] It would appear from several recent opinions that judges have also been paying close attention to the protracted interbranch battles in which some courts have become entangled in trying to develop manageable standards. The lesson judges are drawing from these entanglements is not necessarily that courts cannot prevail in school funding battles with legislatures; in fact, courts eventually do prevail in many of these disputes, especially when they are prepared to resort to threats to close the schools and when they have the media on their side. Rather, recent experience has demonstrated the extensive practical challenges that courts encounter in trying to devise standards that can produce meaningful distinctions between adequate and inadequate spending levels. The language and intent of state constitutional education clauses offer little guidance. Academic costing-out studies that might have provided guidance in the form of expert assessments of funding adequacy are beset by methodological problems and charges of politicization.[109] And judges have not been able to escape these problems by issuing initially deferential judgments that decline to provide specific guidance and then undertaking repeated reviews of legislative efforts to devise acceptable solutions.[110]

Echoing the concerns of federal district courts that rejected the initial challenges to school finance systems in the late 1960s, a number of state courts have
therefore concluded that the experience of the past four decades—particularly
the difficulty of promulgating judicially manageable standards—counsels
against continued judicial entanglement in this area. Rejecting as nonjusticiable
an adequacy challenge in 2007, the Nebraska Supreme Court found in the protracted litigation and numerous school finance rulings in Arkansas, Kansas,
Texas, Alabama, and New Jersey a "landscape . . . littered with courts that have
been bogged down in the legal quicksand of continuous litigation and challenges to their states' school funding systems. Unlike those courts, we refuse to
wade into that Stygian swamp."[111]

Concerns about the legitimacy and capacity of judicial intervention along
with the lessons from long-term supervision are persuading many of today's
judges to terminate long-standing jurisdiction and not to embark on new interventions. As a result, the school finance litigation movement, despite its success
in winning cases that have led on balance to a more equitable distribution of
funds and increased state share of school spending, is unlikely to achieve a
wholesale transformation of school governance and financing, whether in the
sense of securing continued state court jurisdiction or achieving a decisive break
with the traditional reliance on local taxes for funding schools.

Notes

1. School finance suits have been filed in every state but Mississippi, Nevada, Utah, and
Hawaii. For the most current information on school finance litigation, see the website of the
National Access Network (www.schoolfunding.info/states/state_by_state.php3).

2. This concept of three waves of school finance litigation was first advanced by William
E. Thro, "The Third Wave: The Impact of the Montana, Kentucky, and Texas Decisions on
the Future of Public School Reform Litigation," *Journal of Law and Education* 19 (Spring
1990): 219–50. Various scholars have noted problems with this categorization scheme. See,
for example, Richard Briffault, "Adding Adequacy to Equity," in *School Money Trials: The
Legal Pursuit of Educational Adequacy,* edited by Martin R. West and Paul E. Peterson
(Brookings, 2007), pp. 26–27.

3. Arthur E. Wise, *Rich Schools, Poor Schools: The Promise of Equal Educational Opportunity* (University of Chicago Press, 1968); John E. Coons, William H. Clune, and Stephen D.
Sugarman, *Private Wealth and Public Education* (Harvard University Press, 1970).

4. *McInnis* v. *Shapiro,* 293 F.Supp. 327, 335–36 (N.D. Ill. 1968); and *Burruss* v. *Wilker-
son,* 310 F.Supp. 572, 574 (W.D. Va. 1969). However, plaintiffs were victorious in the
Federal District Court of Minnesota, in *Van Dusartz* v. *Hatfield,* 334 F. Supp. 870 (D.
Minn. 1971).

5. *McInnis* v. *Shapiro,* 335.

6. 5 Cal. 3d 584 (1971).

7. 411 U.S. 1 (1973).

8. Paul A. Sracic, San Antonio *v.* Rodriguez *and the Pursuit of Equal Education: The Debate over Discrimination and School Funding* (University Press of Kansas, 2006).

9. For the New Jersey ruling, see 62 N.J. 473 (1973). State courts also invalidated school finance systems in California (1976), Connecticut (1977), Washington (1978), West Virginia (1979), Wyoming (1980), and Arkansas (1983).

10. See Matthew H. Bosworth, *Courts as Catalysts: State Supreme Courts and Public School Finance Equity* (State University of New York Press, 2001), p. 36.

11. These rulings were issued by the state supreme courts in Arizona (1973), Illinois (1973), Michigan (1973), Montana (1974), Idaho (1975), Oregon (1976), Pennsylvania (1979), Ohio (1979), Georgia (1981), New York (1982), Colorado (1982), Maryland (1983), Oklahoma (1987), North Carolina (1987), and South Carolina (1988). See Michael A. Rebell, "Educational Adequacy, Democracy, and the Courts," in *Achieving Higher Educational Standards for All,* edited by Timothy Ready, Christopher Edley Jr., and Catherine E. Snow (Washington: National Research Council, 2002), p. 252, n. 53.

12. The citation for the Kentucky case is 790 S.W.2d 186 (1989); the Montana case, *Helena School District* v. *State,* 769 P.2d 684 (1989); and the Texas case, *Edgewood I.S.D.* v. *Kirby,* 777 S.W. 2d 391 (Tex. 1989).

13. *Tennessee Small School Systems* v. *McWherter,* 851 S.W. 2d 139 (Tenn. 1993).

14. Joshua Dunn and Martha Derthick, "Adequacy Litigation and the Separation of Powers," in *School Money Trials,* edited by West and Peterson, pp. 329–31.

15. These rulings were issued by state courts in Kentucky (1989), Montana (1989), Texas (1989), New Jersey (1990), Alabama (1993), Massachusetts (1993), Tennessee (1993), Arizona (1994), Missouri (1994), Wyoming (1995), North Carolina (1997), Vermont (1997), New Hampshire (1997), Ohio (1997), South Carolina (1999), New Mexico (1999), Maryland (2000), Arkansas (2002), New York (2003), Kansas (2005), and Idaho (2005). Most of the rulings were issued by the state supreme court, but some were handed down by a lower court, and in these cases either no appeal was filed or an appeal was denied by the state supreme court. See Rebell, "Educational Adequacy, Democracy, and the Courts," pp. 252–53, n. 54; Molly Hunter, "School Funding 'Adequacy' Decisions since 1989, Updated May 2007" (National Access Network, 2007) (www.schoolfunding.info/litigation/adequacydecisions.pdf).

16. These rulings were issued in Oregon (1991), Minnesota (1993), North Dakota (1994), Virginia (1994), Rhode Island (1995), Florida (1996), Illinois (1996), Pennsylvania (1999), Wisconsin (2000), Nebraska (2007), and Oklahoma (2007). See Briffault, "Adding Adequacy to Equity," p. 27; Hunter, "School Funding 'Adequacy' Decisions since 1989."

17. The nonoriginalist nature of these rulings has essentially been conceded by leaders of the litigation movement. Rebell has argued: "In the aftermath of Brown, contemporary beliefs and values have, for many judges, endowed the education clauses of state constitutions with a new meaning that has powerful implications for what states must do." And to those who advocate "strictly following the original intent of those who frame our constitutions," he has responded: "At this moment in our history, we need to recognize that a strict focus on the framers' intent undercuts the ever increasing importance of education in the modern era." Michael A. Rebell, "Equal Opportunity and the Courts," *Phi Delta Kappan* 89 (February 2008): 433, 437.

18. Dunn and Derthick, "Adequacy Litigation and Separation of Powers," pp. 332–34.

19. John C. Eastman, "When Did Education Become a Civil Right? An Assessment of State Constitutional Provisions for Education, 1776–1900," *American Journal of Legal History* 42 (January 1998): 1–34, and Eastman, "Reinterpreting the Education Clauses in State Constitutions," in *School Money Trials,* edited by West and Peterson, pp. 55–74; John

Dinan, "The Meaning of State Constitutional Education Clauses: Evidence from the Constitutional Convention Debates," *Albany Law Review* 70 (2007): 927–81.

20. The relevant clause in the Massachusetts Constitution of 1780 is found in pt. II, chap.
V, sec. 2, and states in part: "Wisdom and knowledge, as well as virtue, diffused generally
among the body of the people, being necessary for the preservation of their rights and liberties; and as these depend on spreading the opportunities and advantages of education in the
various parts of the country, and among the different orders of the people, it shall be the duty
of legislatures and magistrates, in all future periods of this commonwealth, to cherish the
interests of literature and the sciences, and all seminaries of them; especially the university at
Cambridge, public schools, and grammar-schools in the towns." Article 3 of the Northwest
Ordinance of 1787 opened with the admonition: "Religion, morality, and knowledge, being
necessary to good government and the happiness of mankind, schools and the means of education shall forever be encouraged." On the hortatory purpose of many education clauses, see
Dinan, "The Meaning of State Constitutional Education Clauses," pp. 939–47.

21. Ibid., pp. 948–51.

22. Ibid., pp. 951–55. This particular language of "intellectual, scientific, moral, and agricultural improvement" is taken from the California Constitution, art. IX, sec. 1. William
Spruance in the Delaware Convention of 1896–97 made clear the difference when he argued,
"I do not like this language 'shall encourage by all suitable means, the promotion of intellectual, scientific and agricultural improvement.' I do not know of any particular encouragement that I care about, except the establishment of schools. . . . [D]o we really want to do
anything more than to say that 'the Legislature shall provide for the establishment and maintenance of an efficient system of free schools'? What shall be taught in them I would have
nothing to do with; I would leave that to the Legislature. Surely we do not want to make
them technical schools, either for the teaching of agriculture or for the teaching of any branch
of science." *Debates and Proceedings of the Constitutional Convention of the State of Delaware
[1896]* (Milford: Milford Chronicle, 1958), pp. 1212–13, quoted in Dinan, "The Meaning
of State Constitutional Education Clauses," p. 954.

23. Dinan, "The Meaning of State Constitutional Education Clauses," pp. 955–58.

24. Ibid., pp. 958–64. Albert Hawley explained in the Nevada Convention of 1864—in
support of an education clause stating in part that "the Legislature shall provide for a uniform
system of common schools, by which a school shall be established and maintained in each
school district at least six months in every year"—that the purpose was to ensure that "any
school-district neglecting to establish and maintain such a school . . . shall be deprived of its
proportion . . . of the public-school fund during such neglect." *Official Report of the Debates
and Proceedings in the Constitutional Convention of the State of Nevada* (San Francisco: Frank
Eastman, 1866), p. 577, quoted in Dinan, "The Meaning of State Constitutional Education
Clauses," p. 960.

25. Nor do the extant constitutional records support the standard scholarly efforts at categorizing the language of these clauses so as to suggest that certain clauses provide greater or
lesser support for judicial superintendence of school finance systems. Erica Black Grubb was
the first to attempt such a categorization, and her four-category scheme has been widely used.
In her view, the weakest clauses merely establish a school system; a stronger set of clauses provides for a thorough and efficient system; an even stronger set of clauses includes language
discussing the purpose or benefit of a quality education; and the strongest clauses either stipu-
late that education is a paramount duty or require the state to perform other specific duties
regarding the education system. Erica Black Grubb, "Breaking the Language Barrier: The

Right to Bilingual Education," *Harvard Civil Rights-Civil Liberties Law Review* 9 (January 1974): 66–70. This categorization was then relied upon by Gershon M. Ratner, "A New Legal Duty for Urban Public Schools: Effective Education in Basic Skills," *Texas Law Review* 63 (February 1985): 777–864. It was brought to the attention of many other scholars by William E. Thro, "To Render Them Safe: The Analysis of State Constitutional Provisions in Public School Finance Reform," *Virginia Law Review* 75 (November 1989): 1639–79. Molly McUsic then advanced a different scheme dividing the clauses into equity and standards clauses and further dividing the latter into four subcategories such that the weakest clauses are those that set bare minimum education standards and the strongest clauses are those that set explicit and significant standards. Molly McUsic, "The Use of Education Clauses in School Finance Reform Litigation," *Harvard Journal on Legislation* 28 (Summer 1991): 307–40. Not only do the constitutional records reveal little support for these purported distinctions among education clauses, but scholars have found little support for any connection between the strength of a state's clause according to these schemes and the likelihood of a court invalidating a school finance system. See William E. Thro, "A New Approach to State Constitutional Analysis in School Finance Litigation," *Journal of Law and Politics* 14 (Summer 1998): 540–42; Paul L. Tractenberg, "Education," in *State Constitutions for the Twenty-first Century,* vol. 3: *The Agenda of State Constitutional Reform,* edited by G. Alan Tarr and Robert F. Williams (State University of New York Press, 2006), pp. 264–66. The limited post-1960s evidence from constitutional records of an intent to promote judicial superintendence of legislative judgments regarding funding levels, most notably concerning the Montana Constitution of 1972 and amendments to the Florida Constitution in 1998 and Oregon Constitution in 2000, is detailed in Dinan, "The Meaning of State Constitutional Education Clauses," pp. 967–78, 979–80.

26. *Campbell County School District* v. *Wyoming,* 907 P.2d 1238, 1257–58 (1995) (citations omitted).

27. 790 S.W.2d 186, 205 (1989). For the entire Kentucky Supreme Court's consideration of the constitutional records, see pp. 205–06.

28. *McDuffy* v. *Secretary of Executive Office of Education,* 415 Mass. 545, 585 (1993). For the court's lengthy consideration of the constitutional records, see pp. 558–606.

29. *DeRolph* v. *State I,* 78 Ohio St. 3d 193, 203 (1997) (internal citations omitted). For the debates in full about the education clause in the Ohio Convention of 1850–851, see *Report of the Debates and Proceedings of the Convention for the Revision of the Constitution of the State of Ohio, 1850–51* (Columbus: S. Medary, 1851), pp. 10–19, 698–700. This passage from the court's opinion has been cited by Michael Rebell. See most recently Michael A. Rebell and Jessica R. Wolff, *Moving Every Child Ahead: From NCLB Hype to Meaningful Educational Opportunity* (New York: Teachers College Press, 2008), p. 23.

30. This was the approach taken, for instance, by the Connecticut Supreme Court in *Horton* v. *Meskill,* the Washington Supreme Court in *Seattle School District No. 1* v. *Washington,* and West Virginia Supreme Court in *Pauley* v. *Kelley.* See John Dinan, "Can State Courts Produce Social Reform? School Finance Equalization in Kentucky, Texas, and New Jersey," *Southeastern Political Review* 24 (September 1996): 445, n. 2.

31. 790 S.W.2d 186, 215 (1989).

32. *Abbott* v. *Burke,* 119 N.J. 287, 315 (1990).

33. Ibid., pp. 408–09.

34. *Montoy* v. *State,* 279 Kan. 817, 845 (2005).

35. This point is made in Briffault, "Adding Adequacy to Equity," pp. 43–44.

36. In fact, the Education Law Center operates a "Starting at 3" project that is funded in part by the Pew Charitable Trusts. According to the program's website, it "promotes and supports legal advocacy to include prekindergarten in school finance litigation and state legislation. The project collects and disseminates research, information and strategies and provides direct technical assistance to attorneys and advocates involved in litigation and policy initiatives to create and expand state prekindergarten programs" (www.startingat3.org/). Lower-court judges in North Carolina and South Carolina have included prekindergarten programs in their remedial orders, but the North Carolina Supreme Court overturned this part of the lower court ruling, and the South Carolina lawsuit is on appeal.

37. *Abbott* v. *Burke*, 153 N.J. 480, 527 (1998).

38. *Abbott* v. *Burke*, 163 N.J. 95, 113, 114 (2000).

39. *Claremont School District* v. *Governor*, 147 N.H. 499, 517 (2002).

40. Gerald N. Rosenberg, *The Hollow Hope: Can Courts Bring About Social Change?* (University of Chicago Press, 1991).

41. Peter Enrich, "Leaving Equality Behind: New Directions in School Finance Reform," *Vanderbilt Law Review* 48 (January 1995): 176.

42. Frederick M. Hess, "Adequacy Judgments and School Reform," in *School Money Trials*, edited by West and Peterson, p. 165.

43. Thomas Downes, "School Finance Reform and School Quality: Lessons from Vermont," in *Helping Children Left Behind: State Aid and the Pursuit of Educational Equity*, edited by John Yinger (Cambridge, Mass.: MIT Press, 2004), p. 285.

44. Enrich, "Leaving Equality Behind," p. 176.

45. Ibid.

46. In a 1991 decision, the Texas Supreme Court suggested a number of reforms that the legislature might enact to comply with the ruling, only to issue a 1992 decision invalidating legislation enacted in the interim that adopted some of the court's suggestions. On the intricacies of the legislative responses to these Texas rulings, see Bosworth, *Courts as Catalysts*, pp. 67–75.

47. Arizona senate president John Greene indicated shortly after a 1994 Arizona Supreme Court ruling that he did not expect the legislature would comply with the decision, arguing, "What are they going to do to us?" In fact, the legislature did not take any action for a year, then eventually acted in 1996. Molly A. Hunter, "Building on Judicial Intervention: The Redesign of School Facilities Funding in Arizona" (Campaign for Fiscal Equity, 2003) (www.schoolfunding.info/resource_center/research/azFinal6.PDF), p. 11.

48. Joe Williams, "The Non-Implementation of New York's Adequacy Judgment," in *School Money Trials*, edited by West and Peterson, pp. 195–212.

49. On the Arkansas legislature's failure to meet a January 1, 2004, court-imposed deadline for conducting a cost study and boosting funding as appropriate, see the history of Arkansas school finance litigation compiled by the National Access Network (www.schoolfunding.info/states/ar/lit_ar.php3).

50. The adoption of state constitutional amendments to preempt or overturn court decisions in other areas is discussed in John Dinan, "Court-Constraining Amendments and the State Constitutional Tradition," *Rutgers Law Journal* 38 (Summer 2007): 983–1039.

51. On Texas, see Bosworth, *Courts as Catalysts*, p. 75; on New Jersey, Douglas S. Reed, *On Equal Terms: The Constitutional Politics of Educational Opportunity* (Princeton University Press, 2001), p. 146, and Dinan, "Can State Courts Produce Social Reform?" p. 438; on recent developments in New Hampshire, Sarah Liebowitz, "School Funds Amendment Voted Down," *Concord Monitor*, May 15, 2008; on Kansas, Richard E. Levy, "Gunfight at

the K-12 Corral: Legislative v. Judicial Power in the Kansas School Finance Litigation," *Kansas Law Review* 54 (May 2006): 1095–1104.

52. On vows by residents of Dallas suburbs to withhold votes in 1996 from judges who issued the Texas Supreme Court rulings from 1989 to 1995, see Bosworth, *Courts as Catalysts*, pp. 90, 228. On the way that the Ohio Supreme Court rulings from 1997 onward figured in judicial elections in 1998, 2000, and 2002, see Peter Schrag, *Final Test: The Battle for Adequacy in America's Schools* (New York: New Press, 2003), pp. 131, 133–34, 140–41. It is not always the opponents who have made school finance rulings an issue in judicial campaigns. Alabama circuit court judge Gene Reese issued a 1993 ruling invalidating the school finance system and then ran (unsuccessfully) for a state supreme court seat in 1994, touting his school finance ruling in his campaign advertising (he then withdrew from the case in 1995). In fact, "Judge Reese's campaign circulated literature categorizing him as 'the judge for educational reform,' and stating, among other things: 'Gene Reese is a tough judge. Last year, he became famous for ruling Alabama's education system unconstitutional and telling a Governor and the Legislature to fix the problem. . . . Now, Gene Reese is running for Alabama Supreme Court—and he will be a tough Justice for change.'" *Ex parte James*, 713 So. 2d 869, 874 (Ala. 1997).

53. Judicial elections in Alabama also produced a reconstituted supreme court that ended judicial intervention in 2002, but school finance rulings were not a key issue in the campaign. Schrag, *Final Test*, pp. 150–51, cited in Dunn and Derthick, "Adequacy Litigation and Separation of Powers," p. 326.

54. All twenty *Abbott* v. *Burke* decisions are available at www.edlawcenter.org/ELC Public/AbbottvBurke/AbbottDecisions.htm.

55. 147 N.H. 499, 520 (2002).

56. On the protracted interbranch conflicts, see Paul A. Minorini and Stephen D. Sugarman, "Educational Adequacy and the Courts: The Promise and Problems of Moving to a New Paradigm," in *Equity and Adequacy in Education Finance: Issues and Perspectives*, edited by Helen F. Ladd, Rosemary Chalk, and Janet S. Hansen (National Research Council, 1999), pp. 201–05. On the use of threats to close the schools, see Alfred A. Lindseth, "The Legal Backdrop to Adequacy," in *Courting Failure: How School Finance Lawsuits Exploit Judges' Good Intentions and Harm Our Children*, edited by Eric A. Hanushek (Stanford, Calif.: Education Next Books, 2006), pp. 67–68.

57. *Hull* v. *Albrecht*, 192 Ariz. 34, 36, 40 (1998).

58. Hunter, "Building on Judicial Intervention," pp. 15, 20.

59. Levy, "Gunfight at the K-12 Corral," pp. 1085–89.

60. Bosworth, *Courts as Catalysts*, p. 105.

61. Ibid., p. 228.

62. For instance, Hunter notes that after the Arizona Supreme Court's 1994 ruling, "the editorial boards of the largest newspapers consistently cajoled or castigated the legislature on the school capital funding issue over the next few years." Hunter, "Building on Judicial Intervention," p. 11. One notable exception is Ohio, where after a 1997 state supreme court ruling "the weight of editorial-page opinion inveighed against judicial overreach" (Hess, "Adequacy Judgments and School Reform," p. 179). For another example of critical media coverage, but one that is confined to a particular ruling in a string of decisions that overall did not necessarily attract critical coverage, see the media reaction to a 1992 Texas Supreme Court ruling, as described in Bosworth, *Courts as Catalysts*, p. 75.

63. Ann E. Flanagan and Sheila E. Murray, "A Decade of Reform: The Impact of School Reform in Kentucky," in *Helping Children Left Behind*, edited by Yinger, p. 203.

64. Rebell and Wolff, *Moving Every Child Ahead*, p. 97 (citations omitted).

65. William A. Fischel, *The Homevoter Hypothesis: How Home Values Influence Local Government Taxation, School Finance, and Land-Use Policies* (Harvard University Press, 2001), p. 152.

66. Flanagan and Murray, "A Decade of Reform," p. 199.

67. On Texas, see Bosworth, *Courts as Catalysts*, p. 78; on Vermont, Downes, "School Finance Reform and School Quality," pp. 285–86; on New Hampshire, Fischel, *The Homevoter Hypothesis*, p. 134.

68. On New Jersey, see Reed, *On Equal Terms*, pp. 138–39. On Tennessee, Vermont, and New Hampshire, see Bosworth, *Courts as Catalysts*, pp. 40–41.

69. A study finding greater increases in per pupil spending in states with school finance judgments as compared with other states is William N. Evans, Sheila Murray, and Robert M. Schwab, "School Houses, Court Houses, and State Houses after *Serrano*," *Journal of Policy Analysis and Management* 16 (January 1997): 10–31. A study finding slower rates of spending increases in states with court orders is Bradley W. Joondeph, "The Good, the Bad, and the Ugly: An Empirical Analysis of Litigation-Prompted School Finance Reform," *Santa Clara Law Review* 35 (1995): 763–824. A study that did not find an increase in spending in court-order states is Michael Heise, "State Constitutional Litigation, Educational Finance, and Legal Impact: An Empirical Analysis," *University of Cincinnati Law Review* 63 (Summer 1995): 1735–66. A study noting that school finance reforms can lead to an increase or a reduction in spending and may be more likely to lead to reductions or slower rates of increase is Caroline M. Hoxby, "All School Finance Equalizations are Not Created Equal," *Quarterly Journal of Economics* 116 (November 2001): 1189–1231. Studies reporting reductions in interdistrict funding disparities in states with court orders as compared with other states include Sheila E. Murray, William M. Evans, and Robert M. Schwab, "Education-Finance Reform and the Distribution of Education Resources," *American Economic Review* 88 (September 1998): 789–812; David Card and A. Abigail Payne, "School Finance Reform, the Distribution of School Spending, and the Distribution of Student Test Scores," *Journal of Public Economics* 83 (January 2002): 49–82; Joondeph, "The Good, the Bad, and the Ugly"; and Reed, *On Equal Terms*, pp. 15–35.

70. Christopher Berry, "The Impact of School Finance Judgments on State Fiscal Policy," in *School Money Trials*, edited by West and Peterson, p. 233.

71. See the data compiled in Kenneth K. Wong, "The Politics of Education," in *Politics in the American States: A Comparative Analysis*, 8th ed., edited by Virginia Gray and Russell L. Hanson (Washington: CQ Press, 2004), pp. 366–67; and Wong, "The Politics of Education," in *Politics in the American States*, 9th ed., edited by Gray and Hanson (2008), p. 359.

72. Bosworth, *Courts as Catalysts*, p. 40.

73. John Yinger, "State Aid and the Pursuit of Educational Equity: An Overview," in *Helping Children Left Behind*, edited by Yinger, p. 39. In terms of scholars who have found evidence of such a connection, Card and Payne, in "School Finance Reform," report "a modest equalizing effect of school finance reforms on the test score outcomes for children from different family background groups," p. 80.

74. A trend in favor of "judicial pullback" and "judicial humility" was discerned by Michael Heise, "Adequacy Litigation in an Era of Accountability," in *School Money Trials*, edited by West and Peterson, p. 263; and was noted (and evidence from additional rulings was provided) by Josh Dunn and Martha Derthick, "Adequately Fatigued," *Education Next* 7 (Summer 2007). In this section I build on their arguments and take note of still more recent evidence in support of such a trend.

75. Rebell recently noted judicial promotion of "institutional reform in the schools not only in regard to desegregation and a range of other areas like bilingual education, gender equity, and special education, but also in a broad array of other social welfare areas like deinstitutionalization of services for the developmentally disabled and prison reform." Taking this litigation as a model for school finance cases, Rebell went on to advocate an "Adequate Education Remedial Oversight" model in which "the court's nominal jurisdiction will probably need to be maintained over a multi-year period in most cases." Michael A. Rebell, "Ensuring Successful Remedies in Education Adequacy Litigation" (Campaign for Educational Equity, 2007) (devweb.tc.columbia.edu/manager/symposium/Files/106_Ensuring%20Successful%20Remedies%2011-04-07.pdf), pp. 5, 9.

76. *Alabama Coalition for Equity* v. *Siegelman* (Ala. 2002); *DeRolph* v. *State,* 97 Ohio St. 3d 1477 (2002).

77. *Tomblin* v. *State Board of Education,* No. 75-1268 (2003); for slip opinion, see pp. 2, 15 (www.schoolfunding.info/states/wv/Tomblin2003.doc).

78. Robert M. Costrell, "The Winning Defense in Massachusetts," in *School Money Trials,* edited by West and Peterson, p. 278.

79. *Campaign for Fiscal Equity* v. *State,* 861 N.E.2d 50 (N.Y. 2006); *Montoy* v. *State,* 282 Kan. 9 (2006).

80. *Campaign for Fiscal Equity* v. *State,* 58.

81. See the history of Tennessee school finance litigation compiled by the National Access Network (www.schoolfunding.info/states/tn/lit_tn.php3).

82. *Lake View School District No. 25* v. *Huckabee* (Ark. 2007).

83. *Campbell County School District* v. *State* (Wyo. 2008)

84. *Londonderry School District* v. *State* (N.H. 2008). It remains to be seen whether this ruling signals a full-scale judicial pullback of the sort seen in other post-2002 rulings. The court ended jurisdiction over a long-running suit; but it may have simply opted to wait for another legal challenge before renewing its intervention.

85. *Abbott* v. *Burke,* M-969/1372 (2009); slip opinion, pp. 43, 44, 49 (www.judiciary. state.nj.us/opinions/supreme/M-969-07%20Abbott%20v%20Burke.pdf)

86. *Neeley* v. *West-Orange Cove,* 176 S.W.3d 746 (Tex. 2005).

87. *Young* v. *Williams,* No. 03-00055/01152 (Cir. Ct., Div. II., Feb. 13, 2007),

88. *Crane Elementary* v. *State,* CV-06-0417-PR (Ariz. 2007).

89. "Major New Case Filed in Illinois," National Access Network, August 28, 2008 (www.schoolfunding.info/news/litigation/8-28-08NewCaseIL.php3).

90. Williams, "Non-Implementation of New York's Adequacy Judgment," p. 201.

91. Dunn and Derthick, "Adequacy Litigation and Separation of Powers," pp. 323–24.

92. A report on Justice Greaney's June 11, 2008, address is posted on the National Access Network website (www.schoolfunding.info/conference/2008/Greaney-QA.pdf).

93. *Lynch* v. *Alabama* (2008) (www.schoolfunding.info/states/al/Lynch-v-State.pdf).

94. "Arizona Gets Ultimatum on Aid for English-Learners," *Education Week,* January 4, 2006, p. 13.

95. *Flores* v. *Horne,* No. 07-15605 (9th Cir. 2008).

96. Docket No. 08-289; 08-294. Quotations at pp. 18 and 23 of the slip opinion.

97. Goodwin Liu, "Education, Equality, and National Citizenship," *Yale Law Journal* 116 (November 2006): 333, 349.

98. Ibid., p. 401.

99. Ibid., n. 337.

100. A recent conference devoted to discussing an enforceable federal right to an adequate and equal education is discussed in Dunn and Derthick, "Adequacy Litigation and Separation of Powers," p. 341.

101. Rebell, "Ensuring Successful Remedies in Education Adequacy Litigation," p. 37.

102. On the ways that courts have overcome the "political question" doctrine, see Dunn and Derthick, "Adequacy Litigation and Separation of Powers," pp. 326–31. On the other hand, for several examples of state court rulings from the 1990s that deemed challenges non-justiciable, in addition to the post-2000 examples discussed here, see Heise, "Adequacy Litigation in an Era of Accountability," pp. 267–68.

103. *Campaign for Fiscal Equity* v. *State,* 861 N.E.2d 50, 58 (2006) (internal citations omitted).

104. *Oklahoma Education Association* v. *State,* 158 P.3d 1058, 1066 (2007).

105. *Young* v. *Williams* (2007), quoted in Raviya H. Ismail and Art Jester, "Ky. School Leaders' Suit Dismissed," *Lexington Herald-Leader,* February 14, 2007.

106. Donald Horowitz, *The Courts and Social Policy* (Brookings, 1977), p. 34.

107. *Hancock* v. *Commissioner of Education,* 443 Mass. 428, 460 (2005) (citations omitted), cited in Costrell, "The Winning Defense in Massachusetts," p. 299.

108. Bosworth, *Courts as Catalysts,* p. 36.

109. On the difficulties occasioned by the commissioning of costing-out studies, see Eric A. Hanushek, "The Alchemy of 'Costing Out' and Adequate Education," and Matthew G. Springer and James W. Guthrie, "The Politicization of the School Finance Legal Process," both in *School Money Trials,* edited by West and Peterson; and Joshua Dunn and Martin West, "Calculated Justice: Educational Research and the Courts," in *When Research Matters: How Scholarship Influences Education Policy,* edited by Frederick M. Hess (Harvard Education Press, 2008), pp. 172–73.

110. Dunn and West, "Calculated Justice," pp. 173–74.

111. *Nebraska Coalition for Educational Equity and Adequacy* v. *Heineman,* 273 Neb. 531, 557 (2007). The Nebraska Supreme Court quoted from a 1995 Rhode Island Supreme Court ruling describing and seeking to avoid what had taken place due to the New Jersey Supreme Court's intervention: "The volume of litigation and the extent of judicial oversight provide a chilling example of the thickets that can entrap a court that takes on the duties of a Legislature." *Pawtucket* v. *City of Sundlun,* 662 A.2d 40, 59 (R.I. 1995).

6

The Judiciary's Now-Limited Role in Special Education

SAMUEL R. BAGENSTOS

The Individuals with Disabilities Education Act (IDEA)—and its predecessor, the Education for All Handicapped Children Act (EAHCA) of 1975—ought to be an ideal context in which to study the courts' role in American education. When Congress enacted the EAHCA, it did so in response to constitutional litigation in twenty-eight states that challenged the exclusion of children with disabilities from public education.[1] The statute incorporated into federal law significant provisions of consent decrees that resolved key cases in Pennsylvania and the District of Columbia: the "zero-reject" principle, under which public schools may not turn away students with disabilities as "uneducable"; and the "least restrictive environment" principle, under which students with disabilities are to be taught alongside students without disabilities to the greatest extent appropriate.[2]

In implementing these principles, themselves born from litigation, the statute takes a proceduralist approach. It requires states to provide a "free appropriate public education" in the least restrictive environment to all children with disabilities but says very little about the *content* of that education. It simply requires the development of an Individualized Education Plan (IEP) for each student with a disability and then imposes a series of administrative and judicial devices for resolving disputes about the content and implementation of a student's IEP.[3] The statute has been criticized from both the left and the right as too legalistic.[4] School superintendents report that parents of children with disabilities "are too quick to threaten legal action to get their way."[5] Shep Melnick asserts that "litigation has increased dramatically" since the statute's passage.[6] And in perhaps the most influential recent critique of court-led social reform, Ross Sandler and David Schoenbrod used a major IDEA class action, *Jose P.* v. *Ambach,* as their primary example of problematic "democracy by decree."[7]

In this chapter, I assess the role and effects of the courts in implementing the IDEA. Perhaps the most surprising empirical conclusion is that courts do not have much of a role in implementing the statute.[8] The statute may well have a major effect on the administration of public schools, and the decisions made by state-level administrative adjudicators under it may make a difference. But to the extent that one is concerned about the role of unelected, politically unaccountable judges in special education, there is little basis for concern. As I show, there is very little litigation under the IDEA. In some class action cases—such as the *Jose P.* case that Sandler and Schoenbrod highlight—the effects of judicial intervention have been significant (for both good and ill). But, by and large, the courts have made little *direct* difference in the treatment of students with disabilities. Courts have a somewhat greater *indirect* effect on the education of students with disabilities, as their (relatively rare) decisions cast a shadow over the (much more frequent) decisions of school administrators. Those decisions have, at the margins, exacerbated one of the problems commentators have attributed to the IDEA: an excessive focus on process over substance. And they have created and maintained a system of public reimbursement of private school tuition that may appear necessary in individual cases but raises substantial equity concerns nonetheless. Considered overall, however, both the strengths and the weaknesses of the IDEA have less to do with the actions of the courts than with those of Congress and the executive branch.

The *Indirect* Effects of Judicial Decisions: The Role of Legal Doctrine

There are two possible ways the courts might affect education when they implement the IDEA. They might do so directly, by ordering schools to take or refrain from certain actions as a remedy for a proven violation of the statute. Or they might do so indirectly, as their legal rulings cast a shadow over the actions of educators, students, and parents.

In view of the limited number of cases brought under the IDEA, the courts have likely had a far greater indirect effect than a direct one on school practices. Teachers, administrators, and their lawyers read and react to court rulings governing school districts, but it is, in the nature of things, impossible to know just how much of an indirect effect judicial rulings have on school practices in this area. One might infer that because the courts are so rarely involved in IDEA cases, teachers and administrators do not think of legal doctrine as particularly relevant to their lives. Of course, one could also draw the opposite inference: maybe there is so little litigation precisely because school districts do a good job of accurately internalizing the rules courts have laid down. An empirical test of these two inferences is beyond the scope of this chapter. But anecdotal evidence suggests that teachers and administrators have at least a general understanding of what the courts are requiring under the IDEA.[9] And Richard Arum's study of school discipline suggests that while teachers are often wrong in their perceptions about the *specifics* of court rulings, they have a pretty accurate understanding of the general *direction* (pro-teacher or pro-student) in which courts rule.[10]

One might therefore hypothesize that judicial decisions are likely to alter schools' conduct when they address the schools' primary obligations under the statute (as opposed to the procedures for judicial enforcement of those obligations); that they are likely to be precisely implemented when they address broad, programmatic questions with clear rules that can be followed by administrators; and that rulings about how much deference school officials should receive will make a particular difference in the conduct of front-line teachers.[11] Considered in this light, judicial decisions under the IDEA have likely had a negative effect on the education of students with disabilities—though the picture is a mixed one, and it is unclear how much blame the courts, as opposed to Congress and the executive branch, deserve for some of those rulings.

The Supreme Court's first decision interpreting the statute, *Board of Education v. Rowley*, addressed the statute's basic standard for determining whether a school district has provided a "free appropriate public education" to its students with disabilities.[12] Two aspects of the Court's decision are significant. First, the Court defined "free appropriate public education" in largely procedural terms:

> Insofar as a State is required to provide a handicapped child with a "free appropriate public education," we hold that it satisfies this requirement by providing personalized instruction with sufficient support services to permit the child to benefit educationally from that instruction. Such instruction and services must be provided at public expense, must meet the State's educational standards, must approximate the grade levels used in the State's regular education, and must comport with the child's IEP. In addition, the IEP, and therefore the personalized instruction, should be formulated in accordance with the requirements of the Act and, if the child is being educated in the regular classrooms of the public education system, should be reasonably calculated to enable the child to achieve passing marks and advance from grade to grade.[13]

Underlining its procedural focus, the Court explained that "Congress placed every bit as much emphasis upon compliance with procedures giving parents and guardians a large measure of participation at every stage of the administrative process as it did upon the measurement of the resulting IEP against a substantive standard," and saw the statute as reflecting the "conviction that adequate compliance with the procedures prescribed would in most cases assure much if not all of what Congress wished in the way of substantive content in an IEP."[14]

Under the *Rowley* test, the instruction that school districts provide to children with disabilities must satisfy all of the statute's *procedural* requirements for the development of an IEP, but it need meet only a very minimal *substantive* standard: it must "permit the child to benefit educationally from that instruction." The Court specifically rejected the notion that the instruction provided to children with disabilities must give them the *same* educational benefit as other children receive—or even an *equal opportunity* to benefit. In applying its rule to the case before it, the Court held that Amy Rowley (a deaf student who had been denied a sign-language interpreter) received a "free appropriate public education" because she was progressing well from grade to grade without the interpreter—even though the evidence was clear that she missed a great deal of what was going on in class without one and would have done much better with one.[15]

The IDEA is commonly criticized as imposing burdensome procedural requirements on school districts that divert the attention of teachers and administrators from educational outcomes.[16] The Supreme Court's decision in *Rowley* is due a substantial share of that criticism. Under the holding of that case, the statute's procedural requirements are frequently the most significant hurdle for school districts; once a district satisfies those requirements, it is typically quite easy to show that the child is receiving *some* benefit from his or her education. *Rowley* thus gives school districts a strong incentive to focus on process rather than substance in special education.

A second aspect of *Rowley* is also important. The Court emphasized that in proceedings for judicial review under the IDEA, courts owe deference to the educational decisions made by school districts. As the Court explained, "The primary responsibility for formulating the education to be accorded a handicapped child, and for choosing the educational method most suitable to the child's needs, was left by the Act to state and local educational agencies in cooperation with the parents or guardian of the child."[17] It is hard to know what effect this rule of deference has had on school districts. For a period of time after *Rowley,* the lower federal courts often blunted the impact of that case's deference holding by ruling that school districts had violated the statutory mandate to place students in the "least restrictive environment"—a question that they characterized as a matter of statutory right rather than of educational method.[18]

But in recent years, prominent federal court decisions have applied *Rowley's* rule of deference in "least restrictive environment" cases as well as in "free appropriate public education" cases.[19] That development sharply limits the degree to which courts can—for good or for ill—overturn school administrators' substantive educational decisions in IDEA litigation.

Two recent IDEA cases, *Schaffer* v. *Weast* (2005) and *Arlington Central School District Board of Education* v. *Murphy* (2006), make it harder for less wealthy parents to present effective challenges to their districts' decisions. *Schaffer* held that the party challenging the content of an IEP (usually the parents) bears the burden of proof, and *Arlington Central* held that a parent who prevails in an IDEA due process proceeding may not recover fees for expert witnesses from the school district. Because an IEP is presumably supported by the school district's expertise, a parent can typically succeed in challenging that IEP only by offering expert testimony. But if parents must pay out of pocket for expert witnesses, they will be less likely to be able to secure the services of those witnesses.[20] At least at the margins, these decisions are part of a "pro-school" trend that further supports the deference that *Rowley* accords.

In two areas, decisions of the Supreme Court have addressed broad, programmatic questions that have likely had a significant impact on school practices. In *Cedar Rapids Community School District* v. *Garret F.,* the Court held that school districts must provide noneducational "related services" to enable children with disabilities to attend school (so long as they need not be performed by a physician), regardless of the cost of those services.[21] This ruling—and an earlier ruling on which the Court relied—undoubtedly contributed to the statute's cost burden of which school districts frequently complain. But it is hard to see the "related services" rule as primarily the doing of the *courts*. In articulating that rule, the Supreme Court merely adopted the views of the U.S. Department of Education. Although Congress has reauthorized the IDEA three times since the Court first announced the rule in 1984, it has never seen fit to change that rule.

Similarly, in *Honig* v. *Doe* the Court read the IDEA as imposing significant limitations on the discipline of students with disabilities.[22] The Court held that the statute's "stay-put" provision prohibited school systems from expelling or suspending students with disabilities for more than ten days without (a) obtaining parental consent or (b) obtaining a court order permitting it. There is no doubt that the IDEA, as so interpreted, has had a substantial effect on schools' disciplinary practices.[23] But again, it is hard to blame this result on the courts. As in *Garret F.,* the Supreme Court in *Honig* merely applied the interpretation adopted by the U.S. Department of Education.[24] And Congress has shown great attention to this question by successively amending the statute to reduce the restrictions it imposes on school discipline practices.[25]

In one other important area, however, it is fair to say that the courts have largely acted on their own. According to data from the Office of Special Education Programs at the U.S. Department of Education, over 56,000 students received IDEA services in private schools, at public expense, during the 2006–07 school year.[26] That number is a direct result of the Supreme Court's decisions, in *School Committee of Burlington* v. *Department of Education* and *Florence County School District Four* v. *Carter*, that parents of children with disabilities who are not receiving an appropriate education in public school have the right unilaterally to remove their children to private school and obtain reimbursement for the tuition.[27] The Court identified the right to reimbursement in the statute's general language authorizing appropriate relief for violations. Although Congress has tinkered with the judicially created reimbursement rule at the margins, it has not confronted the Court's holding head-on. Supporters of the private school reimbursement rule argue that it provides a necessary safety valve for children who simply are not being served. Critics contend that the rule essentially creates two special education systems, "separate and unequal."[28] Because the parent bears the burden of finding the appropriate private school and then must front the tuition pending the resolution of reimbursement proceedings (and risk not obtaining reimbursement if the hearing officer or court concludes that the school was providing adequate services to the child), the beneficiaries of the reimbursement rule are likely to be disproportionately wealthy and educated.

An extreme example is Tom Freston, the former chief executive officer of Viacom, who received an $85 million severance package from his company and then (successfully) litigated all the way to the Supreme Court to demand that the New York City schools reimburse his child's $38,000 annual private school tuition. Freston explained, quite plausibly, that he cared not about the money but about the principle.[29] But it is unlikely that many less well-to-do parents would be able to take advantage of the principle Freston established, because they would have to front the private school tuition for their children in the hope that (someday, perhaps at the end of a long administrative and judicial process) the school district would reimburse them. This result raises substantial concerns about the equity of the reimbursement program courts have created.[30]

The Shockingly Minimal Direct Effects of Individual Cases

The IDEA creates a multistep process for enforcement of its mandates. The statute requires states to permit parents to submit administrative complaints "with respect to any matter relating to the identification, evaluation, or educational placement of the child, or the provision of a free appropriate public education to such child."[31] Since 1997 states have been required to make a mediation process available to resolve such complaints.[32] But if mediation fails—or they simply do not want to engage in it—the parents are entitled to "an impartial due process hearing" before a state administrative tribunal.[33] Aggrieved parties may seek review of the final state administrative decision in federal district court.[34]

Perhaps surprisingly, parents do not invoke these procedures very often, although the number of administrative hearings may be slowly on the rise. A five-year nationwide survey (from 1996 to 2000) by the National Association of State Directors of Special Education (NASDSE) found that, each year, state and local education agencies across the country held approximately 5 due process hearings for every 10,000 students in special education.[35] A subsequent study by the Consortium for Appropriate Dispute Resolution in Special Education (CADRE), who examined the IDEA hearing process on a grant from the U.S. Department of Education, found a higher number—7.9 hearings for every 10,000 students in special education nationwide—but the researchers who conducted the study cautioned that the data might not be reliable owing to mid-study changes in the reporting format.[36]

There is substantial regional variation in hearing rates, however. The NASDSE study found that "nearly 80 percent of all hearings were held in five states—California, Maryland, New Jersey, New York, and Pennsylvania—and the District of Columbia."[37] Among those five states, hearing rates ranged from 3 per 10,000 special education students in California to 24 per 10,000 in New York. In the District of Columbia—a school system well known for its deep dysfunction—a staggering 336 hearings were held each year per 10,000 students in special education.[38]

All told, these sources report that state administrative hearing officers across the country hold somewhere between 3,000 and 5,500 due process hearings a year.[39] But these quasi-judicial processes are administered exclusively by state education agencies, not by the courts. How many of the cases that proceed to administrative hearings move to the next step, an action in court for judicial review?

Very few. The Special Education Expenditure Project (SEEP) estimated, on the basis of a survey of school administrators, that parties initiated only 301 actions for judicial review under the IDEA during the 1998–99 school year.[40] I found that number shocking, so I conducted my own small study using Westlaw's docket databases (which permit full-text searching of all federal district court dockets since January 1, 2000).[41]

My results, set forth in table 6-1, seem to confirm the SEEP's finding that few cases are filed in federal court under the IDEA. Between January 1, 2000, and January 1, 2008, an average of 374 cases that met my criteria were filed each year, with a slight upward trend from 364 in 2000 to a high of 409 in

Table 6-1. *IDEA Cases Filed in Federal District Court by Year, 2000–07*

Year	Number of IDEA cases filed
2000	364
2001	320
2002	360
2003	385
2004	366
2005	403
2006	385
2007	409

2007. (The low was 320 in 2001.) During the same period, the number of children served under the statute each year hovered around 6.6 million during the period. That number averages out to just over 4 cases each year for each of the eighty-nine federal district courts. To give a sense of proportion, 278,272 cases were filed in the federal district courts between April 1, 2006, and March 31, 2007, including 13,942 employment discrimination cases alone.[42]

To be sure, these data do not provide a complete tally of the IDEA cases brought in court in the past eight school years. They do not take into account cases filed in state court—which are an important component of special education litigation in a very few states (Massachusetts being the most significant example)—nor do they necessarily encompass all complaints invoking the IDEA. Pro se complaints (that is, complaints filed by parents without an attorney, which are often not filed in a format that allows the collection of the sort of information I relied on in my search) could easily elude detection.[43] Still, my search of dockets is likely to give a far more accurate picture of federal court IDEA litigation than did earlier studies that looked only at *opinions* included in electronic databases.[44] And it reveals numbers very close to the SEEP's survey-based estimate that about 300 IDEA cases are filed each year.

These numbers help to put in perspective the claims of some commentators that judicial review is a source of massive transaction costs in IDEA cases.[45] Perry Zirkel, for example, argues with considerable force that litigation of IDEA claims adds delay and cost that are not justified by the incremental benefit of adding another layer of review.[46] In his assessment of the benefits of judicial review, Zirkel looks only to *direct* benefits—the chance that a court will overturn an erroneous decision by the state administrative adjudicator. He thus ignores the possible *indirect* benefits of judicial review—such as the possibility that administrative adjudicators, knowing that someone is looking over their shoulder, will make better decisions in the first instance. But even assuming that

Zirkel is correct that the costs of judicial review outweigh the benefits in individual cases, there just are not enough cases to make a significant difference to the aggregate costs of the statute.

Data from the SEEP confirm the point. Although "the estimated average annual expenditure per open litigation case . . . amounted to $94,600 in 1999–2000," aggregate nationwide expenditures on IDEA litigation by school districts were only $56.3 million during that time period, or $9 per special education student.[47] Again, however, regional variations make a difference. Thus the extremely troubled District of Columbia school system, which obtained from Congress a special cap on the attorneys' fees it would be required to pay to prevailing IDEA plaintiffs, was nonetheless ordered to pay $3.24 million in such fees during fiscal years 1999–2001.[48] School systems with similar demographics in their general and special education populations—Oakland, California; St. Louis, Missouri; and San Antonio, Texas—were not required to pay *any* plaintiffs' attorneys' fees in IDEA cases during that period.[49] But note the relatively small numbers here: to be sure, the financially strapped District of Columbia public school system could have found other uses for the $1 million it spent each year on plaintiffs' attorneys' fees during 1999–2001.[50] But that $1 million was a small fraction of the school system's nearly $1 billion budget in fiscal 2001.

This is not to deny that IDEA litigation can create problems of cost and equity. Delay is endemic to litigation, and IDEA litigation is no exception. By the time the judicial process concludes, the record may be stale, and the decision may have little relevance for the child's current situation.[51] And better-off parents are far more likely to be able to take advantage of the litigation process—particularly after the Supreme Court's recent decisions placing the burden of proof on those opposing an IEP and refusing to permit prevailing parents to recover expert witness fees.[52] The point is merely that individual litigation has not had much *direct* effect—one way or the other—on the administration and delivery of education for children with disabilities.

The Uneven, but Still Largely Minor, Direct Effects of Class Action Cases

One set of cases has had a more significant impact on schools—cases brought on behalf of classes of students with disabilities. Even here, it bears emphasizing that the number of IDEA cases is remarkably small. My research was able to uncover less than 100 cases in which class actions had been certified to pursue IDEA claims. I could not find any IDEA class action in the overwhelming majority—more than 99 percent—of school districts. Perhaps this is not surprising. Because federal courts in recent years have tightened requirements for certifying class actions, they have been especially wary of according class treatment to cases brought under statutes that require individualized assessments. The IDEA is such a statute. Its requirement that parents exhaust state administrative (though not judicial) remedies before bringing suit also stands as a barrier to class treatment, as does the recent trend in the federal courts against authorizing private lawsuits to enforce federal conditional-spending statutes.

However, it is in the nature of class action litigation that a single suit can affect a large number of people. IDEA class actions have resulted in consent decrees or litigated injunctions that have had significant effects on some (though far from all) of the nation's largest school districts. As I argue in this section, some of those effects have been quite positive. Others have not, though that may have as much to do with lawyers' strategic choices than with anything inherent in IDEA class action litigation.

New York City provides an apt setting in which to explore the strengths and limits of IDEA class action litigation. New York City has the largest public school system in the nation, with 986,967 students in the 2004–05 school year.[53] The class actions here included the much-studied—and deeply controversial—*Jose P.* case.[54] New York is far from representative of public school districts. Not only is it far more diverse demographically than are most school districts; it has also experienced far more IDEA class action suits. But part of my point is that it is *not* typical for a school district to be a defendant in an IDEA class action; to study those class actions is precisely to study atypical districts. By being subject to more of those suits than any other district, New York City offers an opportunity to begin to assess what works and what does not in systemic IDEA litigation.

Scholars have identified two basic types of institutional reform cases, and two corresponding types of decrees that the parties might negotiate or the court might issue.[55] The first type could be called the "totality" case, in which plaintiffs and their lawyers sue to challenge systemic deficiencies in an institution—deficiencies that touch on all or nearly all of the institution's operations. The second type, typical of more recent litigation, is more focused. Rather than challenge defendants' conduct across the board, plaintiffs in this type of case pick out a few aspects of that conduct and develop an extensive record that those aspects violate the law. The remedial decree in such a case accordingly does not seek to restructure the defendants' entire operation but simply to resolve the particular problem or problems targeted by the suit. There is necessarily some overlap between these two categories. And some cases have started out in one category before shifting into the other. But the two broad categories are nonetheless sufficient for my illustrative purposes. In New York City, focused litigation has been far more successful than has totality litigation.

The story of the *Jose P.* litigation has been told at length elsewhere—most notably in a largely positive assessment by Michael Rebell, one of the plaintiffs' lawyers, and in a basically negative assessment by Ross Sandler and David Schoenbrod.[56] The litigation began in 1979 as a relatively simple class action, *Jose P.* v. *Ambach,* which challenged the school system's failure to promptly evaluate students with disabilities and assign them to appropriate placements. (When the *Jose P.* plaintiffs filed their complaint, more than 14,000 students sat on waiting lists for evaluation or placement.) The *Jose P.* plaintiffs sought a straightforward order requiring the school system to adopt a plan to reduce the backlog and ensure that students receive prompt evaluation and placement. The district judge assigned to the case, Eugene H. Nickerson, granted a preliminary injunction on the basis of the waiting-list violation, but he refused to confine the court's intervention to that narrow issue. Instead, he consolidated the case with a case filed soon after *Jose P.,* which was styled *United Cerebral Palsy* v. *Board of Education.* The *United Cerebral Palsy* plaintiffs had alleged a much broader set of violations of the EAHCA than had the *Jose P.* plaintiffs: "These included a lack of individualized placement procedures, inadequate preparation of individual education programs (IEP), unavailability of "mainstreaming" opportunities, inaccessibility of facilities to the non-ambulatory, a lack of requisite related services, and inefficiencies in the contracting procedures for placement in private school."[57]

The *United Cerebral Palsy* plaintiffs sought a broad-ranging "structural" remedy to address this array of problems.[58] Although Judge Nickerson did not find liability on any ground other than the *Jose P.* plaintiffs' waiting-list claim, he found that violation to be sufficiently intertwined with the *United Cerebral Palsy* plaintiffs' allegations to warrant the sort of broad-ranging remedy those plaintiffs sought.

The parties negotiated, and in December 1979 Judge Nickerson approved, a consent decree that addressed a wide range of issues.[59] New York's Least Restrictive Environment Coalition—a group that includes some of the counsel to the *Jose P.* plaintiffs—summarized the thrust of the decree this way:

> In addition to directing the Board of Education to comply with relevant federal and state laws, the judgment directed the Board of Education to (1) engage in a multi-part planning process for the implementation of a new special education services delivery system, (2) develop a set of operating procedures by which Board of Education staff should undertake the evaluation and service delivery process, (3) increase resources to facilitate timely evaluation and placement, including hiring staff, purchasing office equipment, creating office space and providing instructional materials for

classrooms, (4) develop informational materials for parents to inform them of their rights, and (5) reduce physical barriers that kept children with mobility impairments from participating in programs.[60]

The decree was quite process oriented. It originally required the school system to adopt a set of reforms proposed by the city's then-new special education director, Jerry Gross. The reforms were visionary—though, in the end, not all they were cracked up to be.[61] The Gross plan required "the establishment in each school of a school-based support team (SBST) consisting of a psychologist, social worker, and administrators and teachers from the local school."[62] At the plaintiffs' insistence, the consent decree not only ordered the city to adopt the Gross plan but also "add[ed] specific timelines and resource commitments, explicit procedural protections for the parents, and provisions for periodic reporting and ongoing monitoring to assure compliance."[63] The decree ordered that the waiting list for evaluation and placement be eliminated by April 1, 1980, and that the school system "'make maximum reasonable efforts' in hiring."[64]

Over the next year and a half, lawyers for the plaintiffs, amici curiae, and the school district hammered out two plans to implement different aspects of the decree's requirements. The first, approved by Judge Nickerson in January 1981, set forth "SBST evaluation procedures, standards for the provision of related services, and a detailed description of each program in a full continuum of educational services." This plan, incorporated as an order of the court, "consisted of a 76-page basic plan together with a 185-page appendix." The second plan, which Judge Nickerson approved in an incomplete form in May 1981, "provide[d] detailed information on staffing, supplies, and classroom space issues." Even in its incomplete form, this plan was more detailed than the first one; it "consisted of a 54-page basic plan, an 85-page supplement, and a 200-page appendix."[65]

The *Jose P.* decree has changed through the years, as the parties have agreed on—and the district court has approved—supplemental orders and stipulations. Some of these orders and stipulations have themselves been quite detailed and process oriented. For example, the parties agreed to a stipulation in the spring of 1983 that required the school system "to hire 613 new teachers and 600 psychologists, social workers, or educational evaluators by September 1983."[66] In 1988 the parties agreed to a stipulation that required the school system "to have 960 school psychologists (one-third of which were to be bilingual), 960 educational evaluators (one-third bilingual), and 572 social workers (one-half bilingual)."[67] And in 2003, after the city sought to restructure its procedures for monitoring the decree (as part of Mayor Michael Bloomberg's overhaul of the city's public schools), the parties stipulated that the city could hire the following personnel in lieu of the monitoring personnel required by the decree: "(i) 38 full-time professional school improvement team members with appropriate qualifications, at least 36 of whom will have civil service status above that of the current monitors, and one full-time supervisor; and (ii) 22 professional auditors and 3 supervisors with appropriate qualifications, working full-time for two months in the fall of each year and four months in the spring of each year." The stipulation required the city to provide "adequate clerical support" for those professional staff and to "apprise Plaintiffs twice a month of the progress in hiring and training the staff covered by this subparagraph."[68]

The litigation, which remains active to this day (seven years after Judge Nickerson's death), also remains highly controversial.[69] Supporters argue that it forced the New York City schools to pay attention (and devote resources) to children with disabilities—something the school system was not going to do otherwise. It is clear that both the number of students served by special education programs in New York City and the amount of funding for those programs have increased substantially since the court entered the *Jose P.* consent decree in 1979.[70] A real question, though, is whether the litigation was a necessary cause of that increase in attention and resources. Sandler and Schoenbrod suggest that, even in the absence of litigation, "strong demands for special education arising from parents, educators, and political leaders" would "have forced the [school] board to enhance programs irrespective of federal law, although not likely in the same direction as compelled by Judge Nickerson's remedial decree."[71] But that is just speculation. One could equally speculate that the "strong demands for special education" would be outweighed in the political process by even stronger demands—from many more parents—for improvement in general education. And one might also conclude, from the fact that "New York City had nine school chancellors over the course of the litigation," that "the turmoil in the city's special education programs [was] more a characteristic of the city's schools than something fairly attributable to judicial enforcement of the federal statute."[72] Sandler and Schoenbrod are closer to the mark when they say, of claims that *Jose P.* caused the city to devote greater attention and resources to special education, that "there is no way to prove or disprove this claim because it compares what occurred with what might have been—a hypothetical standard, the results of which vary with the views of the observer."[73]

That the benefits of the *Jose P.* decree are uncertain does not mean they are nonexistent. And some of the criticisms of that decree seem to me quite misplaced. One common criticism is that, as a result of the decree, New York's "regular education system resembles a parking lot full of 1968 cars, while special ed is like a handful of shiny new Cadillacs."[74] One might legitimately criticize giving priority in resource allocation to children with disabilities at the expense of other children with equally compelling needs (though determining whose needs are equally compelling is normatively complex).[75] But to the extent that such a priority is problematic, it is the IDEA that compels it—not the process of litigation. Criticism of that priority is appropriately directed to Congress and not the courts.[76]

But the process orientation and wide-ranging scope of the decree had some significant negative consequences. By writing into law the Gross plan—which seemed like the wave of the future at the time—the decree put the weight of the court behind what was essentially a bet about where the state of professional practice was going to move. In so doing, the decree made it difficult for the New York City schools to respond to evolving professional understandings of what structures of special education administration worked best in promoting good outcomes. The decree's wide-ranging nature seemed to require a change in the basic structure of the city's special education system to be successful, but that structural change limited the city's nimbleness in responding to evidence of the effectiveness and ineffectiveness of the decree in achieving its goals. And it helped to guarantee ongoing judicial oversight of the city's special education program, with no particular end in sight. Although many commentators (including me) would defend judicial intervention in the administration of local public schools in some circumstances, there are undoubted costs (in responsiveness to the public) to decades-long judicial oversight. A handful of other major cities have been the site of long-running IDEA class actions as well, though New York City is an outlier both in the length and in the detailed nature of the judicial oversight in these cases.

Moreover, the decree's focus on hiring personnel and meeting procedural deadlines has given administrators an incentive to shortchange the crucial questions of outcomes. Are children with disabilities being educated in the appropriate settings? And are they receiving education that promotes achievement? In an affidavit filed with the court in 1982, then-chancellor Frank Macchiarola stated the decree had "created a bias in favor of special education placement, whether or not that placement is appropriate."[77] By judging the schools on the basis of how many students they quickly evaluated for and placed in special education, he explained, the decree had "required City defendants to create an organizational machine which will identify and place greatly increasing numbers of handicapped students, and this machine, once created, has taken on a life of its own. Classroom teachers feel they have an obligation to refer students who are not meeting expected standards of academic or behavioral development. Evaluators feel they have an obligation to identify a handicapping condition that explains the child's difficulties."[78] Chancellor Macchiarola decried "the increasing attention focused in this litigation on comprehensible questions of quantity, principally timeliness and numbers of students served, at the expense of questions of quality, such as the appropriateness of diagnostic and placement decisions and the educational effectiveness of services provided to different categories of handicapped students."[79]

Although attributing causation is tricky, more than two decades after the entry of the *Jose P.* consent decree the city of New York continued to have exceptionally high rates of placement of students with disabilities in segregated settings—that is, separate classes or facilities from those in which nondisabled children are placed. The Least Restrictive Environment Coalition described the situation in a 2001 report: "In the 2000–01 school year, more than half (54%) of school aged special education students in New York City spent more than 60% of their time in a self-contained class in a general education school or separate facility for children with disabilities. One in eleven students (8.8%) were in wholly separate facilities and only 45.3% spent 20% or less of their time outside of a general education classroom."[80]

As the report explained, these numbers were significantly worse than the state and national averages, though they had gotten slightly better over time.[81] And on the all-important matter of educational outcomes, the report stated that "outcomes have become worse," though some improvements have occurred over the seven years since the report was issued.[82] Just over 2 percent of students in New York City's special education programs are "declassified"—that is, determined no longer to need special education—each year.[83] And those who remain in special education—particularly those in more restrictive settings—have substantially lower graduation rates and higher dropout rates than do general education students.[84] These outcomes are "far worse than those for special education students in New York State and across the nation."[85] And black and Hispanic students are placed in special education—and in more restrictive settings within special education—at disproportionate rates.[86]

The overall record of the still-pending *Jose P.* litigation is mixed at best, and it leaves substantial reasons for concern about its process orientation and its broad-ranging scope. The results in *Jose P.* contrast sharply with those in another IDEA class action brought against the city of New York. In *Ray M.* v. *Board of Education,* attorneys sued on behalf of a class of preschoolers with disabilities to challenge the city's failure to provide services in the least restrictive environment. The plaintiffs filed suit in federal district court in 1994, the court certified the plaintiff class in 1995, and the parties entered into a consent decree in 1999, which (after a brief extension) terminated in June 2002. The *Ray M.* litigation focused on a single issue (integration) in a single part (preschool) of the city's special education system. The consent decree in *Ray M.* focused to a far greater extent than its counterpart in *Jose P.* on the substance of educational practices, rather than on timelines for processing evaluations. The *Ray M.* litigation ended after less than ten years, while the *Jose P.* litigation is finishing its third decade. And the *Ray M.* litigation has been remarkably successful on its own terms. At the time they initiated the litigation, plaintiffs' counsel estimated that 80 percent of New York City's preschoolers with disabilities were served in segregated settings. By the 2005–06 school year, just over 50 percent of preschoolers with disabilities were served in *integrated* settings.[87]

The New York City experience suggests that it is wrong to think about the effectiveness of judicial intervention in special education as an acontextual matter. Rather, the effectiveness of IDEA class actions there has seemed to turn on the scope of the litigation and the orientation of the remedy. The more wide-ranging the case, and the more process-oriented the remedy, the less likely is litigation to be successful in achieving desirable outcomes. But there is nothing special about *courts* in this account. Efforts by legislatures and administrative agencies to make broad-ranging changes to school systems' conduct by imposing process-oriented rules are likely to be just as unsuccessful as are similar efforts by courts.[88] Indeed, detailed, process-oriented regulation (now pejoratively called "command-and-control" regulation) was very much in vogue in legislatures and administrative agencies during the 1970s, as the *Jose P.* case was filed and proceeded to judgment. Incentives- and outcome-based regulation is now understood to be far superior. And, as Sabel and Simon have shown, consent decrees in institutional reform litigation—including IDEA class actions— have increasingly embraced the new outcome-based model.[89] The limitations of cases like *Jose P.* are limitations of the ambition and form of regulation they adopt. They do not reflect *inherent* limitations of courts and judges.

Conclusion

What, then, can be said about the effect of judicial intervention under the IDEA? The most significant conclusion is that the *direct* effects of judicial intervention are much less than one might expect. Outside of the few districts that are defendants in IDEA class actions, a school district will only rarely be found defending its compliance with the statute before a judge. But that does not mean the role of the courts is insignificant. Class action consent decrees can have a major effect on the way schools provide education to students with and without disabilities—and, as the New York experience shows, the success or failure of those decrees can depend a great deal on whether they are structured in a broad-ranging and process-oriented way or in a narrowly focused and outcome-oriented way. And the courts have adopted rules—such as the "some benefit" standard in *Rowley* and the private school reimbursement rule in *Burlington* and *Florence County*—that have exacerbated the IDEA's own process orientation and that have raised significant questions of educational equity. It is the adoption of those sorts of programmatic rules, and not the adjudication of particular disputes under the statute, that likely accounts for the courts' greatest effect on schooling in the implementation of the IDEA.

These empirical findings shed significant light on much-debated normative questions about the statute. The statute has been criticized as imposing an adversarial model on the education of children with disabilities, with substantial transaction costs that divert time and resources away from the education of students with disabilities and those without them. But my analysis should suggest that those criticisms miss the mark to a significant extent. With the exception of Washington, D.C., school systems by and large do not face any significant federal litigation under the IDEA. For good or for ill, and notwithstanding the legalistic nature of the statute, the federal courts have very little involvement in the administration of education for individuals with disabilities.

Notes

1. Thomas Hehir and Sue Gamm, "Special Education: From Legalism to Collaboration," in *Law and School Reform: Six Strategies for Promoting Educational Equity,* edited by Jay P. Heubert (Yale University Press, 1999), p. 212.

2. Ibid.; R. Shep Melnick, *Between the Lines: Interpreting Welfare Rights* (Brookings, 1994).

3. 20 U.S.C. 1415.

4. From the left, see David Neal and David L. Kirp, "The Allure of Legalization Reconsidered: The Case of Special Education," *Law and Contemporary Problems* 48 (Winter 1985): 63. From the right, see Wade F. Horn and Douglas Tynan, "Time to Make Special Education 'Special' Again," in *Rethinking Special Education for a New Century,* edited by Chester E. Finn Jr., Andrew J. Rotherham, and Charles R. Hokanson Jr. (Washington: Thomas B. Fordham Foundation and Progressive Policy Institute, 2001).

5. Jean Johnson and Ann Duffett, "'I'm Calling My Lawyer': How Litigation, Due Process, and Other Regulatory Requirements Are Affecting Public Education" (Public Agenda, 2002), p. 9.

6. See Melnick, *Between the Lines,* p. 140.

7. Ross Sandler and David Schoenbrod, *Democracy by Decree: What Happens When Courts Run Government* (Yale University Press, 2003), pp. 45–112.

8. Although the conclusion is surprising, it accords with the findings of a much earlier study by Paul T. Hill and Doren L. Madey, "Educational Policymaking through the Civil Justice System," R-2904-ICJ (Santa Monica, Calif.: RAND Institute for Civil Justice, 1982).

9. Anna B. Duff, "How Special Education Policy Affects Districts," in *Rethinking Special Education for a New Century,* edited by Finn and others, pp. 135–59.

10. Richard Arum, *Judging School Discipline: The Crisis of Moral Authority* (Harvard University Press, 2003), pp.127–58.

11. These hypotheses are by and large consistent with the findings of Hill and Madey, "Educational Policymaking."

12. *Board of Education* v. *Rowley,* 458 U.S. 176 (1982).

13. Ibid., pp. 203–04.

14. Ibid., pp. 205–06.

15. Ibid., pp. 209–10.

16. For example, Neal and Kirp, "The Allure of Legalization Reconsidered"; Patrick J. Wolf and Bryan C. Hassel, "Effectiveness and Accountability (Part 1): The Compliance Model," in *Rethinking Special Education for a New Century,* edited by Finn and others; Perry A. Zirkel, "The Over-Legalization of Special Education," *West's Education Law Reporter,* vol. 195 (2005), p. 35.

17. *Board of Education* v. *Rowley,* 207.

18. Mark C. Weber, "The Transformation of the Education of the Handicapped Act: A Study in the Interpretation of Radical Statutes," *U.C. Davis Law Review* 24 (Winter 1990): 349.

19. For example, *Hartmann* v. *Loudoun County Board of Education,* 118 F.3d 996 (4th Cir. 1997).

20. Kelly D. Thomason, "The Costs of a 'Free' Education: The Impact of *Schaffer* v. *Weast* and *Arlington* v. *Murphy* on Litigation under the IDEA," *Duke Law Journal* 57 (November 2007): 457.

21. *Cedar Rapids Community School District* v. *Garret F.,* 526 U.S. 66 (1999).

22. *Honig* v. *Doe,* 484 U.S. 305 (1988).

23. For a highly critical assessment of the IDEA's impact in this regard, see Anne Proffitt Dupre, "A Study in Double Standards, Discipline, and the Disabled Student," *Washington Law Review* 75 (January 2000): 1–96.

24. *Honig* v. *Doe,* 325 and n. 8.

25. Mark C. Weber, "Reflections on the New Individuals with Disabilities Education Improvement Act," *Florida Law Review* 58 (January 2006): 34–39.

26. "Students Ages 6 through 21 Served under IDEA, Part B, by Disability Category, Educational Environment and State: Fall 2006" (www.ideadata.org/tables30th/ar_2-2.xls).

27. *Florence County School District Four* v. *Carter,* 510 U.S. 7 (1993); *School Committee of Burlington* v. *Department of Education,* 471 U.S. 359 (1985).

28. Daniel McGroarty, "The Little-Known Case of America's Largest School Choice Program," in *Rethinking Special Education for a New Century,* edited by Finn and others, p. 293.

29. Joseph Berger, "Fighting over When Public Should Pay Private Tuition for Disabled," *New York Times,* Mach 21, 2007.

30. A recent analysis concludes that public schools spend about $922 million a year on private school reimbursement for students with disabilities, about a quarter of 1 percent of the aggregate annual budget of public schools in the United States. That is a small percentage, and while cash-strapped school districts could surely use that money for other things, the cost is not terribly significant. Jay P. Greene and Marcus A. Winters, "Debunking a Special Education Myth," *Education Next* 67 (Spring 2007): 67–71.

31. 20 U.S.C. 1415(b)(6)(B).

32. Ibid., 1415(e).

33. Ibid., 1415(f).

34. Ibid., 1415(i)(2).

35. General Accounting Office, "Special Education: Numbers of Formal Disputes are Generally Low and States Are Using Mediation and Other Strategies to Resolve Conflicts" (www.gao.gov/cgi-bin/getrpt?GAO-03-897 [2003]).

36. "Summary of National Dispute Resolution Data—Rates per 10,000 Special Education Students Enrolled" (www.directionservice.org/pdf/DP%20Complaints%202005-06%20per%2010K.pdf [November 7, 2007]); Dick Zeller, "Cautions for Those Who Would Interpret State Dispute Resolution Data Reports" (www.directionservice.org/cadre/statecomprpts.cfm, [January 16, 2008]).

37. General Accounting Office, "Special Education," pp. 13–14.

38. Ibid., p. 14. The CADRE study found that an even more staggering 2,445 hearings were held in the District of Columbia during the 2005–06 school years even though the D.C. public schools had only 11,505 students in special education. See "Summary of National Dispute Resolution Data." But the researcher who conducted that study warns against relying on its data because of changes in reporting formats. See Zeller, "Cautions for Those Who Would Interpret State Dispute Resolution Data Reports."

39. See General Accounting Office, "Special Education," p. 13; "Summary of National Dispute Resolution Data."

40. Special Education Expenditure Project, "What Are We Spending on Procedural Safeguards in Special Education, 1999–2000?" (Palo Alto, Calif.: Center for Special Education Finance, 2003), p. 7. See also General Accounting Office, "Special Education," p. 1. n. 2.

41. A study of dockets is preferable to a study of published opinions—even opinions published on an online service such as Westlaw—because an enormous proportion of cases are resolved without any opinions being filed. Margo Schlanger and Denise Lieberman, "Using Court Records for Research, Teaching, and Policymaking: The Civil Rights Litigation Clearinghouse," *University of Missouri–Kansas City Law Review* 75 (Fall 2006): 164–65; Peter Siegelman and John J. Donohue III, "Studying the Iceberg from Its Tip: A Comparison of Published and Unpublished Employment Discrimination Cases," *Law and Society Review* 24, no. 5 (1990): 1133–70. To formulate a search, I first read a random sampling of dockets from cases I knew to have been brought under the IDEA. I identified these cases by searching for published district court opinions containing the phrase "Individuals with Disabilities Education Act." This might have led my later docket search to be underinclusive—if some of the dockets in cases that did not result in published opinions used different language to describe the case and cause of action than did the dockets I read. Since there is no reason that the language used to describe a case in a federal court docket (which is entered at the time the complaint is filed) would have anything to do with the form in which the court subsequently disposes of the case (published opinion or otherwise), I doubt this is a significant problem. The cases were filed under a variety of administrative office "nature of suit" codes, but all of them contained one or more of three things: a citation to 20 U.S.C. 1400, 1401, or 1415 (the opening provisions of the IDEA, and the provision that authorizes judicial review in IDEA cases, respectively); the words "handicapped child" or "handicapped children's protection" (a reference to a statute that amended the IDEA, the Handicapped Children's Protection Act); or the words "handicap" or "disability" (or their derivatives) within two or three words of the word "education." Accordingly, I searched in all federal district court dockets since January 1, 2000, for dockets containing one of the three statutory citations, the word "handicapped" adjacent to the world "child" (or its derivatives), or the words "handicap" or "disability" (or their derivatives) within five words of the word "education." I entered the following search on the DOCK-DCT-ALL database, adding a date restriction of cases filed after January 1, 2000: "20 usc 1400" "20 usc 1401" "20 usc 1415" (handicapped /1 child!) ((handicap! disabilit!) /5 education). (I chose five words, rather than three, for inclusiveness.) That search brought up many IDEA cases, but it also brought up literally hundreds of public accommodations suits filed under the Americans with Disabilities Act by an organization called Disability Rights Enforcement Education Services (DREES) (a frequent plaintiff in the federal courts in California). For a discussion of the cases brought by DREES, see Samuel R. Bagenstos, "The Perversity of Limited Civil Rights Remedies: The Case of 'Abusive' ADA Litigation," *University of California Los Angeles Law Review* 54 (October 2006): 1–36. Because those cases had nothing to do with education or the IDEA, I revised the search to

exclude any docket that contained the organization's name. (To the search in note 42, I added: percent "disability rights enforcement education service.") I reviewed each of the more than 500 dockets that exclusion eliminated and found that none involved IDEA cases.

42. "U.S. District Courts—Civil Cases Commenced, by Basis of Jurisdiction and Nature of Suit, during the 12-Month Period Ending March 31, 2006 and 2007" (www.uscourts. gov/caseload2007/tables/C02Mar07.pdf).

43. Theodore Eisenberg and Margo Schlanger, "The Reliability of the Administrative Office of U.S. Courts Database: An Initial Empirical Analysis," *Notre Dame Law Review* 78 (August 2003): 1455–96.

44. Perry A. Zirkel and Anastasia D'Angelo, "Special Education Case Law: An Empirical Trends Analysis," *West's Education Law Reporter* 161, no. 2 (2002): 731–53.

45. Kevin J. Lanigan, "Nasty, Brutish . . . and Often Not Very Short: The Attorney Perspective on Due Process," in *Rethinking Special Education for a New Century*, edited by Finn and others; Perry A. Zirkel, "'Transaction Costs' and the IDEA," *Education Week*, May 21, 2003; Zirkel, "The Over-Legalization of Special Education."

46. Zirkel, "The Over-Legalization of Special Education."

47. Special Education Expenditure Project, pp. 5, 8.

48. General Accounting Office, "Special Education," p. 6.

49. Ibid.

50. "D.C. Public Schools Face Spending Pressures in FY2001" (www.dcwatch.com/ schools/ps010906.htm.)

51. Zirkel, "The Over-Legalization of Special Education."

52. *Arlington Central School District Board of Education* v. *Murphy*, 548 U.S. 291 (2006) (expert witness fees); *Schaffer v. Weast*, 546 U.S. 49 (2005) (burden of proof). For a good discussion of the point, see Thomason, "The Costs of a 'Free' Education."

53. "Overview of the 100 Largest School Districts" (http://nces.ed.gov/pubs2008/100_ largest/overview.asp).

54. For the district court's order refusing to vacate the consent decree—probably the most significant *published* order in the case—see *Jose P.* v. *Ambach*, 557 F. Supp. 1230 (E.D.N.Y. 1983).

55. Margo Schlanger, "Civil Rights Injunctions over Time: A Case Study of Jail and Prison Court Orders," *New York University Law Review* 81 (May 2006): 550–630; Charles F. Sabel and William H. Simon, "Destabilization Rights: How Public Law Litigation Succeeds," *Harvard Law Review* 117 (February 2004): 1016–1101.

56. Michael A. Rebell, "*Jose P.* v. *Ambach*: Special Education Reform in New York City," in *Justice and School Systems: The Role of the Courts in Education Litigation*, edited by Barbara Flicker (Temple University Press, 1990); Sandler and Schoenbrod, *Democracy by Decree*. Unless otherwise noted, information about the case comes from these two sources.

57. Rebell, "*Jose P.* v. *Ambach*," p. 32.

58. Ibid.

59. The decree and numerous subsequent amendments and stipulations are available at www.advocatesforchildren.org/josep.php (July 2008).

60. Least Restrictive Environment Coalition, "Still Waiting, after All These Years . . . : Inclusion of Students with Special Needs in New York City Public Schools" (New York, 2001), p. 21.

61. Even Michael Rebell, the plaintiffs' lawyer who most strongly defends the litigation, became disillusioned with the Gross plan, though he understates the degree to which the adoption of the plan in the original decree had continuing effects later in the litigation. See

Rebell, "*Jose P.* v. *Ambach,*" p. 35: "What the lawyers for both sides did not fully appreciate at the outset, however, was that Dr. Gross's reorganization plan did not constitute a proven educational system that could be fully implemented over time if sufficient resources were provided. Rather, it was an imaginative proposal for beginning a structural reform process whose direction and substance would be subject to ongoing reformulation."

62. Ibid., pp. 33–34.

63. Ibid., p. 34.

64. Ibid.

65. The quotations in this paragraph are from ibid., p. 36.

66. Ibid., p. 42.

67. Ibid., p. 43.

68. *Jose P.* v. *Mills,* 96 Civ. 1834, 79 Civ. 560, 79 Civ. 2562 (June 4, 2003).

69. At this writing, the most recent activity on the court's docket for the case was recorded on January 21, 2009.

70. See Rebell, "*Jose P.* v. *Ambach,*" p. 44; Sandler and Schoenbrod, *Democracy by Decree,* pp. 88–89. The most recent Mayor's Management Report for the New York City Department of Education shows that special education enrollments continue to increase, even as overall enrollments are decreasing (www.nyc.gov/html/ops/downloads/pdf/_mmr/doc.pdf).

71. Sandler and Schoenbrod, *Democracy by Decree,* p. 94.

72. Mark Tushnet, "'Sir, Yes, Sir!': The Courts, Congress, and Structural Injunctions," *Constitutional Commentary,* vol. 20 (Spring 2003), p. 201.

73. Sandler and Schoenbrod, *Democracy by Decree,* p. 94.

74. Kay S. Hymowitz, "Special Ed: Kids Go In, but They Don't Come Out," *City Journal* (Summer 1996).

75. Mark Kelman and Gillian Lester, *Jumping the Queue: An Inquiry into the Legal Treatment of Students with Learning Disabilities* (Harvard University Press, 1997); Mark Kelman, "The Moral Foundations of Special Education Law," in *Rethinking Special Education for a New Century,* edited by Finn and others.

76. Tushnet, "Sir, Yes, Sir!"

77. Quoted in Sandler and Schoenbrod, *Democracy by Decree,* p. 69.

78. Quoted in ibid., p. 69.

79. Quoted in ibid., p. 70.

80. Least Restrictive Environment Coalition, "Still Waiting, after All These Years," p. 22.

81. Ibid., pp. 22–23.

82. Ibid., p. 25.

83. Ibid., pp. 25–26. The most recent Mayor's Management Report shows that the declassification percentage remains just over 2 percent (www.nyc.gov/html/ops/downloads/pdf/_mmr/doe.pdf).

84. Least Restrictive Environment Coalition. "Still Waiting, after All These Years," pp. 26–28.

85. Ibid., p. 27.

86. Ibid., pp. 29–35.

87. See the statistics collected by the New York State Education Department at http://cscrviccs.nysed.gov/sepubrep/mainservlet?f=report0506&school=300000010000#Indicator%206:%20Preschool%20LRE.

88. Compare Tushnet, "Sir, Yes, Sir!"

89. For a quite positive account of one IDEA class action on this score, see Sabel and Simon, "Destabilization Rights," p. 1028.

7

Pass or Fail? Litigating High-Stakes Testing

MICHAEL HEISE

The nation's sustained appetite for education reform includes a taste for test-based accountability.[1] Through standardized tests tied to various rewards and sanctions, policymakers seek to increase student achievement and enhance student, teacher, and school accountability for academic progress. In some cases, the consequences of poor test performance can be quite severe. For students, results from such "high-stakes" tests frequently determine their eligibility to graduate, advance from one grade to the next, or enter a particular curricular track.[2] Grade promotion decisions are particularly important as research consistently illustrates that involuntary grade retention correlates with a student's likelihood of dropping out.[3] Because the high school diploma (or its equivalent) is a threshold requirement for access to higher education, the military, and many higher-paying jobs and careers, students who lack a high school diploma begin their adult lives at a great disadvantage. Teachers also face testing consequences, for the results can provide access to necessary teaching certificates and licenses. Most states impose tests on would-be teachers, but a number do so for teachers seeking recertification as well.

I am grateful to the editors, Dawn M. Chutkow, Nicole Heise, and Michelle Yetter, for their input on earlier versions of this chapter. The reference librarians at Cornell Law School also provided excellent research assistance.

Standardized tests incident to the federal No Child Left Behind Act (NCLB) illustrate a related—though distinct—consequence of high-stakes testing.[4] Under NCLB, annual test results are used to determine whether schools and districts are achieving adequate yearly progress.[5] An array of penalties awaits those schools and districts that fail to demonstrate necessary progress.[6] Although these are high-stakes tests in the sense that unsatisfactory results give rise to sanctions, they differ from other forms of high-stakes testing in that adverse consequences affect schools and districts rather than individual students.

Largely because of these various consequences high-stakes standardized testing poses a threat to the education status quo as well as to individual and institutional interests. If modern U.S. education history is any indication, reform measures that threaten the status quo or entrenched interests inevitably attract litigation. High-stakes testing policies are no exception, and the resulting litigation contributes to the growing congestion surrounding educational policy and the law.

Although high-stakes testing policies generate litigation, less clear is *how* litigation influences high-stakes testing policies. That relationship warrants careful attention as it illustrates how law can influence education policy as well as inhibit efforts to use the law to that end.

Litigation's assault on high-stakes tests over a number of decades appears to have had at least two broad effects. First, litigation (and even the mere threat of litigation) has prompted states and districts to develop tests that are less vulnerable to legal challenge. Past litigation failures have also made them more attentive to due process and equal protection concerns. Furthermore, the broad legal parameters for these tests are now generally understood. So as long as states and districts keep them within the general legal boundaries, courts will remain reluctant to intervene. Greater attention to high-stakes tests' legal dimensions, combined with the growing popular demand for greater accountability, have diminished the threat of lawsuits against high-stakes testing.

Second, policymakers have reduced legal exposure by delaying the implementation of tests and making them more forgiving. This has meant fewer failing students, teachers, or schools, and in turn fewer disgruntled plaintiffs seeking legal redress. Although current tests provide greater legal insulation, they are less efficacious as a lever for meaningful education policy reform.

High-stakes testing policies did not emerge in a policy vacuum. Thus it is important to examine the broad legal terrain in which they are rooted before considering the three major types of high-stakes tests and the litigation challenging them. Although recent litigation trends indicate increased judicial reluctance to upset well-designed high-stakes testing policies, important challenges endure, with consequences for education policy.

Legal Terrain for High-Stakes Testing

High-stakes tests have moved to a central position in current educational policy debates and gained favor with many (but not all) parents, taxpayers, and policy-makers for two primary reasons. One is the sustained effort to eliminate the historical bias against certain student subgroups and give them greater access to educational opportunities. The emergence of standardized tests in the mid-1900s—notably the Scholastic Aptitude Test (SAT)—reflected a growing desire to democratize access to leading higher educational institutions, long dominated by wealthy graduates of prominent New England boarding schools.[7] Objective standardized tests diluted the importance of more subjective teacher grading, which had worked against less-advantaged students.

A second—and more current—factor is a lingering unease with the performance of American students and schools, especially since the publication of *A Nation at Risk,* a government report on education issued in 1983. The educational establishment's persistent unwillingness or inability to assume accountability for student, teacher, and school performance only heightens this anxiety. A paucity of helpful and meaningful data on student and school performance over time and across school districts and states also contributes to the anxiety over the condition of American education. Standardized tests—whether linked to any consequences for students, teachers, or schools—can contribute such data.

Recognizing the need for educational equity and quality, all levels of government—federal, state, and local—helped to develop and implement various tests. Historically, the federal government's role in this respect is quite limited, while state governments enjoy broader police and regulatory powers, and all fifty state constitutions say something about education.[8] Local authority flows largely from state delegation. Although all three layers of government have the legal authority to establish and implement high-stakes tests, specific sources of authority vary.

After a long history of comparative disengagement, the federal government is now fully engaged with K–12 education policy with the development of high-stakes tests through the No Child Left Behind Act of 2001 (NCLB).[9] NCLB's scope is considerable as it implicates every public K–12 school, regardless of whether it receives Title I funding.[10] NCLB's cornerstone is an expansion of school accountability pivoting on determinations of adequate yearly progress for student academic achievement determined through annual testing.[11]

Congress invoked its spending clause authority to pass NCLB, and over the years courts have interpreted this authority quite broadly. In 1987 in *South Dakota* v. *Dole,* the Supreme Court indicated a willingness to defer to Congress to define the contours of Congress's spending clause authority.[12] This deference is not unlimited, however. Whenever Congress exercises this authority, it must make clear the conditions for federal funding so that states can make informed decisions about whether to participate.[13] In a recent challenge to NCLB by the city of Pontiac, Michigan, local school districts raised questions about the responsibility for costs flowing from the act.[14] Although the district court dismissed the lawsuit, in 2008 a federal appeals court reinstated the action, concluding that NCLB violated the spending clause's clear-statement requirement.[15] The Sixth Circuit Court decision in *Pontiac,* if it withstands appeal, hints at possible limits to federal authority in the K–12 area.

Although it is too early to dismiss the *Pontiac* decision as an outlier, if Congress desires to do so it can easily fix any offending aspects of NCLB. Moreover, NCLB is due for reauthorization, which will almost certainly prompt a revisiting of the statute's major components. While the Court may impose upon Congress the need to engage in some technical fixing, nothing in the *Pontiac* decision even hints that Congress lacks the constitutional authority to promote high-stakes testing policies through the spending clause. Thus Congress will likely continue to force states to confront a potentially stark choice: submit to NCLB and comply with, among other requirements, such testing, or forgo federal Title I funds.

State governments may possess broad authority to promote citizen welfare, but various state laws impose constraints on that authority. For example, state governments typically share the federal government's commitment to equal protection as well as substantive and procedural due process. Unlike the federal constitution, however, all state constitutions express some textual commitment to education.[16] Local governmental units, including school districts and boards, face similar constraints even in areas where a state has delegated specific authority.

A large concern of testing's opponents is that tests may violate students' rights to due process and equal protection. The principal sources of these individual rights are the Fifth and Fourteenth Amendments of the U.S. Constitution, related state constitutional protections, and Title VI of the 1964 Civil Rights Act.

Tests that regulate access to high school diplomas in particular may implicate a student's property and liberty interests. Both the Fifth and Fourteenth Amendments protect students from the deprivation of "life, liberty, or property, without due process of law."[17] State constitutions offer due process protections as well.[18] In addition, procedural safeguards generally endeavor to ensure that any governmental action that interferes with a student's property interests in education is fair. A critical safeguard in the context of high-stakes exams is adequate notice. Other factors that might influence a court's assessment of procedural due process are the availability of remedial programs to needy students along with adequate opportunities to retest. An important substantive due process concern is a test's curricular validity, while equal protection becomes an issue when test pass rates vary across student groups. Federal law, including Title VI, also contains numerous and varied protections against discrimination based on race, ethnicity, gender, and other factors.

High-Stakes Tests and Litigation

Many high-stakes tests implemented across the nation in recent decades have attracted litigation. As the efficacy of efforts to roll back testing improved, schools, school districts, and states responded by adjusting their testing programs to ensure greater insulation from legal challenges. Since 2000, efforts to protect high-stakes tests from disruptive court decisions have been, on balance, quite successful.

High-Stakes Tests

High-stakes testing gained prominence in the 1970s with the emergence of the minimum competency test (MCT), which was soon overshadowed by the standards and assessment movement. The current NCLB regime—including its requirements for adequate yearly progress—changed the testing landscape markedly, in part by holding schools and districts accountable for poor student performance. Unlike MCTs, annual NCLB-required tests do not directly implicate students in the consequences for poor performance.

MINIMUM COMPETENCY TESTS. Responding to fears that social promotion policies, unfocused curricula, and diluted academic standards had debased the value of the high school diploma, states began requiring students to pass MCTs as a condition for high school graduation to ensure that they possess some minimal mastery of core academic subjects.[19] Any student entitled to graduate without passing an MCT typically receives a "certificate of attendance" rather than a full academic diploma.[20] Introduced in Oregon in 1973, MCTs quickly spread to other states, reaching thirty-six states by 1979, with eighteen states requiring satisfactory performance as a condition for graduation.[21]

It remains unclear whether MCTs—a precursor to standards-based accountability—helped resurrect the integrity of the high school diploma without unduly discouraging more students, particularly those from low-income households, from completing high school. Research on this question generates mixed results.[22] What is clear is that students—in some cases, many students—fail MCTs, and these failures distribute unevenly across various student subgroups.[23]

Although most states found it relatively easy to enact MCT legislation, implementation encountered substantial political and legal impediments related to MCT failure rates: initial failure rates (of eighth- or ninth-grade students) sometimes exceeded 30 percent.[24] Because rates among non-white students and students from low-income households exceeded those of their white counterparts, legal pressure against the tests increased.[25] Many states sought relief from the resulting pressure (both legal and political) by simply lowering the passing threshold used for the MCT, which drove the student failure rate below 5 percent (and frequently below 1 percent) by the time the initial cohort of students was poised to graduate from high school.[26] Scholars note that, among other factors, "equal protection and due process" concerns resonated among state policymakers when setting MCT failure thresholds.[27]

Whereas MCTs dwelled on students' exam results, most of the state education reforms launched after 1983 adopted a more comprehensive view of the education system. To better assess student progress toward state standards, many states articulated (or refined) their education standards, tethered the curriculum to the new standards, and aligned the exit exams with both the curriculum and standards. In addition, states expanded the universe of accountability from the individual student to the student's school and school district.

No Child Left Behind and High-Stakes Tests: The Federal Government Steps In. At its core, NCLB leverages state-created standards and assessments, increases transparency by disseminating data on progress, and imposes consequences on local schools and districts for insufficient annual student progress. As commentators note, standardized tests are the fuel that runs the NCLB engine.[28] Test scores must be generated annually for all students in grades 3 to 8 (and for one grade in high school), aggregated to the school level, and then disaggregated for a number of student subgroups, including those defined by race, ethnicity, and family income, as well as special education and limited English proficiency status.[29] All of these scores are used to assess whether a school is achieving adequate yearly progress (AYP). Although states currently enjoy significant latitude in establishing annual proficiency benchmarks, the NCLB requires academic proficiency in virtually all students by 2014.[30]

Unlike MCTs, NCLB-required tests do not directly implicate individual students in the consequences for poor performance. Instead, accountability for AYP failure falls on schools and districts. Because students are insulated from the adverse consequences from NCLB tests, the tests have attracted less litigation (let alone successful litigation) than MCTs.[31] Worse still from a policy perspective is that even if individual students were held to account for NCLB test performance, it might not accomplish much. As Paul Peterson has pointed out, NCLB's "simplistic dichotomy" (between achieving AYP or not doing so) provides little incentive for most students or much probative textured information about student progress toward specific educational objectives.[32]

A sliding scale of consequences befalls schools that do not achieve AYP.[33] Federally aided public schools that fail to do so are designated institutions "in need of improvement."[34] Schools failing to achieve AYP for two consecutive years must develop an improvement plan after receiving technical assistance from the U.S. Department of Education.[35] Also, students assigned to such schools are eligible to select another public school within the district.[36] Schools that fail to demonstrate AYP for three consecutive years must provide, at district expense, tutoring services to students attending the schools.[37] After four consecutive years, schools must undertake one of several measures, ranging from replacing school staff to implementing a more challenging curriculum.[38] Under NCLB, a school that fails to achieve AYP for five consecutive years runs some risk of having to engage in significant restructuring, including surrendering to district control, dissolving, or reconstituting as a charter school.[39]

As some observers note, "schools that fail to make AYP will likely be deemed failures, which in turn will generate pressure on state and local officials to do something to avoid that label."[40] This characterization stems not from NCLB but from the media, which "have translated 'in need of improvement' to mean 'failing.'"[41] One policy risk here is that the popular perception of schools that fail to achieve AYP will feed on itself and thereby reduce the likelihood that the schools can improve in the future.

Although sanctions for failing to achieve AYP are directed at schools, a broad array of key public school constituencies have various stakes in a school district's success. These constituencies include educators, students, and parents. As education professionals, teachers and administrators do not want their schools to be characterized as "in need of improvement" or worse. Similarly, it is fair to assume that students assigned to such schools (as well as their parents) would at the very least prefer additional publicly funded school options.[42]

Fallout from underperforming schools certainly extends to state and local politicians, many of whom are held vicariously liable for school success. As states increasingly centralize the control of education policy, governors' interest in the fate of public schools increases. Moreover, homeowners remain economically tied to local public school performance, especially in affluent suburban neighborhoods where public school reputations (real or perceived) influence home values.[43] A desire to protect home equity exists independent of whether the homeowner has school-age children. Local economic and business interests, especially among those with critical skilled-labor requirements, also have an important stake in the success of local public school systems. These varied interests—combined with the democratic accountability systems of public schools—help ensure the salience of political economy for education policy.

TESTING TEACHERS. Another persistent public concern surrounding testing involves teacher quality. Some of this anxiety relates to the academic preparation of those seeking to become teachers, significant procedural barriers to entry into the teaching profession, and robust collective bargaining and public civil servant protections for existing teachers. Partly in response to such misgivings, NCLB expressly requires that only "highly qualified" teachers staff classrooms for core academic subjects.[44]

To allay concerns about teacher quality and respond to NCLB requirements, many states and districts impose high-stakes tests on teachers as well as would-be teachers. Although testing policies vary across states, teacher tests fall into three broad categories. The most common test applies to those seeking to enter the teaching profession, that is, those seeking a professional credential (certificate or license) necessary for employment as a public school teacher. The second category consists of competency (or recurrency) tests for teachers who already possess a teaching credential and desire to renew that credential or convert it from a temporary into a permanent teaching credential. The third category—and the least common—comprises tests for teacher merit pay schemes, promotion schedules, or dismissal procedures.

High-Stakes Testing Litigation

As the consequences of high-stakes testing increased for entities ranging from students to states, so too did the litigation seeking to blunt those consequences. Much of the litigation pursued one or a combination of three broad claims: due process, equal protection, or statutory rights (notably Title VI). Litigation (and its threat) led to many changes in test policies—including delayed implementation, increased resources for students who struggle with such tests, and more forgiving pass rates—all of which reveal policymakers' increased sensitivity to legal exposure.

FLORIDA AND *DEBRA P.* In 1976 Florida lawmakers passed the Educational Accountability Act, which included an exit exam requirement for high school graduation.[45] Students who failed were provided remediation classes as well as another chance to pass the test thirteen months later. A student who failed the test for a second time received only a certificate of high school attendance.[46] Non-white students failed the initial test at a rate three times greater than the rate for white students.[47] Results from the second administration of the test resembled the first: non-white students failed at a far higher rate than white students.[48] Students denied a high school diploma because they failed to pass Florida's exit exam sued the state, arguing in part that the implementation of Florida's exit exam requirement violated their due process and equal protection rights.

Student claims were anchored in testing notice and preparation defects. After finding that students possessed a property right in a high school diploma, the trial court concluded that the state had failed to provide adequate notice before altering high school diploma requirements and thereby violated procedural due process.[49] The court also determined that the thirteen-month remediation program was insufficient to offset the potential harm attributable to the ten years of instruction provided before the development of the exit exam.[50] Due process was also violated, concluded the court, because the state's curriculum did not adequately align with the material covered in Florida's exit exam.[51]

In addition, the trial court found that Florida's exit exam posed equal protection problems. When combined with Florida's past de jure segregation policies, evidence of disproportionate failure rates across various student subgroups indicated that the exit exam discriminated against non-white students.[52] However, the distribution of failure rates, along with the state commissioner of education's anticipation of disproportionate failure rates, did not support a judicial finding of intentional discrimination.[53] Despite the absence of any intentional discrimination, the trial court enjoined the state of Florida from withholding high school diplomas from students who failed the exit exam.

The state's appeal fell on similarly skeptical ears. After quickly agreeing with the trial court on the nature of the equal protection and procedural due process problems, the appeals court dwelled on the exit exam's validity and relation to the instruction that Florida students received in class. The appeals court concluded that it could not determine whether the exit exam was sufficiently related to the curriculum because of the meager direct evidence on this issue admitted at trial. Thus the case was remanded back to the trial court for a hearing on the issue.

On remand, both parties submitted lengthy testimony from a platoon of experts, and the district court judge was persuaded that Florida's official curriculum, as implemented by a majority of the state's teachers, provided students with a fair opportunity to learn what was necessary to pass the state's exit exam. Moreover, by then enough time had passed so that every Florida student would have attended schools the courts deemed unitary. The injunction was removed, and upon affirmance by the appeals court, Florida was permitted to implement its exit exam in full in 1984—years after the initial trial court ruling that enjoined the exam's full implementation.[54]

The *Debra P.* litigation saga included several important outcomes. First, it demonstrated that litigants can successfully impede the implementation of high-stakes tests, at least those with procedural and substantive defects. Second, although litigants delayed implementation of Florida's exit exam, their success was ultimately reversed. In time, all of Florida's students were attending judicially decreed unitary schools for their entire elementary and secondary education. Florida educators further refined the curriculum to better align with the content of the exit exam. After various appeals and remands, the circuit court concluded in 1984 that Florida's use of the exit exam was permissible and that it could deny high school diplomas to those who failed the exit exam.[55] Third, the final opinion in the *Debra P.* litigation hints at the courts' increased reluctance to impede satisfactorily designed testing programs.

THE TEXAS EXIT EXAM: *GI FORUM.* Like their Florida counterparts, Texas policymakers sought to improve student performance through the imposition of a high school exit exam. In 1985, after a decade-long struggle over the direction of school reform in Texas, state lawmakers implemented the Texas Educational Assessment of Minimum Skills (subsequently replaced by the Texas Assessment of Academic Skills, TAAS) as one piece of a larger school reform initiative.[56] The Texas Assessment of Knowledge and Skills (TAKS), introduced in 2003, replaced TAAS.[57] Results from the TAKS were used to assess not only students but also schools and school districts.

Where necessary, both TASS and TAKS provided students with remedial assistance and multiple opportunities to pass the exit exam. Under TAAS, students were permitted eight chances to pass before the completion of their senior year.[58] Even more indulgent, the current TAKS gives students an unlimited number of chances to pass. Moreover, students who leave high school without a full academic diploma can continue taking TAKS and will receive a diploma retroactively upon passing.[59]

Notably, the transition from TASS to TAKS also involved a temporary reduction in the required passing threshold (from 70 to 60 percent).[60] Under the more forgiving threshold, the student pass rate jumped from 40–50 percent to 80–90 percent. The results helped squelch public outcry and reduced the number of students positioned to legally challenge TAKS.[61]

Despite supplemental resources, multiple opportunities to pass TAKS, and a reduced failure rate, some students failed TAKS and were denied high school diplomas. As in Florida, test failure rates distributed unevenly across various student subgroups and were highest among African American and Hispanic students. Representing minority students who failed the exit exam and were denied high school diplomas, attorneys from the Mexican American Legal Defense Fund (MALDEF) sued the state of Texas, alleging that its exit exam violated the students' equal protection, due process, and statutory rights. However, only the statutory Title VI claim proceeded to trial.

Within the Title VI context, the court dwelled on the stark disparity in pass rates between white and non-white students. Expert witnesses from both sides agreed that the pass-rate disparity was high, with an adverse effect on non-white students, and that statistically significant, though lower, disparities existed in the cumulative exam pass rates.[62] On the basis of largely uncontested statistical evidence, the trial court in *GI Forum* concluded that the plaintiffs had established a prima facie discrimination claim against the state's exit exam.[63]

Even so, Texas policymakers successfully defended their exit exam as a legitimate exercise in educational policymaking authority notwithstanding the exit exam's heavy impact on non-white students. The trial court concluded that the exit exam was intended to advance education reform in Texas and that the high-stakes graduation requirement was justified, in part, because it "encouraged learning."[64] The court also rejected the plaintiff's assertion that equally effective yet less disparate alternatives to the exit exam existed.[65] Moreover, the court noted that the state provided adversely affected students remedial classes expressly geared toward the exit exam. Consequently, the court ruled against the students and declined to interfere with the implementation of the Texas exit exam.

As commentators note, the *GI Forum* decision supports three distinct interpretations, each with markedly different implications for policymakers.[66] First, the decision may be narrowly understood as a failure by the plaintiffs to rebut the state's arguments about the efficacy of TAKS policy in advancing school reform. Second, the decision may also reflect the court's deference to states when it comes to establishing minimal standards necessary for graduation. Third, the decision may reflect lessons that Texas policymakers drew from Florida's legal struggle with its exit exam. Critical TAKS components—the supplemental resources for struggling students, unlimited number of chances to succeed, and a temporarily reduced failure rate—appeared to anticipate legal challenges moored in both substantive and procedural due process claims and to reflect Texas lawmakers' awareness of the legal exposure created by high-stakes exit exams.

CALIFORNIA. In 1999 California joined a growing number of states requiring the successful completion of a statewide exit exam for receipt of a full high school diploma.[67] Students begin taking the California High School Exit Exam (CAHSEE) in the tenth grade and are afforded multiple opportunities to retake the exam. CAHSEE was implemented in conjunction with a larger statewide effort to bolster academic standards and assessments.[68]

Testing began in 2001 and affected students planning to graduate in 2004. By the summer of 2002, however, less than one-half of the class of 2004 had passed the exam.[69] Moreover, Hispanic, African American, and low-income students passed at far lower rates.[70] No doubt mindful of likely legal and political blowback, the California Board of Education voted to delay denying diplomas to students who could not pass CAHSEE until 2006. As graduation for the class of 2006 approached and the prospect of denying thousands of California high school diplomas loomed, a class-action lawsuit was filed in state court to enjoin the state from withholding diplomas from students who had failed the exit exam.

In *Valenzuela* v. *O'Connell,* the trial judge enjoined CAHSEE's implementation for another year, arguing that the harm to the state in delaying implementation was outweighed by the harm arising from denying otherwise qualified students their high school diplomas.[71] Harms to the students entailed equal protection and the right to an education. Anxious to appeal the injunction and obtain definitive guidance from the California Supreme Court, the state sought to bypass the court of appeals. In the court's view, however, the controversy could be sidestepped by sending the matter to the state appellate court rather than deciding the merits of the state's challenge to the trial court's injunction.[72]

After hearing from both parties at oral argument and numerous others in amici curiae briefs, the three-judge appellate panel vacated the trial court's preliminary injunction. While the appellate court agreed with the trial court that the plaintiffs were likely to prevail on their denial of equal educational opportunity claims, it nonetheless concluded that the injunctive relief was an improper encroachment upon legislative terrain.[73] Favoring the state's high-stakes test, the appellate court ruling prompted a negotiated settlement between the litigating parties.[74]

The appellate court indicated that the trial court's injunction prohibiting CAHSEE's full implementation injected the judicial branch too deeply into legislative terrain.[75] Thus, it noted, the trial court's remedy impermissibly limited policymakers' discretion to bring CAHSEE into constitutional compliance.[76] Although the political question doctrine remains murky, litigation efforts seeking to influence high-stakes testing policies invariably push the envelope of the separation-of-powers principle.[77] A clear distinction does not typically exist between those seeking judicial assistance in protecting a student's procedural and substantive due process rights and those seeking to simply evade traditional political processes.

The appellate court's decision to vacate the trial court's preliminary injunction sparked considerable criticism. Many argued that both courts failed to appreciate fully the extent to which CAHSEE would infringe on students' due process rights.[78] Drawing on survey data, some also complained that not all students were provided with the instruction necessary to prepare for the exam, a factor that weighed heavily in Florida's *Debra P.* decision.

Despite the plaintiffs' disappointment with the outcome in *O'Connell,* the settlement prompted by the appellate court's decision culminated in new state legislation providing important help for students struggling with CAHSEE.[79] Students are now entitled to two additional years of instruction if they have not passed the exam by the end of their senior year. This supplemental instruction focuses on preparing students for the exam. In addition, students whose primary language is not English are entitled to receive two additional years of language instruction to better enable them to pass the exam.

TEACHER TESTING LITIGATION. The legal terrain for teacher high-stakes testing differs considerably from that for students. For one thing, teachers and school districts are bound by collective bargaining rights, in addition to general employment and contract law. Significant legal challenges in this context pertain to the various high-stakes tests used for teacher recertification and for dismissing existing teachers. Despite the array of tests used by districts and states, most legal challenges revolve around teachers' due process and equal protection rights. Due to the employment context, Title VII, a federal statute addressing employment discrimination, comes into play.

Along with fair notice, a critical due process concern involves the test's psychometric validity. Simply put, any test that seeks to measure teacher competence must reliably measure some defensible construct of teacher competence. To assess test validity, courts frequently ask whether appropriate validation techniques were used, such as those put forth in the *Uniform Guidelines on Employee Selection Procedures* (adopted by the U.S. Equal Employment Opportunity Commission) or in the *Standards for Educational and Psychological Testing* (adopted by the American Psychological Association).

With the growing use of National Teacher Examinations (NTEs) by states, districts, and schools, much litigation has focused on content validity. In *United States* v. *South Carolina,* judges upheld the state's use of NTEs for initial hiring as well as teachers' pay classification decisions after finding ample evidence of the NTE's content validity. An opposing judicial view of the NTE's content validity is found in *Georgia Association of Educators, Inc.* v. *Nix* (1976).[80] In *Nix,* the court concluded that Georgia's requirement of a minimum NTE score for a six-year teaching certificate was arbitrary as no effort had been made to validate the specific cutoff score and its intended purpose. Despite conflicting case law, courts appear increasingly reluctant to upset a state's and district's use of a professionally recognized test, so long as there is evidence of a serious effort to establish the validity of the test for the purpose used.

High-stakes teacher tests have also been challenged on the basis of teacher equal protection claims, as in *United States* v. *South Carolina.*[81] In this case, the federal government sued South Carolina (and numerous educational agencies and officials) for relying on NTEs in its teacher certification program. Like many other states, South Carolina officials had been using high-stake test results for decades. And as in many states, NTE results broke along racial lines and prompted claims of racial discrimination. The plaintiffs felt that teachers' rights guaranteed by the Fourteenth Amendment and Title VII had been compromised by South Carolina's use of the test results. Although the legal mechanics of the Fourteenth Amendment and Title VII differ in important technical ways, a few basic principles link the legal claims.

Under conventional Fourteenth Amendment analysis, even if a state's policy to use high-stakes teacher tests for teacher certification (and other) purposes is race-neutral on the surface, courts will consider whether sufficient evidence of an intent to discriminate exists by assessing whether test results skew along racial, gender, or ethnic lines. In *South Carolina,* a review of more than three decades of teacher high-stakes testing did not uncover evidence of discriminatory intent.

This meant that South Carolina only needed to prove its use of teacher testing was "rationally related" to its stated policy goal of improving public education. In concluding that South Carolina's reliance on NTEs was not irrational from a policy perspective, the court gave considerable weight to the extensive efforts to validate NTE and certification minimums with policy objectives relating to basic teacher competence.[82]

As for Title VII considerations, the plaintiffs succeeded in establishing that a disproportionate number of non-white teacher applicants failed to receive certification because they had not achieved the necessary minimum NTE score. Under the statute, the legal burden then shifted to South Carolina officials to justify such a result. Emphasizing once again the importance of psychometric test validation efforts, the court concluded that the state had sustained its evidentiary burden and upheld South Carolina's use of NTEs.[83]

It is no surprise that policies designed to link teacher performance assessments and student high-stakes test results trigger litigation. In one such case, *Sherrod* v. *Palm Beach County School Board* (2003), the Palm Beach County (Florida) school board initiated proceedings to dismiss a teacher for incompetence.[84] At that time, Florida law required school boards to base annual teacher assessments "primarily" on student performance on state and local tests, including the Florida Comprehensive Assessment Test.[85] Despite the school board's overwhelming evidence of teacher incompetence, it did not include any student performance data from Florida's high-stakes tests.[86] Concluding that applicable Florida law did not provide for any discretion in the matter, a Florida court in 2006 reversed the teacher's dismissal.[87]

Ironically, a Florida law designed to boost student achievement through high-stakes tests was successfully used by incompetent teachers in *Sherrod* to reverse their dismissals on procedural grounds. Recognizing that motivated students may succeed on high-stakes tests *despite* teacher incompetence, Florida lawmakers quickly amended the relevant state statute to prevent such an outcome in the future.[88]

High-Stakes Testing's Legal Future

The most recent explications of the judiciary's posture toward legal challenges to state high-stakes exit exams are reflected in the *GI Forum* and *O'Connell* decisions. Standing alone or in conjunction with the earlier *Debra P.* decision, these two decisions signal firmer judicial resistance to litigation efforts seeking to dislodge exit exams and other test-based accountability policies. The trend of several decades of litigation aimed at disrupting high-stakes testing policies suggests that judges are becoming hesitant to second-guess policymakers who carefully design and implement high-stakes tests.

At the same time, litigation continues to influence such programs. The mere specter of litigation—including lawsuits unlikely to prevail—imposes concrete costs on policymakers inclined to pursue high-stakes testing. For cash-strapped states, the potential financial costs might be sufficient to prompt states to lower student proficiency thresholds in an effort to reduce legal exposure. Furthermore, the nation's ongoing experience with NCLB suggests that political pressure might be a more efficacious means of blunting the consequences of poor test results. For example, no doubt in response to growing political pressures, George W. Bush's education secretary, Margaret Spellings, displayed a robust appetite for granting cities, districts, and states assorted waivers from NCLB requirements.[89] As commentators note, the waiver process, though formally channeled through administrative law, contains a healthy political lobbying dimension.[90]

High-Stakes Testing and School Finance Litigation

Other costs may be incurred by school finance advocates who successfully leverage poor high-stakes test results into legal claims for increased educational spending, principally through adequacy lawsuits.[91] Although school finance litigation and high-stakes testing movements began independently, the emergence of adequacy theory in school finance litigation helped forge a link between the two. Results from high-stakes tests—particularly poor results—provide critical evidence for litigants seeking a court declaration that schools or districts are "inadequate" as a matter of state law.

Litigation in Kansas provides an example of this relationship.[92] The Kansas constitution, as amended in 1966, mandates that the legislature "make suitable provision for finance of the educational interests of the state."[93] In 1992 Kansas lawmakers enacted the School District Finance and Quality Performance Act (SDFQPA) to meet its constitutional duty.[94] The SDFQPA created a statewide property tax and a statewide system for collecting and disbursing property tax revenues. Although the SDFQPA presumes equal per pupil spending, district-specific weighting factors modify this presumption. In addition, the SDFQPA established a guaranteed per pupil spending floor along with an accountability system tied to state minimum student performance standards in specific subjects.[95] Despite the guaranteed spending floor, a school finance lawsuit challenging the SDFQPA succeeded in 2003.[96]

The state's student proficiency standards—a necessary component under NCLB—played a critical role in the courts' assessment of whether the Kansas school finance system passed state constitutional muster. At trial, NCLB test results were essential to the court's conclusion that the SDFQPA violated the state's constitution.[97] Although part of the trial court decision was reversed on appeal, even the Kansas Supreme Court construed educational adequacy in terms of student achievement measured in relation to NCLB test requirements.[98]

Notably, both the plaintiffs *and* defendants in Kansas turned to NCLB student test results to support their respective legal positions. They used 2002 and 2003 math and reading proficiency scores for fifth, eighth, and eleventh grade students to substantiate the large achievement gaps between and across various student cohorts.[99] This evidence, noted the court, was both "informative and disturbingly telling."[100] Nevertheless, the defendants stated that even these gaps were not enough to preclude the schools and districts from achieving AYP under NCLB. They argued, unsuccessfully, that achieving AYP under NCLB precluded a finding that the schools and districts provided an inadequate education.[101] Setting aside debates about whether the Kansas courts correctly interpreted NCLB data for school finance purposes, the critical point is that the courts construed a key school finance concept—educational adequacy—in terms of student academic outcomes prompted by the high-stakes testing requirement imposed by NCLB.

As litigants are beginning to find, however, results from high-stakes testing—long presumed to be a *sword* for plaintiffs in school finance lawsuits—may also be used as a *shield* by districts and states to defend against claims that resources are inequitably or inadequately distributed, as illustrated by the torturous school finance litigation in Texas.[102] In 2005, after protracted litigation, the Texas Supreme Court decided to focus on student test results rather than inputs such as per pupil spending.[103] The court concluded that Texas was required to fund public K–12 education to achieve a "general diffusion of knowledge."[104] The court declared that it would adopt a "plainly [test] result-oriented" perspective to assess whether the state was meeting its constitutional obligation.[105] In rejecting the plaintiffs' argument that per pupil spending gaps contributed to the disparities in student achievement, the court endeavored to separate student inputs (resources) and outcomes (test results). To justify this decision, the Texas court noted that even though per pupil spending differences remained static, student test scores improved.[106] Moreover, student test scores increased even though the tests and the material covered in them had become more difficult.[107]

Teacher Testing

As with student high-stakes testing, courts appear increasingly unlikely to strike down properly designed high-stakes teacher tests. Aside from critical procedural due process concerns, notably fair notice, what makes teacher testing more complicated than student testing is the difficulty in aligning the test with a measurable outcome. Simply put, it is easier to reach a consensus on how to operationalize desired student outcomes than on desired teacher outcomes. To complicate matters, teacher competency can be plausibly assessed either by tests designed to gauge teacher skill levels or by student achievement tests. Whether a teacher's effectiveness should be measured by student improvement continues to be debated, particularly in states and districts that are considering various teacher merit pay schemes. Central to this debate is uncertainty about the connection between the quality of teaching and student learning. Hence courts in general seem less inclined to intrude into substantive policy disputes about these factors.

Conclusion

Litigation trends involving test-based accountability shed some light on the dynamics between law and education policy. Courts began to intervene in this policy area in response to the early design limitations of one popular form of high-stakes test—high school exit exams—as well as the vestiges of segregated schooling. Once formerly segregated districts achieved unitary status and tests paid greater attention to students' due process concerns, courts became more reluctant to interfere with these testing policies. As high-stakes testing grew in popularity, other variants appeared, such as the annual testing connected with the No Child Left Behind legislation. These developments further embedded test-based accountability systems into the American educational landscape. Although some policymakers continue to question the usefulness of high-stakes tests, few disagree about their potential consequences for students, schools, and districts.

Even if one thinks courts should be more aggressive in halting efforts to impose high-stakes tests, a critical point to consider is that high-stakes tests generate valuable data on student academic performance. To ensure that such data will continue to be gathered, districts and states should be able to require testing even if test performance does not implicate a student's status in school. That is to say, even if courts reversed present trends and prohibited high-stakes tests, schools and districts should be able to administer no-stakes standardized tests and disseminate the results.

One helpful model in this regard emanates from NCLB and involves the National Assessment of Educational Progress (NAEP) program. Before NCLB, state participation in NAEP tests was purely voluntary. NCLB requires that participating states administer annual student performance tests in math, reading, and science in part to determine whether a school or district has achieved adequate yearly progress under NCLB. Although states are required to participate in NAEP, the results, however bad, have no adverse consequence for the states (aside from potentially negative publicity).[108] If anything, NAEP participation generates comparative information across states and helpful student perform-ance data, all of which serve important policy functions.

For better or worse (or, more accurately, for better *and* worse), high-stakes testing currently dominates the American K–12 educational landscape. The pol-icy stakes surrounding the fate of test-based accountability systems are high. The multidecade litigation effort to impede the implementation of test-based accountability systems illustrates how the law and litigation inform high-stakes testing policy. Over the past decades, policymakers have modified high-stakes tests to reduce their exposure to adverse court decisions. Consequently, well-designed high-stakes tests are less likely to encounter litigation in the future. As the legal exposure recedes, fighting over test-based accountability policies will migrate even further from the legal arena and into the political arena. In insu-lating high-stakes tests from legal attack, however, policymakers have reduced testing's efficacy as a lever for education policy reform. Such an outcome illus-trates, once again, the congested and complicated interplay between law and education policy.

Notes

1. See Paul T. O'Neill, "High Stakes Testing Law and Litigation," *Brigham Young University Education and Law Journal,* 2003 (2003): 623, noting that the number of states imposing some form of high-stakes exam has "consistently risen over the last decade" and that the number is likely to "continue to climb."

2. See National Research Council, *High Stakes: Testing for Trackings, Promotion, and Graduation,* edited by Jay P. Heubert and Robert M. Hauser (Washington: National Acade-mies Press, 1999), p. 1.

3. See generally Shiri Klima, "The Children We Leave Behind: Effects of High Stakes Testing on Dropout Rates," *Southern California Review of Law and Social Justice* 17 (Fall 2007): 3.

4. *No Child Left Behind Act of 2001,* P.L. 107-110, 115 Stat. 1425 (2002) (codified at 28 U.S.C. 6301–6578 [Supp. II 2002]). To be sure, many other standardized tests involve various forms of "high stakes." For college-bound students seeking admission into selective colleges and universities, the SAT and ACT are obvious examples. However, this chapter focuses on litigation prompted by three major high-stakes standardized tests imposed on stu-dents, teachers, and schools: minimum competency (or "exit") exams, teacher competency (or certification) exams, and annual testing incident to the No Child Left Behind Act.

5. 20 U.S.C. 6311(b)(3).

6. See, for example, ibid., 6316(b)(7)(C)(i)–(vi).

7. For a summary of public opinion support for testing, see Jennifer C. Braceras, "Killing the Messenger: The Misuse of Disparate Impact Theory to Challenge High Stakes Educational Tests," *Vanderbilt Law Review* 55 (May 2002): 1127–28; Rebecca Zwick, *Rethinking the SAT: The Future of Standardized Testing in University Admissions* (New York: Routledge, 2004), p. 109. For recent critiques of college admissions practices at elite, selective

colleges and universities, see, for example, Daniel Golden, *The Price of Admission: How America's Ruling Class Buys Its Way into Elites Colleges—and Who Gets Left Outside the Gates* (New York: Three Rivers Press, 2007); Jerome Karabel, *The Chosen: The Hidden History of Admission and Exclusion at Harvard, Yale, and Princeton* (New York: Houghton Mifflin, 2005).

8. Jessica R. Berenyi, "'Appropriate Action,' Inappropriately Defined: Amending the Equal Educational Opportunities Act of 1974," *Washington and Lee Law Review* 65 (Spring 2008): 643, n. 23.

9. P.L. 107-110, 115 Stat. 1425 (codified in scattered sections of 20 U.S.C.).

10. NCLB involves every state as all receive some level of federal Title I funding. However, not every school district within a state receives Title I funds. Nevertheless, various (but not all) parts of NCLB apply even to districts that do not receive Title I funds. For a helpful summary of NCLB's key parts, see James E. Ryan, "The Perverse Incentives of the No Child Left Behind Act," *New York University Law Review* 79 (June 2004): 944.

11. 20 U.S.C. 6311(b)(2) (Supp. II 2002).

12. 483 U.S. 203 (1987).

13. Ibid., p. 207.

14. *School District of City of Pontiac* v. *Spellings (Pontiac I)*, 05-CV-71535-D, 2005 WL 3149545 (E.D.Mich. November 23, 2005).

15. *School District of City of Pontiac* v. *Secretary of United States Department of Education (Pontiac II)*, 512 F.3d 252 (6th Cir. 2008), *vacated en banc* May 1, 2008.

16. Berenyi, "Appropriate Action," p. 643, n. 23.

17. U.S. Constitution, Fifth Amendment, and Fourteenth Amendment, sec. 1.

18. See, for example, Cal. Const. art. I, sec. 3, subdiv. (b)(4), which provides that "nothing in this subdivision supercedes or modifies any provision of this Constitution, including the guarantees that a person may not be deprived of life, liberty, or property without due process of law."

19. See Thomas S. Dee, "Learning to Earn," *Education Next,* vol. 2003, no. 3 (2003), p. 65.

20. See, for example, Tenn. Code Ann. sec. 49-6-6001 (2001).

21. See Jeri J. Goldman, "Political and Legal Issues in Minimum Competency Testing," *Educational Forum* 48 (June 1984): 207–16. It is important to note, however, that many states that made successful passage of MCT a condition for full high school graduation delayed the implementation of the graduation requirement to reduce legal exposure. See Thomas S. Dee, "The 'First Wave' of Accountability," in *No Child Left Behind?: The Politics and Practice of School Accountability,* edited by Paul E. Peterson and Martin R. West (Brookings, 2003), p. 217, n. 12.

22. For a discussion, see Dee, "First Wave," pp. 233–34.

23. See Frederick M. Hess, "Refining or Retreating? High-Stakes Accountability in the States," in *No Child Left Behind?* edited by Peterson and West, p. 70.

24. Ibid.

25. See Doris Ball and Darryl Paulson, "Back to Basics: Minimum Competency Testing and Its Impact on Minorities," *Urban Education* 19 (April 1984): 5–15.

26. See Hess, "Refining or Retreating?" p. 70.

27. Ibid.

28. See Ryan, "Perverse Incentives," p. 940.

29. 20 U.S.C. 6311(b)(2)(C)(v)(II).

30. Ibid., 6311(b)(2)(F).

31. As discussed in chapter 10, thus far litigation has not disrupted NCLB's core testing components.

32. Paul E. Peterson, "A Lens That Distorts," *Education Next,* vol. 2007, no. 4 (2007), p. 48.

33. Sec. 6316(b)(5), (8). A stricter set of consequences befalls schools that receive Title I funding and do not achieve AYP. Although Title I public schools are a subset of the entire population of public schools, over one-half of all public K–12 schools receive Title I funds. See Ryan, "Perverse Incentives," p. 942, n. 46.

34. Sec. 6316(a)(1)(B).

35. Sec. 6316(b)(1)(a).

36. Sec. 6316(b)(1)(E)(i).

37. Sec. 6316(b)(5)(B).

38. Secs. 6316(b)(7)(C)(iv)(I)–(VI).

39. Sec. 6316(b)(8)(B).

40. Ryan, "Perverse Incentives," p. 945.

41. Ibid.

42. How many students provided school options would exercise them is a matter of dispute. See, for example, Jay Mathews, "The Wrong Yardstick," *Washington Post,* April 3, 2008, p. W22.

43. See, for example, Sandra E. Black, "Do Better Schools Matter? Parental Valuation of Elementary Education," *Quarterly Journal of Economics* 114 (May 1999): 578, noting a correlation between student test scores and home values.

44. 20 U.S.C. 6319(a)(2).

45. Fla. Stat. 232.245(3) (1977).

46. Results from a third administration of the test, released during the trial, were consistent with results from the prior two iterations. Of the students required to take the test, 5.8 percent failed to pass before the end of their senior year in high school. Of those that failed, the failure rate of black students was approximately ten times that of white students. *Debra P. v. Turlington (Debra P. I),* 474 F.Supp. 244, 249 (M.D. Fla. 1979), *aff'd in part, vacated in part (Debra P. II),* 644 F.2d 397 (5th Cir. Unit B 1981), *remanded to* 564 F.Supp. 177 (M.D. Fla. 1983), *aff'd sub nom. Debra P. by Irene P. v. Turlington (Debra P. III),* 730 F.2d 1405 (11th Cir. 1984).

47. See *Debra P. I,* 248–49. See also Betsy A. Gerber, "High Stakes Testing: A Potentially Discriminatory Practice with Diminishing Legal Relief for Students at Risk," *Temple Law Review* 75 (Winter 2002): 868–69.

48. *Debra P. I,* 248–49; Gerber, "High Stakes," pp. 868–69.

49. *Debra P. I,* 266, 267.

50. Ibid.

51. Ibid., p. 265.

52. Ibid., p. 255–56.

53. Ibid., p. 254–55.

54. *Debra P. v. Turlington,* 564 F. Supp. 177 (M.D. Fla. 1983), *aff'd sub nom. Debra P. by Irene P.,* 730 F.2d 1405 (11th Cir. 1984).

55. *Debra P. by Irene P. v. Turlington,* 730 F.2d 1405, 1416 (11th Cir. 1984).

56. For a discussion of the Texas Assessment of Academic Skills as well as its even more rigorous successor, the Texas Assessment of Knowledge and Skills, see Keith L. Cruise and Jon S. Twing, "The History of Statewide Achievement Testing in Texas," *Applied Measurement in Education* 13 (January 2000): 329–30; O'Neill, "High Stakes Testing Law and Litigation," p. 649.

57. Tex. Educ. Code Ann. 39.025.

58. *G.I. Forum Image De Tejas* v. *Texas Education Agency,* 87 F.Supp. 2d 667, 673 (W.D. Tex. 2000).

59. Tex. Educ. Code Ann. 39.025.

60. See Frederick M. Hess, "Refining or Retreating? High-Stakes Accountability in the States," in *No Child Left Behind?* edited by Peterson and West, p. 74.

61. Ibid.

62. See Olatunde C. A. Johnson, "Disparity Rules," *Columbia Law Review* 107 (March 2007): 397–98, n. 106.

63. *GI Forum,* 676.

64. Ibid., p. 681.

65. Ibid., pp. 681–82, referencing *Debra P. by Irene P.,* 1416.

66. See, for example, Johnson, "Disparity Rules," p. 399.

67. See Cal. Educ. Code, 60850 ff.

68. See Arturo J. González and Johanna Hartwig, "Diploma Denial Meets Remedy Denial in California: Tackling the Issue of Remedies in Exit Exam Litigation after the Vacated *Valenzuela* v. *O'Connell* Preliminary Injunction," *Santa Clara Law Review* 47 (2007): 716.

69. Ibid., p. 718.

70. Ibid., p. 719.

71. *Valenzuela* v. *O'Connell,* CPF-06506050 (Super. Ct. of Cal., County of San Francisco, March 23, 2006).

72. *O'Connell* v. *Superior Court,* JCCP-4468, slip op. (Cal. May 24, 2006).

73. *O'Connell* v. *Superior Court,* 47 Cal.Rptr.3d, 147, 157 (Ct. App. 2006).

74. For a discussion of the settlement, see González and Hartwig, "Diploma Denial," pp. 743–51.

75. *O'Connell* v. *Superior Court,* 47 Cal.Rptr.3d, 162–66.

76. Ibid., p. 165.

77. See, for example, Robert J. Pushaw Jr., "Justiciability and Separation of Powers: A Neo-Federalist Approach," *Cornell Law Review* 81 (January 1996): 395–512.

78. See, for example, González and Hartwig, "Diploma Denial," pp. 740–43.

79. A.B. 347, 2007 Leg., 2007-08 Sess. (Cal. 2007) (www.leginfo.ca.gov/pub/07-08/bill/asm/ab_0301-0350/ab_347_bill_20071012_chaptered.pdf [July 2008]), amending sections 1240, 35186, 52378, and 52380 of the California Education Code.

80. 445 F. Supp. 1094 (D.S.C. 1977), *aff'd mem. sub. nom. National Educ. Ass'n* v. *South Carolina,* 434 U.S. 1026 (1978); 407 F. Supp. 1102 (N.D. Ga. 1776).

81. 445 F. Supp. 1094.

82. 407 F. Supp. 1107.

83. Ibid., p. 1114.

84. 963 So.2d 251 (FL. App. 4 Dist., 2006).

85. Florida Stat. Annot. Ch. 1012.34(3) (2003).

86. *Sherrod* v. *Palm Beach County School Board,* 963 So.2d 251–53.

87. Ibid., p. 253.

88. Florida Stat. Annot. Ch. 1012.34(3) (2008).

89. See, for example, Kristina P. Doan, "No Child Left Behind Waivers: A Lesson in Federal Flexibility or Regulatory Failure?" *Administrative Law Review* 60 (Winter 2008): 216–18.

90. See generally Tim Conlan and John Dinan, "Federalism, the Bush Administration, and the Transformation of American Conservatism," *Publius* 37 (Summer 2007): 278–89;

Michael Heise, "The Unintended Legal and Policy Consequences of the No Child Left Behind Act," *Nebraska Law Review* 86 (2007): 124, n. 28.

91. See, for example, Michael Heise, "Adequacy Litigation in an Era of Accountability," in *School Money Trials: The Legal Pursuit of Educational Adequacy,* edited by Martin R. West and Paul E. Peterson (Brookings, 2007), pp. 262–66; Marshall S. Smith, "What's Next?" *Education Week,* January 5, 2006, pp. 66, 70; Martin R. West and Paul E. Peterson, "The Adequacy Lawsuit: A Critical Appraisal," in *School Money Trials,* edited by West and Peterson, pp. 1, 6; Michael A. Rebell, "Educational Adequacy, Democracy, and the Courts," in *Achieving High Educational Standards for All: Conference Summary,* edited by Timothy Ready and others (Washington: National Academies Press, 2002); James S. Liebman, "Implementing *Brown* in the Nineties: Political Reconstruction, Liberal Recollection, and Litigatively Enforced Legislative Reform," *Virginia Law Review* 76 (April 1990): 378; compare James E. Ryan, "Standards, Testing, and School Finance Litigation," *Texas Law Review* 86 (May 2008): 1224, who disagrees with the conventional wisdom.

92. *Montoy* v. *State (Montoy II),* 102 P.3d 1160, 1164 (Kan. 2005) (per curiam), republished with concurring opinion *(Montoy III),* 120 P.3d 306 (Kan. 2005), supplemented by *(Montoy IV)* 112 P.3d 923 (Kan. 2005).

93. Kans. Const. art. VI, sec. 6.

94. School District Finance and Quality Performance, 1992 Kan. Sess. Laws 280.

95. Charles Berger, "Equity without Adjudication: Kansas School Finance Reform and the 1992 School District and Quality Performance Act," *Journal of Law and Education* 27 (January 1998), p. 28.

96. *Montoy* v. *State (Montoy I),* No. 99-C-1738, 2003 WL 22902963, *49 (Kan. Dec. 2, 2003).

97. Ibid., *45.

98. *Montoy II,* 1164.

99. *Montoy I, *47.

100. Ibid.

101. Ibid., *41

102. See Ryan, "Standards, Testing, and School Finance Litigation," p. 1224.

103. See *Neeley* v. *W. Orange-Cove Consolidated Independent School District,* 176 S.W.3d 746, 769–70 (Tex. 2005).

104. Ibid., 788.

105. Ibid.

106. Ibid., 789–90.

107. Ibid.

108. See, for example, Heise, "Unintended Legal and Policy Consequences," p. 119.

8

School Choice Litigation after Zelman

MARTIN R. WEST

In the highest profile decision of its 2002 term, the Supreme Court ruled in *Zelman* v. *Simmons-Harris* that Cleveland's fledgling school voucher program did not, in permitting low-income parents to use government funds to send their children to parochial schools, violate the First Amendment's ban on the establishment of religion.[1] Proponents of private school choice, led by President George W. Bush, hailed the ruling as the Court's most important education decision since *Brown* v. *Board of Education.*[2] Indeed, the president saw a direct connection between the two decisions. In *Brown,* the Court had ordered that the nation no longer operate two school systems, one for white children and another for blacks. In the Cleveland case, Bush said, the Court had affirmed that "our nation will not accept one education system for those who can afford to send their children to a school of their choice and another for those who can't."[3]

Yet for all of the fanfare, *Zelman* was hardly the final judicial intervention in the debate over school choice. This is not because it is a narrow or ambiguous decision. Despite the 5-4 split among the justices, the majority opinion provides unusually clear guidance on how to design a school voucher program in order to survive a challenge under the U.S. Constitution. Nor was the policy question at

I would like to thank Jessica Goldberg for her assistance in preparing this chapter and Clint Bolick and Jonathan Zimmerman for insightful comments.

stake unimportant. Because the inclusion of religious schools is vital to the growth of private school choice programs, uncertainty about its constitutionality was a major obstacle to their expansion. An adverse decision binding across all fifty states would have been devastating to the school voucher movement, at least in the short run.

Even so, programs that expand private school choice continue to face a bewildering array of legal challenges. Most of this activity has taken place in state courts, far below the radar of national policy discussions. Yet these post-*Zelman* challenges, which have so far been almost uniformly successful, continue to shape the pace and trajectory of choice-based reform. Three of the seven school voucher programs enacted nationwide between 2003 and 2006 have been found to be in violation of state constitutions, along with a fourth that had been in place since 1999. Significantly, two of these decisions were based on perceived violations of the education clauses of state constitutions rather than concerns about improper relations between church and state. Programs offering tax credits for donations to scholarship funds, an innovation embraced by advocates of private school choice largely because they appeared less susceptible to legal challenge, have meanwhile expanded at a steady clip. In April 2009, however, the U.S. Court of Appeals for the Ninth Circuit ruled that an Arizona tax credit program may unconstitutionally restrict parental choice by allowing participating organizations to award scholarships for only religious schools.

If anything, then, the pace of litigation has quickened in the years following *Zelman,* as school choice programs have proliferated and become more varied in their design. This is as expected. Not only are vouchers, tuition tax credits, and even charter schools controversial as a matter of public policy; they also provide alternatives to and thereby threaten the district-based system of education provision that has long been dominant in the United States. The courts provide groups with a stake in that system—most prominently, teachers unions, but also local school boards and allied advocacy organizations—with additional opportunities to block their enactment or limit their growth. Moreover, the lack of clear constitutional guidance or relevant precedent on many of the issues raised by modern school choice programs gives judges substantial discretion to issue decisions that reflect their ideological preferences or political needs.

The ongoing legal battle over private school choice, which I survey in this chapter, is thus a natural extension of a broader political conflict that has now raged for more than half a century. In the end, it is politics that will determine whether school choice initiatives move past the fringes of the American education system and become widespread. In the short run, however, both adverse judicial rulings and the uncertainty created by ongoing legal challenges continue to influence the design of programs and to constrain the growth of choice-based reform. Their net effect is to make the incremental pace of the expansion of parental choice in education all the more so.

The Road to *Zelman*

The Supreme Court's ruling in *Zelman* marked the end of the first wave of school voucher litigation, a wave dominated by the question of the permissibility of voucher use at religious private schools under the establishment clause of the U.S. Constitution. To resolve this issue, the Court was forced to carve a path through its own confusing and seemingly contradictory precedents concerning government aid to religious institutions, many of which dealt specifically with education. Its decision thus also served to culminate a decades-long reorientation away from tight restrictions on all such aid and toward broad approval of programs allowing government funds to reach religious schools on a nondiscriminatory basis via the independent decisions of private individuals.[4]

The widely acknowledged (and often ridiculed) difficulties in the Supreme Court's jurisprudence concerning aid to religious schools originate with its 1947 decision in *Everson* v. *Board of Education,* in which the Court articulated two competing principles that have guided its decisionmaking in this area.[5] On the one hand, said the Court, "No tax in any amount, large or small, can be levied to support any religious activities or institutions." In the very next paragraph, however, it held that the government "cannot exclude individual Catholics, Lutherans, Mohammedans, Baptists, Jews, Methodists, Non-believers, Presbyterians, or the members of any other faith, or lack of it, from receiving the benefits of public welfare legislation." Both principles, which came to be known as no aid (or strict separation) and nondiscrimination (or neutrality), represent attempts to discern the implications of the establishment clause's requirement that the government "make no law respecting an establishment of religion." A bare majority of five justices concluded in *Everson* that the program in question, through which the state of New Jersey provided free transportation to students attending religious schools, offered a general welfare benefit to individuals rather than aid to religious institutions. While quick to emphasize that nothing would prevent New Jersey from offering transportation only to students attending public schools, they were reticent to conclude that the state could not make transportation available to all students without regard for the type of school they chose to attend.

Although nondiscrimination won the day in *Everson,* in subsequent decisions the Court came to prioritize the no-aid principle. Most worrying for advocates of school vouchers was *Committee for Public Education* v. *Nyquist* (1973), in which the Court struck down a set of "parochiaid" programs enacted by New

York that included a partial reimbursement program for parents paying private school tuition.[6] The Court's decision emphasized the fact that the benefits offered by the state were available only to private schools and those who attended them. The legislature's stated intent for the programs was to forestall a decline in private school attendance that threatened to "aggravate an already serious fiscal crisis in public education." Nonetheless, because approximately 85 percent of the private schools in New York were religious, the Court concluded that their "primary effect" was to advance religion. Under the three-pronged test articulated in its 1971 *Lemon* v. *Kurtzman* decision, in which the Court had struck down a Pennsylvania law providing funds for teacher salaries and instructional materials for secular subjects in religious schools, this finding alone was sufficient to invalidate the program.[7] It was not necessary to inquire into the other two prongs of the Lemon test, which also required that aid programs have a "legitimate secular purpose" and not result in the "excessive entanglement of church and state."

Still, the Court dropped a footnote into its *Nyquist* decision suggesting that the "significantly religious character of the statute's beneficiaries might differentiate the present cases from a case involving some form of public assistance (e.g. scholarships) made available generally without regard to the sectarian-nonsectarian, or public-nonpublic nature of the institution benefited." A decade later, in *Mueller* v. *Allen,* the Court confirmed that this distinction indeed mattered, upholding a Minnesota program that offered a modest tax deduction for educational expenses, despite the fact that the vast majority of families claiming the deduction did so for private school tuition—and that 96 percent of those families sent their children to religious schools.[8] Justice William Rehnquist's majority opinion rejected the use of statistical criteria to discern the program's primary effect, emphasizing instead that the financial benefit was "neutrally available" to all parents and that its use to support religious instruction was "ultimately controlled by the private choices of individual parents."

The *Mueller* decision, however, was an outlier during a period in which the no-aid principle more often held sway in a string of cases dealing mainly with programs providing various types of benefits directly to religious schools. Most notably, in *Aguilar* v. *Felton* (1985) the Court invalidated New York City's use of Title I funds to pay the salaries of public school teachers who provided remedial instruction in secular subjects for low-income students on the campus of religious private schools.[9] Despite the program's clear secular purpose, the majority found that the observation system the city had established to monitor the content of Title I classes resulted in excessive entanglement of church and state. The program's constitutionality was already in doubt in light of past decisions suggesting that the mere presence of full-time government employees on religious school campuses constituted a symbolic endorsement of the schools' beliefs. *Aguilar,* however, suggested in addition that the very same measures New York City had adopted to ensure that its program conformed to the establishment clause ensured that it did not. The predictable (and expensive) result of the Court's decision was the nationwide proliferation of mobile classrooms outside of religious private schools in which teachers funded through Title I offered exactly the same services they had previously offered inside.[10]

Yet *Mueller* had suggested that the Court viewed programs that directly aided religious schools differently from those that did so only indirectly, as a result of the independent decisions made by students or their parents. Two subsequent cases confirmed the importance of this distinction. In *Witters* v. *Washington Department of Services for the Blind* (1986), the justices unanimously ruled that the establishment clause did not prohibit the state of Washington from allowing a student with an eye condition to use aid generally available to disabled students to attend a religious college in preparation for a career as a pastor.[11] Seven years later, a closely divided Court heard the case of James Zobrest, a deaf student who wished to attend a Catholic high school accompanied by an interpreter funded in part through the federal Individuals with Disabilities Education Act. The school district had rejected his request, and the Ninth Circuit agreed that the provision of an interpreter would violate the establishment clause. The Supreme Court's 5–4 decision in *Zobrest* v. *Catalina Foothills School District* reversed this outcome, again emphasizing the importance of independent choice. "By according parents freedom to select a school of their choice," wrote Chief Justice Rehnquist for the majority, "the statute ensures that a government-paid interpreter will be present in a sectarian school only as a result of the private decision of individual parents."[12]

As the Supreme Court continued to wrestle with the issue of aid to religious schools, the nation's first publicly funded school voucher programs were enacted, both in urban school districts with a history of deep educational dysfunction.[13] First out of the gate was the Milwaukee Parental Choice Program, established in 1990 at the urging of leaders in the local black community and Wisconsin's Republican governor, Tommy Thompson.[14] Voucher use was initially limited to secular private schools, in part because of constitutional concerns, but was expanded to religious schools in 1995 in order to accommodate growing demand. The Ohio legislature enacted the Cleveland Scholarship and Tutoring Program that same year, shortly after a federal district court, having declared a "crisis of magnitude" in the city's schools, placed the entire Cleveland Metropolitan School District under the state's control.[15] As in Milwaukee, voucher eligibility was limited to low-income students living within the central city school district.

Both programs were beset by legal challenges from their inception. The Milwaukee Teachers Education Association enlisted the head of the local chapter of the National Association for the Advancement of Colored People (NAACP) to serve as lead plaintiff in its first complaint, filed expeditiously in the summer of 1990 in an attempt to prevent the program's launch. Because the program did not yet include religious schools, the establishment clause was irrelevant. Instead, the plaintiffs alleged that the program violated three provisions of the state constitution. The trial court judge dismissed their complaints, allowing the program to get off the ground, but the state court of appeals invalidated the program as an unconstitutional local bill (because it applied only to Milwaukee) midway through the following school year. The program's status remained in doubt until the Wisconsin Supreme Court reversed that ruling in March 1992.[16]

Subsequent litigation following the Milwaukee program's expansion and the enactment of Cleveland's led eventually, after many twists and turns, to a mixed set of outcomes. Applying the criteria of independent choice and neutrality between religious and secular alternatives articulated in *Mueller, Witters,* and *Zobrest,* the Wisconsin Supreme Court in 1998 and the Ohio Supreme Court in 1999 deemed the inclusion of religious schools acceptable under both federal and state constitutions.[17] In 2000, however, a divided panel of the Sixth Circuit Court of Appeals found that the Cleveland program had the primary effect of advancing religion in violation of the establishment clause as applied in *Nyquist.*[18]

It was Ohio's appeal of this last decision that brought the issue of school vouchers before the Supreme Court. The justices had previously declined to review the 1998 decision upholding the Milwaukee program and a similar Arizona Supreme Court decision the following year upholding a tuition tax credit program.[19] However, the disagreement between the Wisconsin and Ohio Supreme Courts, on the one hand, and the Sixth Circuit, on the other—in part with respect to the very same program—made it likely that they would agree to hear the case. In fact, the Court granted certiorari in *Zelman* v. *Simmons-Harris* in September of 2001.

As Clint Bolick, who litigated the case on behalf of participating families, points out, the facts of the *Zelman* case presented advantages for both sides: "The program was a response to abysmal conditions in the Cleveland public schools, which cast it as a remedial program rather than an effort to aid religious schools; but the majority of children (roughly ninety-six percent) were enrolled in religious schools."[20] The Sixth Circuit panel had noted that the modest size of the vouchers, which were limited to $2,250 and 90 percent of tuition costs even for the city's poorest families, meant that religious schools were often the only feasible private option for participating students. The disproportionate share of voucher students attending religious schools also reflected the fact that the city's two largest secular private schools had converted to charter status so as to receive more state funding and that none of the suburban public school districts surrounding Cleveland had agreed to accept voucher students. Taking a broader perspective, research by Jay Greene showed that only 16.5 percent of Cleveland students using public funds in schools of choice (a category including magnet and charter schools) in the 1999–2000 school year attended religious schools.[21] Whatever the cause or context, however, the statistical evidence gave the voucher program a decidedly religious flavor.

Yet a majority on the Supreme Court ultimately deemed the preponderance of voucher students attending religious schools irrelevant. "The constitutionality of a neutral aid program," wrote Chief Justice Rehnquist in an opinion joined in full by five justices, "simply does not turn on whether and why, in a particular area, at a particular time, most private schools are run by religious organizations, or most recipients choose to use the aid at a religious school." What mattered instead was that the program offered aid "to a broad class of citizens who, in turn, direct government aid to religious schools wholly as a result of their own genuine and independent choice." The Court refrained from overturning its decision in *Nyquist,* noting instead that the programs invalidated in that case were designed to benefit religious schools and that the *Nyquist* court had not ruled on the constitutionality of a genuinely neutral aid program. As a result, it was able to present its decision in *Zelman* as one "in keeping with an unbroken line of decisions rejecting challenges to similar programs."

As was commonly the case on the Rehnquist court, it was Justice Sandra Day O'Connor who provided the pivotal fifth vote to uphold the Cleveland program. O'Connor's approach to indirect aid programs had been a matter of speculation owing to her dissent in *Zobrest,* in which she had voted to dismiss the case on a technicality and declined to reach a decision on its substance. In *Zelman,* however, she embraced the logic of *Zobrest* in full, writing separately to emphasize that the decision in no way marked "a dramatic break from the past." Her concurrence also emphasized that the question of whether an indirect aid program offered "true private choice" should be addressed by considering "all reasonable educational alternatives to religious schools that are available to parents." Citing the Greene study, she noted that religious schools played only a minor role in the city's overall system of school choice.

Zelman, it seems, arrived at the Supreme Court at precisely the right time for advocates of private school choice. By the turn of the twenty-first century, the Court's understanding of the situations in which government aid could reach religious schools had already changed. Consider the 1997 decision in *Agostini* v. *Felton,* in which the Court, having taken the highly unusual step of inviting a challenge to one of its own recent precedents, overturned *Aguilar* and allowed teachers funded through Title I to reenter religious private schools.[22] Citing *Witters* and *Zobrest,* the Court rejected its earlier assumptions that the mere presence of government employees on religious school campuses "constitutes a symbolic union between government and religion" and that "all government aid that directly aids the educational function of religious schools is invalid." What mattered instead was that the program did not "give aid recipients any incentive to modify their religious beliefs or practices in order to obtain program services." In other words, what mattered was neutrality. School voucher programs, given the central role they allowed for parental decisions over where to send their child to school, were even easier to fit within this emerging legal framework.

While conservative appointments to the Court clearly contributed to this reorientation, changes in the political climate surrounding private school choice were also critical.[23] Rapid growth in the number of private schools operated by non-Catholic denominations led evangelical Christian groups to reverse their position on the issue of government aid—from staunch opposition to vigorous support—and meant that voucher programs could no longer be seen as benefiting a single sect. And while the concept of private school choice had once been tainted by its association with efforts to resist integration, by the 1990s inner-city minorities had emerged as its most vocal supporters. Although the traditional civil rights organizations did not switch sides, new groups like the Black Alliance for Educational Options, which filed an amicus brief in *Zelman,* provided the justices with tangible evidence of this transformation.

Moreover, school voucher programs had now been operating in two major cities for some time, and the sky had not fallen. On the contrary, the justices were presented with evidence suggesting that participating families in both Milwaukee and Cleveland were quite satisfied with their private schools, that they seemed to be benefiting academically, and that the public school systems they left were responding in positive ways to the new competition. While the strength of the social science evidence supporting urban school voucher programs as a reform strategy continues to be debated, its very existence enabled the Institute for Justice, the public interest law firm that coordinated the defense of both the Milwaukee and Cleveland voucher programs, to highlight the implications of an adverse decision for educational equity. Their *Zelman* brief emphasized the fact that the Cleveland program was, first and foremost, an attempt to provide disadvantaged students in a long-troubled school system with new educational options.[24]

The end result of these developments was a definitive victory for advocates of private school choice: a decision that established clear and easily satisfied criteria to ensure a program's consistency with the establishment clause. Both school voucher and tuition tax credit programs provide aid to religious schools only as directed by the independent choices of parents. There is some ambiguity, especially in light of Justice O'Connor's retirement, as to whether and how broad an array of secular educational options in addition to neighborhood public schools is essential in order for a voucher program to survive constitutional scrutiny. Even so, meeting this requirement does not appear to be an important obstacle to the creation of new programs. All but a handful of states have charter school laws, and most urban school districts now offer parents some measure of choice among traditional public schools. The voucher program enacted in 2003 by Congress for Washington D.C., where more than one-quarter of students now attend charter schools, for example, is clearly acceptable under any plausible interpretation of the requirement for secular options. Subject only to the U.S. Constitution, it has not been challenged in the courts.

The Return to the States

While the victory for private school choice in *Zelman* was real, it was also incomplete. It did not end the legal battle but rather returned it to the state court systems in which it had begun. And while the Supreme Court's evolving understanding of the establishment clause in the years leading up to the *Zelman* decision had created an environment hospitable to private school choice programs, the legal terrain in the states is far less certain. Not only do many state constitutions contain their own language concerning aid to religious schools, but they also include provisions dealing with the organization and governance of state school systems that provide additional grounds for challenging the validity of new choice initiatives.

The pace of adoption of school voucher programs has accelerated since 2002, ensuring that state courts will continue to have ample opportunities to engage the issue. Along with the federal program in Washington D.C., programs for low-income students in specific districts have been enacted in Colorado (2003) and Louisiana (2008). Statewide programs for all special education students, students with particular disabilities, or students in foster care have been passed in Ohio (2003), Utah (2005), Arizona (two programs in 2006), and Georgia (2007). Ohio also enacted a statewide program for students in schools performing poorly under the state's accountability system in 2005.[25] In the twelve years between the creation of the Milwaukee program and *Zelman,* in contrast, only three voucher programs had been enacted nationwide: Cleveland's and two Florida programs launched in 1999.

Programs expanding private school choice through the tax code have also proliferated. While tax deductions or credits for educational expenses had long existed in states such as Iowa (1987), Illinois (1999), and Minnesota (1983), they offered only modest benefits that were not readily available to low-income families. The key policy innovation came in 1997, when Arizona enacted a tax credit for individuals making donations to organizations that offer students partial scholarships to attend private schools. Similar tax credit programs for corporations donating to scholarship organizations have now been enacted in Florida (2001), Pennsylvania (2001), Iowa (2006), Rhode Island (2006), Arizona (2006), and Georgia (2008). The number of students attending private schools with assistance from such programs far surpasses the number using vouchers issued directly by the government.

Religion Clauses of State Constitutions

At first glance, the most daunting legal obstacles to the spread of private school choice programs are state constitutional provisions concerning aid to religion, most of which are far more specific than the First Amendment. Roughly thirty-seven states have so-called Blaine amendments, which take their name from James G. Blaine, a nineteenth-century U.S. senator who proposed that a similar clause be added to the U.S. Constitution. Though their language varies, these provisions typically prohibit the use of government funds to "aid" or "benefit" religious institutions or schools. In some cases, they forbid aid from reaching religious institutions either "directly or indirectly." Twenty-nine state constitutions include "compelled support" clauses that prohibit the legislature from requiring citizens to support a religious ministry without their consent. Thirteen states have both types of restrictions; only Maine, North Carolina, and Louisiana have neither.[26]

As if to offer a reminder of the threat posed by these provisions, a trial court judge in Florida invalidated that state's Opportunity Scholarship Program (OSP) on Blaine amendment grounds less than two months after the *Zelman* decision.[27] Enacted in 1999, the program offered vouchers to students attending public schools that received an "F" grade from the state's accountability system twice in any four-year period. In linking voucher eligibility to school performance ratings, the OSP was the model for the public school choice provisions of No Child Left Behind and the more recent Ohio program. Several public school parents and organizations backed by the state's National Education Association (NEA) and American Federation of Teachers (AFT) affiliates (which subsequently merged) challenged the program under both the state and federal constitutions immediately following its enactment. The plaintiffs voluntarily dropped their First Amendment challenge in light of the *Zelman* decision but continued to litigate the case under the Florida Constitution. Judge P. Kevin Davey's August 2002 decision acknowledged the "salutary purpose of this legislation" but nonetheless concluded that "such a purpose does not grant this court the authority to abandon the clear mandate of the people as enunciated in the Constitution." An appeal from Governor Jeb Bush, the named defendant in the case, allowed the OSP to remain in operation temporarily. But the decision served to warn of what could lie ahead for newly enacted voucher programs.

State court decisions before *Zelman,* however, confirm that neither Blaine amendments nor compelled support provisions necessarily preclude the enactment of school voucher programs. The key interpretive issue is whether vouchers constitute aid only to students or also to the schools they choose to attend. The Wisconsin Supreme Court rejected challenges to the Milwaukee program based on both types of provisions, concluding that their state's constitution prohibited nothing more than what was already forbidden by the First Amendment.[28] Similarly, the Ohio Supreme Court rejected a challenge to the Cleveland program based on a compelled support provision.[29] The Vermont Supreme Court did rule in 1999 that a compelled support provision required the exclusion of religious private schools from the state's long-standing town-tuitioning program, through which students in towns that do not maintain a high school are provided with funds to attend a public or private school of their choice.[30] Interestingly, however, the same program included religious schools for the bulk of its history dating back to the nineteenth century, and the state Supreme Court had ruled in 1994 that such an arrangement was not precluded by the federal establishment clause (ignoring the issue of compelled support altogether).[31]

At least in the case of Blaine amendments, one reason state courts have avoided more expansive interpretations may be their sordid history.[32] Most of these amendments originated in the late 1800s, when public schools were ostensibly nonsectarian but in fact deeply infused with Protestant theology. Official Catholic doctrine at the time opposed the emergence of state-controlled school systems and required parents to seek out a suitable religious education for their children. Efforts by American Catholics to win public funding for the maintenance of parochial schools helped fuel the rise of anti-Catholic nativist sentiment that Senator Blaine attempted to exploit with his 1875 proposal to amend the U.S. Constitution. The original Blaine amendment would have applied the provisions of the First Amendment to the states while explicitly prohibiting them from appropriating funds to support schools under the control of a religious sect. Although the proposal narrowly failed to win the necessary supermajority support in the U.S. Senate, twenty-two states adopted similar provisions in the half-century following its defeat. In fact, Congress often required that newly formed states during this period include such language in their founding documents as a condition of joining the union.

Some legal scholars and historians have questioned whether all of the no-aid provisions of state constitutions can be fairly tainted by an association with anti-Catholicism. Steven Green, for example, asserts that they are best understood as part of a broader struggle to ensure the fiscal stability of emerging common school systems in which religious animus played only a small role.[33] He also suggests that many of the states that adopted no-aid clauses before the

Blaine amendment proposal did so "in the absence of any controversy over Catholic schooling or any nativist agitation."[34] Even so, Justice Clarence Thomas, in a 2000 opinion joined by Chief Justice Rehnquist and Justices Anthony Kennedy and Antonin Scalia, concluded in very general terms that "hostility to aid to pervasively sectarian schools has a shameful pedigree that we do not hesitate to disavow."[35]

Thomas's statement suggests another reason state courts may be reluctant to strike down school voucher programs on Blaine amendment grounds: to avoid the possibility of an appeal to the U.S. Supreme Court. A strong case can be made that to deny the same level of financial support to students attending religious schools as is provided to similar students attending nonreligious private schools amounts to discrimination based on religion. For religious families, such a policy might be overturned as a violation of their right to the free exercise of their religion as protected by the First Amendment. Moreover, the equal protection clause of the Fourteenth Amendment, as interpreted by the Court, requires that all religion-based classifications be subject to strict scrutiny. This means that in order to survive a constitutional challenge, states would be required to show that they have a compelling interest in preventing aid from reaching religious schools. In *Widmar* v. *Vincent* (1981), the Court rejected Missouri's use of the Blaine amendment and compelled support clauses of its state constitution to justify denying religious groups equal access to facilities at the University of Missouri.[36] An analogous decision concerning school vouchers would control the application of these clauses in all fifty states and would imply that any school choice program would have to include religious schools on equal terms with other private schools in order to survive constitutional scrutiny.

The Supreme Court had an opportunity to issue such a decision in *Locke* v. *Davey* (2004), which involved a college student in Washington denied a merit scholarship for which he had qualified because he was training to be a minister.[37] A 7-2 majority declined to do so, but on the narrow grounds that states had historically been allowed to withhold funding for the vocational training of clergy. It concluded that the funding of future ministers fell within the "play in the joints" between the free exercise and establishment clause of the First Amendment; while Washington could allow its citizens to use government funds to prepare for the ministry, it was not obligated to do so simply because it made funds available to students training for other professions. The Court evaded the issue of the origins of Washington's Blaine amendment by accepting the state's contention that its policy was guided by a different provision of the state constitution. As a result, although Blaine amendments and compelled support provisions can be interpreted in accordance with the establishment clause of the U.S. Constitution, they continue to loom as a potential barrier to school voucher programs in many states.

Tuition tax credit programs, in contrast, largely avoid this difficulty. Consider the argument of the Arizona Supreme Court in *Kotterman* v. *Killian*, a 1999 decision rejecting a challenge to the state's landmark program allowing dollar-for-dollar credits of up to $500 for individuals donating to scholarship funds.[38] Plaintiffs had alleged that the program violated several clauses of the state's constitution, including its aid clause requirement that "no tax shall be laid or appropriation of public money made in aid of any church, or private or sectarian school, or any public service corporation." The court noted, however: "No money ever enters the state's control as a result of this tax credit. Nothing is deposited in the state treasury or other accounts under the management or possession of governmental agencies or public officials. Thus, under any common understanding of the words, we are not dealing here with 'public money.'" As the decision went on to explain, a court ruling that a tax credit constitutes public money would effectively be forced to argue that all money is the government's, and that individuals are allowed to keep a certain portion of it for their own private use. It would also call into question such long-established practices as allowing tax deductions for donations to private schools and religious charities.

As the first decision dealing with a tax credit program designed to provide voucher-like scholarships for low-income students, the *Kotterman* precedent is significant. While state court decisions are not formally binding on courts in other states, they are often considered persuasive authority. At least with respect to state religion clauses, then, the tax credit mechanism has an important advantage over school vouchers. The programs in Florida, Pennsylvania, Rhode Island, Georgia, and Ohio have so far avoided legal challenge.

Education Clauses of State Constitutions

Most challenges to private school choice programs allege violations of not only religion clauses but also state constitutional provisions concerning the governance and organization of public schools. And while the Supreme Court's establishment clause jurisprudence influences and may ultimately constrain the interpretation of state religion clauses, courts face no such pressures when applying their own state's education clauses. Decisions from state high courts on matters of state law are not subject to federal review. Twice since 2004 they have resulted in the elimination of legislatively enacted voucher programs.

The first to fall was also the nation's first post-*Zelman* private school choice program, enacted by the Colorado legislature in April 2003.[39] Low-income, low-achieving students in eleven school districts whose performance the state had rated as "low" or "unsatisfactory" were to be eligible for vouchers funded through a mixture of state and local tax revenues. Caps on participation were to be gradually raised until they reached 6 percent of enrollment in each district, by which point up to 21,000 students statewide could have been using vouchers to attend private schools. Opponents filed suit before the program's implementation, however, alleging (among other things) that it violated the Colorado Constitution's guarantee that locally elected school boards "shall have control of instruction in the public schools of their respective districts."

The Colorado Supreme Court had in 1999 rejected a challenge to the state's charter school law based on this same clause.[40] The Denver school board had alleged in *Board of Education No. 1 in the City and County of Denver v. Booth* that the charter statute, by empowering the state board of education to require school districts to approve specific charter applications, infringed on its constitutionally protected authority. The court rejected this complaint, finding the constitution's grant of "general supervision" over public education to the state board sufficient to justify granting it the power to approve local charter schools. Although this interfered to some extent with local control of instruction, it did not have the effect of "usurping the local board's decision-making authority or its ability to implement, guide, or manage the educational programs for which it is ultimately responsible." At the same time, the court ruled that while the state board could order the approval of the charter application, it could not require the district to actually open the school or rubber-stamp all of the terms in the applicant's proposal. Rather, it determined that the state board's directive merely required the district to negotiate with the applicant over the "issues necessary to permit the applicant to open a charter school."

In its 2004 decision in *Owens v. Colorado Congress of Parents,* the court interpreted the guarantee of local control more broadly.[41] Despite the fact that the constitution mandates only that local school boards control "instruction in the public schools," it nonetheless held that requiring districts to divert local revenues to private schools through vouchers was invalid. Interestingly, the court relied heavily in its reasoning on a 1982 decision rejecting a challenge to the state's school finance system in which it had linked local control of instruction with the power to control locally raised funds.[42] In light of this precedent, the voucher program would undermine local control "by stripping local districts of any discretion over the character of instruction participating students will receive at district expense."

The implications of the *Owens* decision for other choice initiatives are limited, as only a handful of state constitutions contain specific guarantees of local control.[43] But the case illustrates the range of potential obstacles for school choice programs in state constitutions. Read alongside the same court's decision in *Booth* only five years earlier, it also suggests that state courts may be more willing to defer to the intent of the legislature when considering charter school programs, which generally face less intense political opposition, than when evaluating school vouchers.[44]

In contrast, the Florida Supreme Court's 2006 decision striking down the Opportunity Scholarship Program as a violation of its constitution's mandate to maintain a "uniform, efficient, safe, secure, and high-quality system of free public schools" may be more consequential.[45] Almost all state constitutions contain broad statements along these lines directing the legislature to make provision for public education. The choice of adjectives varies from state to state, with common formulations including "adequate," "uniform," "thorough and efficient," and "high-quality." Best known for their central role in school finance litigation, uniformity clauses were also used in early lawsuits challenging school voucher initiatives. Most courts easily dismissed these challenges, however, on the grounds that such provisions established a floor for legislative efforts to provide educational opportunities, not a ceiling. The Wisconsin Supreme Court, for example, concluded in 1992 that the Milwaukee voucher program "merely reflects a legislative desire to do more than what is constitutionally mandated."[46]

In *Bush* v. *Holmes,* a 5-2 majority on the Florida court found justification to depart from this pattern in the rarely used interpretive principle of *expressio unius est exclusio alterius,* or "the expression of one thing implies the exclusion of another." The Florida Constitution clearly obligates the legislature to provide public funds for public schools. This, the court reasoned, implies that it "prohibits the state from using public monies to fund a private alternative to the public school system," despite the fact that the constitutional text contains no such prohibition. The majority also faulted the program for failing "to ensure that the private school alternative to the public school system meets the criterion of uniformity" because private schools participating in the program were not required to follow the state's curricular standards or to employ only state-certified teachers. As Martha Derthick and Joshua Dunn have noted, however, "the uniformity clause, whatever it may mean, clearly applies only to public schools."[47]

Taken at face value, the sweeping logic of the decision would seem to call into question the full panoply of Florida programs that allow students to use public funds to attend private schools. It could also extend to charter schools, virtual schools, and other programs specifically designed to allow departures from "uniformity" within the public school sector. The court made a weak effort to distinguish such programs, suggesting that they are "structurally different from the OSP, which provides a systematic private school alternative to the public school system." But it is difficult to see what could distinguish the OSP from, among others, the state's popular McKay Scholarship Program for special education students that was enacted alongside it.

The decision in *Bush* v. *Holmes* was unusual in still another respect. As previously discussed, the trial court had in 2002 used the state's Blaine amendment to strike down the OSP, a decision that was later upheld by the appellate court.[48] Upon first hearing the case in 1999, however, the trial court had invalidated the program on the basis of the uniformity clause without considering the Blaine amendment challenge. In 2001 the Florida Supreme Court declined to review the appellate court's reversal of that decision, implicitly agreeing that the uniformity clause challenge was without merit.[49] While it is impossible to gauge the court's motivations in invalidating the program on the basis of an issue that it had already considered and rejected, it is reasonable to suspect that it sought to ensure that its decision would not be subject to federal review. Having found reason to reject the OSP under the uniformity clause, it was able to ignore the Blaine amendment complaint altogether.[50]

The Florida Supreme Court went on to stymie an attempt by supporters of private school choice to amend the state's constitution so as to undo the court's handiwork. In April 2008, the state's Taxation and Budget Reform Commission, a constitutionally mandated body convened once every twenty years to examine and propose state policy reforms, had submitted two amendments intended to restore the OSP and secure the status of the state's other private school choice programs.[51] The first would have repealed the state's Blaine amendment and substituted language stating that an individual or entity cannot be barred from participating in a publicly funded program because of religious belief. The second would have made clear that the state could carry out its educational obligations "at a minimum and not exclusively" by financing a uniform system of public schools.[52] The Florida Education Association challenged both proposals on the grounds that the commission had exceeded its constitutional mandate by proposing amendments unrelated to taxation or the state budgetary process. And the Florida Supreme Court ordered that they be removed from the ballot just seven weeks before the November election, reversing trial and appellate court decisions that had rejected the union's complaint.[53]

The decision in *Bush* v. *Holmes* is noteworthy not only because it marked the very first time that an established private school choice program had been discontinued, but also because it may provide a model for courts hostile to choice in other states. As mentioned earlier, most state constitutions contain language similar to that relied upon by the Florida court, and nothing in the tortured logic of the decision would suggest that it is limited to programs similar in design to the OSP, or even to programs including private schools. The contortions the court was forced to make in order to reach its preferred outcome may limit its influence, leading courts instead to look back to past decisions in Wisconsin and Ohio rejecting challenges to voucher programs under uniformity clauses. It is already clear, however, that the decision will at least serve as a model for continued challenges to school choice programs of all stripes across the nation.

Recent and Ongoing Litigation

The dust having momentarily settled in Florida, Arizona reemerged as the central battleground in the judicial conflict over private school choice, with three cases challenging four distinct programs decided within a span of six weeks in early 2009. Named plaintiffs in the cases included the Arizona affiliates of the NEA and AFT, the Arizona School Boards Association, the American Civil Liberties Union of Arizona, and the People for the American Way. The Institute for Justice, which opened its first state chapter in Arizona in 2001, intervened on behalf of program beneficiaries in all three.

While the major parties to the three cases were familiar, the challenges were in other respects atypical. Two involved idiosyncratic complaints against programs offering tax credits for donations to scholarship funds, programs of the kind that have elsewhere avoided legal challenge since Arizona's own *Kotterman* decision. Equally unusual was litigation involving two small voucher programs enacted in 2006. Modeled after Florida's McKay Scholarship Program, the challenged Arizona programs provide vouchers to students eligible for special education services or in foster care. Politically popular and seemingly consistent with the system of private placement under the federal Individuals with Disabilities Education Act (which permits students unable to receive appropriate instruction in public schools to enroll in religious or secular private schools), voucher programs for special education students in Florida, Georgia, Ohio, and Utah have not faced a court challenge.

The challenge to the individual tax credit program, initially filed in federal court in 2000 on the heels of *Kotterman*, alleged that the program violates the establishment clause by permitting participating organizations to provide scholarships only for schools of a particular religious denomination. This, the plaintiffs argued, means that the program as implemented does not offer parents genuine private choice as required under *Zelman*. The defendants responded that the program offers private choice not only to taxpayers claiming the credit, but also to parents accepting a scholarship, thus achieving "a double attenuation separating the state and religion."[54] They also asserted that the program should be evaluated within the context of the full range of choices available to Arizona parents, which includes both interdistrict open enrollment and charter schools in the public sector.

A Ninth Circuit panel including the famously liberal Stephen Reinhardt issued its decision in *Winn* v. *Garriott* in April 2009, embracing the plaintiffs' argument in full and remanding the case to the district court to ascertain whether participating organizations in fact limit the distribution of scholarships as alleged.[55] While the decision stopped short of ruling that scholarship tax credit programs in general are unconstitutional, absent a successful appeal it will limit the range of organizations able to offer scholarships in comparable tax credit programs—including the parallel program for corporate donations enacted by the Arizona legislature in 2006.

Interestingly, just weeks earlier a state appellate court had rejected a challenge to that program, deeming it consistent with the principles articulated in both *Kotterman* and *Zelman*.[56] Confronted with the same establishment clause issue as the Ninth Circuit, the Arizona court emphasized that any discrimination based on religion under the program is performed by participating organizations in distributing scholarships or by schools in admitting students, not by the state itself. The conflicting application of precedent by the two courts highlights the extent to which the precise parameters of private school choice under the U.S. Constitution remain uncertain, leaving judges at least limited room to impose their own views.

The irony in the outcome of the Ninth Circuit case is that the tax credit mechanism adopted by Arizona in order to avoid Blaine amendment challenges appears to have created a new legal pitfall; there is little doubt after *Zelman* that a similar program providing funds to parents directly in the form of vouchers would be acceptable as a matter of federal law. Still, the rationale behind the tax credit approach in states with strong constitutional prohibitions on aid to religious schools was confirmed by the near-simultaneous invalidation of Arizona's new voucher programs.

The Supreme Court of Arizona in *Cain* v. *Horne* upheld an appellate-level ruling that the voucher programs for special education and foster care students violate the aid clause of the Arizona Constitution, which states: "No tax shall be laid or appropriation of public money made in aid of any . . . private or sectarian school."[57] The court rejected the notion that the vouchers constituted aid to students rather than schools, arguing that such an interpretation "would nullify the Aid Clause's clear prohibition." "That the checks or warrants first pass through the hands of parents," it said, "is immaterial." The court thus ignored the appellants' argument that the aid clause would still ban direct grants to private schools for such purposes as facilities or teacher salaries even were the programs found to be valid. It also failed to distinguish the voucher programs from other Arizona programs in which beneficiaries use public funds to attend private schools at both the K–12 and postsecondary levels, thereby calling into question their status.

The decision was a major disappointment for voucher proponents. A decade earlier in *Kotterman* the same court had expressed concerns about the origins of the state's aid clause that it seemed would incline it toward a narrower interpretation. Having deemed the clause irrelevant because the program involved a tax benefit rather than an appropriation of public funds, the court nonetheless went on to examine the history of Blaine amendments in state constitutions. After describing the proposed federal Blaine amendment as a "clear manifestation of religious bigotry," it conceded that because Arizona did not enter the union until the twentieth century, its aid clause might not fall into the same category. If in fact it were shown to be related, however, the court said that it "would be hard pressed to divorce the amendment's language from the insidious discriminatory intent that prompted it."[58]

The *Cain* decision, in contrast, made no mention of religious animus. It traced the origins of the aid clause instead to the framers' desire to foster a "strong public school system . . . by prohibiting appropriation of funds from the public treasury to private schools." Moreover, because Arizona's is one of the few state constitutions that prohibits aid to both private and religious schools, the decision provides no grounds for an appeal that would give the U.S. Supreme Court an opportunity to consider the use of Blaine amendments to ban aid from reaching religious private schools through neutral programs of private choice.[59]

The only bright side of the decision for advocates of private school choice is that the court did not have the opportunity to invalidate the programs on the basis of the education clause of the Arizona constitution, which, much like Florida's, mandates the "establishment and maintenance of a general and uniform public school system." The plaintiffs did not include a uniformity clause challenge in their initial complaint but hastily added one in light of the Florida Supreme Court's decision in *Bush* v. *Holmes*. The appellate court essentially ignored this aspect of the plaintiffs' argument after basing its decision on the aid clause.[60] The issue was not addressed in the appeal.

Conclusion

Though filed in different venues and on widely varying grounds, recent and ongoing legal challenges to private school choice programs follow a common pattern that was established well before the Supreme Court issued its decision in *Zelman.* The programs most commonly targeted are those offering vouchers to low-income students in failing schools or districts, all but one of which have been challenged and two of which have been eliminated or kept from starting as a result of judicial intervention. In contrast, voucher programs for other populations and tuition tax credit programs have, with the exception of those in Arizona, not been touched. The legal status of tax credits differs in part from that of vouchers because they do not involve government appropriations—a factor that may explain why state legislatures are increasingly turning to this alternative. But it is hard to see why a voucher program for special education students should be constitutional while one for low-income students is not.

Plaintiffs in the cases invariably include organizations representing the public school system or its employees. Typically they are joined by advocacy groups such as the People for the American Way opposed to the use of government funds in religious institutions regardless of whether it is individuals who ultimately make that decision. Rather than focus on a single issue, however, their complaints typically take a "shotgun" approach, offering an assortment of charges based on multiple constitutional provisions in the hopes that courts will find merit in at least one. The diverse and constantly evolving nature of their complaints suggests that their fundamental objection to private school choice is not legal but policy based.[61] It is therefore unfortunate that they persist in asking the courts to revisit policy decisions made by more representative bodies.

Notes

1. 536 U.S. 639 (2002).

2. 347 U.S. 483 (1954).

3. "President Lauds Supreme Court School Choice Decision," press release, July 1, 2002 (www.whitehouse.gov/news/releases [October 1, 2008]).

4. Douglas Laycock, "Why the Court Changed Its Mind about Government Aid to Religious Institutions: It's a Lot More than Just Republican Appointments," *Brigham Young University Law Review* 2008, no. 2 (2008): 275–94.

5. 330 U.S. 1 (1947).

6. 413 U.S. 756 (1973).

7. 403 U.S. 602 (1971).

8. 463 U.S. 483 (1983).

9. 473 U.S. 402 (1985).

10. William W. Bassett, "Changing Perceptions of Private Religious Schools: Public Money and Public Trust in the Education of Children," *Brigham Young University Law Review* 2008, no. 2 (2008): 243–74.

11. 474 U.S. 481 (1986).

12. 509 U.S. 1 (1993).

13. There are also long-standing programs in Vermont and Maine through which students in towns that do not maintain a high school are provided with funds to attend a public or private school of their choice.

14. Frederick M. Hess, *Revolution at the Margins: The Impact of Competition on Urban School Systems* (Brookings, 2002).

15. *Reed* v. *Rhodes,* 1 F. Supp. 2d 705 (U.S. Dist. 1995).

16. *Davis* v. *Grover,* 480 N.W.2d 460 (Wis. 1992).

17. *Jackson* v. *Benson,* 578 N.W.2d 602 (Wis.), *cert. denied,* 525 U.S. 997 (1999); *Simmons-Harris* v. *Goff,* 711 N.E.2d 203 (Ohio 1999).

18. *Simmons-Harris* v. *Zelman,* 234 F.3d 945 (6th Cir. 2000).

19. *Kotterman* v. *Killian,* 972 P.2d 606 (Ariz.), *cert. denied,* 528 U.S. 921 (1999).

20. Clint Bolick, "The Constitutional Parameters of School Choice," *Brigham Young University Law Review* 2008, no. 2 (2008): 335–51.

21. Jay P. Greene, "The Racial, Economic, and Religious Context of Parental Choice in

Cleveland," prepared for the annual meeting of the Association for Policy Analysis and Management, Washington D.C., November 5, 1999.

22. 521 U.S. 203 (1997).

23. James Forman Jr., "The Rise and Fall of School Vouchers: A Story of Religion, Race, and Politics," *UCLA Law Review* 54 (February 2007): 547–604; Laycock, "Why the Court Changed Its Mind about Government Aid to Religious Institutions."

24. Brief of the Institute for Justice in *Taylor* v. *Simmons-Harris,* June 27, 2002.

25. The Utah legislature also passed a universal voucher plan in 2007 that voters subsequently rejected in a statewide referendum. See Clint Bolick, "Voting Down Vouchers," *Education Next* 8 (Spring 2008): 46–51.

26. Richard D. Komer, "School Choice: Answers to Frequently Asked Questions about State Constitutions' Religion Clauses," Institute for Justice, updated September 2006 (www.ij.org [October 1, 2008]).

27. *Holmes* v. *Bush,* CV 99-370, slip op. (Fla. Cir. Ct. August 5, 2002).

28. *Jackson* v. *Benson,* 602.

29. *Simmons-Harris* v. *Goff,* 203.

30. *Chittenden* v. *Town Sch. Dist.* v. *Dep't of Educ.,* 738 A.2d 539 (Vt. 1999); *cert denied, Andrews* v. *Vermont Dep't of Educ.,* 528 U.S. 1066 (1999).

31. Komer, "School Choice."

32. Joseph Viteritti, "Blaine's Wake: School Choice, the First Amendment, and State Constitutional Law," *Harvard Journal of Law and Public Policy* 21 (Summer 1998): 657–718.

33. Steven K. Green, "The Blaine Amendment Reconsidered," *American Journal of Legal History* 36 (January 1992): 38–69.

34. Steven K. Green, "The Insignificance of the Blaine Amendment," *Brigham Young University Law Review* 2008, no. 2 (2008): 312.

35. *Mitchell* v. *Helms,* 530 U.S. 793 (2000).

36. 454 U.S. 263 (1981).

37. 540 U.S. 712 (2004).

38. *Kotterman* v. *Killian,* 606.

39. Lance Fusarelli, "Will Vouchers Arrive in Colorado?" *Education Next* 4, no. 4 (2004): 51–55.

40. 984 P.2d 639 (Colo. 1999).

41. 92 P.3d 933 (Colo. 2004).

42. 649 P.2d 1005 (Colo. 1982).

43. Richard Briffault, "The Local School District in American Law," in *Besieged: School Boards and the Future of Education Politics,* edited by William G. Howell (Brookings, 2005), pp. 24–55.

44. Although similar percentages of Americans support school vouchers and charter schools, the share opposed to charter schools is much lower as many Americans remain undecided. See William G. Howell, Martin R. West, and Paul E. Peterson, "The 2008 Education Next-PEPG Survey of Public Opinion," *Education Next* 8 (Fall 2008): 12–26.

45. *Bush* v. *Holmes,* 919 So. 2d 392 (Fla. 2006).

46. *Davis* v. *Grover,* 460; *Jackson* v. *Benson,* 602. See also *Simmons-Harris* v. *Goff,* 203, which rejected a uniformity clause challenge to the Cleveland voucher program but struck it down as an unconstitutional local bill, forcing the legislature to reenact the program.

47. Joshua Dunn and Martha Derthick, "Florida Grows a Lemon," *Education Next* 6 (Summer 2006): 11. For useful critiques of the decision in *Bush* v. *Holmes,* see Irina Manta, "Missed Opportunities: How the Courts Struck Down the Florida School Voucher Program,"

Saint Louis University Law Journal 51 (Fall 2006): 185–202; Jason A. Pfeil, "Casenote: No Vouchers for You! The Supreme Court of Florida's Avoidance of Inconvenient Precedent in *Bush* v. *Holmes,*" *Florida Coastal Law Review* 8 (Summer 2007): 173–89.

48. *Bush* v. *Holmes,* 886 So. 2d 340 (Fla. 1st DCA 2004).

49. *Bush* v. *Holmes,* 797 So. 2d 668 (Fla. 1st DCA 2000); *Holmes* v. *Bush,* 790 So. 2d 1104 (Fla. 2001).

50. Bolick, "Constitutional Parameters of School Choice."

51. Mary Ellen Klas, "School Voucher Amendment Headed to Voters in November," *Miami Herald,* April 26, 2008 [www.lexisnexis.com.us/lnacademic [October 1, 2008]).

52. To increase its chances of passing, the Second Amendment was paired with a requirement that school districts spend 65 percent of overall funding on classroom instruction, a policy popular with voters in other states.

53. *Ford* v. *Browning,* 33 Fla. L. Weekly S 641 (Fla. 2008).

54. Brief of Appellees filed by the Institute for Justice in *Winn* v. *Killian,* September 7, 2005.

55. No. 05-1574 (9th Cir. 2009).

56. *Green* v. *Garriott,* 552 Ariz. Adv. Rep. 21 (Ariz. Ct. App. 2009).

57. 202 P.3d 1178 (Ariz. 2009).

58. 972 P.2d 606 (Ariz. 1999).

59. However, in November 2008 the Institute for Justice filed a federal lawsuit challenging Washington state's use of its Blaine amendment to prohibit students entitled to private placement under the Individuals with Disabilities Education Act from attending religious schools. "Freeing Special Needs Students from Religious Discrimination in Washington State," press release, November 11, 2008 (www.ij.org/index.php?option=com_content&task =view&id=2454&Itemid=165 [May 15, 2009]).

60. 183, P.3d 1269 (Ariz App. 2008).

61. Indeed, the general counsel for the National Education Association appears to have admitted as much. See Clint Bolick, *Voucher Wars: Waging the Legal Battle for School Choice* (Washington: Cato Institute, 2003).

9

Talking about Religion: Separation, Freedom of Speech, and Student Rights

JOSHUA M. DUNN

Education and religion have repeatedly collided in court. Most of these collisions have occurred under the First Amendment's establishment clause, which forbids laws "respecting an establishment of religion." Moreover, most of the Supreme Court's decisions defining the meaning of the establishment clause have been driven by conflicts over education policy. The results have not been encouraging, with the Court inflicting on school officials a doctrinal farrago that seems designed not to clarify but to generate legal uncertainty and litigation. Because of this confusion, few areas of constitutional law receive the derision heaped on the Court's establishment clause jurisprudence, which a Fifth Circuit opinion despaired of as a "vast, perplexing desert."[1] If federal judges are baffled, what hope can there be for school boards, principals, and teachers?

Of course, not all legal issues at the intersection of religion and education are unclear. A 1995 joint statement on religion and the public schools signed by a variety of secular and religious organizations—including the American Civil Liberties Union (ACLU) and Christian Legal Society (CLS)—noted that "while there are some difficult issues [remaining], much has been settled."[2] Many of these and the earlier controversies have been the result of school officials' misunderstanding of the law. Their confusion is not so surprising given the dogmatic-sounding metaphor of separation of church and state that the Court has grafted

I would like to thank Becca Siegel and Kyla Walstad for their research assistance.

onto the establishment clause, and that many have improperly taken to mean that schools are to be "religion-free zones." Even so, the past three decades have witnessed the domestication of part of this inhospitable region of the law—but not because of establishment clause litigation, with the notable exception of school choice and the Court's clear but closely divided opinion in *Zelman* v. *Simmons-Harris* (2002).[3]

Rather, religious litigants, tired of losing establishment clause cases, began relying on the First Amendment's free speech clause, which forbids laws "abridging the freedom of speech." The doctrines the Court has developed under this clause, such as viewpoint and content neutrality, are relatively clear and robust. Since religion naturally involves expression, religious groups recognized that a large number of their establishment clause disputes, such as those over access to school facilities, could also be framed as free speech claims. Under the Court's "public forum doctrine," the government generally cannot restrict access to facilities open to other groups on the basis of the content of someone's speech. As a result, religious litigants saw far greater success with this new strategy, often winning unanimous decisions before the Supreme Court.

At the same time, some important issues remain unresolved because of the peculiar status of free speech in K–12 education arising out of the Court's most significant school speech decision in *Tinker* v. *Des Moines* (1969).[4] Until recently, the Court was able to address many of these issues without relying on *Tinker,* but that will be unlikely in the next round of litigation over religious speech. In *Tinker,* the Court declared that students' free speech rights do not stop at the schoolhouse door but added the somewhat vague caveats that speech creating a "substantial disruption" of school activities or that "impinges upon the rights others" could be censored. To confuse matters even more, the Court in later cases invoked another standard holding that schools do not have to tolerate speech that undermines their "basic educational mission."[5] The central controversies regarding students' free speech rights flow from the attempts to make sense of this very loose language. Most recently, *Morse* v. *Frederick* (also known as "Bong Hits for Jesus") offers a glimpse of the nettlesome legal disputes over these questions that are on the horizon.[6] Because the disputes over student speech, at least the most contentious ones, hark back to religion, the courts remain unable to clearly define the contours of student free speech rights in public schools.

Examining how establishment clause jurisprudence created this educational confusion and prompted the turn to freedom of speech will help clarify the coming disputes over religious speech that will be litigated under *Tinker* and its progeny. Most important, the Court should resist the temptation to rely on a school's "basic educational mission" to justify upholding restrictions on speech and should instead rely on traditional doctrines such as viewpoint neutrality.

While the "basic educational mission" of schools would appear to grant substantial discretion to school officials, its vagueness would undoubtedly invite litigation, forcing the Court to formulate inscrutable distinctions (as it has under the establishment clause), as well as policy judgments about the purposes of public education that the Court is ill equipped to make.

Establishment Clause Chaos

Since *Everson* v. *Board of Education* (1947), which marks the beginning of modern establishment clause jurisprudence, the Supreme Court has decided sixty-seven establishment clause cases.[7] More than half of them involved K–12 education.[8] In *Everson* the Court declared that the Constitution "erected a wall of separation" between church and state that is "high and impregnable." But the Court's decision implied the separation would be difficult to maintain when it invoked the two contradictory principles of no aid and of nondiscrimination. These competing positions would come to be known as strict separation and accommodation.[9]

At issue in *Everson* was a New Jersey school district policy reimbursing parents for the cost of transporting their children to private schools, including parochial ones. Under state law, school districts had the authority to regulate the transportation of students. The Court's majority ruled: "No tax in any amount, large or small, can be levied to support any religious activities or institutions, whatever they may be called, or whatever form they may adopt to teach or practice religion." Thus *Everson*'s principle of separation meant that the government could give no aid directly to religion. But the majority also decided that the program was constitutional since the aid went to parents rather than to schools. Relying on a principle of nondiscrimination, the Court said that New Jersey could not be forbidden from "extending its general state law benefits to all its citizens without regard to their religious belief." The dissenters agreed that the establishment clause required separation but argued that the principle mandated that the program be struck down. This disagreement foreshadowed the deeply subjective and incoherent application of the principle of separation that was to come.

Some of the problems surfaced just five years after *Everson,* in *Zorach* v. *Clausen* (1952), when the Court upheld a program allowing public school students time for religious instruction during the school day off school grounds.[10] In justifying the decision, Justice William O. Douglas noted that a truly consistent application of separation would lead to obviously absurd results: "Churches could not be required to pay even property taxes" and "municipalities would not be permitted to render police or fire protection to religious groups." Thus as long as religion exists, church and state will inevitably have some interaction, and some aid will inevitably go to religious organizations. The confusions created by the doctrine of separation led Robert M. Hutchins to complain a decade later: "[The] wall has done what walls usually do: it has obscured the view. It has lent a simplistic air to the discussion of a very complicated matter. Hence, it has caused confusion whenever it has been invoked. Far from helping to decide cases it has made decisions unintelligible. The wall is offered as a reason. It is not a reason; it is a figure of speech."[11]

Nonetheless, by the early 1960s, separation had won the day over nonpreferentialism. As the Court applied the principle of separation, it reached clear but controversial decisions outlining what separation required. What accounted for the clarity, however, was the simplicity of the issues rather than the principle. In *Engel* v. *Vitale* (1962) and *Abington* v. *Schempp* (1963), for example, the Court ruled respectively that state-mandated school prayer and devotional Bible reading violated the principle.[12] These were but two of the Court's frequent countermajoritarian decisions on church-state issues. Gallup polls since *Engel* show substantial majorities supporting prayer in public schools, for instance.[13] Moreover, many states simply refused to comply with these decisions.[14] Even though controversial, public school prayer and Bible reading allowed for relatively straightforward remedies and thus provided little help in evaluating other more complicated controversies such as state aid to religious schools.

In 1971 the Court tried to clarify the meaning of separation and its concomitant principle of no aid to religion with a three-pronged test, enunciated in *Lemon* v. *Kurtzman* I.[15] In *Lemon* the Court struck down a Pennsylvania law that allowed the state to reimburse private schools for teachers' salaries and instructional materials. The Court held that government action (1) must have a secular legislative purpose, (2) cannot have the primary effect of advancing or inhibiting religion, and (3) must not create an excessive entanglement with religion. The test was supposed to provide a clear standard by which to evaluate possible violations of the no-aid requirements undergirding the principle of separation. However, the *Lemon* test created only the illusion of clarity. In practice, it was impossible to employ consistently and produced even greater uncertainty and confusion.

For example, the first prong could require courts to strike down legislation with clear secular effects if it was promoted for religious reasons.[16] This has forced courts to assess the motivations of lawmakers, which the latter can simply disguise to satisfy this aspect of the test. Consider the status of moments of silence under the Court's jurisprudence. Under the first prong of the *Lemon* test, the Court struck down Alabama's mandated moment of silence for student "meditation or voluntary prayer" in *Wallace* v. *Jaffree* (1985).[17] It found that the legislative history of the law indicated that the purpose of the state legislature was religious and not secular. But if states want a moment of silence and do not broadcast their religious motivations, the legislation can pass judicial scrutiny. According to the National Conference of State Legislatures, a dozen states have such legislation, some of which predates *Wallace* v. *Jaffree.* Furthermore, nearly twenty states allow teachers to require such moments in their classes at the teacher's discretion.[18]

Perhaps the most problematic part of the *Lemon* test is that prongs two and three seem contradictory, or at least in tension with each other. How can one know the primary effect of a government action without close monitoring of a religious organization? But that monitoring risks excessive entanglement.[19] As a result, many Supreme Court justices have called for the *Lemon* test to be abandoned. Even more troubling, the Court has not always relied on the *Lemon* test. This inconsistency led Justice Antonin Scalia to ridicule the Court's invocation of the test in *Lamb's Chapel* v. *Center Moriches Union Free School District:* "Like some ghoul in a late-night horror movie that repeatedly sits up in its grave and shuffles abroad after being repeatedly killed and buried, *Lemon* stalks our establishment clause jurisprudence once again, frightening the little children and school attorneys of Center Moriches Union Free School District."[20]

Not surprisingly, as establishment clause precedents accumulated, the Court came to bizarrely contradictory positions that it made no meaningful attempt to justify. For example, the Court held that it was constitutional to provide bus rides for children attending religious schools but not from a religious school to a museum for a field trip.[21] It also decided that the government could not subsidize science and history instruction at religious schools but that it could subsidize religious organizations instructing students in proper sexual behavior.[22] And most famously, it ruled that the government could provide pupils at religious schools with books but not maps.[23] This last absurdity led an exasperated Senator Daniel Patrick Moynihan to inquire about the constitutional status of atlases.[24]

The Court's confused and confusing interpretation of the establishment clause has been paralleled by criticism of both the metaphor of separation and the *Lemon* test. The historical evidence presented by constitutional scholars such as Phillip Hamburger and Daniel Dreisbach casts substantial, even overwhelming, doubt on the notion that the authors of the First Amendment intended the establishment clause to separate church and state in the way the Court has maintained.[25] Akhil Amar and Phillip Munoz have argued that the establishment clause was a "federalism" clause, which was there to protect states.[26] "To apply the clause against a state government," says Amar, "is precisely to eliminate its right to choose whether to establish a religion—a right clearly confirmed by the establishment clause itself."[27] Thus attempts to do so will necessarily strain and contort the clause's language.

If the *Lemon* test and its application had only been incoherent, religious groups would have simply had the same complaint as everyone else, but they found it inherently and unconstitutionally hostile to religion. Indeed, when applying the second prong of the *Lemon* test, the Supreme Court did not ask if the principle or primary effect was to advance religion but whether government action aided religion at all. "The constitutional requirement of 'primary secular effect,'" observed Harvard Law's Laurence Tribe, has "become a misnomer; while retaining the earlier label, the Court has transformed it into a requirement that any non-secular effect be *remote, indirect, and incidental.*"[28] The reason for this transformation was that the no-aid standard at the core of *Lemon* and *Everson* was itself oriented against religion. As John Jeffries and James Ryan of the University of Virginia Law School have noted, "the blurred margins of the no-aid policy should not disguise its effect. *Everson* drew the line between permissible support for education and impermissible aid to religion very far to one side."[29] As a result, most religious litigants of the past four decades lost their Court disputes over K–12 education, particularly up to the mid-1990s, when their claims relied on the establishment clause.[30]

Since the mid-1990s, the Court has become slightly more "accommodationist." In *Agostini* v. *Felton* (1997), it overturned its twelve-year-old ruling from *Aguilar* v. *Felton* (1985), which had struck down the reimbursement of public employees who were sent to parochial schools to provide remedial instruction for low-income school students.[31] In *Mitchell* v. *Helms* (2000), the Court upheld lending educational materials to religious schools under chapter 2 of the Education Consolidation and Improvement Act of 1981.[32] Most significantly, in 2002 the Court upheld the constitutionality of school vouchers in *Zelman* v. *Simmons-Harris.*[33]

The obvious reason for the Supreme Court's more accommodating stance toward religion was the gradual change in its composition with the addition of more conservative justices during the 1980s and 1990s. Of course, Justices Scalia and Clarence Thomas have been the most accepting of government aid to religion, with Justice Anthony Kennedy generally but not always joining them. Even Justice Stephen Breyer, typically part of the Court's liberal bloc, has voted to uphold government aid in some cases, as in *Mitchell* v. *Helms.* While these changes in personnel were important, legal scholars have increasingly recognized that it is an insufficient explanation. Douglas Laycock, John Jeffries, and James Ryan, for example, have all argued that the decline of anti-Catholicism along with the rise of evangelical support for government aid to private schools helped create a strong religious coalition opposed to the Court's no-aid doctrine.[34]

Despite the trend toward accommodation, confusion over religion in public schools persists. Although there is no precedent precluding any reference to Christmas or Easter break, many schools and school districts have chosen the more benign "winter and spring break" simply to avoid crossing a still extremely blurry line between acceptable and unacceptable religious activity. At times, this strategy has angered religious parents and students (and Fox News) who find scrubbing such seasons of all religious references to be a sign of hostility to religion.[35]

The clearest principle that can be divined about what schools can and cannot do concerning holidays is that school officials should make certain to surround religious elements with sufficiently secular material. The Court established this requirement in *Lynch* v. *Donnelly,* which upheld the display of a crèche on public property because it was surrounded by secular seasonal displays such as a Santa Clause house.[36] This standard, if one can call it that, was nicknamed "the two Rudolphs and a Frosty" rule, implying that religious themes on public property are acceptable if diluted by secular displays. Of course, government officials cannot know how many secular displays are needed to satisfactorily dilute religious symbols. There is also disagreement about what counts as a secular display. In *Allegheny* v. *ACLU,* the Court struck down a courthouse display of a crèche but upheld the display of a menorah alongside a Christmas tree, reasoning that Christmas trees had become a secular symbol of the season.[37] Some protested the Court's declaration, however, arguing that anything reminding an observer of Christmas inevitably points to Christianity and that any attempt to pick and choose secular and religious displays is therefore an exercise in judicial willfulness.[38]

The opaqueness of legal doctrine in this area is also illustrated by the profoundly unhelpful advice provided by legal guidebooks for administrators and teachers. One book suggests "there should be no worship or devotional services nor religious pageants or plays of any nature held in the school. However, certain programs may be conducted if a secular purpose is clearly served. . . . School choirs and assemblies may be permitted to sing or play holiday carols, as long as these activities are held for entertainment purposes rather than religious purposes." In the event of conflicts over displays of generic religious mottos used by the government such as "In God We Trust," the guide offers, "only time will reveal how the courts will address these emerging conflicts."[39] According to another such book, "decisions about what to do in December should begin with the understanding that public schools may not sponsor religious devotions or celebrations; study about religious holidays does not extend to religious worship or practice. Does this mean that all seasonal activities must be banned from the schools? Probably not." Furthermore, "school concerts that present a variety of selections may include religious music. Concerts should, however, avoid programs dominated by religious music, especially when these coincide with a particular religious holiday."[40] These books essentially tell school administrators to be as careful as possible and hope they will not be sued.[41]

While the incoherence of the Court's doctrine is primarily responsible for ongoing litigation, another reason has been the mobilization over the last three decades of "New Christian Right" public interest law firms determined to counteract the legal efforts of the American Civil Liberties Union (ACLU). Jay Sekulow, the chief counsel of the American Center for Law and Justice (ACLJ), believes that school officials legitimately fear "mutual lawsuits" from the ACLU and religious public interest firms.[42] One of the ACLJ's allies, the Alliance Defense Fund (ADF), undertakes an annual "Christmas project" to inform thousands of school districts that it will provide free legal representation from its battalion of attorneys against attempts by the ACLU and others to eliminate religious expression from schools.[43] One example, among many, of the ACLJ and ADF attempting to counteract the ACLU came in Wilson, Tennessee. The ACLU petitioned the court to stop religious activity such as a "See You at the Pole" prayer meeting by Christian students and the singing of Christmas carols at kindergarten Christmas celebrations. In response, the ACLJ provided representation for school officials while the ADF represented parents opposed to the ACLU request. The ACLU lost on most of its claims.[44] The websites of the ACLJ, ADF, and other religious legal firms such as Liberty Legal Institute (LLI), Thomas More Law Center (TMLC), Liberty Counsel (LC), and Rutherford Insitute (RI) contain descriptions of dozens of similar lawsuits.[45]

Rescuing Religion

Even as criticism of its establishment clause jurisprudence grew, the Supreme Court persisted in its decades-long confusion largely because the justices could not agree on what could replace its unwieldy doctrines. For religious groups, this persistence called for a change in legal strategy. Following loss after loss under the establishment clause, attorneys for the New Christian Right recognized that many of their issues could be brought on free speech grounds. This move has to be one of the most successful political legal strategies of the past thirty years. While New Christian Right attorneys certainly did not set out to save the principle of the separation of church and state, its "rickety judicial edifice might have collapsed of its own weight," note Christopher Eisgruber and Lawrence Sager, had it not been for its "collision" with "other more stable doctrines," particularly those found in the Court's free speech jurisprudence.[46]

Compared with the establishment clause, free speech doctrine is guided by relatively transparent principles, or at least principles that the average school principal or teacher without specialized legal training can understand. Viewpoint and content neutrality, two principles at the core of the Court's free speech jurisprudence, proved critical in the marriage of religion and speech in the context of schools. Viewpoint neutrality simply means that the government cannot prohibit speech because it dislikes the motivating ideology of the speaker. Content neutrality forbids restrictions based on content unless the speech falls under a well-defined exception to protection such as defamation, obscenity, or incitement.

These doctrines are closely associated with the Court's "public forum" doctrine, which outlines guidelines concerning free speech on government property. A public forum is government property that has traditionally been open to free expression, such as a park or sidewalk. A limited or designated public forum is public property specifically opened for public expression, such as school facilities that the public can use after hours. While the government can establish the time, place, and manner of restrictions on public and limited public forums, these restrictions are subject to strict scrutiny. Thus free speech doctrine provided a ready-made alternative for religious groups when defending students' right of access to school property. Under the Court's establishment clause jurisprudence, however, access to public property for such groups would clearly count as aid to religion, thus violating the core principle of separation. Hence religious litigants had to convince the Court that free speech should "trump" separation.[47]

The first and most important case testing this legal strategy, *Widmar* v. *Vincent* (1981), addressed access to university facilities by religious groups and served as "arguably the breaking point in the development of modern Establishment Clause doctrine."[48] The logic of this case powerfully influenced the relationship between religion and education in secondary schools. In *Widmar* the Court ruled in favor of a Christian student group that had been denied access to the use of facilities at the University of Missouri at Kansas City.[49] The university believed that under the Court's establishment clause, jurisprudence allowing university property to be used for religious worship or teaching would violate the principle of separation. The student group, with the assistance of a Christian Legal Society attorney, argued that under the Court's public forum doctrine, government officials are not allowed to discriminate on the basis of viewpoint. The group lost before the district court, which considered religious speech to be different from "secular intellectual activities," but then proceeded to win resoundingly on appeal. Writing for the Eighth Circuit, Judge Gerald Heaney, a liberal stalwart, rejected the lower court's ruling, saying, "We begin with the proposition that religious speech, like other speech, is protected by the First Amendment." Heaney's opinion also used free speech analysis to argue that the university's policy violated the establishment clause: the "university's prohibition on worship and religious teaching also hopelessly entangles it in the delicate tasks of defining religion, determining whether a proposed event involves religious worship or teaching, and then monitoring events to ensure that no prohibited activity takes place."[50] While obviously referencing the *Lemon* test, this portion of the opinion clearly drew on the doctrine of viewpoint neutrality. To say that religious speech is somehow a separate category of speech that can be prohibited from a public forum would require the government to make messy and hopelessly subjective judgments about which viewpoints are acceptable and which are not.

On appeal, the university argued that the Eighth Circuit's decision created a "fiberglass pole" in order to "spring over the Establishment wall."[51] The Supreme Court, in an 8-1 decision, disagreed. Writing for the majority, Justice Lewis F. Powell said the university was attempting to create more separation than the establishment clause required and in doing so fell afoul of the free exercise and free speech clauses. The Court ruled that when creating a public forum, as the university had, government officials must not make content-based restrictions against religious speech.

The Court's decision applied only to public colleges and universities, so at the urging of religious groups Congress extended *Widmar*'s rationale to secondary schools with the Equal Access Act of 1984. The act made it "unlawful for any public secondary school which receives Federal financial assistance and which has a limited open forum to deny equal access or a fair opportunity to, or discriminate against, any students who wish to conduct a meeting within that limited open forum on the basis of the religious, political, philosophical, or other content of the speech at such meetings." It did provide exceptions for groups that might "materially and substantially interfere with the orderly conduct of educational activities within the school."[52] As well, schools could simply ban all noncurricular student clubs.

The Court addressed the Equal Access Act in *Westside Community Schools* v. *Mergens* (1990).[53] In this case, school administrators at Westside High School in Omaha, Nebraska, denied the request of a group of students to form a Bible club because all student clubs had to have a faculty sponsor and having a faculty sponsor in this instance would imply the school's endorsement of religion. The students, represented by Jay Sekulow of the ACLJ, sued claiming that the school's decision violated the Equal Access Act. In response, the school challenged the act's constitutionality.[54] On both issues, the Court ruled for the students, holding that the school's decision violated the Equal Access Act and that the act did not violate the establishment clause. While eight justices ruled in favor of the students, they were highly fractured, particularly on the establishment clause question. In fact, the case provides a clear contrast between the straightforward application of free speech doctrine and the contortions required under establishment clause precedent.

In a convoluted application of the *Lemon* test, Chief Justice William Rehnquist and Justices Sandra Day O'Connor, Byron White, and Harry Blackmun argued that the act did not require schools to "endorse" religion and thus was constitutional. By this time Justice O'Connor had begun advocating that *Lemon*'s effects test be replaced with an endorsement test.[55] Justice Kennedy, joined by Justice Scalia, rejected the endorsement test, contending that the school inevitably endorses a religious club "if the club happens to be one of the many activities that the school permits students to choose." To Kennedy and Scalia, there was no constitutional violation as long as student participation in the club was voluntary. Justices Thurgood Marshall and William Brennan agreed that the act was constitutional but wanted to call on the school to vigorously disassociate itself from any appearance of endorsement of religious clubs.

In his dissent, Justice John Paul Stevens pointed out that since the act forbade content discrimination, schools would now be required to allow the "Ku Klux Klan or the Communist Party" access to school facilities. Stevens argued that schools must be able to "shape the educational environment" of their schools. But because of the Court's decision, "if a high school administration continues to believe that it is sound policy to exclude controversial groups, such as political clubs, the Ku Klux Klan, and perhaps gay rights advocacy groups from its facilities, it now must also close its doors to traditional extracurricular activities that are noncontroversial but not directly related to any course being offered at the school."

All the same, the Court continued to extend its public forum protections to religious groups seeking to use school property. In *Lamb's Chapel* v. *Center Moriches Union Free School District* (1993), it struck down a school district policy that allowed non-school secular groups access to school facilities but forbade non-school religious groups access even though both were discussing similar topics.[56] According to the Court, the school district was engaging in unconstitutional viewpoint discrimination. The Court applied the same reasoning in *Good News Club* v. *Milford Central School* (2001).[57] Here the school district had opened up its facilities to community residents after school hours. The Good News Club was run by local residents and asked to use the facilities to conduct programs for six- to twelve-year-olds in which children would sing songs, pray, memorize Bible verses, and listen to Bible lessons. The district refused the club's request, saying that the religious nature of its activities could be considered religious worship and thus fell outside the district's acceptable use policies. Once again, the Court ruled that this was unconstitutional viewpoint discrimination.

Despite this impressive set of victories, religious groups have not been universally successful in using the free speech strategy. In *Sante Fe School District* v. *Doe* (2000), the Court struck down a school district policy allowing for student-initiated and -led prayer before football games.[58] According to the majority, this practice was not really student initiated and thus should not receive the protections for private speech. According to Michael McConnell, a leading First Amendment clause scholar and former Tenth Circuit judge, this case combined with others indicated the Court was establishing some consensus on the establishment clause: "emerging Establishment Clause jurisprudence can be seen as a specialized application of the state action doctrine." If the action can be attributed to private parties, then "any attempt to censor or discriminate against private religious activity would, at a minimum, raise serious questions under the Free Speech and Free Exercise Clauses."[59] If the speech is attributable to the government, then it violates the establishment clause.

While leaving no one completely happy, this standard does make the job of attentive school officials much easier. The law is so clear and well established now, notes Jay Sekulow, that the only explanation for the decisions of some school districts to deny access to religious groups is "blatant hostility." However, resistance to the law appears "isolated," and most school districts "are catching up."[60] Some school administrators have tried to prohibit disfavored clubs by claiming that all their student clubs are curricular and therefore do not fall under the requirements of the Equal Access Act. This is how school officials in Louisville, Colorado, defended their decision not to allow a Bible club. The school district had a Gay-Straight Alliance Club but argued that it was related to the curriculum since the school's health classes study sexual orientation. The school district made the same argument for other student groups such as Amnesty International, Peace Jam, and multicultural clubs. Two months after the ACLJ filed a lawsuit, the school district changed its policy to allow the Bible club.[61]

The same story has played out in other school districts, except that Gay-Straight Alliance Clubs have been denied access by school authorities.[62] When these decisions are challenged in court, school districts typically lose. In *Mergens,* the Court went out of its way to warn school districts against classifying favored student clubs as curriculum-related entities as a way of engaging in viewpoint discrimination against clubs school authorities dislike. According to the Court, a curriculum-related club "is one that has more than just a tangential or attenuated relationship to courses offered by the school." In *Mergens,* the school argued that since the school's math teachers often encouraged their students to play chess, the student chess club was curriculum related. The Court rejected that reasoning and said the existence of such clubs meant the school had created a limited public forum.

Schools can escape the requirements of the Equal Access Act, of course, by eliminating all noncurricular clubs. But this risks a political backlash. In Salt Lake City, Utah, the school board banned all noncurricular clubs after a Gay-Straight Alliance requested to meet on school property. At trial, the board's policy was upheld by a federal district court. But the decision generated so much opposition from the community that the board had to reverse itself and recognize the club.[63]

On access to school facilities, the legal advice books depart markedly from suggestions based on policies implicating the establishment clause. Instead of caveats and qualifications, they give straightforward declarations. "Although schools do not have to open or maintain a limited open forum," states one book, "once they do, they may not discriminate against a student group because of the content of its speech."[64] Another says that even though the issue is "emotionally charged," schools "that provide a limited open forum may not permit certain groups to use school facilities while denying others."[65] Since the law is so clear, one would expect litigation to continue to decline.

The Return to *Tinker*

Noticeably absent so far in this analysis has been any discussion of *Tinker* v. *Des Moines.* Since the Court's public forum doctrine has only a limited reach, ultimately the conflict over religious speech will have to confront this decision. It is here that strange political coalitions are forming between religious public interest law firms and their usual opponents such as the ACLU.

Tinker famously announced in 1969 that students and teachers do not shed their rights at the schoolhouse door. However, the Court qualified this categorical language to censor speech that was likely to materially disrupt the educational process and could "impinge upon the rights of others." Thus instead of creating firm guidelines, the Court's standard necessitated a case-by-case analysis of whether student expression caused a substantial disruption. As a result, *Tinker* prompted seemingly endless litigation during the 1970s and early 1980s on everything from sideburns to student elections. The Court tried to distinguish between the political speech at issue in *Tinker,* which revolved around three students wearing black armbands to protest the Vietnam War, and restrictions on appearance: "The problem posed by the present case does not relate to regulation of the length of skirts or the type of clothing, to hair style or deportment." However, it took little legal creativity for attorneys to argue that hair length and other attributes of personal appearance could be political statements. Because of the vagueness of "substantial disruption," the courts often reached divergent results on similar issues.

The Supreme Court did nothing to clarify students' free speech rights until *Bethel School District* v. *Fraser* (1986) and *Hazelwood School District* v. *Kuhlmeier* (1988). In *Fraser,* school officials suspended a student for an extended and "elaborate sexual metaphor" in a speech nominating a classmate for vice president of the student body. The Court held that school districts can censor "vulgar and lewd" speech.[66] The Court also included language that would eventually frighten religious groups in *Morse* v. *Frederick.* Writing for the majority, Chief Justice Warren Burger said, "The First Amendment does not prevent the school officials from determining that to permit a vulgar and lewd speech such as respondent's would undermine the school's basic educational mission." The Court made no attempt to define "basic educational mission," leaving some uncertainty about the status of *Tinker*'s substantial disruption standard.

In *Kuhlmeier,* the Court upheld the decision of a school principal to censor articles in the school newspaper.[67] Since the school sponsored the newspaper, the Court held that such school-sponsored speech is not protected by *Tinker*. The Court reiterated that a school need not tolerate speech contrary to its basic educational mission but left the phrase undefined.

This phrase would be a significant issue when the Court revisited student speech nearly twenty years later in *Morse* v. *Frederick*. At issue in *Morse* was the 2002 suspension of Joseph Frederick, a Juneau, Alaska, high school student, for displaying a banner saying "BONG HiTS 4 JESUS" as the Olympic torch passed by the school on its way to the winter games in Salt Lake City. The school had given students and faculty permission to leave class for the event. The school's principal, Deborah Morse, confiscated the banner and suspended Frederick for ten days. When his suspension was upheld by the school board, Frederick sued the district and Principal Morse in federal court alleging violation of his civil rights and requested punitive and compensatory damages. At trial, the district court ruled in favor of the school board and Principal Morse. But the Ninth Circuit overturned the district court, setting up the board's and principal's appeal to the Supreme Court.

After the Court granted certiorari, the intersection of religious interests with *Tinker* were revealed. Superficially, the issue in *Morse* did not appear to be of particular interest to religious groups. Christians, one suspects, would normally be disinclined to defend the right of a student to associate drug use, however opaquely, with Jesus. But to the horror of Christian groups along with free speech advocates, the school district argued in its brief that schools should be able to censor student speech that is inconsistent with their "basic educational mission" and that the district's action should be upheld because the student's language was "offensive." Religious groups feared that if the Court accepted this standard, schools would be free to define their basic educational mission as they wished and thus religious speech that offended some students could be construed as undermining that mission.

In response, a politically strange coalition of groups submitted amicus briefs to the Court in defense of the student. Religious legal associations such as the ACLJ, CLS, LLI, LC, and ADF found themselves on the same side as the Lambda Legal Defense and Education Fund and the ACLU. A common theme of the religious groups' amicus briefs was that the school district was really arguing that it should be able to engage in viewpoint discrimination. The LLI said that allowing schools to prohibit speech on the basis of their self-defined "basic educational mission" would simply give them a "standardless discretion to censor student speech" and "would destroy the fundamental protections in

Tinker and sanction political and religious viewpoint discrimination." The LLI also said the Court could not rely on "other existing doctrines" such as its public forum doctrine to "protect student speech if *Tinker* were undermined in this way."[68] The ACLJ argued that the school district had "engaged in blatant viewpoint-based censorship of student speech in a context where an otherwise identical banner from the *opposite* viewpoint (e.g., 'Jesus Says "No Drugs"') would have been permissible. A school's basic educational mission does not confer blanket authorization for viewpoint suppression of student speech."[69]

The religious amici explicitly urged the Court to announce that school officials have no right to punish speech simply because it offends others. The CLS contended that "*Tinker* itself provides a basis for rejecting the request for essentially unchecked authority to regulate student speech on the ground that it offends others. The *Tinker* Court declared that school officials may not prohibit speech based on 'a mere desire to avoid the discomfort and unpleasantness that always accompany an unpopular viewpoint.'"[70]

The Court ruled in favor of the school district, but because of the divided majority did so on very narrow grounds. For religious groups, the decision was decidedly mixed. In his majority opinion, Chief Justice John Roberts explicitly rejected the district's position that schools should be able to censor offensive speech. "After all," he wrote, "much political and religious speech might be perceived as offensive to some." The issue, according to Roberts, was that Frederick's banner could be "reasonably viewed as promoting illegal drug use." He made no reference to the basic educational mission of schools but did note that *Fraser* had not relied on *Tinker*'s substantial disruption test and had provided other grounds for restricting student speech.

However, Justice Samuel Alito's concurring opinion would be the controlling one. He joined the Court "on the understanding that (a) it goes no further than to hold that a public school may restrict speech that a reasonable observer would interpret as advocating illegal drug use and (b) it provides no support for any restriction of speech that can plausibly be interpreted as commenting on any political or social issue." Thus the Court in *Morse* really just carved out another exception to *Tinker,* allowing schools to restrict speech advocating illegal drug use. For the ACLU and the religious amici, this was small comfort since the Court was sanctioning viewpoint discrimination, something that neither *Fraser* nor *Kuhlmeier* had done.

Given the peculiar circumstances of the case, Justice Breyer's partial concurrence and dissent seemed particularly sensible. Apparently following the old legal adage "bad facts make bad law," Breyer argued that allowing school officials to restrict speech under such bizarre circumstances as in this case would be "unlikely to undermine basic First Amendment principles," whereas carving out a viewpoint-based restriction to do so raised "serious concerns." Instead the

Court should have avoided the First Amendment question and addressed only whether the principal was entitled to qualified immunity, which requires finding in favor of a government official unless his or her conduct violates "clearly established statutory or constitutional rights of which a reasonable person would have known." The circumstances surrounding the case and the Court's obvious difficulty in deciding it indicated that Principal Morse certainly could not have been expected to know that she was violating the student's rights.[71]

The significance of *Morse* then is uncertain. The facts alone—how many students routinely unfurl signs of dubious semantic content at city parades during school hours—could restrict its influence. However, it points the way to looming conflicts that almost certainly will demand the Court's attention. Unfortunately, the Court's precedents make it unclear how these issues will be resolved, and *Morse* itself has already proved ripe for manipulation by lower courts. The Court could establish clear rules that would greatly simplify the task of school officials, or it could, because of internal divisions, muddle through in much the same way it has done on the establishment clause.

Most conflicts in the offing involve religious speech that school officials deem offensive. The most prominent case in the lower courts, *Harper* v. *Poway Unified School District,* was the real target of several of the amicus briefs in *Morse.* In this case, a San Diego student, Tyler Harper, wore a T-shirt to school that said, "I will not accept what God has condemned," and "Homosexuality is shameful. Romans 1:27." He wore the shirt on the school district's officially sanctioned Day of Silence in 2004, which was intended to promote tolerance of gays and lesbians. After he refused to remove the T-shirt, school officials forced Harper to sit in the principal's office all day, made him undergo counseling, and had a deputy sheriff photograph him and question him about his religious beliefs.

With the support of the ADF, Harper sued, requesting an injunction. A federal district court denied his request, at which point his appeal to the Ninth Circuit also failed. However, the Ninth Circuit panel, in an opinion written by the well-known liberal Stephen Reinhardt, essentially upheld the ability of the school officials to engage in viewpoint discrimination. Relying on language from *Tinker* sanctioning suppression of speech to protect the rights of others, Judge Reinhart's opinion said that schools should be able to restrict the expression of "derogatory and injurious remarks directed at students' minority status such as race, religion, and sexual orientation." Such speech, he said, "violates the rights of other students" and really constitutes "verbal assaults that may destroy the self-esteem of our most vulnerable teenagers and interfere with their educational development."[72] This reasoning implies that viewpoints that can be interpreted as critical of someone's race, religion, or sexual orientation can be suppressed.[73]

In its amicus brief in *Morse,* the Christian Legal Society noted that the National School Boards Association's brief had defended Reinhardt's decision, revealing "the scope of the power they seek" from the Court.[74] The ADF's brief in *Morse* explicitly asked the Court to rule in a way that would effectively overturn the Ninth Circuit's decision in *Harper*. However, in March 2007, before deciding *Morse*, the Court addressed *Harper*, but in a very peculiar way. Harper had petitioned the Court for certiorari. Instead of just denying cert, the Court took the unusual step of vacating the decision and sending it back to the Ninth Circuit to be declared moot since Tyler Harper had already graduated from high school. The Court's decision allowed for the issue to be relitigated while simultaneously removing any precedential value of Reinhart's decision.

In light of the Court's decision, Tyler Harper's sister, Kelsie, asked the district court to reconsider its previous judgment in the case. The judge, John Houston, denied her request, however, and showed how the reasoning of *Morse* could be manipulated to accommodate almost any restriction on speech. The court agreed that in *Morse* "the majority made it clear its decision is limited to speech concerning illegal drug use." At the same time, Judge Houston said that the reasoning presented in *Morse* lends support for a finding that the speech at issue in the instant case may properly be restricted by school officials if it is considered harmful."[75] Quite implausibly, the opinion simply expanded the physical harm caused by drug use emphasized in Justice Alito's controlling concurrence to include emotional harm.

A similar case, *Nuxoll* v. *Indian Prairie School District,* has been working its way through the Seventh Circuit. Again, a school-sponsored Day of Silence was at the center of the controversy. This time a student was punished for wearing a T-shirt saying "Be Happy, Not Gay" the day after the school's Day of Silence. The student was represented by the ADF, but the ACLU of Illinois also supported the student's claim, indicating the durability of the coalition in *Morse*. The Seventh Circuit granted an injunction allowing the student to wear the T-shirt but declined to rule on the constitutionality of the school's speech code, which had been the basis for censoring the student. Judge Richard Posner, writing for the panel, rejected the school district's claim that it was simply protecting the rights of students who have derogatory comments directed toward them: "A school can—often it must—protect students from the invasion of their legal rights by other students. But people do not have a legal right to prevent criticism of their beliefs or for that matter their way of life."[76] However, even Judge Posner's reasoning opened the door to restrictions based on psychological harm. Ignoring Alito's concurrence, he cited some of Chief Justice Roberts's discussion of the harmful psychological effects of drugs.[77]

No one knows, of course, how the Court will resolve the issues raised by *Harper* and *Nuxoll*.[78] Historically, the conservative bloc on the Court has been more likely to give substantial discretion to school officials. In *Morse,* Justice Thomas argued on originalist grounds to overturn *Tinker,* which would vastly expand the authority of school officials. However, his position allows him to vote for what he thinks is appropriate under the Court's precedents as long as others do not call for the interment of *Tinker*. But even though the conservatives seem more willing to support school officials, they have also been calling for more accommodation of religion in public schools. This bloc would likely defend religious speech as long as it did not fall in one of the exceptions to *Tinker* carved out in *Fraser, Kuhlmeier,* and *Morse*.

Given the spirited defense of student rights offered by the liberal bloc, one would expect its members to vote to strike down restrictions on student free speech rights. But there is some tension in this bloc, exhibited particularly by Justice Stevens. In *Mergens,* Stevens would have granted substantial discretion to school officials because of the disruptive nature of certain viewpoints, precisely the opposite position he took in *Morse*. His dissent in *Morse,* however, was so strong and categorical in opposing viewpoint restrictions that it seems unlikely that he and his fellow dissenters would uphold these sorts of restrictions.

Conclusion

Whatever the term "basic educational mission" means, it is safe to say that when teachers and administrators concentrate on avoiding litigation, they are distracted to some degree from accomplishing that mission. Unfortunately, the confusion over establishment clause violations is likely to continue since the Supreme Court seems incapable of clarifying the clause's meaning. With the ACLU ready to sue on one side and Christian public interest firms ready on the other, school officials will simply face the difficult task of not antagonizing either side.

Despite the uncertainty as to how the Court will rule on students' free speech rights, at the very least, it should avoid falling into a doctrinal morass, as it has with the establishment clause. It could do so by explicitly overruling *Tinker*. This obviously is unlikely. After nearly forty years of life under *Tinker,* it seems a bit late to put the expressive T-shirts back in the dresser. The best that can be hoped for is that the Court will try to limit the grounds for litigation while also protecting core free speech rights of students.

The application of free speech principles to religious speech provides hope that the Court can establish clear doctrines that will limit litigation. The apparently durable coalition between New Christian Right public interest firms and the ACLU indicates that some legal comity is possible. Given their nature, legal rules will never eliminate litigation, but they can be clear enough that school officials and students (and their parents) can assess the legal merits of their claims without excessive difficulty. Naturally, school officials and the National School Boards Association would prefer far more leeway in restricting student speech. However, their legal goals seem to be premised on the mistaken belief that the Court would grant them that unlimited discretion. Today it seems unimaginable that the Court would either explicitly overturn *Tinker* or, through a cascading list of exceptions, overturn it in effect. Instead the choice is between the Court hewing to traditional free speech principles or generating an indeterminate and ever-changing doctrine based on the basic educational mission of public schools.

Unfortunately, the possibility of confusion and more litigation is certainly lurking in the "basic educational mission" language of *Bethel* and *Fraser,* which was ignored in *Morse* and thus remains undefined, "waiting to be invoked by school boards in other cases."[79] While the ACLU and religious amici in *Morse* expressed fear that this standard would provide a limitless basis for suppression of speech, it would more likely create a limitless basis for litigation. The National School Boards Association, it could be argued, made a mistake in asking the Court to grant schools the authority to restrict speech because it violated their basic educational mission. Should the Court rely on this standard, it almost certainly would not wash its hands of the issue and allow school officials to define its meaning without judicial oversight. The Court and lower federal courts would be repeatedly called on to define the phrase's meaning and what is actually necessary to accomplish it. Defining the basic educational mission of schools requires knowing what sorts of educational practices advance and undermine that mission. Some have even argued that the Court must engage in a deep analysis of the particular mission of schools to form a suitable free speech doctrine for students.[80] But engaging in this sort of investigation would thrust the Court into debates over educational policy that it is ill equipped to resolve.[81] Moreover, since it is probably impossible to define "basic educational mission" with any degree of precision, the Court would risk drawing inscrutable distinctions, just as it has done with the metaphor of separation.

Should the Court resort to the basic educational mission of schools as a standard, it should say, as Douglas Laycock has argued, that the "basic educational mission of the public school is not inconsistent with, and cannot be defined to be inconsistent with, the First Amendment's core commitment to freedom of political and religious speech."[82] Doing so would go far to confine the standard and provide some discernible boundaries about what school officials can and cannot do.

Notes

1. *Helms* v. *Picard,* 151 F.3d 347 (5th Cir. 1998).
2. "Joint Statement of Current Law on Religion in the Public Schools," April 12, 1995 (www.aclu.org/religion/schools/16146leg19950412.html [July 30, 2008]).

3. 536 U.S. 639 (2002).

4. 393 U.S. 503 (1969).

5. *Bethel School District* v. *Fraser,* 478 U.S. 675 (1986).

6. 127 S. Ct. 2618 (2007).

7. 330 U.S. 1 (1947).

8. For a list of all establishment clause cases, see www.firstamendmentcenter.org/faclibrary/libraryreligion.aspx?topic=establishment_clause_supreme_court_cases_topic&subheading=n (July 26, 2008).

9. To complicate matters, even the narrowest reading of the establishment clause implies separation. If it only prevents established churches such as the Church of England, there still is obviously some separation between church and state. The confusions follow from the principle of no aid rather than just the language of separation.

10. 343 U.S. 306 (1952).

11. Robert M. Hutchins, "The Future of the Wall," in *The Wall between Church and State,* edited by Dallin H. Oaks (University of Chicago Press, 1963), p. 19.

12. *Engel* v. *Vitale* 370 U.S. 421 (1962); and *Abington Township School District* v. *Schempp* 374 U.S. 203 (1963).

13. See Linda Lyons, "The Gallup Brain: Prayer in Public Schools," December 10, 2002 (www.gallup.com/poll/7393/Gallup-Brain-Prayer-Public-Schools.aspx [August 22, 2008]).

14. See Joseph Viteritti, *"The Last Freedom: Religion from the Public School to the Public Square* (Princeton University Press, 2007), p. 107.

15. 403 U.S. 602 (1971).

16. Laurence Tribe, *American Constitutional Law,* 2nd ed. (Minneola, N.Y.: Foundation Press, 1988), p. 1211, notes that "a legislature might vote to increase welfare benefits because individual legislators feel religiously compelled to do so."

17. 472 U.S. 38 (1985).

18. National Conference of State Legislators, "States with Moments of Silence or School Prayer Legislation" (www.ncsl.org/magazine/MomentofSilence.htm [July 31, 2008]).

19. Justice Byron White noted this problem in his partial concurrence and dissent in *Lemon*: "The Court thus creates an insoluble paradox for the State and the parochial schools. The State cannot finance secular instruction if it permits religion to be taught in the same classroom; but if it exacts a promise that religion not be so taught—a promise the school and its teachers are quite willing and, on this record, able, to give—and enforces it, it is then entangled in the 'no entanglement' aspect of the Court's Establishment Clause jurisprudence."

20. *Lamb's Chapel* v. *Center Moriches Union Free School District,* 508 U.S. 384 (1993).

21. *Everson* v. *Board of Education* (1947); and *Wolman* v. *Walter,* 433 U.S. 229 (1977).

22. *Lemon* v. *Kurtzman* (1971); and *Bowen* v. *Kendrick,* 487 U.S. 589 (1989).

23. *Board of Education* v. *Allen,* 392 U.S. 236 (1968); and *Wolman* v. *Walter* (1977).

24. 124 *Cong. Rec.* 25661 (1978).

25. See Philip Hamburger, *Separation of Church and State* (Harvard University Press, 2002); and Daniel Dreisbach, *Thomas Jefferson and the Wall of Separation between Church and State* (New York University Press, 2003).

26. See Akhil Amar, *The Bill of Rights: Creation and Reconstruction* (Yale University Press, 1998); and Phillip Munoz, "The Original Meaning of the Establishment Clause and the Impossibility of Its Incorporation," *University of Pennsylvania Journal of Constitutional Law* 8 (2006): 585–639.

27. Amar, *Bill of Rights,* pp. 33–34.

28. Tribe, *American Constitutional Law,* p. 1215.

29. John C. Jeffries Jr. and James E. Ryan, "A Political History of the Establishment Clause," *Michigan Law Review* 100 (2000): 289.

30. On education policy alone, the Court struck down a Kentucky law requiring the posting of the Ten Commandments in schools, *Stone* v. *Graham,* 449 U.S. 39 (1980); a nonsectarian prayer at public school graduation, *Lee* v. *Weisman,* 505 U.S. 577 (1992); and the creation of a public school district inhabited solely by Hasidic Jews, *Kiryas Joel Village* v. *Grumet,* 512 U.S. 687 (1994).

31. *Agostini* v. *Felton,* 521 U.S. 203 (1997); and *Aguilar* v. *Felton,* 473 U.S. 402 (1985).

32. 530 U.S. 793 (2000).

33. 536 U.S. 639 (2002).

34. Douglas Laycock, "Why the Court Changed Its Mind about Government Aid to Religious Institutions: It's a Lot More than Just Republican Appointments," *Brigham Young University Law Review* 2008, no. 2 (2008): 292, also cites the rise of the free-market argument for vouchers along with the support of minority parents in inner cities for school choice programs as important parts of this change: "As this coalition joined Catholics in demanding money for private schools, and as Protestant hostility to Catholics faded further into the past, aid to private schools looked less like a special interest demand for Catholics and more like a way to accommodate the needs and preferences of a wide variety of Americans. It became much more apparent that this was not just about aiding Catholics, and not just about aiding religion; it became much easier to see the issue in terms of neutrality and private choice."

35. For example, in 2002 a Roman Catholic parent unsuccessfully sued the New York City Department of Education for its policy allowing a Jewish Menorah to be displayed during Hannukah and the Islamic Star and Crescent during Ramadan but forbidding the display of a nativity scene during the Christmas season. *Skoros* v. *City of New York,* 437 F.3d 1 (2nd Cir. 2004). Similarly, in 2004 a parent sued the Maplewood, New Jersey, School District for adopting a policy banning all religious music at seasonal celebrations. The parent argued that this signaled not government neutrality toward religion but unconstitutional hostility to religion. After several years of procedural wrangling, the case finally went to trial in the summer of 2008. See Melanie Bingston, "3rd Circuit Lets Suit Proceed on Religious Music in School," First Amendment Center (Nashville, Tenn., October 12, 2006) (www.firstamendment center.org/news.aspx?id=17526 [July 30, 2008]).

36. 465 U.S. 668 (1984).

37. 492 U.S. 573 (1989).

38. For a spirited presentation of this position along with the idea that separation of church and state is tied up with Christianity and thus hopelessly religious itself, see Stephen Feldman, *Please Don't Wish Me a Merry Christmas* (New York University Press, 1997).

39. Nathan L. Essex, *School Law and the Public Schools: A Practical Guide for Educational Leaders,* 2nd ed. (Boston: Allyn & Bacon, 2002), pp. 35–36, 38.

40. Charles C. Haynes and others, *The First Amendment in Schools: A Guide from the First Amendment Center* (Nashville, Tenn.: First Amendment Center, 2003), p. 56.

41. Similar advice can be found in William C. Bosher and others, *The School Law Handbook: What Every Leader Needs to Know* (Alexandria, Va.: Association for Supervision and Curriculum Development, 2004); and in "Religious Holidays and Public Schools: Questions and Answers" (www.clsnet.org/clrfPages/pubs/pubs_holida5.php [July 30, 2008]). The latter

is a joint statement sponsored by groups such the Christian Legal Society, National Education Association, and American Jewish Committee.

42. Jay Sekulow, interview with author, August 12, 2008.

43. See Alliance Defense Fund, "Christmas Project" (www.alliancedefensefund.org/christmas/aboutchristmas.php [July 30, 2008]).

44. *Doe* v. *Wilson County School System,* No. 3:06-0924, 2008 (M. D. Ten., May 29, 2008).

45. An important part of this story has been the changing politics behind establishment clause litigation. Initially, most Protestants, motivated by anti-Catholicism, supported the idea of the separation of church and state since it was seen as a way of denying benefits to Catholic institutions. But the years since *Everson* have witnessed a decline in anti-Catholicism and an increasing willingness, particularly by evangelical Protestants, to work with Catholics to defend religious interests. One can see this change represented in the religious legal firms discussed here. The Thomas More Law Center represents believers of all stripes but, given its name, obviously has Catholic sensibilities. In fact, it was founded with the support of Tom Monaghan, the founder of Domino's Pizza and generous funder of Catholic causes. However, one could hardly detect a difference in the types of cases litigated by the TMLC and other religious public interest firms coming out of evangelical Protestantism. For an excellent history of the changing politics surrounding the establishment clause, see Jeffries and Ryan, "Political History," p. 2000.

46. Christopher Eisgruber and Lawrence Sager, *Religious Freedom and the Constitution* (Harvard University Press, 2007), p. 33.

47. For a thorough account of the free speech strategy of the "New Christian Right" legal movement, see Steven P. Brown, *Trumping Religion: The New Christian Right, the Free Speech Clause, and the Courts* (University of Alabama Press, 2002).

48. Michael W. McConnell and others, *Religion and the Constitution,* 2nd ed. (New York: Aspen, 2006), p. 622.

49. *Widmar* v. *Vincent,* 454 U.S. 263 (1981).

50. *Chess* v. *Widmar,* 635 F.2d 1310 (8th Cir. 1980).

51. *Widmar* v. *Vincent,* Brief of Petitioners, pp. 52–53.

52. 20 U.S.C. 4071–74.

53. 496 U.S. 226 (1990).

54. Sekulow played a large role in litigating free speech cases on behalf of religious groups. He had his first significant victory using the free speech argument with *Board of Airport Commissioners* v. *Jews for Jesus,* 482 U.S. 569 (1987), where he successfully challenged the Los Angeles International Airport's prohibition on all "First Amendment Activities."

55. Justice O'Connor's endorsement test, which she initially advocated in *Lynch* v. *Donnelly,* has assumed a prominent role in establishment clause jurisprudence over the past two decades. However, the precise nature of this role is not clear. It could be seen as a separate test, or as a replacement for *Lemon's* effects test as O'Connor seemed to advocate. Even if it were to supplant the *Lemon* test, one should not expect more consistent results than the *Lemon* test has produced. As Michael McConnell has noted in "Religious Freedom at a Crossroads," in *The Bill of Rights in the Modern State,* edited by Geoffrey Stone and others (University of Chicago Press, 1992), p. 148, "Whether a particular governmental action appears to endorse or disapprove religion depends entirely on the presuppositions of the observer, and there is no 'neutral' position outside the culture, from which to make this assessment."

56. *Lamb's Chapel* v. *Center Moriches Untion Free School District* (1993).

57. 533 U.S. 98 (2001).

58. 530 U.S. 290 (2000).

59. Michael McConnell, "State Action and the Supreme Court's Emerging Consensus on the Line between Establishment and Private Religious Expression," *Pepperdine Law Review* 28 (2000): 681.

60. Sekulow, interview, August 12, 2008.

61. American Center for Law and Justice, "ACLJ Gets School District to End Religious Discrimination against Student Bible Club," March 19, 2003 (www.aclj.org/news/read.aspx? ID=220 [July 31, 2008]).

62. See First Amendment Center, "Gay-Straight Club Can Meet at Fla. High School" (www.firstamendmentcenter.org/news.aspx?id=20359 [July 31, 2008]).

63. *East High Gay/Straight Alliance* v. *Board of Educ.*, 81 F. Supp. 2d 1166 (D. Utah 1999).

64. Haynes and others, *First Amendment,* p. 47.

65. Essex, *School Law,* p. 31.

66. 478 U.S. 675 (1986).

67. 484 U.S. 260 (1988).

68. *Morse* v. *Frederick,* 127 S. Ct. 2618 (2007), Brief of the Liberty Legal Institute as Amicus Curiae in Support of Respondent, p. 2.

69. *Morse* v. *Frederick,* Brief of the American Center for Law and Justice as Amicus Curiae in Support of Respondent, p. 2.

70. *Morse v. Frederick,* Brief of the Christian Legal Society as Amicus Curiae in Support of Respondent, p. 13.

71. Justice Breyer's position on qualified immunity was recently adopted by his colleagues. Under *Saucier* v. *Katz,* 533 U.S. 194 (2001), federal judges had to follow an "order of battle" rule requiring them to determine whether a constitutional violation had occurred before they could grant qualified immunity. The Court effectively overturned *Saucier* in a unanimous decision in *Pearson* v. *Callahan* No. 07–751 (2009).

72. *Harper* v. *Poway Unified School District,* 445 F.3d 1167 (9th Cir. 2005).

73. Judge Alex Kozinski, who dissented in the case, argued that "the 'rights of others' language in *Tinker* can only refer to traditional rights, such as those against assault, defamation, invasion of privacy, extortion and blackmail, whose interplay with the First Amendment is well established."

74. *Morse* v. *Frederick,* Brief of the Christian Legal Society as Amicus Curiae in Support of Respondent, p. 12.

75. *Harper* v. *Poway Unified Sch. Dist.,* Civ. No. 04CV1103 JAH, 9 (S.D. Cal. February 11, 2008), Order Denying Plaintiff's Motion for Reconsideration.

76. *Nuxoll* v. *Indian Prairie School District,* 523 F.3d 668 (7th Cir. 2008).

77. For an interesting analysis of how some courts are distorting *Morse* to sanction restrictions on student speech, see Clay Calvert, "Misuse and Abuse of *Morse* v. *Frederick* by Lower Courts: Stretching the High Court's Ruling Too Far to Censor Student Expression," *Seattle University Law Review* 32 (2008): 1–34. I would like to thank Ron Schildge for alerting me to Calvert's analysis.

78. Similar issues surround pro-gay speech in communities with more socially conservative dispositions. In 2008 a Florida federal district judge struck down restrictions that a principal had placed on speech advocating gay rights. The case came out of a rural school district in the Florida panhandle. The facts of the case made it obvious that the principal engaged in censorship completely unjustified under the court's precedents. See *Gillman* v. *Holmes County School District,* Opinion and Order, 5:08cv34-RS-MD, Filed June 24, 2008.

79. Douglas Laycock, "High Value Speech and the Basic Educational Mission of a Public School: Some Preliminary Thoughts," *Lewis and Clark Law Review* 12 (2008): 114.

80. See Richard W. Garnett, "Can There Really Be 'Free Speech' in Public Schools?" *Lewis and Clark Law Review* 12 (2008): 45–59.

81. For an analysis of the difficulties courts have experienced using educational research, see Joshua Dunn and Martin West, "Calculated Justice: Education Research and the Courts," in *When Research Matters: How Scholarship Influences Education Policy,* edited by Richard Hess (Harvard Education Press, 2008), pp. 155–76.

82. Laycock, "High Value Speech," p. 115.

10

Litigation under No Child Left Behind

MARTHA DERTHICK

The No Child Left Behind Act (NCLB) has not—as of the spring of 2009—generated a large volume of litigation. This may seem puzzling in view of the widespread litigiousness of U.S. society in regard to schools and the length, complexity, and extreme controversy surrounding the law itself. Surely, one supposes, there must be language in the legislation on which to hang lawsuits. Early in 2004, when the two-year-old law began to bite in local districts, widespread opposition developed, and news stories, citing school administrators and officials of teachers unions, predicted a flood of lawsuits.[1] There has been no flood. I have been able to identify only a dozen suits, more or less, but some of these have been important enough to raise constitutional questions. Taken together, they constitute a varied and revealing spectrum of NCLB's impact on the operation of the country's schools.

The suits fall into two groups: those that originate with the state and local governments and public employees that have borne the considerable burden of meeting NCLB's demands, and those that originate with plaintiffs making claims on behalf of the students whom the law purports to benefit. The distinction is rough rather than precise, in that plaintiffs in the first group also ordinarily claim to be serving the interests of students. I take up these two groups separately and then consider explanations of why there has not been

I thank Nanette Asimov, Angela A. Ciolfi, and John Dinan for their help.

more litigation under this law. By and large, the fights over NCLB—and there have been many fights over NCLB, which is overdue for legislative reauthorization—have been carried on in legislative, executive, and even electoral forums. In the presidential campaigns of both 2004 and 2008, candidates found that they could win applause by attacking the act. This was true especially for Democrats in primary contests, given the power and prevalence of teachers unions within the party.

The statutory background, in brief, is that NCLB was enacted in 2001 as a reauthorization of the Elementary and Secondary Education Act (ESEA), the basic federal law applying to K–12 schools. It intervenes more broadly and deeply than any of its predecessors, which since the original passage in 1965 have focused on disadvantaged students. Every school and every school child are affected. In exchange for federal funds, NCLB requires the states to attain universal proficiency in reading and mathematics by the 2013–14 school year, a goal that literally no one believes to be realistic. In the meantime, they must make "adequate yearly progress" (AYP). They must adopt academic content standards for the core subjects of reading/language arts and mathematics, and must test students on these subjects each year in grades 3 to 8 and at least once in high school.

States are required to set escalating performance targets, expressed as percentages of students who pass the test. The performance targets apply not just to the whole school population, but also to subgroups: the racial and ethnic groups that are present in the school, low-income students, students with disabilities, and students with limited English proficiency. Schools that meet the targets are deemed to have made AYP. Schools that fail to make AYP two years in a row are labeled "in need of improvement" and must prepare an improvement plan. They also must offer students choice—that is, the option of transferring to a public school within the district that is not "in need of improvement." If they fail to improve for a third straight year, they must provide supplemental educational services (SES), or free tutoring, to needy students. Further failures lead to more drastic sanctions, including "restructuring."[2]

Officials as Plaintiffs

First into the courtroom fray from the official side were two school districts at opposite ends of the country but with the common characteristic of a large Spanish-speaking enrollment. Reading, Pennsylvania, was the first in the country to file, followed soon by Coachella Valley Unified School District in California. Both sued their state governments in state courts, claiming that English-only tests were unfair to students with limited English proficiency.

Underlying these suits was the requirement that students be tested annually in math and reading, and that school districts' performance be judged by the results. What was unfair to the students was therefore unfair as well to the districts, which would suffer the public shame and sanctions that came with poor ratings. Tests originated with the states, but the federal law provided that students with limited English proficiency be assessed in "a valid and reliable manner" with "reasonable accommodations" and "to the extent practicable, . . . in the language and form most likely to yield accurate data on what such students know and can do in academic content areas, until such students have achieved English language proficiency."[3]

Reading was the fifth largest among Pennsylvania's 501 school districts. Two-thirds of its 16,000 students were Hispanic, and 15 percent had limited English proficiency. In 2003 the Pennsylvania Education Department found that thirteen of the district's nineteen schools failed to meet the stipulated benchmarks of the testing regime. The district responded with a lawsuit, protesting that many of its students could not even read the tests, which the state supplied in English only, and that the state did not provide the resources necessary to comply with the standards.[4] The state's largest teachers union filed a friend-of-the-court brief supporting the district.

Coachella Valley's suit against California was filed in June 2005. The district was joined by eight other districts in Southern California and one from the San Francisco Bay area, the California Association for Bilingual Education, and Californians Together, a statewide coalition devoted to improving the education of English language learners (ELLs). The population of ELL students was estimated at 1.6 million children, or 1 in 4 attending the state's public schools. Together, these plaintiffs employed three law firms, one specializing in education law and two in civil rights litigation. They argued that California was failing to meet the standards set by NCLB for testing ELLs.

The Pennsylvania suit failed quickly. In 2004 a three-judge Commonwealth Court panel ruled unanimously that testing in a student's native language was not mandatory but was required only to the extent that it was "practicable." The court held also that the level of state support for the district was irrelevant to evaluation of the district's progress, and that the district had not proved that it needed more resources to comply.[5] Beyond the issue of language, Reading also attacked the statistical methodology underlying AYP determinations and argued that the state department of education allowed an illegally small range of appeals of AYP determinations, violating the district's due process rights. A state trial court upheld the latter claim and ordered the state to hear a wider range of appeals.[6]

The Coachella Valley case has had a more complicated history. In response to a petition of the defendants, it migrated briefly to a federal district court, which found the motion to intervene moot and remanded the case to the state. Two years later, in May 2007, a judge in the San Francisco Superior Court ruled that he lacked authority to issue a writ of mandamus commanding the state to comply with NCLB because the state's duties under that act were discretionary, and further that the state's method of language assessment was not an abuse of discretion. He made clear his reluctance to intervene: "Rational people could differ as to whether administration of NCLB assessments in a second language, or in multiple additional languages, is . . . feasible, or desirable, or otherwise appropriate. The test for this court . . . is not to choose among competing rational alternatives and then mandate the judicially chosen one. To the contrary, decisions such as how to assess student performance for purposes of NCLB are best left to other branches of government." In 2008 the Coachella Valley plaintiffs appealed this decision, arguing that the state's duties under NCLB were mandatory, not discretionary. The Coachella Valley District, in which nineteen of twenty-one schools had failed to make AYP for four straight years, was being threatened with appointment of a state trustee. Sixty percent of the district's 18,000 students were ELLs.[7]

As opposition to NCLB rose between 2003 and 2004, state attorneys general considered whether to take legal action. In Wisconsin, Attorney General Peg Lautenschlager issued an opinion holding that the state had no legal obligation to implement the law because Congress failed to adequately fund the testing and other actions the law required.[8] However, only one attorney general, Connecticut's Richard Blumenthal, ventured into court.

Blumenthal acted in 2005 after his state's education commissioner, Betty J. Sternberg, got into the modern media equivalent of a street brawl with U.S. Secretary of Education Margaret Spellings. Sternberg, who had spent much of her twenty-four-year career in Connecticut's education department developing the state's tests, protested: "We won't learn anything new about schools by giving these extra tests." Having instituted tests in 1984, Connecticut had been administering them annually in grades four, six, and eight, whereas NCLB required that they be given also to grades three, five, and seven. Sternberg said that the money spent on the added tests could be put to better use. Spellings shot back in an op-ed piece in the *Hartford Courant* that the state was acting like a child who did not want to be tested, and in a TV interview on PBS said it was "un-American" to resist a law that was meant to close the achievement gap between whites and blacks—a gap that was much higher in Connecticut than the national average. Sternberg demanded an apology. It took the intervention of Connecticut's Republican governor, M. Jodi Rell, to get these two warring officials to sit down together.[9]

In the midst of this confrontation, Blumenthal, a Democrat, announced that he would file suit against the federal government. In August he made good on that threat, with equivocal support from Governor Rell, who was not present at his press conference.[10] Blumenthal complained to a federal district court in

Connecticut that Secretary Spellings was violating a provision of federal education law—dating from 1994, initially authored by Republicans who were trying to protect state governments from unfunded mandates, and reincorporated in NCLB—that says, "Nothing in this act shall be construed to . . . mandate a State or any subdivision thereof to spend any funds or incur any costs not paid for under this act." He also complained that Spellings had denied, "without any basis in scientific research," Connecticut's requests for three waivers relating to the federally prescribed testing regime. (NCLB repeatedly pays homage to scientific research.) Connecticut wished to continue to test biennially instead of annually. It wished to phase ELLs in over a period of three years rather than testing them immediately, or within a year in the case of language arts. And in regard to special education students, it sought the option of testing at their instructional level rather than their grade level. "A tenth grade special education student who is learning fractions and decimals should not be required to take a test in algebra," the attorney general said. He added that the state could not opt out of NCLB or fail to comply without suffering severe penalties in the loss of federal funds, which amounted to roughly $436 million a year, or 5.8 percent of the state's $7.5 billion education budget. Teachers unions—the Connecticut Education Association and the National Education Association (NEA)—filed amicus briefs on behalf of the state, but no other state attorneys general joined Blumenthal. The Connecticut State Conference of the National Association for the Advancement of Colored People (NAACP) intervened on behalf of Secretary Spellings.

Connecticut lost this suit in two stages. First, in September 2006 Judge Mark R. Kravitz dismissed the state's claims that the secretary was violating the unfunded mandate portion of the act, inasmuch as Connecticut had yet to suffer any penalties for noncompliance. Nor was it at immediate risk of losing federal funds. In the absence of enforcement measures that penalized the state, the court lacked jurisdiction, Kravitz said. He also ruled that the secretary's denial of waiver requests was not reviewable because she had unfettered discretion to deny them. However, he allowed the state to proceed with its claim that the U.S. DOE had acted arbitrarily and capriciously in denying the state's request for waivers.[11] This claim did not fall until the spring of 2008, when Judge Kravitz dismissed Connecticut's arguments in an opinion that was often critical of the state's presentation of its case.[12]

The Connecticut case developed in such a way that Kravitz never ruled on the merits of what most observers—and Kravitz himself—regarded as the core question: the import of the unfunded mandates provision. The judge was obviously disappointed: "It is truly unfortunate that the Court is unable to reach this issue because the State failed adequately to raise it . . . . Regrettably, the result is that over a year and one-half after the Motion to Dismiss Ruling, the

State is no closer to a determination of this very important issue." In May 2008 Blumenthal appealed to the Second Circuit, asking it to rule on the issue of unfunded mandates.

Another suit filed in the early wave of state and local resistance to NCLB focused squarely on unfunded mandates. This was *Pontiac* v. *Spellings*, brought in the spring of 2005 by a coalition of nine school districts in Pontiac, Michigan (largely African American), Laredo, Texas (largely Hispanic), and Vermont (largely rural and white), along with a mix of local and state chapters of the NEA. The leader in this action was the NEA, the largest teachers union in the country with 2.7 million members, which financed the suit and whose general counsel, Robert H. Chanin, was the chief litigator.[13] The NEA tried but failed to find a state government that would join it as a plaintiff.[14]

From the start, *Pontiac* v. *Spellings* was all about money, the meaning of the unfunded mandates provision in NCLB, and the meaning also of the spending clause of the U.S. Constitution. And it was complemented by a drumbeat of complaint from the NEA and congressional Democrats about the failure of the Bush administration to recommend appropriations that would match the authorizations in the act. The NEA kept an annual tally of the multibillion-dollar shortfall and claimed that NCLB was making education worse by causing state and local governments to divert funds that could have been better used.

In the litigation, plaintiffs told a federal appellate court: "This case raises a question of first impression regarding the proper construction of Section 9527(a) of the No Child Left Behind Act . . . the resolution of which is of great importance not only to the twenty parties in this case but to states, school districts and education associations nationwide."[15] The disputed section of NCLB reads, in its entirety: "Nothing in this Act shall be construed to authorize an officer or employee of the Federal Government to mandate, direct, or control a State, local educational agency, or school's curriculum, program of instruction, or allocation of State or local resources, or mandate a State or any subdivision thereof to spend any funds or incur any costs not paid for under this Act."

When the case came before Judge Bernard A. Friedman of the Eastern District of Michigan, he denied Spellings's motion to dismiss the complaint for lack of standing, and he did not assert, as Judge Kravitz had in Connecticut's case, that the plaintiffs needed to exhaust administrative remedies. The plaintiffs in this case possessed no such remedies, which was, ironically, an advantage. But he granted Spellings's motion to dismiss for failure to state a claim, finding her argument "convincing" that Section 9527(a) only barred unauthorized actions by federal officers or employees and did not limit the obligation of states and school districts to comply fully with the substantive requirements of NCLB whether or not the federal government paid the added costs.

The plaintiffs appealed to the Sixth Circuit. Amicus briefs came from Connecticut, five other states, and the District of Columbia, the governor of Pennsylvania, the American Association of School Administrators (AASA), and an ad hoc group of state and local officials from California. To the surprise of many lawyers and the litigants, a three-member panel ruled 2-1 for the plaintiffs in January 2008.[16]

In arguing that Friedman had misconstrued Section 9527(a), the plaintiffs relied both on legislative history and Supreme Court interpretations of the spending clause. For legislative history, they went back to 1994 and analyzed the arguments made for including the language that became section 9527(a) of NCLB in the Goals 2000 Education Act, the School to Work Opportunities Act, and the Improving America's Schools Act, which was a reauthorization of the ESEA of 1965, the basic federal statute for aid to education and predecessor of NCLB. They distinguished between what they called the "no-federal-control proviso" in the opening part of the section and the "no-state-or-local-funds proviso" at the end, which is more commonly referred to as "unfunded mandates." This latter portion was the focus of their appeal. They argued that the legislative debates of 1994 confirmed "what is readily apparent from the plain language of that provision—that the provision is intended to impose a broad prohibition against requiring states or school districts to spend their own funds for NCLB compliance, including compliance with requirements that are imposed by the [act] itself."

In making their constitutional argument, the plaintiffs seemed to behave strategically in citing a prior decision of the Sixth Circuit, which held, in *Coleman* v. *Glynn* (1993), "The key to the analysis [of a spending clause statute] should be the following principle of statutory construction arising from our system of federalism: '[I]n return for federal funds, the states agree [by contract] to comply with federally imposed conditions and such conditions must be imposed 'unambiguously' and 'with a clear voice.'" This ruling harked back to a Supreme Court decision of 1981, *Pennhurst State School* v. *Halderman*, which is the foundation of the clear statement rule as applied to federal grant programs. In its analysis, the Sixth Circuit majority cited a much more recent Supreme Court case, *Arlington Central School District Board of Education* v. *Murphy* (2006), in which the Court found that a school district was not obligated to pay expert fees to parents of a disabled child who had gone to court under the Individuals with Disabilities Education Act (IDEA). IDEA provides for the award of reasonable attorneys' fees to parents who prevail in a lawsuit, but the Court concluded that states had not been clearly told that they must also pay expert fees. IDEA, which is enacted under the spending clause, thus failed the clear statement test in this case.

The Second Circuit majority forthrightly embraced the constitutional argument:

> Because statutes enacted under the Spending Clause of the United States Constitution must provide clear notice to the States of their liabilities should they decide to accept federal funding under those statutes, and because we conclude that the NCLB fails to provide clear notice as to who bears the additional costs of compliance, we REVERSE the judgment of the district court and REMAND this case for further proceedings consistent with this opinion.[17]

But before long this bombshell was defused. At the beginning of May, a majority of the circuit's judges voted to rehear the case en banc, which meant that the opinion of January was vacated and the case was restored to the docket as a pending appeal.[18] Thus NCLB's most momentous legal issue remains unresolved. If it does go back to the trial court for a determination of whether federal funding fully covers the cost of complying with NCLB, the trial will be long and complicated and employ many expert witnesses.[19]

A relatively recent filing recalls where this cluster of officially inspired suits began—namely, with the testing of students who are not proficient in English. One of the most outspoken official critics of NCLB is Tom Horne, a lawyer, long-time school board member, and former state legislator who was elected superintendent of public instruction in Arizona in 2002 and reelected in 2006. While endorsing the tripartite principles of "standards, assessment, and accountability," Horne has insisted that "when a central bureaucracy attempts to manage a complex continent-wide system, extreme dysfunction results."[20] He has been angered in particular by rules that doom schools with a large number of ELLs to failure. (In the argot of NCLB, these students are also known as "limited English-proficient" [LEP] students.) There are many such schools in the border state of Arizona, and, anticipating that they would fail to make AYP, Horne in 2003 sought to negotiate with the DOE an understanding to protect them. He thought he had a deal, though it was oral only, "in order that it not be copied by other states." When the DOE reneged, Horne sued in a federal district court in Arizona. The court ruled, as had Kravitz in Connecticut, that it lacked jurisdiction because the plaintiff had not exhausted administrative remedies. Horne proceeded to do that, which took another year, and then refiled in June 2008.

Horne's petition explains that "in return for Arizona's support of NCLB," the DOE agreed that the Arizona Department of Education "would include the test scores of all LEP students; however, any school that failed to make AYP as a result of such scores could appeal that determination." The DOE and the superintendent would have discretion "to grant such appeals and authorize schools to exclude the test scores of LEP students within the first three years of English instruction at the school solely for AYP calculation purposes." Arizona was not trying to avoid giving the tests or recording the results; it was trying only to avoid the "inappropriate skewing" of AYP scores that resulted from having to treat LEP students as one of the defined subgroups by which school performance was measured. In 2005 a DOE audit of Arizona's compliance with NCLB objected to the state's practice. Horne thereupon sued, charging that the DOE had been "arbitrary and capricious" in pulling the switch on Arizona.[21]

He went one step farther. At the time of his 2008 filing, the DOE had recently adopted regulations exempting LEP students from a school's AYP calculations for one year. To the court, Horne complained that this too was arbitrary and capricious in that it was "not based on any scientific research or study," echoing, as had Connecticut's complaint, a phrase that recurs in the law. In a speech to the Heritage Foundation, Horne said:

> Rather than give the three years' grace period that is in the Arizona system, and that [the] federal government had agreed to, it imposed a one-year grace period, which is now the federal nationwide policy. There is no recognized expert in the country, not one in the country, who would say that it is possible to bring a significant percentage of students coming here from Mexico, or any other country where English is not the native language, to academic proficiency in English, and able to pass reading and math tests in English, after only one or two years. High standards are desirable. Requiring something that is impossible is inane.

Finally, there was the less noticed case of a solitary public school teacher, Brian K. Kegerreis, who filed suit in a federal district court in Kansas claiming that NCLB is unfair and unconstitutional because it holds school personnel accountable if students fail to perform adequately. In particular, he argued that the AYP standards set forth in NCLB cannot be met and that the consequences would injure him and other teachers. The court ruled that Kegerreis failed to show that the United States waived sovereign immunity with respect to his claim and granted the defendant's motion to dismiss.[22]

Children's Advocates as Plaintiffs

Suits on behalf of the student beneficiaries of NCLB are hardly more numerous than suits on behalf of aggrieved state and local governments, and no more successful. Most, but not all, of these suits have been brought by advocacy groups that are sustained by foundation grants.

An early suit brought by the Center for Law and Education—actually two suits, both filed in the U.S. District Court for the District of Columbia—complained that committees established by the U.S. DOE to develop regulations under NCLB did not ensure an equitable balance between representatives of parents and students, on one hand, and educators and education officials, on the other. The DOE was using a process called negotiated rulemaking, which had been authorized by Congress in the Negotiated Rulemaking Act of 1990 and incorporated in NCLB. The court held that none of the plaintiffs had standing and that the Negotiated Rulemaking Act barred judicial review of agency action relating to the establishment of a negotiated rulemaking committee.[23]

Another early target of advocacy plaintiffs was the failure of schools and school districts to implement the requirements that followed if they did not make AYP for at least two years in a row. Schools were supposed to respond by first offering choice and after another year SES. Early in 2003, the Association of Community Organizations for Reform Now (ACORN), along with parents, sued school administrations in New York City and Albany, charging that they had not informed parents of eligible children of their options. The plaintiffs further alleged that the school districts had illegally rejected thousands of transfer and SES requests. A federal district court ruled that NCLB vests sole authority to enforce violations of NCLB in the secretary of education and does not contemplate enforcement by private plaintiffs.[24] Explicitly, at least, the law does not contain a private right of action, the "third remedial tool" that Shep Melnick refers to in chapter 2.

Actions taken by two national advocacy groups apropos school choice in Southern California in 2006 did not quite attain the status of a lawsuit but approached near enough to warrant description. In March the Alliance for School Choice and the Coalition on Urban Renewal and Education filed formal complaints with the school districts of Los Angeles and Compton, California, charging that they were not properly implementing the choice provisions of NCLB. Los Angeles was an extreme case in that it had a very large number of students, at least 250,000, who were eligible for transfers, whereas only 527 students (0.2 percent of the eligible population) had received transfers. In Compton, no transfers had taken place. Nationwide, in the 2006–07 school year, only 45,000 students, less than 1 percent of the eligible total, used the choice option.[25] Thus these California districts were extreme examples of a widespread condition. Clint Bolick, head of the alliance and a well-known activist on behalf of school choice, hoped to make examples of the two districts. They were charged with failing to make information about transfers available to parents in a clear and timely way.[26]

The alliance's press release explained that because NCLB does not provide for a private right of action, parents and their organizational partners must file complaints in the first instance with the school districts. Several months later, Bolick said there soon would be a lawsuit, adding that the threat of one would force Secretary Spellings to deal with the problem of poor compliance.[27]

Even without a lawsuit, Spellings and the DOE took several actions in an effort to improve compliance. Spellings gave a speech in April 2006 that alluded to the California filings and called for strict observance of the law's requirement on choice. In May she sent a letter to every state linking the "unacceptably low" transfer rate to poor implementation and warned of "significant enforcement action." She also instructed California to produce a statewide plan to implement choice. California, with other states, was also selected to receive intensive monitoring of its transfer programs to make sure that parents were made aware of their options.[28] No suit was filed, but Bolick may have been correct in supposing that the threat of one prompted Spellings to act.[29]

Late in 2006, in New Jersey, the Seton Hall University School of Law Center for Social Justice filed a class action lawsuit on behalf of Newark parents complaining that the district had failed to notify those whose children were in failing schools of their rights to choice and SES. A federal district judge dismissed the suit on the grounds that the law was not privately enforceable. This decision was appealed to the Third Circuit, which affirmed the dismissal.[30]

Cognizant of the difficulty that other plaintiffs had encountered in basing action directly on the NCLB act, two legal advocacy organizations in Virginia in 2008 sought a writ of mandamus under state law to compel the superintendent of Roanoke schools to offer choice to students in a failing elementary school, Forest Park. This was, they argued on behalf of parents, a "clear and unequivocal duty" under NCLB that the superintendent had failed to perform. Filed in August in the Circuit Court for the City of Roanoke, the petition was denied in November. The city attorney called the request for a writ of mandamus "extraordinary" and maintained the writ should be used only to uphold "a clear and unequivocal right," which did not exist in this case. The judge did not address the issue of mandamus but ruled on the facts, which included the city's having closed Forest Park as an elementary school in order to turn it into a middle and high school. The plaintiffs chose not to appeal.[31]

As a strategy for improving student achievement, the testing regime with sanctions against failing schools was only one part of a long and complicated act. Another important part consisted of provisions governing the qualifications of teachers. The act required that in schools receiving Title I funds, which are designed to benefit low-income students, all teachers hired to teach core academic subjects after the 2002–03 school year must be "highly qualified," and that by the end of the 2005–06 school year, all school districts must employ only highly qualified teachers. Schools receiving Title I funds were required to inform individual parents when a teacher who was not highly qualified taught his or her child for more than four weeks.

The standard set for high qualification was that teachers hold a bachelor's degree, meet state certification or licensure requirements, and demonstrate subject-matter competence. The law also stipulated that certification or licensure requirements must not be waived on an emergency, temporary, or provisional basis.

California became the state in which the highly qualified teacher provisions were legally tested. Public Advocates, a nonprofit firm in San Francisco with a wide-ranging antipoverty and civil rights mission, filed three lawsuits between 2003 and 2007. The first two were in state courts and the third was in a federal district court. Although Public Advocates did the litigating, the named plaintiffs were Californians for Justice, the California ACORN, and individual parents of children in Title I schools.

The first suit, filed at the beginning of 2003 against the state's Board of Education and Department of Education, claimed that California's definition of a highly qualified teacher failed to meet the federal standard. The state was not requiring full certification, and it required only eighteen units of college course work in the subject to be taught, less than a typical college major. In addition to the lawsuit, the board received an angry letter from Representative George Miller, the California Democrat who was one of the principal authors of NCLB—in fact, *the* principal author of the provisions governing teacher qualifications.[32] In reaction, the Board of Education adopted a new and more exacting standard, and a superior court judge declared the case moot.[33]

In the second suit, filed in August 2005, the defendant was the state's Commission on Teacher Credentialing. Plaintiffs charged that it was allowing interns, on an emergency basis, to be considered highly qualified by issuing an Individualized Internship Certificate (IIC). Although their petition pointed out that this new credential fell short of NCLB requirements, Public Advocates chose to rest the case on state procedural grounds—that the commission had acted without advance notice or opportunity for public comment and failed to submit the proposed action to a state agency that must approve new regulations. A superior court judge ruled for the plaintiffs, citing the procedural defects that they had charged. He ordered the commission to revoke the roughly 4,000 IIC credentials that it had issued.[34]

Having won these two victories at the state level, Public Advocates next tried to land a bigger fish. In 2007 it brought suit against the U.S. DOE, charging that its regulations on teacher qualifications violated the law. At issue was a parenthetical phrase in the law stating that full state certification could include "certification obtained through alternative routes." The phrase was meant to facilitate entry of teachers who have not followed a standard teacher-training curriculum. The suit alleged that the DOE's regulations eviscerated an "explicit" statutory standard by allowing teachers who were still in training, and thus merely *participating* in alternative routes to certification, to be judged highly qualified. Public Advocates argued that the law required *completion* of the alternative route. The stakes were high, inasmuch as 100,000 teachers nationwide were alleged to be currently benefiting from the regulatory "loophole," 10,000 of them in California alone.[35] Federal district judge Phyllis J. Hamilton, after negotiating a passage through NCLB, the Administrative Procedure Act, and *Chevron* v. *Natural Resources Defense Council* (1984), concluded in 2008 that the challenged DOE regulation, with its relaxed interpretation of the alternative route, was reasonable and not contrary to the discernible intent of Congress.[36]

Finally, a case that did not conform to the usual pattern of advocacy organizations as plaintiffs was brought in 2005 by two Illinois school districts—Ottawa High School District and Ottawa Elementary School District 141—along with the parents of four students in special education. The parents claimed that NCLB had impermissibly compromised the IDEA, which requires that each special education student have an individualized education program. The plaintiffs complained that NCLB undermined this requirement by treating special education students as a distinct subgroup whose test results helped determine a school's performance.

A federal district court in Chicago dismissed the suit in 2007, ruling that the plaintiffs lacked standing because they had suffered no concrete injuries. On appeal, a panel of the Seventh Circuit reversed the district court on the issue of standing but concluded nonetheless that the suit was "too weak to justify continued litigation."[37]

Alternatives to Litigation

The foregoing history richly illustrates the range of issues embedded in NCLB. However, suits have emerged in a trickle rather than a flood, and even the trickle has slowed over time. Potential litigants have evidently calculated that their chances of success are too poor to justify the considerable costs of a lawsuit. If so, this history, with the potential exception of *Pontiac* v. *Spellings,* amply supports their calculation. Plaintiffs have almost always lost.

Foremost among the potential litigants who are missing from this story are the state attorneys general, with the exception of Connecticut's Blumenthal. It is a striking and ironic feature of NCLB litigation that a teachers union, not the state governments, has led the attack on the law as an unfunded mandate. This would seem to be the states' fight, but their lawyers, the attorneys general, have for the most part sat it out. None joined Blumenthal in his lawsuit. When he filed an amicus brief in support of the *Pontiac* plaintiffs, he was joined only by Delaware, Illinois, Maine, Oklahoma, Wisconsin, and the District of Columbia (New Mexico would join later). And Blumenthal's own office, if Judge Kravitz's acerbic comments are to be credited, fell short in addressing the mandates issue.

The likely explanation is that the attorneys general thought this fight neither a political nor a legal winner, plus they ran the obvious risk of alienating the Bush administration. It is an uphill fight to sue the federal government, and state governments in recent decades have concentrated instead on developing the art of defending themselves in the Supreme Court.[38] Mostly elected, and mostly hoping to attain higher offices (governor or senator, usually), the attorneys general do a lot of litigating in pursuit of populist causes. Their target of choice is corporations that can be charged with defrauding the public. Thus they present themselves as defenders of the weak and vulnerable, among whom most people would not count state governments. The public greeting on Blumenthal's home page says: "Welcome. As the public's lawyer I am here to defend state laws, protect consumers and insure our children and seniors are safe from abuse and neglect." As another example, the following mission statement is posted on the door of the Office of the Attorney General of Louisiana, which I encountered in 2008 as a tourist in Baton Rouge: "Protection of the Citizens of the State. Protection of the Environment. Investigation of Illegal Activities. Legal Representation for the State."

Education—in contrast, say, to environmental protection, consumer protection, Indian law, water resources, or tobacco—has not been among the subject specialties of the attorneys general. Their association lacks even a committee on the subject, and a book that describes their powers and responsibilities says virtually nothing of it.

In the main, the state governments and school districts on which the burdens of NCLB fall have used political and administrative means to defend themselves, often combining the two. They have complained vociferously, and their complaints are not of a legalistic kind. When Virginia applied for NCLB funds, the president of the state's Board of Education said in a cover letter that the state was applying "only under strong protest." He said that while there was much good in the law—no one disputes its aims of improving school performance and closing racial and other achievement gaps—the method of determining AYP was "irrational and lacks common sense, certainly as applied to Virginia. As a consequence, the AYP results for Virginia will be seriously flawed."[39]

It is not possible to take Congress to court for lacking reason and common sense, for intervening too deeply, or for departing from tradition, much as state and local school officials might wish to. Instead they have asked the U.S. DOE for administrative concessions and asked their legislative representatives for support in this effort. In doing so, they have gained more concessions outside of court than in.

In August 2005, the Civil Society Institute, an organization headed by the social activist and MacArthur Fellowship winner Pam Solo, issued a report sympathetically detailing the state and local rebellion against NCLB. In addition to litigation, the report identified four main areas of protest activity. One was legislative. Fifteen states had weighed legislation to opt out of NCLB. Four states had considered legislation that would prohibit the use of state resources for NCLB implementation. Seven states had passed resolutions critical of NCLB through both chambers of the legislature. Another class of activity fell under the heading of "opting out, waivers and exceptions." All but ten states had sought an exemption or waiver or some other alteration of NCLB requirements. Several districts in Illinois had chosen not to accept Title I money, thereby relieving themselves of an obligation to implement the law. Fourteen states were participating in an NCLB cost consortium sponsored by the Council of Chief State School Officers (CCSSO) to assess the costs of implementation. Connecticut had released a report finding that implementation would increase state costs by $41.6 million through fiscal 2008, and that local districts would bear sizable added costs as well. New Mexico's study put the added state costs at $10.1 million to $17.7 million a year and the local costs at $71 million to $108 million a year. "Failing school" studies constituted the final category. Nine states had issued reports detailing the detrimental impact of federal testing requirements and punitive actions on state education systems. Many schools had already been penalized for not meeting NCLB benchmarks; almost 11,000 had been subject to federal sanctions in the current year.[40]

The U.S. DOE, while firmly denying that a grassroots rebellion was under way, nevertheless made concessions to stanch it. Section 9401 of the ESEA permits the DOE to grant waivers of many of the substantive requirements of NCLB. It was slow to use this authority to address complaints about the rigidity of the act. Between 2002 and 2004, not one of the 118 waivers it approved gave substantive relief under NCLB. But this changed in 2005 and 2006, when it granted six state waivers that allowed selected districts to begin the required "improvement" of lagging schools by offering SES ahead of school choice, thus reversing the order prescribed in the law. Four more waivers of this kind were granted to states in 2007. For example, Virginia, one of the most rebellious states, learned in August 2005 that in the coming school year, four of its districts—Alexandria City, Henry County, Newport News City, and Stafford County—could begin the improvement of "failing" schools with SES. A year later, the DOE renewed the waiver for those four districts. A year after that, Virginia learned that this same waiver had been renewed for two of the original districts (Newport News and Henry County) and granted for five others (Fairfax, Fauquier, Greene, and Henrico Counties, and Hampton City) for the first time.[41]

Another type of waiver that the DOE began granting selectively allowed local educational agencies to provide SES themselves, upon application to the state educational agency, rather than contracting out. Yet another, which received a good deal of attention, allowed selected states to use so-called growth models to track individual student achievement from one year to the next as a way of determining AYP, rather than rely on absolute test results.

Not all concessions have taken the form of waivers granted to individual states upon application, which are easy to verify because they must be reported to Congress and are also posted in the *Federal Register* and eventually on the department's website. The U.S. DOE also negotiates with states over the content of their individual plans for implementing NCLB, and from time to time it has announced generally applicable rules changes that have increased flexibility. Summarizing these would take too much space here.[42] Enough has been said to reinforce the point that courts are not where the action is. Not only are administrative routes more likely to succeed than litigation, using them is likely to be a necessary precondition for successful litigation. Judges will want to know, as Judge Kravitz did in Connecticut, that states have exhausted their administrative remedies.

Protecting Students' Rights

School children per se have essentially no political resources, and their parents are limited to small-scale organizations and informal advocacy. However, numerous advocacy organizations, the largest of them financed by major foundations such as Gates, Ford, Casey, Hewlett, and Packard, purport to speak for them. For these organizations—the ACORNs of the education politics and policy world—litigation is their lifeblood. They live to sue. For that purpose, NCLB has been both a hindrance and a help. As an instrument on which to rest lawsuits, it has been almost entirely useless, as the preceding history shows. Indirectly, however, it has benefited the plaintiffs in school finance lawsuits, who can deploy the abundantly generated data on failing schools to support their cases.

In the history of NCLB, one can detect the advocacy organizations' struggle to find grounds for legal action: recall the failure of the Alliance for School Choice to file suit at all, or Public Advocates' modest victory in California that rested on state procedural grounds. The main explanation for this difficulty lies both in NCLB, which does not contain an express grant of a private right of action, and in recent Supreme Court jurisprudence, which has propounded an increasingly narrow interpretation of implied rights of private action.[43] Some of the suits described earlier took the route of administrative law, arguing that state or federal administrative agencies acted contrary to the statute. But here, too, plaintiffs have been frustrated. Courts have repeatedly deferred to agency interpretations of the law. Standing has also sometimes posed an obstacle. After a detailed and doctrinally nuanced analysis of the cases, Benjamin M. Superfine of the University of Illinois at Chicago concluded that the courts have not constituted an effective venue for addressing implementation problems or for enforcing NCLB provisions.

To show that NCLB has been hard to enforce through the courts, however, understates its effect on litigation, which can occur indirectly in suits ostensibly on other subjects. Leaders of the adequacy litigation movement and scholars have noted the impact of NCLB on school finance cases. These have traditionally focused on funding disparities among school districts, but increasingly they have been broadened to also focus on legal issues relating to standards, testing, and accountability. As this change took place, much of the impetus came from the implementation of NCLB, which produced a windfall of data on failing schools for the plaintiffs' use.[44]

Another example of a lawsuit in which a major litigant sought to use NCLB indirectly—though in this instance unsuccessfully—comes from the long-running case of *Flores* v. *Arizona,* which since 1992 has pitted a class of parents in the Nogales Unified School District against the state, with counsel from the Arizona Center for Law in the Public Interest. The case arises under the Equal Educational Opportunities Act (EEOA) of 1974, in which Congress decreed that "no State shall deny equal educational opportunity . . . by the failure . . . to take appropriate action to overcome language barriers that impede equal participation by its students in its instructional programs." Flores charged that Arizona was failing to meet its obligations under this act, and a federal district judge ruled in her favor in 2000. The suit dragged on without resolution, and in 2006 the leaders of the Arizona legislature—speaker of the House and president of the Senate—entered as intervenors and tried to argue, among other things, that because NCLB had been enacted, the suit should be dismissed. The district court disagreed, and in upholding its judgment, a three-judge panel of the Ninth Circuit read the intervenors a firm lesson in the differences between EEOA and NCLB. "Intervenors fail to appreciate the distinct purposes of the EEOA and the NCLB," it said. "The first is an equality-based civil rights statute, while the second is a program for overall, gradual school improvement. . . . Importantly, this very gradual improvement plan does not set as an objective immediate equalization of educational opportunities for each . . . student." The EEOA, by contrast, was a "rights-enforcing law" and as such could not tolerate the "ephemeral compliance" that could come with the year-to-year vagaries of school test scores.[45] Clearly, the EEOA had more bite in court.

What Next?

That NCLB has not provided ample grounds for litigation so far does not necessarily mean that it never will. The law is awaiting reenactment, and, as of

2009, many interests are jockeying to influence the outcome. Some of them want to make the law more litigation-friendly.

Federal-state tensions over NCLB did not disappear with time. On the contrary, they mounted sharply in 2007 as an attempt at reauthorization got under way in Congress. Schools all across the country were complaining that testing was unfair, especially as it was being applied to ELLs, and most especially to those who were foreign born and had arrived in this country with little or no formal education. As a politically pregnant example, there were many such students in the Washington, D.C., metropolitan area, so that any reader of the *Washington Post* could not fail to be aware of the anger of education officials in Virginia and its northern suburbs, who pleaded with federal education officials for more flexibility in administering reading tests. Federal officials, unyielding, threatened Virginia with the loss of funds. In 2007 many schools in Arlington, Fairfax, and Loudoun Counties—big suburban systems in the shadow of the capital, with pride in their schools—failed to make AYP. In recently rural but rapidly urbanizing Prince William County, where minorities account for nearly half of the population of 370,000 and illegal immigration is a prominent issue, nearly half of the county's seventy-nine schools did not meet the standards. Old Bridge Elementary School in Woodbridge fell short, just barely, solely because of poor reading scores among ELLs. "It's a bitter pill to swallow," Old Bridge principal Anita Flemons said. "If you think I'm a little upset about it, you are right."[46] In these disputes, Virginia's school administrators had strong bipartisan support from the state's Senate and House delegations as well as the governor and members of the state legislature. The legislature toyed with a law that prescribed a date for withdrawing from the NCLB if the DOE did not bend. Democratic governor Timothy M. Kaine did not favor withdrawing but did endorse the Board of Education's request for waivers. Secretary Spellings traveled down I-95 to Richmond to try to calm Virginia down.

A group of sixty-five Republicans in the U.S. House, including the minority whip, introduced a bill that would have allowed states to opt out of NCLB with no loss of funds. Many Republicans in Congress had always had doubts about the law but swallowed them in 2001 and 2002 in deference to a new president. Six years later, when the president was both deeply unpopular and a lame duck, they ceased to feel obliged. More surprisingly, so did some former Bush administration officials, once high-ranking members of the U.S. DOE, who stepped forth as critics. Governors and leaders of two state education organizations—the CCSSO and the National Association of State Boards of Education—collaborated in a call for revisions. The CCSSO said the DOE should be required to approve waiver applications that demonstrated proposed policies would achieve the law's goal of universal proficiency by the 2013–14 school year, a measure that, if adopted, could give rise to litigation and much dispute over standards of proof. The AASA, representing district superintendents, objected that the state organizations had not gone far enough. Teachers unions remained highly critical, as they had been all along. A new president of the American Federation of Teachers (AFT) in the summer of 2008 said that NCLB should be abandoned—it was "too badly broken to be fixed."[47] Democratic presidential candidates attacked it, and Democratic activists with an interest in education became divided over what the party should do next.

In this chaos, the Democratic education leaders in Congress, Representative George Miller and Senator Edward M. Kennedy, tried to maintain optimism and to advance their own proposals for fixing the law, which would have left it essentially intact. But by the end of 2007, they had given up on renewing it before the 2008 election.

Among the many organizations advancing proposals for change at this time were two that sought amendments specifically for the purpose of making it easier for aggrieved parents to bring suit to enforce the law's provisions. The Education Trust, with a seventeen-year record of campaigning for school reform, affirmed support for the essential elements of the original law and said that rather than asking too much of schools, NCLB had asked too little. The Education Trust would have toughened the law to demand equitable distribution of state and local funds and to require annual auditing of states and selected school districts by the DOE's inspector general to measure progress. It called for a private right of action to enable parents to enforce their rights through litigation.[48]

A somewhat oblique proposal of the same sort in 2007 came from a fifteen-member ad hoc commission on NCLB that was constituted by the Aspen Institute, a global think tank, with foundation financing (Gates, Kauffman, Joyce, MacArthur, Carnegie, and Spencer). Cochaired by two former governors, Tommy G. Thompson of Wisconsin and Roy E. Barnes of Georgia, the commission placed emphasis on giving more power to parents. Among several proposals to that end was one for "enhanced enforcement options," which would seem to be a euphemism for private rights of action. States would be required to "establish a procedure to allow individuals or groups of citizens to bring their complaints against the district or state to the state." If not satisfied there, citizens could appeal to the U.S. DOE, and if not satisfied there, they could appeal to a state court. An "analogous procedure" would be established for individuals who had complaints about the DOE's implementation of the law, which meant, presumably, that they could appeal to a federal court.[49]

Among members of the commission was Christopher Edley, dean of the law school at the University of California–Berkeley and a leading advocate of private rights of action in education. To the *San Francisco Chronicle*, he spoke more forthrightly than did the commission:

As of now, parents and the public cannot get in the courthouse door to argue that officials are failing to live up to their statutory obligations. If the state fails to enforce environmental regulations against a polluter, members of the public can not only go to the ballot box, they can also go to court. That is true in countless areas, and it ought to be true in education.[50]

In general, it has not been true in education, perhaps because federal aid has typically been targeted at institutions—school districts—rather than individuals. NCLB was not exceptional in omitting a private right of action.[51] Where individuals are the beneficiaries, as with Education for All Handicapped Children, later renamed the Individuals with Disabilities Education Act, access to the courts has been liberally granted. IDEA is a rights-creating statute; one of its purposes is "to ensure that the rights of children with disabilities and parents of such children are protected." Each eligible child is entitled to an individualized education program. The act contains numerous procedural safeguards, and IDEA has been litigated more often and more successfully than NCLB.

It would be rash to predict what will emerge from Congress when it takes up NCLB in the presidency of Barack Obama. When Obama's stimulus package became law early in 2009 with added billions for K–12 education, Representative George Miller, the liberal chair of the House Committee on Education and the Workforce and a leader of the attempt to renew NCLB, predicted that renewal would now be a lot easier.[52] But making it easier for parents to sue has not been on Miller's agenda. "I'm not there yet," he told the *San Francisco Chronicle* in response to the recommendations of Edley and the commission. If Miller is not "there," a private right of action is unlikely to appear in a revised NCLB.

Conclusion

NCLB has been a political anomaly. Politicians generally prefer to dispense pleasure rather than pain. That they should have inflicted as much pain on school administrators and teachers as they did in NCLB is puzzling, but they seem to have taken a perverse pride in 2001 and 2002 in ignoring the established interest groups of elementary and secondary education, including organized teachers, administrators, and state and local boards. Nor were the National Governors Association or National Conference of State Legislators invited to the negotiating table. Analyses of the legislative politics associated with passage of the law have emphasized the enhanced influence of "expert" analysts in think tanks and the exclusion of the parties principally at interest, who were disdained for being self-regarding and wedded to the status quo.[53]

Perhaps Congress was acting in frustration. It had passed many laws since 1965 in an attempt to improve school performance. The pace of lawmaking picked up considerably in the early 1990s with a series of enactments, but students did not seem to do better even as Congress tried harder. With leadership from a freshly elected Republican president who was in a hurry to seize education reform from the opposing party, federal officeholders concluded that the federal government was not doing enough to reward success and sanction failure in education.[54] NCLB, advanced as a solution, employed sanctions rather than rewards, and state and local officials reacted with the resentment one would expect. Lawsuits were of no practical use.

If there is one thing that seems to unite the Democrats, who have a strong grip on the government following the election of 2008, it is a desire to spend more money on schools, and they may find a way to be less punitive and more remunerative—while honoring accountability—by offering performance pay for teachers. Teachers would get more money if students made better progress, and there may be a willingness to define progress more broadly, not just by measuring test results in a limited set of subjects. The Aspen Institute's commission, in the coercive spirit of the original NCLB, recommended that teachers prove they can raise test scores before being considered "highly qualified" under the law. The president of the NEA responded that the proposal would pit teachers against each other and label one out of four teachers as unqualified and ineffective. Similarly, principals would be barred from working in schools with poor children unless they could prove that they are effective leaders. Presumably, in the commission's world, parents would be able to sue school districts and states to remove principals who were not effective leaders.

NCLB may someday, if the practitioners of advocacy litigation have their way, evolve into a rights-creating law, in the manner of EEOA, and thus be more usable for aggrieved parents and their advocates. It did not get there in its original incarnation.

Notes

1. Andrea Almond, "Educators Expect Flood of Lawsuits Targeting Federal No Child Left Behind Act," Associated Press, November 1, 2004 (www.lexisnexis.com/us/lnacademic/delivery [July 2, 2008]).

2. For a lucid and parsimonious explanation of NCLB, see Frederick M. Hess and Michael J. Petrilli, *No Child Left Behind: Primer* (New York: Peter Lang, 2006).

3. PRNewswire, "CABE and Californians Together to Hold a Press Conference on NCLB Assessment Lawsuit against the State of California," April 6, 2005 (www.lexisnexis.com/us/lnacademic/delivery [July 2, 2008]).

4. Mark Scolforo, "School District Loses Challenge to Performance Rating," Associated

Press state and local wire, August 7, 2004 (www.lexisnexis.com/us/lnacademic/delivery/ [July 2, 2008]); and Almond, "Educators Expect Flood of Lawsuits".

5. Scolforo, "School District Loses Challenge."

6. Benjamin Michael Superfine, "Using the Courts to Influence the Implementation of No Child Left Behind," *Cardozo Law Review* 28 (November 2006): 779.

7. "Judge Dismisses Lawsuit Seeking Standardized Testing in Spanish," Associated Press state and local wire, May 22, 2007 (www.lexisnexis.com/us/lnacademic /delivery [July 2, 2008]). See also *Coachella Valley Unified School District* v. *State of California,* Case CPF-05-505334 (www.sfgov.org/courts [November 9, 2008]); Mary Ann Zehr, "A San Francisco Judge Rules that English-Only Tests are OK," May 22, 2007, and "Another Take on *Coachella Valley Unified School District* v. *California,*" May 23, 2007 (http://blogs.edweek. org/edweek/learning-the-language/2007/05 [November 11, 2008]).

8. Chuck Haga, "Ruling Ignites Schools Debate; Wisconsin Bucked No Child Left Behind," *Minneapolis Star-Tribune,* June 17, 2004 (www.lexisnexis.com/us/lnacademic/ delivery [July 2, 2008]).

9. Alison Leigh Cowan, "At the Front of the Fight over No Child Left Behind," *New York Times,* April 18, 2005, and Cowan, "Rell Aides Set for Talks on Federal School Bill," *New York Times,* April 14, 2005 (www.lexisnexis.com/us/lnacademic/delivery [July 5, 2008]); Michael Dobbs, "Conn. Stands in Defiance on Enforcing 'No Child,'" *Washington Post,* May 8, 2005, p. A10.

10. Sam Dillon, "Connecticut to Sue U.S. over Cost of School Testing Law," *New York Times,* April 6, 2005 (www.lesixnexis.com/us/lnacademic/delivery [July 5, 2008]); Connecticut Attorney General, "State Sues Federal Government over Illegal Unfunded Mandates under No Child Left Behind Act," press release, August 22, 2005 (www.ct.gov/ag [June 15, 2008]); Robert A. Frahm, "No Child Lawsuit Disputed," *Hartford Courant,* August 23, 2005 (www.courant.com/news/local [August 24, 2005]).

11. Sam Dillon, "Connecticut Case Advances," *New York Times,* September 28, 2006, p. A18; *State of Connecticut* v. *Margaret Spellings,* 453 F. Supp. 2d 459; 2006 U. S. Dist. LEXIS 69552, September 27, 2006.

12. *State of Connecticut* v. *Margaret Spellings,* 2008 U.S. Dist. LEXIS 34434, April 28, 2008.

13. Sam Dillon, "Teachers' Union and Districts Sue over Bush Law," *New York Times,* April 21, 2005; Michael Dobbs, "NEA, States Challenge 'No Child' Program," *Washington Post,* April 21, 2005 (www.lexisnexis.com/us/lnacademic [July 5, 2008]); "Teachers Sue over No Child," *Daily Progress* (Charlottesville, Va.), April 21, 2005, p. B2.

14. Julia Koppich, "A Tale of Two Approaches—The AFT, the NEA, and NCLB," *Peabody Journal of Education* 80 (April 2005): 137–55.

15. *Pontiac School District* v. *Secretary of the United States Department of Education,* Opening Brief of Plaintiffs-Appellants, March 22, 2006 (www.nea.org//lawsuit/images/appeal brief.pdf [July 25, 2008]).

16. For a pessimistic estimate of the suit's prospects, see John R. Munich and Rocco E. Testani, "NEA Sues over NCLB: The Bucks Are Big, but the Case Is Weak," *Education Next* 5 (Fall 2005) (www.hoover.org/publications [November 11, 2006]).

17. *School District of the City of Pontiac* v. *Secretary of the United States Department of Education,* No. 05-2708, 512 F. 3d 252; 2008 U.S. App. Lexis 198; 2008 FED App. 0006 (6th Cir.)

18. U.S. Court of Appeals for the Sixth Circuit, 2008 U.S. App. Lexis 12121, May 1, 2008.

19. Rocco E. Testani and Joshua A. Mayes, "Accountability Left Behind," *Education Next* 4 (Summer 2008): 43–45.

20. "Blasting Away at NCLB," Heritage Foundation speech, April 24, 2007 (www.ade. state.az.us/administration/superintendent [July 24, 2008]).

21. *Horne* v. *Spellings,* Complaint for Declaratory Judgment, June 19, 2008 (www.ade.az. gov/pio/Press-Releases/2008/pr06-23-08 [July 25, 2008]).

22. *Brian K. Kegerreis* v. *United States of America,* 2003 U.S. Dist. LEXIS 18012, decided October 9 2003.

23. *Center for Law and Education* v. *United States Department of Education,* 209 F. Supp. 2d 102, 2002 U.S. Dist. LEXIS 8945, and 315 F. Supp. 2d 15, 2004 U.S. Dist. LEXIS 5266.

24. Superfine, "Using the Courts to Influence the Implementation of No Child Left Behind"; *Association of Community Organizations for Reform Now* v. *New York City Department of Education,* 269 F. Supp. 2d 338; 2003 U.S. Dist. LEXIS 10929, decided June 20, 2003.

25. "Report Roundup," *Education Week,* January 21, 2009, p. 5.

26. "National Test Cases Filed against Los Angeles and Compton School Districts Demanding Public School Transfer Options under No Child Left Behind Act," press release, March 23, 2006 (www.allianceforschoolchoice.org [January 20, 2008]).

27. Claudio Sanchez, "California Schools Could Lose Aid over 'No Child' Law," July 6, 2006 (www.npr.org/templates/story [January 20, 2008]).

28. "In Major Speech, Secretary Spellings Takes Seriously Public Schools Lack of Transfer Options," press release, April 5, 2006 (www.allianceforschoolchoice.org [January 20, 2008]); Sam Dillon, "Most States Fail Demands Set Out in Education Law," *New York Times,* July 25, 2006, p. A14; "States Face Federal Review on NCLB Choice, Tutoring," *Education Week,* February 28, 2007 (www.lexisnexis.com/us/lnacademic [July 3, 2008]).

29. If so, this was an exceptional event. There is no detectable pattern in NCLB of administrators acting in anticipation of legal action in order to deter it. As this essay shows, they have not had much to fear from lawsuits.

30. "Seton Hall Law School Files Suit to Compel Newark Public Schools to Comply with the No Child Left Behind Act," press release, November 30, 2006 (http://law.shu.edu/ administration/public_relations/press_releases/2006 [July 31, 2008]); Emily Goldberg, Seton Hall University School of Law, telephone interview with author, August 4, 2008, and telephone message, February 17, 2009.

31. Angela A. Ciolfi, e-mail message to author, February 12, 2009; David Harrison, "Forest Park Parents Lose Claim on Choice of Schools," *Roanoke Times* (www.roanoke.com/ news/roanoke/wb/184590 [Febuary 12, 2009]).

32. Hess and Petrilli, *No Child Left Behind,* p. 64.

33. Nanette Asimov, "State Faces Lawsuit over Teachers' Qualifications," *San Francisco Chronicle,* January 24, 2003 (www.lexisnexis.com/us/lnacademic [July 8, 2008]); Asimov, e-mail message to author, July 9, 2008.

34. Bob Egelko, "Suit Filed over State's Teacher Credentialing," *San Francisco Chronicle,* August 3, 2005, and "State Illegally Labeled Teachers as 'Qualified,'" *San Francisco Chronicle,* November 3, 2005 (www.lexisnexis.com.us/lnacademic [July 8, 2008]).

35. Public Advocates, "U. S. Department of Education Waters Down Teacher Quality, NCLB Lawsuit Charges," press release, August 21, 2007 (www.publicadvocates.org [January 7, 2008]).

36. *Sonya Renee* v. *Margaret Spellings,* 2008 U.S. Dist. LEXIS 49369.

37. "NCLB Trumps IDEA, Appeals Court Rules," *Education Week,* February 20, 2008 (www.edweek.org/ew/articles [February 26, 2008]).

38. Emily Myers and Lynne Ross, eds., *State Attorneys General: Powers and Responsibilities* (National Association of Attorneys General, 2007), chap. 22.

39. Kate R. Kaminski and others, *Virginia School Law Deskbook,* vol. 2: *Reference on Legal Issues* (LexisNexis and Virginia School Boards Association, 2004), p. 16.

40. "NCLB Left Behind: Report Finds 47 of 50 States in 'Some Stage of Rebellion' against Controversial Law," August 17, 2005 (www.resultsforamerica.org [June 10, 2008]).

41. Information about waivers can be found on the department's website, www.ed.gov.

42. See Hess and Petrilli, *No Child Left Behind,* pp. 126–31.

43. Superfine, "Using the Courts to Influence the Implementation of No Child Left Behind"; more generally, see John C. Jeffries and others, *Civil Rights Actions: Enforcing the Constitution* (New York: Foundation Press, 2007).

44. Superfine, "Using the Courts to Influence the Implementation of No Child Left Behind"; Andrew Rudalevige, "Adequacy, Accountability, and the Impact of the No Child Left Behind Act," in *School Money Trials: The Legal Pursuit of Educational Adequacy,* edited by Martin R. West and Paul E. Peterson (Brookings, 2007), pp. 243–61; and Michael Heise, "The 2006 Winthrop and Frances Lane Lecture: The Unintended Legal and Policy Consequences of the No Child Left Behind Act," *Nebraska Law Review* 86 (2007): 119.

45. *Flores* v. *Arizona,* 516 F. 3d 1140, 2008 U.S. App. LEXIS 4005.

46. Maria Glod and Michael Alison Chandler, "N. Va. Schools Set Back on 'No Child' Test Goals," *Washington Post,* August 24, 2007, p. A1.

47. Sam Dillon, "Union Chief Will Propose Wider Role For Schools," *New York Times,* July 14, 2008, p. A11.

48. "Summary of Education Trust Recommendations for No Child Left Behind Reauthorization," January 1, 2006 (www2.edtrust.org [July 28, 2008]).

49. Aspen Institute, *Beyond NCLB: Fulfilling the Promise to Our Nation's Children, 2007* (www.aspeninstitute.org [July 28, 2008]).

50. Nanette Asimov, "Education Act Changes Proposed; Panel Urges Allowing Suits against Schools," *San Francisco Chronicle,* February 14, 2007 (www.lexisnexis.com.us/lnacademic [July 28, 2008]).

51. Jack Jennings, telephone interview with author, July 23, 2008.

52. See http://blogs.edweek.org/edweek/campaign-k-12/2009/02/miller_stimulus_changes_the_co.html (February 18, 2009).

53. Elizabeth H. DeBray, *Politics, Ideology and Education* (New York: Teachers College Press, 2006), pp. 122–25, 148–51. In an intriguing essay in 2003, political scientist Jennifer Hochschild takes up the question of why accountability founded on testing became a political winner without the support of public school professionals or even the public. In polls the public gave a general endorsement to accountability yet attached higher priority to discipline, safety, extracurricular activities, and the work ethic. If politicians had embraced the voters' agenda for improving schools, they would have looked in a different direction altogether. Focusing on the growth of accountability measures that took root first in state governments, Hochschild locates critical specialized support in state supreme courts that were deciding school finance cases, business leaders who wanted better-trained workers, college professors and organized academic disciplines who framed the standards, and commercial test preparers. "Rethinking Accountability Politics," in *No Child Left Behind? The Politics and Practice of Accountability,* edited by Paul E. Peterson and Martin R. West (Brookings, 2003), pp. 110–20. Entrenchment of accountability measures at the state level may have led national

politicians in 2001–02 to believe that they were conforming to the standard American practice of shaping national policy in keeping with state precedents. But the very complicated and prescriptive law they constructed was received locally as an arbitrary, punitive piling on rather than a reasonable extrapolation from experience.

54. On the politics of NCLB, see Martin R. West and Paul E. Peterson, "The Politics and Practice of Accountability" and Andrew Rudalevige, "No Child Left Behind: Forging a Congressional Compromise," both in *No Child Left Behind?* edited by Peterson and West; Patrick J. McGuinn, *No Child Left Behind and the Transformation of Federal Education Policy, 1965–2005* (University Press of Kansas, 2006); and Kevin R. Kosar, *Failing Grades: The Federal Politics of Education Standards* (Boulder, Colo.: Lynne Rienner, 2005).

11

Still Judging School Discipline

RICHARD ARUM AND DOREET PREISS

In short, in the earliest public schools, teachers taught, and students listened. Teachers commanded, and students obeyed. Teachers did not rely solely on the power of ideas to persuade; they relied on discipline to maintain order.

—CLARENCE THOMAS

Justice Clarence Thomas, in his concurring opinion in *Morse* v. *Frederick* (2007), relied heavily on scholarship from progressive historians to argue that public education in this country was originally established with the intention of socializing youth as law-abiding citizens.[1] Other Supreme Court justices have spoken out in a similar fashion. Antonin Scalia, for example, noted in a 2006 speech at the Georgetown Law School that "the founders considered discipline to be a necessary part of education . . . because it taught respect for the rule of law." Following "the court's application of due process to school affairs

We would like to thank Martin West for editorial suggestions and the collaborating researchers who worked with Arum on several related projects that laid the empirical foundation for this chapter. Lauren Edelman, Calvin Morrill, and Karolyn Tyson collaborated on the School Rights Project; Irenee Beattie and Josipa Roksa collaborated on the analysis of appellate court cases; Melissa Velez assisted with the analysis of the School Rights Project and Harris Public Opinion Data; and Abby Larson contributed to a comparative cross-national project on school discipline.

and the increasing role of litigation in society," Scalia maintained, "swift and effective punishment of even a non-physical sort, has been all but banished from today's public school classrooms."[2]

Judicial concern for the extent to which school authority has been undermined by adversarial legal challenges stretches well beyond the more conservative elements of the Court. In *Morse* v. *Frederick,* for example, Justice Stephen Breyer filed a separate opinion, in part concurring with and dissenting from the conservative majority: "Students will test the limits of acceptable behavior in myriad ways better known to school teachers than to judges; school officials need a degree of flexible authority to respond to disciplinary challenges; and the law has always considered the relationship between teachers and students special." Breyer continued, "Under these circumstances, the more detailed the Court's supervision becomes, the more likely its law will engender further disputes among teachers and students. Consequently, larger numbers of those disputes will likely make their way from the schoolhouse to the courthouse. Yet no one wishes to substitute courts for school boards, or to turn the judge's chambers into the principal's office."

The justices' opinions and commentary articulate some of the critical empirical questions about the role of law in contemporary public education. To what extent is Breyer's concern that court involvement in school disciplinary issues will trigger a flood of lawsuits supported by the record of legal challenges over the past several decades? Is Scalia correct in surmising that the extension of due process protections to students facing disciplinary sanctions and increasing litigation in this area has affected school disciplinary practices and undermined school authority? If so, what have been the educational consequences for America's youth?

Courts have clearly become increasingly involved in regulating U.S. schooling, particularly school discipline. While changes in student behavior and school disciplinary climates emanate from a multiple and complex set of social factors—including changes in family structure, labor force organization, communal voluntary organization, and popular culture—changes in the law have had a marked effect on school practices as well as on taken-for-granted assumptions that principals, teachers, parents, students, and others have long held about how authority and discipline in schools should be structured.[3] To understand this influence of the courts, it is important to examine both "the law on the books" (that is, the extent and contours of litigation, related statutes, and administrative regulations) and "law in action" (that is, legalized organizational forms and practices, educator and student understanding of legal entitlements, and the way in which legal rights are mobilized in schools). This is a critical area of research as student interaction with school institutional authority is one of the primary mechanisms by which youth come into contact with and internalize societal norms, values, and rules. Indeed, school discipline and the moral authority of educators are essential components of youth socialization.

Court Decisions: Landmark Cases

The Supreme Court, in a set of landmark cases in 1969 and 1975, affirmed that students do not "shed their constitutional rights to freedom of speech or expression at the schoolhouse gate" and granted "rudimentary" due process protections to students facing school suspensions and exclusion.[4] Before 1969, no significant school discipline cases reached the Supreme Court. However, several cases during this earlier period set the stage for the landmark cases that provided challenges to the traditional exercise of public school discipline. The Warren court's decision in *In re Gault* (1967), for example, granted due process rights to youth in juvenile courts, an important precedent to the future expansion of due process rights to students. A year later, in *Epperson* v. *Arkansas* (1968), the Court ruled that Arkansas law was in violation of the First Amendment for mandating the firing of any teacher who taught or used a text teaching evolution. Though not directly related to school discipline, this ruling was often cited in school discipline cases because it "emphasized the need for affirming the comprehensive authority of the States and of school officials, *consistent with fundamental constitutional safeguards,* to prescribe and control conduct in schools."[5] These cases set important legal precedents, foreshadowing and shaping the orientation of the court when it adjudicated future legal challenges.

By contrast, the period from 1969 to 1975, the student rights contestation period, was characterized by frequent legal challenges to the regulation of student behavior.[6] In 1969 *Tinker* v. *Des Moines Independent Community School District* was decided by the Supreme Court. Three Iowa students had worn black armbands as a sign of protest to the "hostilities in Vietnam," and their fathers had filed a complaint in the federal district court to block disciplinary measures by the school district. The district court upheld the school's authority, finding its actions constitutional and reasonable to prevent disturbances to school order. However, in both the court of appeals and in the Supreme Court, the judges were divided on this case. While the majority opinion acknowledged that neither students nor teachers abdicate their constitutional rights to freedom of speech when they enter school grounds, it also acknowledged the need to affirm the authority of states and school officials to control school conduct. The problem, it continued, "lies in the area where students in the exercise of First Amendment rights collide with the rules of the school authorities."[7] Ultimately, the Court decided that a student may express his opinion "if he does so without 'materially and substantially interfer[ing] with the requirements of appropriate discipline in the operation of the school' and without colliding with the rights of others."[8] Although the two dissenting justices worried that the Court's ruling would usher in "a new revolutionary era of permissiveness" that would inevitably undermine school authority, *Tinker* v. *Des Moines* was decided in favor of the students, greatly broadening the existing conceptualization of student rights.[9]

To this day, the most important court decision affecting how schools approach student discipline is *Goss* v. *Lopez,* decided by the Supreme Court in 1975. During a patriotic assembly at Central High School in Columbus, Ohio, in 1971, student unrest turned into a week of demonstrations and disturbances to normal school functioning. According to Central's principal Calvin Park, a group of black students were "disgruntled" because no comparable assembly existed for Black History Week. As a result, "scores of students refused to return to classes from the assembly in protest."[10] Demonstrations continued the following week, and other local schools experienced similar racial tensions. Hundreds were involved in the disturbances, and about seventy-five students were suspended. However, many of the suspended students claimed to have only watched but not taken an active role in the demonstrations. Nevertheless, the students were suspended for up to ten days without formal hearings or notification of the specific charges against them. Students were not afforded an opportunity to present evidence on their behalf, and because protests blocked the building, parents were unable to attend the necessary Board of Education meeting to ensure their children's return to school. The full suspensions were carried out and became part of the students' permanent record. Some students were transferred to adult schools without their consent. Outraged parents and the local chapter of the National Association for the Advancement of Colored People (NAACP), aided by local civil rights lawyer Denis Murphy and lawyers from the Office of Economic Opportunity (OEO) legal services, brought their grievances to court. In the end, the lawyers selected nine named plaintiffs for the case. Dwight Lopez, a nineteen-year-old student from Central High became the first-named plaintiff because of his "ethnic-sounding" name and articulate speech.

Rather than merely contest the specific suspensions enacted by the school authorities, the students' lawyers sought to "set up a federal appellate-level challenge that was potentially capable of establishing student rights to due process as broadly as possible in school disciplinary procedures."[11] Because the nine suspended students challenged the constitutionality of the Ohio state law "empowering principals to suspend students with few procedural guidelines," their case skipped straight to the federal judiciary, strategically denying school officials an opportunity to settle the case.[12] In *Lopez* v. *Williams,* the case heard by the U.S. District Court for the Southern District of Ohio, the verdict favored the students. Although the court emphasized the overall authority of school officials in disciplinary matters, it also applied constitutional limitations to that authority:

The primacy of the educator in the school has been unquestioned by the Courts. The Courts have consistently reaffirmed the right of school administrators to manage their school systems without interference from the Courts, so long as the basic commands of the Constitution are honored. . . . Remembering that school officials are better suited to make decisions affecting their institutions, the Court nonetheless is constitutionally bound to insure that the student be afforded the minimum procedural process mandated by the Constitution.[13]

Central High School appealed the district court's decision, arguing that because education is not a constitutionally protected right, the students did not have an assumed right to an uninterrupted education. In *Goss* v. *Lopez,* however, the Supreme Court rejected the school's claim and upheld the district court's opinion. Finding that Ohio's laws mandated free and compulsory education for children of a certain age, the court pointed out that the state itself created a situation in which students do indeed have reasonable claims to a public education. In a 6-3 decision, the Supreme Court ruled the suspensions invalid and ordered that the students' records be expunged of all references to this incident. In addition, it set a landmark precedent in granting "rudimentary" due process rights to students suspended from school for fewer than ten days, as well as "more formal protections" for students facing longer exclusions. Then in *Wood* v. *Strickland* (1975), the Court established that a public school educator had the responsibility to maintain "knowledge of the basic unquestioned constitutional rights of his charges" and that knowingly violating such rights would subject the individual to risk of personal liability and damages.[14]

Although *Tinker, Goss,* and *Wood* exemplify the Court's pro-student orientation during the student rights contestation period, the court climate changed over time. Since 1975 the Supreme Court has on the whole been less favorable toward students. In *Ingraham* v. *Wright* (1977), for example, the Burger court ruled that corporal punishment could not be considered "cruel and unusual punishment" under the Constitution and could continue in schools. In *New Jersey* v. *T.L.O.* (1985), the first major case involving drug possession to reach the Supreme Court, the majority ruled that school officials should be able to search students without a warrant or probable cause but in keeping with the "reasonableness" of the search. Both these cases demonstrated the Court's "renewed willingness to consider constitutional rights less applicable to schoolchildren than to other citizens."[15] The court climate changed for various reasons, including the growing public concern about the level of violence and disorder in public schools, a change in the political climate following the end of the Vietnam era, and the preponderance of increasingly conservative judicial appointments.

More recently, court cases have involved enforcement of zero-tolerance policies (regarding weapons, violence, drugs, and alcohol), as well as claims by students and their parents against schools for not maintaining and providing adequate disciplinary climates.[16] These cases have by and large continued the post-1975 pattern of the Supreme Court's sympathy with schools facing challenges to their disciplinary authority.

In 1995 the Supreme Court adjudicated *Vernonia School District* v. *Wayne Acton,* a drug-related search-and-seizure case that challenged a school district's drug-testing/urinalysis policy. Concerned about the sharp increase in student drug use and potential risks associated with drug consumption and athletic competition, an Oregon school district, along with parents at a parent "input night," voted to implement a urinalysis drug-testing policy for all student athletes. The policy required all students and their parents to give written consent to the testing, which included urinalysis testing at the beginning of the sports season as well as random weekly testing of 10 percent of all athletes during the season. When a seventh-grade student was excluded from the school's football program because he failed to consent to the testing, he and his parents filed suit, claiming the policy violated his Fourth Amendment rights, as well as a provision of the Oregon State Constitution. Following the precedent set in *T.L.O.*, the Court found that the constitutionality of such a policy hinged upon the reasonableness of the search. Because the drug-testing policy was reasonable in light of the district's demonstrated drug problems (especially related to students involved in interscholastic athletics), and because this type of policy was relatively unobtrusive, the Court found that the school's policy did not violate the Fourth Amendment.

The Supreme Court also weighed in on *Board of Education of Independent School District No. 92 of Pottawatomie County* v. *Lindsay Earls* (2002). In this particular case, several students and their parents brought suit against the Tecumseh District School Board, claiming that its urinalysis testing policy for all students participating in extracurricular activities violated their constitutional protections against unreasonable searches. While the district court originally favored the school board, its decision was reversed by the U.S. Court of Appeals for the Tenth Circuit. Before establishing a "suspicionless" drug-testing program, stated the court, the school board would have to sufficiently demonstrate a drug problem among those tested, such that testing that group would address the identified problem. According to the court of appeals, because the board had not established such a problem among the population tested, its policy violated their Fourth Amendment rights. Although the court of appeals found for the students owing to the lack of evidence to justify the board's policy, the Supreme Court declared that individual suspicion was not required in such a case. Echoing *T.L.O* (1985) and *Vernonia* (1995), it emphasized that although the students do retain some rights when they enter the schoolhouse, their Fourth Amendment rights differ from their rights elsewhere. Because the state is responsible for maintaining discipline, health, and safety in public schools, a student's privacy may be limited, and students may be subjected to greater controls while on school property. The Supreme Court concluded that the board's policy was a reasonable means of detecting and preventing drug use among its students. As in *T.L.O.* and *Vernonia,* the Court supported the school and reversed the court of appeals' prior pro-student ruling.

The Supreme Court also recently decided one of the first major peer-to-peer sexual harassment cases. In *Aurelia Davis, As Next Friend of Lashonda D., Petitioner* v. *Monroe County Board of Education* (1999), the mother of fifth-grade student Lashonda sued the county board of education, the school superintendent, and the school principal, alleging that her daughter was the victim of persistent sexual harassment by one of her classmates. According to the mother's claims, no disciplinary action was taken even though the harassment had been reported to school authorities, and there was no effort to separate the two students. Lashonda's mother charged that the school board's deliberate indifference created an "intimidating, hostile, offensive, and abusive school environment" that violated Title IX of the Education Amendments of 1972.[17] For this violation, she sought monetary and injunctive relief. While the district court originally dismissed the suit on the grounds that student-on-student harassment was not an adequate reason to seek compensation under Title IX, the U.S. Court of Appeals for the Eleventh Circuit reversed that decision, but it also granted the school board's motion for a rehearing and eventually reaffirmed the district court's original dismissal.

The appeals court ruling, however, did not have much traction in the Supreme Court. In a 5-4 split decision, the Court declared that in cases of student-on-student harassment, a private damages action may be claimed against a public school board if and when (a) "the school board acted with deliberate indifference to known acts of harassment in the school board's programs or activities," and when (b) "the harassment was so severe, pervasive, and objectively offensive that it effectively barred the victim's access to an educational opportunity or benefit." In this case, the Court declared that it could not be proven beyond doubt that the mother would not be able to provide evidence in support of her claims. Therefore dismissing the Title IX claim would be an error. Although the dissenting justices argued that Title IX does not equate accepting federal funds with ceding power over day-to-day disciplinary issues to the federal government, in the end, the Court reversed the lower court's ruling.

The *Davis* case is particularly interesting in that it exemplifies an increasing number of cases in lower courts in which students and families have sued

schools for failing to provide adequate school discipline and for permitting bul-
lying, sexual harassment, or other forms of school violence (including rampage
school shootings).[18] In these cases, schools have been sued for both disciplining
students and for not disciplining them.

The latest school discipline case to reach the Supreme Court at the time of
this writing, *Morse* v. *Frederick* (2007), continues the pro-school trend. Joseph
Frederick had displayed a banner that read "BONG HiTS 4 JESUS" during a
parade in support of the torch relay for the Winter Olympic Games in Salt Lake
City. Although the parade took place on a public street and the students stood
on a public sidewalk, school participation at the event was mandated, so Principal Deborah Morse ordered Frederick to take down the sign. He refused and
received a ten-day suspension. Frederick challenged his suspension in court,
claiming that his First Amendment rights had been violated. A federal appeals
court in San Francisco favored Frederick and found Principal Morse liable for
damages for violating Frederick's First Amendment rights, whereas the Supreme
Court considered the banner a clear violation of the school's antidrug policy. In
a 6-3 majority decision, the Court found for the principal.

The split decision revealed the court's difficulties in defining the precise limits of free speech in schools. Despite the precedent set in *Tinker,* the Supreme
Court justices were "deeply split over what weight to give free speech in public
schools."[19] According to Chief Justice John Roberts, the principal's actions were
reasonable; failing to act would have sent a powerful and undesirable message to
her students. In addition, he emphasized, "The First Amendment does not
require schools to tolerate at school events student expression that contributes to
those [illegal drug] dangers."[20] Justice Thomas went further in his definition of
the limits of free speech in schools, urging that *Tinker* be overturned for "it cannot seriously be suggested that the First Amendment 'freedom of speech'
encompasses a student's rights to speak in public schools."[21] Although Justice
Breyer voted with the majority and believed that the principal should not be
liable for monetary damages, he did not sign the chief justice's opinion because
he found the First Amendment issue in schools to be particularly cloudy and
felt the case did not lend itself to generating greater judicial clarity or guidance
on this issue.

The dissenting justices, on the other hand, asserted that the majority opinion
distorted the First Amendment by "carving out pro-drug speech for uniquely
harsh punishment." Justice John Paul Stevens wrote that the majority's decision
"finds no support in our case law and is inimical to the values protected by the
First Amendment."[22] Though in the end the case ruling constrains student
rights, the divided opinion indicates that the extent of students' free speech
rights, aside from political or religious speech, is not easily defined. While the
media responded to the *Morse* v. *Frederick* decision with headlines announcing

that the case had placed "limits" on student rights, the court case in no way challenged the "rudimentary due process" provisions for minor day-to-day school discipline mandated by the *Goss* decision.[23] The case thus ultimately failed to alter significantly the general contours of student rights affecting authority relationships in schools that had been previously established by past Supreme Court decisions.

Court Decisions: Appellate Case Patterns

Although every school in the nation must adhere to the rulings in these few landmark cases, they do not encompass the full universe of legal challenges to school discipline. Thus in order to gain a better understanding of the court climate regarding school discipline, we examine all appellate-level federal and state court cases in which school efforts to discipline and control students have been challenged.[24] Our survey includes cases involving the use of state agents (such as the police) acting on behalf of school authorities to deal with students in the vicinity of school grounds. We exclude from this analysis all instances of conflicts between schools and teachers (such as teacher dismissal cases) and between schools and non-student outsiders (such as drug and weapon-free-zone cases that did not involve students), as well as student rights cases focused exclusively on free speech issues (that is, those not combined with the school's use of suspension, expulsion, corporal punishment, transfer, and so on). We also exclude cases in which students allege that school authorities have breached their duty to maintain safety in the school and protect students from harm.

From this set of cases it appears that both the frequency of legal challenges and the content and direction of outcomes have varied greatly over time. Because this analysis focuses solely on appellate-level cases, it excludes the vast majority of litigation that was either settled before hearing or never reached state and federal appellate courts. Our research methods (described in the following paragraphs) gauge the overall prevalence of legal challenges that contemporary educators face. We focus first on the appellate-level court cases as these cases define case law, generate media coverage, influence public perceptions, and can be tracked over time as an empirical indicator of the broad parameters that shape court climate toward school discipline.

Before the social and political shifts of the late 1960s and early to mid-1970s, no major legal challenges to school officials and school authority had reached the federal Supreme Court, and such cases occurred only sporadically at the state and federal district appellate levels. Viewing common schools as a public function providing instruction in wisdom, virtue, and the ideals of the nation, parents and students seldom questioned disciplinary actions of school authorities.[25] However, as conceptions of youth rights began to shift (in part because of

Figure 11-1. *K–12 Frequency of Public School Discipline Court Cases, 1960–2007*

Number of cases

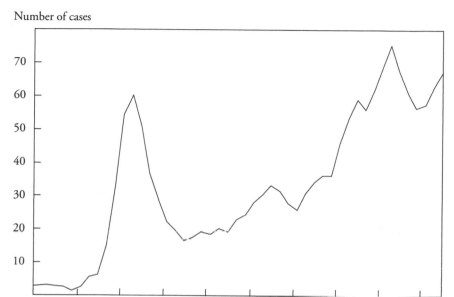

the Twenty-sixth Amendment's lowering of the legal voting age in 1971), and as citizens across the country began questioning the government's involvement in Vietnam, students and parents also began to question and challenge school disciplinary practices.

This newfound willingness to challenge school authority became evident in the surge of discipline-related litigation during the student rights contestation period of the late 1960s. After hovering at an average level of only 3.5 relevant public school K–12 cases a year from 1960 to 1967, the numbers reaching the appellate level swelled to an average of 39.1 cases a year between 1968 and 1975 (three-year moving averages are presented in figure 11-1), thanks in part to increased institutional support from public interest legal advocacy groups and OEO legal services.[26] After important legal precedents were set and institutional support waned, the average number of cases declined to 24.5 a year in the post-contestation period of 1976 to 1992.[27] The number of legal challenges to school discipline then rose sharply from 1993 to 2002, reaching levels even higher than those of the student rights contestation period. The number of appellate cases rose to 51.7 a year between 1993 and 2002 and 55.6 between 2003 and 2007, with a peak of 76 cases in 2000 and a slight drop to 65 cases a year in 2007. We present the overall number of cases, rather than a relative measure calculated per

Figure 11-2. *Content and Outcomes of K–12 Public School Discipline Court Cases, 1960–2007*

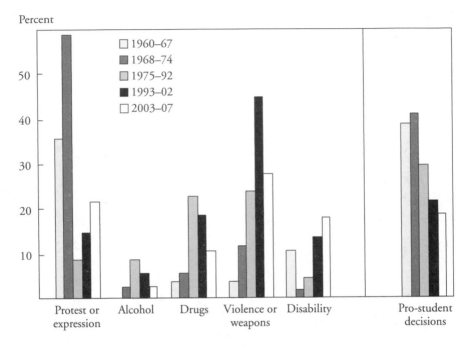

Percent

Legend:
☐ 1960–67
■ 1968–74
☐ 1975–92
■ 1993–02
☐ 2003–07

Categories: Protest or expression, Alcohol, Drugs, Violence or weapons, Disability, Pro-student decisions

public school enrollment, given that media coverage and individual understandings are a product of the former rather than latter indicator. A measure of state and federal court cases calculated per enrolled students would demonstrate similar upward trends, more than doubling from the 1976–92 period to the 2003–07 period.

In addition, the substance of the discipline cases brought before the courts varied over time (figure 11-2). Protest and free expression cases, which were matters commonly adjudicated during the student rights contestation period, decreased from 59 percent of K–12 public school discipline cases in 1968–74 to only 8 percent of cases in 1975–92.[28] More recently, courts have witnessed a reemergence of these issues: by 2003–07, 23 percent of court cases—including *Morse* v. *Frederick*—involved either political protest or freedom of expression issues. Cases involving alcohol and drugs rose during the intermediate periods that coincided with national attention to the nation's "War on Drugs" and since then have diminished.

While cases related to alcohol and drugs have steadily declined, those connected with weapons and violence have increased to 40 percent of all K–12 public school discipline cases since 1993. The rate of violence and weapons cases over the past decade and a half is now more than three times the rate of 1968–74. In addition, more school discipline court cases involve student disability, as special protections for students with disabilities have been increasingly mandated and invoked. Between 2003 and 2007, 18 percent of K–12 public school discipline court cases included discussion of student disability status. Over time, courts in general have become less favorable to student claims in court. However, given that the number of court challenges has increased in recent decades, the likelihood of a school facing a legal environment in which a student has recently been successful in a court challenge over school discipline has not significantly diminished.

Challenges to discipline involving free speech or protest dominated the courts during the 1960s and 1970s, as some students wore armbands to protest the war and others flaunted the dress code in order to protest the status quo.[29] In today's climate of zero-tolerance policies and legal regulations affecting students with disabilities, violence- and weapons-related infractions and laws related to student disability status are increasingly adjudicated in the courts. In other words, the court's procedures and doctrines for a set of problems occurring in an earlier era have had to be revised and applied in complex ways to meet current school conditions.

Legal Mobilization: Institutional Origins and Current Prevalence

Although accounts of legal challenges to school disciplinary measures often focus on the students, parents, and school officials involved in the suit, institutional actors have also played a crucial role in this type of litigation. Some trace the rights consciousness underlying student and parent reaction to school authority and disciplinary measures to the United Nation's Universal Declaration of Human Rights in 1945, which identified children and youth as a population deserving individual rights and protections in international law.[30] While this certainly could have affected the way students and families conceived of their rights within and outside of schools, the overt questioning of school authority in the United States and the emergence of this type of litigation were more directly stimulated by the federal government's establishment of the OEO Legal Service Program in 1965 and the program's Center for Law and Education, opened at Harvard University in 1969 and funded to support high-impact appellate-level legal work on education.

As noted earlier, few cases relevant to school discipline emerged before 1969, but with institutional assistance, including support from private and corporate foundations for public interest legal advocacy, landmark cases such as *Goss* v. *Lopez* were developed and shaped the court climate that schools faced. These groups did not merely represent the students' interests, however, or those of administrators and teachers. They clearly had a vested interest in the outcomes themselves. Professional groups representing schools and administrators emphasized the importance of maintaining school authority, whereas others often backed the students' cause. In *Goss* v. *Lopez* (1975), for example, groups such as the National Committee for Citizens in Education, the American Civil Liberties Union, the NAACP Legal Fund, and the Children's Defense Fund filed significant amici curiae briefs on behalf of the students. Their goal was not only to defend the named students in the case but also to set up "rudimentary" due process rights for all students in order to protect them from "unwarranted government-exercised authority."[31]

Although national groups were not involved in all discipline cases, when they were, as in *Goss*, their motivations stretched far beyond the immediate cases before them. After playing an important role in promoting and shaping the particular legal field that dealt with student disciplinary challenges during the student rights contestation period, federal support for these efforts was significantly limited following the mid-1970s. Today other advocacy organizations—such as Lambda Legal Defense and Education Fund, the Alliance Defense Fund, and the Disability Rights Legal Center—have taken up this role, joining earlier advocacy groups arguing on behalf of students and schools as they question and challenge the prominent issues of the day, including issues related to school practices dealing with students' sexual orientation, religious expression, and disability accommodation.

Notwithstanding the institutional efforts of public interest lawyers, empirical evidence suggests that litigation in this area is increasingly used strategically and instrumentally by families from relatively privileged origins to promote the interests of their children. Attempts to identify the extent to which legal challenges are associated with social background and privilege can focus on either the sources of the cases that appear in court or the prevalence of legal mobilization reported by individuals in schools.

In earlier empirical work, Irenee Beattie, Josipa Roksa, and Richard Arum examined the characteristics of schools that were cited in appellate court cases from 2000 to 2002.[32] They found that, on average, appellate court cases emerged from secondary schools with 28.7 percent non-white students; the proportion of non-white students in the national population of secondary schools was 37.1 percent (the latter weighted for enrollment size to be comparable to the court case data); appellate cases also emerged from schools with more educational resources per student (student/teacher ratios of 16.3 compared with 17.5).

National surveys of teachers and administrators have provided evidence of similar associations between school characteristics and the prevalence of educators facing legal challenges. In a reanalysis of a Harris public opinion survey of approximately 600 teachers and administrators conducted for Common Good in 2003, Melissa Velez and Arum linked individual reports to school-level data and examined the proportion of public school educators (that is, a combined sample of both teachers and administrators) who reported that either they or someone they know personally had been sued by a student or parent.[33] The distribution of reports of legal challenges suggests that educators have the greatest likelihood of adversarial involvement with the legal system if they are located in suburban schools where white students are prevalent. Educators in suburban schools with less than 70 percent non-white students have a 46.9 percent probability of having experienced contact with adversarial legal challenge, compared with 40.2 percent of educators in all other schools. This disparity is particularly striking as students in urban, predominately non-white schools have been thought to face disproportionately high rates of punitive school discipline.[34] Although much of the development of student rights emerged from concern with non-white students in urban areas (for example, *Goss* v. *Lopez* originated when students were disciplined for protesting against the lack of an African American curriculum in Central High School in Columbus, Ohio), educators in those settings had only a 41.3 percent probability of contact with legal challenge.

More recently, in collaboration with colleagues working on the School Rights Project (Lauren Edelman, Calvin Morrill, and Karolyn Tyson), we conducted a national telephone survey of 600 high school teachers and administrators on perceptions and experiences of the law in schools. Teachers and administrators reported high levels of being threatened with lawsuits for school-related matters. Fifteen percent of public school teachers and 55 percent of public school administrators contacted have been threatened with such suits. For administrators with more than fifteen years of experience in the position, the prevalence of threats of legal challenge increased to 73 percent. Administrators' actual experience of lawsuits was considerably lower than the threat of legal action but was still relatively high and the source of considerable professional anxiety, given that these cases—following *Wood* v. *Strickland* (1975)—run the risk of vulnerability to personal liability claims. Fourteen percent of public high school administrators with fifteen years of work experience report the occurrence of such events. While public school administrators today often experience legal threats or actual suits, we again find that these legal challenges are concentrated in schools where more privileged students are concentrated. Administrators in public schools with more than half of students eligible for free lunches are significantly less likely than others to report having been sued for a school-related matter (only 3 percent versus 11 percent). When we restricted our national sample solely to administrators working in urban public schools with high proportions of disadvantaged youth (that is, schools in which more than half of the students are eligible for free lunch), we found—albeit with a sample of only sixteen cases—not a single report of administrators being sued for a school-related matter.

Not surprisingly, legal mobilization generally appears to depend on the availability of economic resources to pursue such challenges. It seems that regardless of the institutional and political origins of student rights found in the *Goss* decision—a case in which public interest lawyers intervened to remedy the plight of urban non-white students exercising their right to dissent politically—legal mobilization in schools today largely reflects patterns of socioeconomic inequalities. As the institutional basis for socially and economically disadvantaged students to pursue legal remedy has waned, the law has increasingly become a tool employed by families with the resources to pursue such action. In the School Rights Project surveys of 5,490 students in twenty-four high schools across three states (New York, North Carolina, and California), we found that white students were nearly twice as likely as non-white students to report having pursued a formal legal remedy for a perceived rights violation.[35]

Legal Understandings and School Disciplinary Practices

Court decisions, lawsuits, and threats of legal challenges are only a small fraction of the law's manifestation in schools as organizations. Law and Society scholars have long recognized that legal mobilization is a relatively rare occurrence—a small tip of a much larger legal dispute pyramid.[36] To appreciate how law has shaped everyday school practices, it is necessary to see how legal understandings have come to underlie many assumptions about school organizational practices. School discipline today is profoundly influenced by legal understandings, regardless of whether lawsuits are ever threatened or pursued. Furthermore, these legal understandings are only partly and indirectly related to formal regulation and case law, which is often ambiguous or even contradictory. We highlight here the extent to which both students and educators have developed an expansive definition of legal rights of students with respect to school discipline, the relationship between this sense of legal entitlement and school disciplinary practices, and perceptions of the fairness and legitimacy of various school disciplinary practices.

While courts in general have become less sympathetic to students since the legal challenges of the student rights contestation period from the late 1960s through the mid-1970s, the legal environment in this area remains highly ambiguous, as prior case law decisions still define and provide the legal parameters to which school disciplinary practices must adhere. At the same time, student legal entitlements have been institutionalized in the form of extensive state statutes and administrative regulations. The institutionalization and legalization of student due process protections go well beyond appellate case law. Since education policies and practices vary across schools, districts, and states, we highlight disciplinary practices in the nation's largest school district to give a sense of the extent to which law has come to permeate school practices.

Public school parents at the start of each school year in New York City receive a twenty-eight-page pamphlet entitled "Citywide Standards of Discipline and Intervention Measures: The Discipline Code and Bill of Student Rights and Responsibilities, K–12." Schools require parents and students to return a signed form acknowledging that they are familiar with the guidelines in this document. The brochure identifies 112 infractions, the range of possible disciplinary responses, and guidance interventions associated with each type of incident. "The Right to Freedom of Expression and Person" section explains the scope of this right in expansive detail, with official materials noting that these freedoms include not only the right to "be free from corporal punishment" but also the explicitly stated right to "decline to participate in the Pledge of Allegiance or stand for the pledge." In addition, the brochure includes a section entitled "The Right to Due Process," which identifies ten specific components of this guarantee:

1. be provided with the Discipline Code and rules and regulations of the school;

2. know what is appropriate behavior and what behaviors may result in disciplinary actions;

3. be counseled by members of the professional staff in matters related to their behavior as it affects their education and welfare within the school;

4. know possible dispositions and outcomes for specific offenses;

5. receive written notice of the reasons for disciplinary action taken against them in a timely fashion;

6. due process of law in instances of disciplinary action for alleged violations of school regulations for which they may be suspended or removed from class by their teachers;

7. know the procedures for appealing the actions and decisions of school officials with respect to their rights and responsibilities as set forth in this document;

8. be accompanied by a parent/adult in parental relationship and/or representative at conferences and hearings;

9. the presence of school staff in situations where there may be police involvement;

10. challenge and explain in writing any material entered in their student records.[37]

The extent to which these due process protections are formalized and extended broadly to students goes well beyond any narrow reading of the *Goss* decision. A New York City public school principal attempting to discipline a student would have to comply with the due process protections specified in the list, consider the range of options allowed by the district for the specific infractions occurring, and reference relevant additional regulations and safeguards. For example, the pamphlet on discipline notes that "students with disabilities are entitled to additional due process protections described in Chancellor's Regulation A-443" and "when a student is believed to have committed a crime, the police must be summoned and parents must be contacted (see Chancellor's Regulation A-412)."[38] In addition, ten other specific "Chancellor's Regulations" are referenced in the document (A-420, A-421, A-449, A-450, A-750, A-801, A-820, A-830, A-831, A-832) in addition to the acknowledgment that all procedures must also comply with relevant "State Education Law and Federal Laws."[39] While school officials "must consult the Disciplinary Code when determining which disciplinary measure to impose," they also are required to consider "the student's age, maturity, and previous disciplinary record . . . the circumstances surrounding the incident leading to the discipline; and the student's IEP, BIP and 504 Accommodation Plan."[40] While it is likely that given the size of the district, New York City public schools are more bureaucratized and formalized in terms of the institutionalization and legalization of school discipline than smaller districts are, the scale, scope, and level of complexity of the legal regulations affecting day-to-day school disciplinary practices appear quite formidable.

Since the student rights contestation period, judges, legislators, and policymakers have also continued to expand legal entitlements to particular groups of students, most notably to students classified as disabled, including those with learning, physical, or behavioral handicaps (among them, psychological disorders that are themselves associated with the manifestation of student misbehavior). While courts were considering and extending due process protections to students in the *Goss* decision, federal legislators began recognizing disabled students as deserving of extended civil rights protections, first in Section 504 of the Rehabilitation Act of 1973 and then in the Education for All Handicapped Children Act of 1985, later known as the Individuals with Disabilities Education Act (IDEA).[41] Through subsequent federal reauthorization, including the Americans with Disability Act of 1990 and the 1997 amendments to the original legislation, special education students gained additional protections relating to school discipline—particularly if infractions were defined as an outcome of the individual's disability.

As a result of the ambiguity found in formal law, including legislative statutes and administrative regulations, and the expansion of legal rights to particular groups of students, educators and students have developed a set of legal understandings based on a broad and expansive definition of the scale and scope of student legal entitlements in this domain. Following the *Goss* decision, students have been granted rudimentary due process protections when facing minor disciplinary action and more formal due process protections when facing more serious forms of discipline (such as long-term expulsion or suspension). The *Goss* decision noted that due process protections for short-term suspensions should entail procedural safeguards such that "the student be given oral or written notice of the charges against him and, if he denies them, an explanation of the evidence the authorities have and an opportunity to present his side of the story." More formal due process protections may include the right of students to "summon the accuser, permit cross-examination, and allow the student to present his own witnesses. In more difficult cases, he (the disciplinarian) may permit counsel."

In our School Rights Project survey, we specifically asked which of these due process protections were required when students faced various disciplinary sanctions. We sought information on individual perceptions, since student and educator beliefs about rights are likely to have real consequences for school authority relations and disciplinary procedures even though they many not correspond precisely with the actual formal "law on the books." We found wide expectation of formal due process protections for students facing major disciplinary actions, and even an expectation of these legal entitlements for those facing minor day-to-day discipline. Of the public school students in our sample, 61.9 percent believed that if faced with long-term suspension/expulsion, they were legally entitled to some form of formal due process protections (that is, at least one or more of the following: a formal disciplinary hearing, opportunity to be represented by legal counsel, opportunity to confront and cross-examine witnesses bringing the charges, or opportunity to call witnesses to provide alternative versions of the incident). Approximately one-third of these students also believed that they were legally entitled to some form of formal due process protection when their grades were lowered for disciplinary reasons (33.3 percent), they were suspended from extracurricular activities (36.1 percent), or they faced in-school suspension (35.4 percent). We found teacher and administrator expectations of required student due process protections to be even greater. When asked about lowering student grades for disciplinary reasons, for example, approximately half of public school teachers and administrators responded that this action was prohibited and could not even be considered; for the remaining educators who did think such disciplinary actions were permissible, 32 percent reported that students subject to such disciplinary sanctions were entitled to formal due process protections.

These expansive perceptions of legal rights and court challenges to school disciplinary practices have led many schools to pull back from traditional forms of school discipline. Where courts have been more favorable to students, schools have been particularly likely to abandon the use of corporal punishment as well as to adopt fewer school rules and disciplinary practices that students consider strict.[42] In recent decades, and in the context of legal ambiguity and pervasive challenges to traditional forms of authority, schools have moved away from disciplinary practices that rely on the judgment, discretion, and action of professional educators and turned instead to the use of school security guards, uniformed police, technical surveillance, security apparatuses, and zero-tolerance policies. The latter techniques are often ill suited to the pedagogical task of enhancing the moral authority of educators to support the socialization of youth—which, as already mentioned, entails the internalization of norms, values, and rules.[43]

We have found in the School Rights Project that increased perceptions of student legal entitlements correlate with decreased reports of the fairness of school discipline. This mirrors James Coleman's finding that Catholic school students in the 1980s were significantly more likely to perceive school discipline to be fairer than public school students who possessed far greater formal legal protections.[44] Although school cultures today reflect a generalized sense of legal entitlements among both educators and students, school practices in many settings have become increasingly authoritarian, with student misbehavior often subject to criminalization and formal legal sanction. These internal contradictions intensify students' sense of the unfairness of school discipline—they see that rights exist in principle, but that school discipline in practice is becoming formalized and administratively institutionalized in a manner considered unfair and illegitimate. Longitudinal research has demonstrated that students who believe school discipline is unfair are more likely to disobey teachers, disrupt classroom instruction, and in general fail to develop behaviors conducive to educational success or related positive outcomes in the course of life.[45]

Conclusion

Our research suggests that schools are currently at a historical crossroads with respect to the law and school discipline.[46] On the one hand, citizens, legislators, judges, and policymakers are recognizing and questioning the role of law in the regulation of the traditional domain of school discipline and authority relations.[47] This attention could lead to changes in statutory or case law that could reduce expectations of student legal entitlements and the prevalence of court challenges to school authority in this country. On the other hand, the institutional forces responsible for the current conditions—which Robert Kagan has associated with the rise of "adversarial legalism"—may well have deepened, become diffused, and broadened in recent decades.[48] These forces, coupled with changes in the political climate or judicial orientation, might be sufficiently powerful to keep schools moving away from disciplinary practices that traditionally relied on professional educators' judgment and discretionary authority. Ironically, although such a movement celebrates and enhances the legal rights and entitlements of students, the formalization and bureaucratization of school disciplinary procedures accompanying it tends to replace traditional professional discretionary authority with authoritarian administrative procedures that can have a negative impact on youth socialization.

As various social and political actors consider legal regulatory reforms, it is important to recognize that the expansion of students' legal entitlements has not only had unintended consequences on the capacity of schools to socialize youth effectively, but it has also increased the potential for student dissent in U.S. schools—whether of a political, religious, or other ideological character. At the same time, individual students and their families are now able to contest what they perceive as unfair disciplinary sanctions or rights violations. These gains have come at a cost, however, in that the resolution of school disciplinary matters has increasingly moved—as Justice Breyer feared—from the schoolhouse to the courthouse.

Notes

1. For example, the opinion cites Lawrence Cremin, William Reese, Carl Kaestle, and Maris Vinovskis. *Morse* v. *Frederick*, 551 U.S. 393 (2007).

2. Scalia paraphrased and directly quoted in "Georgetown News," Georgetown University (http://explore.georgetown.edu/news/?ID=19322 [July 2008]).

3. Richard Arum, *Judging School Discipline: The Crisis of Moral Authority* (Harvard University Press, 2003).

4. See *Tinker* v. *Des Moines*, 393 U.S. 503 (1969); and *Goss* v. *Lopez*, 419 U.S. 565 (1975).

5. *Tinker* v. *Des Moines*, 507. Emphasis added.

6. Arum, *Judging School Discipline*.

7. Ibid., p. 506. According to the First Amendment of the U.S. Constitution, "Congress shall make no law respecting an establishment of religion, or prohibiting the free exercise thereof; or abridging the freedom of speech, or of the press; or the right of the people peaceably to assemble, and to petition the government for a redress of grievances."

8. *Burnside* v. *Byars*, 363 F.2d 744, 749 (U. Ct. App. 5th Cir. 1966).

9. Ibid., p. 518.

10 "Racial Strife Hits Schools," editorial, *Columbus Dispatch*, January 20, 1979, sec. 1, p. 19, as quoted in Arum, *Judging School Discipline*.

11. Arum, *Judging School Discipline*, p. 40.

12. Ibid.

13. *Lopez* v. *Williams*, 372 F. Supp. 1284–85 (S.D. Ohio E. Div. 1973).

14. *Wood* v. *Strickland,* 420 U.S. 308, 322 (1975).

15. Arum, *Judging School Discipline,* p. 75.

16. In *United States* v. *Alfonso Lopez Jr.* (1995), a twelfth-grade student was charged in a federal grand jury indictment of violating the Gun-Free School Zone Act (GFSZA) of 1990 after carrying a concealed handgun and bullets to school. The Supreme Court found that the act concerns and intrudes upon areas traditionally handled by the states (namely, education, criminal sanctions, and commerce). According to the Court, if a state believes that harsh criminal sanctions are necessary to deter students from bringing weapons on school grounds, it is within the state's, and not Congress's, power to enact such sanctions. Although the Court often tended to sympathize with the struggles of schools in the face of disciplinary challenges in the post-student-rights contestation period, in this case the question was decided in favor of state rights.

17. Title IX of the Education Amendments of 1972 prohibits a student from being "excluded from participation in, being denied the benefits of, or being subjected to discrimination under any education program or activity receiving Federal financial assistance," 20 U.S.C. 1681(a). According to the petitioner in this case, the abusive environment her daughter suffered violated her rights under Title IX.

18. See, for example, Katherine Newman, *Rampage: The Social Roots of School Shooting* (New York: Basic Books, 2004), p. 185.

19. Quoted in Linda Greenhouse, "Vote against Banner Shows Divide on Speech in Schools," *New York Times Online* (www.nytimes.com/2007/06/26/washington/26speech. html [July 2008]).

20. Quoted in ibid.

21. Justice Thomas as quoted in ibid.

22. Justice Stevens as quoted in ibid.

23. Quoted in Bill Mears, "'Bong Hits 4 Jesus' Case Limits Student Rights" (nn.law. com/2007/LAW/06/25/free.speech [July 2008]).

24. In Lexis-Nexis, we used the search string "student w/p discip! or expulsion or expel! or supen! or punish!" For more detail, see Arum, *Judging School Discipline.*

25. For a historical discussion of how law shaped education in the United States, see David Tyack, Thomas James, and Aaron Benavot, *Law and the Shaping of Public Education, 1785–1954* (University of Wisconsin Press, 1987).

26. Arum, *Judging School Discipline,* p. 52.

27. Ibid., p. 53.

28. Ibid., pp. 57, 58.

29. See *Tinker* v. *Des Moines.*

30. See Abby Larson. "Rights Consciousness and Mobilization: Youth and Student Rights in Comparative Contexts," prepared for the meeting "Improving Learning Environments in Schools: Lessons from Abroad," La Pietra, Florence, Italy, May 13–14, 2008.

31. Arum, *Judging School Discipline,* p. 80.

32. Irenee Beattie, Richard Arum, and Josipa Roksa, "Zero Tolerance School Discipline and Student Rights: Changes in Court Climates and Legal Contestation, 1960–2002," paper prepared for annual meeting of the American Sociological Association, San Francisco, Calif., August 2004.

33. Richard Arum and Melissa Velez, "The Disparate Impact of Adversarial Legalism: Variation in Legal Contexts across Schools and Patterns of Racial Disadvantage," paper prepared for Association for Public Policy Analysis and Management conference, Atlanta, Ga., October 2004.

34. See, for example, Pedro Noguera, *City Schools and the American Dream: Reclaiming the Promise of Public Education* (New York: Teachers College Press, 2003).

35. Calvin Morill and others, "Legal Mobilization in Schools: Toward a Neo-Institutional Theory of Racial Differences in Perceived Rights Violations and Redress among Youth," paper prepared for Law and Society Association meeting, Montreal, Canada, May 2008.

36. Richard E. Miller and Austin Sarat, "Grievances, Claims, and Disputes: Assessing the Adversarial Culture," *Law and Society Review* 15 (Special Edition, 1981): 525–56.

37. New York City Department of Education, *Citywide Standards of Discipline and Intervention Measures: The Discipline Code and Bill of Student Rights and Responsibilities, K–12, Effective September 2008*.

38. Ibid., pp. 1–2.

39. Ibid., p. 6.

40. Ibid., p. 3.

41. Court decisions around this time also began to single out disabled students for special protections. For example, in 1972 the U.S. District Court for the District of Columbia found that the school district was under an "affirmative duty to provide" special education students with due process before "excluding, suspending, expelling, reassigning and transferring" them from school. See *Peter Mills* v. *Board of Education of the District of Columbia*, 348 F. Supp. 866 (D.C. Cir 1972).

42. Arum, *Judging School Discipline*.

43. Ibid.

44. See James Coleman, Sally Kilgore, and Tom Hoffer, *High School Achievement: Public, Private and Catholic Schools Compared* (New York: Basic Books, 1982).

45. See Arum, *Judging School Discipline*, chap. 5.

46. An examination of the Supreme Court docket at the time of writing provides few clues to the possible direction of court decisions. Currently the Supreme Court is considering *Safford Unified School District* v. *Redding* (No. 08-479), a case involving both the search and seizure requirements outlined earlier in *T.L.O*, as well as the issue of a public school educator's qualified immunity. The case involves a suit for damages against an assistant principal and public school system in rural Arizona. The case alleges that a thirteen-year-old female student's rights were violated when an assistant principal subjected the girl to a search conducted by the school nurse and a second female school employee for prescription drugs that she was suspected of distributing to her peers. Although the student was never touched by school officials, she was required to undress down to her undergarments. During Supreme Court hearings on the case, "Several justices appeared troubled by the search, but also seemed loath to second-guess school officials confronted with a variety of dangerous substances" (Adam Liptak, "Court Debates Strip Search of Student," *New York Times*, April 21, 2009).

In addition to the *Safford* case, the Supreme Court recently declined to hear the appeal of a student who received corporal punishment, a decision that underscores the Court's pro-school orientation. In June 2004 Jessica Serafin was paddled by her San Antonio charter school's principal because she left campus to buy breakfast. At the time of the paddling, Jessica was eighteen years old. According to court papers, she did not consent to the paddling and asked to withdraw from the school in order to avoid the wooden paddle, dubbed "Ole Thunder" by school officials. Despite her request, Jessica was restrained and struck by the paddle several times, necessitating a visit to the hospital emergency room. In her lawsuit, Serafin cited assault and battery, negligence, false imprisonment, and violations of her Fourteenth Amendment due process rights. While the Court granted rudimentary due process rights to students in *Goss* v. *Lopez* (1975), in *Ingraham* v. *Wright* (1977) it concluded that corporal punishment was not cruel and unusual punishment and that the due process clause of the Fourteenth Amendment did not require notice and a hearing before its administration. Both the district and appeals courts followed the *Ingraham* decision, claiming that corporal punishment only violates substantive due process rights when it is "arbitrary, capricious, or wholly unrelated to the legitimate state goal of maintaining an atmosphere conducive to learning." Though Serafin's appeal asked the Supreme Court to revisit its stance on students' due process rights, by declining to adjudicate the case in June of 2008, the Court signaled that its continued pro-school direction is likely. Ruling by the U.S. Court of Appeals for the Fifth Circuit (October 2007), as quoted in Mark Walsh, "The Supreme Court and Corporal Punishment," *Education Week—The School Law Blog* (http://blogs.edweek.org/edweek/school_law/2008/06/the_supreme_court_and_corporal.html [June 2008]).

47. See, for example, Phillip Howard, *Life without Lawyers: Liberating Americans from Too Much Law* (New York: W. W. Norton, 2009); or Peter Schuck and Richard Zeckhauser, *Targeting in Social Programs: Avoiding Bad Bets, Removing Bad Apples* (Brookings, 2006).

48. Robert Kagan, *Adversarial Legalism: The American Way of Law* (Harvard University Press, 2001).

Contributors

RICHARD ARUM
New York University

SAMUEL R. BAGENSTOS
University of Michigan

MARTHA DERTHICK
University of Virginia

JOHN DINAN
Wake Forest University

JOSHUA M. DUNN
University of Colorado–Colorado
Springs

CHESTER E. FINN JR.
Thomas B. Fordham Institute

LANCE D. FUSARELLI
North Carolina State University

MICHAEL HEISE
Cornell University

FREDERICK M. HESS
American Enterprise Institute

R. SHEP MELNICK
Boston College

DOREET PREISS
New York University

JAMES E. RYAN
University of Virginia

MARTIN R. WEST
Brown University

Index

Alphabetization is letter-by-letter (for example, "Educational Accountability Act" precedes "Education clauses").